SEXUAL LIFE IN ANCIENT GREECE

SEXUAL LIFE IN ANCIENT GREECE

HANS LICHT

Translated by
J. H. FREESE

Edited by
LAWRENCE H. DAWSON

DORSET PRESS
New York

This edition published by Dorset Press,
a division of Barnes & Noble, Inc.

1993 Dorset Press

ISBN 1-56619-495-4

Printed and bound in the United States of America

M 9 8 7 6 5 4 3 2

CONTENTS

PART I

INTRODUCTION

CONTENTS

Contents

PART II

Contents

ABBREVIATIONS

Anth. Pal.: *Anthologia Palatina* (see p. 259 ff.).

Ath.: *Athenaei Naucratitae deipnosophistarum libri xv*, ed. G. Kaibel, 3 vols. (Leipzig, B. G. Teubner, 1887–90) (see p. 285).

Brandt-Amores: Commentary on Ovid's *Amores*.

Brandt-Ars: Commentary on Ovid's *Ars Amatoria*.

CAF: *Comicorum Atticorum Fragmenta*, ed. T. Kock, 3 vols. (Leipzig, B. G. Teubner, 1880–8.)

CIA: *Corpus Inscriptionum Atticarum*, 4 vols., with Supplements (Berlin, 1873–90).

CIGr.: *Corpus Inscriptionum Graecarum*, 5 vols. (Berlin, 1828–77), vols. i and ii, ed. by Aug. Boeckh, vol. iii by Joh. Franz, vol. iv by Ernst Curtius and Adolf Kirchoff, vol. v (*Indices*) by Hermann Roehl.

CIL: *Corpus Inscriptionum Latinarum*, 15 vols., with Supplements (Berlin, 1862–1905); edited by Mommsen, Hübner, O. Hirschfield, Karl Zangemeister, W. Henzer, and others.

FHG: *Fragmenta Historicorum Graecorum*, ed. C. and T. Müller, 5 vols. (Paris, Didot, 1841–83.)

PLG: *Poetae Lyrici Graeci*, ed. Th. Bergk, vols. ii and iii. (4th ed. Leipzig, B. G. Teubner, 1882.)

TGF: *Tragicorum Graecorum Fragmenta*, ed. A. Nauck. (2nd ed. Leipzig, B. G. Teubner, 1889.)

SEXUAL LIFE IN ANCIENT GREECE

INTRODUCTION

Greek Ideals of Life

Although youth was regarded by the Greeks as the most precious possession, and its joys, amongst them love in particular, as the greatest happiness, yet other ideals must not be left unnoticed.

In Homer, Nestor calls after Athene as she disappears in the clear sky: " But, O Queen, be propitious and grant me fair renown, to me myself and to my children, and to my reverėd wife " (*Odyssey*, iii, 380).

We may say that these words express the moral ideals of the Greeks. The inclusion of wife and children proves that it is not only a question of victory in war or in athletic contests, but that in addition ideal wishes for life in general are indicated.

According to Pindar (*Pythia*, i, 99) happiness is the first object to be striven for, the second is an honourable reputation; he who has met with and holds fast to both has found the highest crown.

Naturally, by the side of these more ideal possessions there are also material goods which appeared to the Greek worth striving for and which he prayed the gods to grant him. So far as I know, Theognis (*Theognis*, 255) is the first who puts health as the happiness most worth striving for by the side of that previously mentioned, next to it as the most pleasant thing, " to attain what one loves," an ideal which came from the soul of the Greeks, so that, as Aristotle attests (*Eth. Eudem.*, i, 1, and *Eth. Nic.*, i, 8), this wish was inscribed on the vestibule of the sanctuary of Leto at Delphi.

The intentional vagueness of the words of Theognis—" to attain what one loves "—has led one so well acquainted with the history of Greek culture as Burckhardt (J. Burckhardt, *Griechische Kulturgeschichte*, ii, 368) to express the doubt: "that it therefore remains uncertain whether the poet is here speaking of love properly so called, or only in general terms of wishes which are to be fulfilled." Burckhardt, like so many learned men who have written bulky volumes on Greek culture, was not aware that the Greek knew two kinds of love, that between man and woman and that between those of the same sex (homosexual). For this reason Theognis expresses himself with seeming vagueness, but intelligibly enough for one who understands Greek culture, when he wishes every one of his readers that which is pleasant to him and what he himself longs for. That in these words the ideal of youth was always before the soul of Theognis himself, since all his life long his heart drew him towards the boy, will be clear from the chapter dealing with the homosexual literature of the Greeks.

The correctness of the explanation of the passage of Theognis here given is also shown by a comparison with a poem by the famous Sappho, frag. 5 (Diehl):

To ANACTORIA [1]

Some think a gallant navy on the sea,
And some a host of foot or horse, to be
Earth's fairest thing; but I declare
the one we love more fair.

Right easy is the proof, that all may know
How true my saying is, for Helen, though
Much mortal beauty she might scan,
judged him the fairest man

Who in the dust Troy's majesty defiled,
Nor rather of her parents dear and child
Had thought, but, Cypris-led, astray
cherished an ill love's way;

For nowise hard is *woman's will* to sway
If from home thoughts she lightly turn away.
So now fair Anactoria be
in memory nigh to thee

Whose sweet foot-fall I would more gladly hear,
And the bright glory of her face see near,
Than Lydian chariots in the field
and foot with spear and shield!

[1] Translation by C. R. Haines, M.A., in his *Sappho, the Poems and Fragments*, Broadway Translations, Geo. Routledge & Sons, Ltd., 1926.

Full well we know that mortals may not fare
In all things well: albeit to crave a share
In what is well *is not denied,*
if Heaven be on our side.

Anactoria was apparently in Lydia.

It is to be observed that here also (in the fourth verse of the original) the expression is purposely vague and the words chosen are intentionally ambiguous, but the meaning is: whether you now as a woman crave for a woman, as a man for a woman, or as a man for a boy.

However this may be, this much is beyond doubt, that beauty and love especially belong to the joys of life desired by the Greeks and proclaimed by their poets as ideal. This is clear from every page of a Greek author, but it may be enough to quote the charming little song (*PLG.*, iii, Scholion 8), which the Greeks certainly may have sung often enough under the influence of wine when the joy of living is intensified:—

"Best for mortal man is health; second best, charming personal beauty; third, wealth obtained without fraud; fourth, to be young amongst one's friends."

Cheerful enjoyment of life generally is already reckoned by Solon, the famous wise man, statesman, and poet, as one of the possessions worth striving for, and other great intellects (such as Pindar, Bacchylides, and Simonides) entirely agree with him. Indeed, the culture of the Greeks is entirely and solely a song of praise on Hedone (ἡδονή), that is, the cheerful enjoyment of life, especially of the joys of love. The inmost nature of the Greeks is naked sensuality, which, indeed, rarely becomes brutality—as in the case of the Romans—but yet impresses its stamp upon their collective life, while the confession of sensuality or its manifestations in life is unchecked by rigorous state laws or the hypocritical condemnation of public opinion. That this statement is not exaggerated will be clear from this book, which shows that the whole life of the Greeks (not only their private life) represents solely an exultant creed of sensuality. Hence, apart from certain isolated exceptions, the great thinkers of Greece have also recognized the right of sensual enjoyments; indeed, have even claimed them as a matter of course as a happiness of man. Not until he was an old man did Sophocles (Plato, *Republic*, i, 329*c*) pronounce the well-known judgment that old age is to be praised, since it sets us free from the servitude of sensuality; as will be shown later, the great poet's ideas on the subject were essentially different.

Athenæus (*Ath.*, xii, 510*b*), who quotes this view of the aged Sophocles, then reminds us of an opinion of Empedocles, according to which mankind once knew no other goddess save the goddess of love, in whose honour they celebrated the festivals of life.

The Omnipotence of Sensuality in Greek Life

Even the gods, as early as the times of the Homeric poems, succumb to the desire for sexual gratification. To be able to assist the Greeks in their desperate struggle, Hera resolves to charm her husband, Zeus, by wantonness. She adorns and attires herself most carefully, as is described by Homer (*Iliad*, xiv, 153), who takes pleasure in breadth of detail, but, not content with that, she also borrows from Aphrodite, under a false pretext, "the magic girdle of love and longing, which subdues the hearts of all the gods and of mortal dwellers upon earth." Aphrodite obeys the sublime queen of heaven, "and loosed from her bosom the broidered girdle, wherein are fashioned all manner of allurements; therein is love, therein is longing and dalliance—beguilement that steals the wits of the wise." Thereupon the sublime goddess repairs to Hypnos, the god of sleep, whom she requests to lull Zeus to sleep after she has enjoyed the pleasures of love with him, that she may have a free hand to help the Greeks.

Hypnos, terrified, flatly refuses the dangerous commission of the goddess, and not until she has promised him under a solemn oath one of the Graces as a reward, does he consent. He repairs with Hera to the mountains of Ida, from the heights of which Zeus is looking down upon the combat between Greeks and Trojans. Hypnos changes himself into a bird, and perches on a lofty fir-tree, to wait for the end of the love-scene between Zeus and Hera, on the description of which Homer spends more than sixty lines.

Hera invents various reasons why she has decked herself out in such a manner, and, by the pretended excuse that she is going on an important journey, arouses the desire of the god, who is infatuated with her beauty. Zeus tells her that he has never yet been so excited by a woman as he is now at the sight of her, and proceeds to enumerate, with a naïveté certainly to be found nowhere else in the world's literature, for the benefit of his wife (!), an imposing list of women who had rested in his arms without his having ever felt half so much excitement as on the present occasion.

To his desire that they should unite at once and on the spot in the enjoyment of love, Hera raises the objection that they might be seen here by one or other of the gods, and proposes to repair with him to the bridal-bed in the palace of Olympus, where she will comply with his wishes.

" Then in answer to her spake Zeus the cloud-gatherer : ' Hera, fear thou not that any god or man shall behold the thing ; with such a cloud shall I enfold thee withal, a cloud of gold. Therethrough might not even Helios discern us twain, albeit his sight is the keenest of all for beholding.' Therewith the son of Cronos clasped his wife to his arms, and beneath them the divine earth made fresh-sprung grass to grow, and dewy lotus, and crocus, and hyacinth, thick and soft, that upbare them from the ground. Therein lay the twain, and were clothed about with a cloud, fair and golden, wherefrom fell drops of glistening dew. Thus in quiet slept the Father on topmost Gargarus, by sleep and lover overmastered, and clasped in his arms his wife."

If this scene in the fourteenth book of the *Iliad* is a hymn of the omnipotent rights of sensuality, such as could never again have found its poetical expression with an equally self-evident naïveté, yet even the *Oydssey* knows of a unique instance of the glorification of the victorious power of beauty. I mean the episode in the eighth book of the *Odyssey* (viii, 266, etc.) (later to be given in greater detail), in which Aphrodite makes a cuckold of her husband, the insignificant, limping Hephæstus, and abandons herself together with the handsome Ares, the war-god in the vigour of youth, to the certainly illegitimate, but for that reason only sweeter, joys of a forbidden love. But the deceived husband, instead of painfully concealing his disgrace, summons all the gods to witness the piquant spectacle, in which the two lovers are exposed naked and in closest embrace to lascivious eyes. Homer concludes the description of this love-scene with the words: "But to Hermes said the lord Apollo, son of Zeus: 'Hermes, son of Zeus, messenger, giver of good things, wouldst thou in sooth be willing, even though ensnared with strong bonds, to lie on a couch by the side of golden Aphrodite?' Then the messenger, Argeiphontes, answered him: 'Would that this might befall, lord Apollo, thou archer god—that thrice as many bonds inextricable might clasp me about and ye gods, aye, and all the goddesses, too, might be looking on, but that I might sleep by the side of golden Aphrodite.' So he spoke and laughter arose among the immortal gods."

Thus there is not a word of blame nor even of moral indignation; only jest and merriment prepare this mockery of marriage fidelity by the goddess of love herself for the blessed immortals. The whole love-episode is a hymn of sensuality naked and unconcealed and an almost brutal justification of what is called " sin " after the modern triumphal march of spurious morality.

Athenæus (xii, 511*c*) further draws attention to the fact that according to a remark of Theophrastus, no one calls the life of the virtuous Aristeides happy, but they do those of the Sybarite Sminidurides and Sardanapalus.[1]

Heracleides Ponticus (*Ath.*, xii, 512*a*), a pupil of Plato and himself a famous philosopher, had written a book " On Pleasure ", many passages of which have been preserved. For instance, in it it is affirmed and proved that luxury in the conduct of life, and especially voluptuousness, is a right reserved for the governing classes, whereas work and toil fall to the lot of slaves and the poor ; and that all who prize luxury and voluptuousness are broad-minded men of fine character, and hence more to be esteemed than others. This is also shown in the case of the Athenians, who, in spite of, or rather because of, their sensual conduct of life, developed into the heroic people of the victors of Marathon.

Such trains of thought cannot be subscribed to unconditionally ; it is only important in this connection to register these views as very significant in the general opinion as to the right of sensuality. The great poet Simonides (*PLG.*, frag. 71) openly asked : " Would the life of mortals be delightful without sensual happiness ? Is not even the life of the blessed gods unenviable without this ? " Indeed, the historian Megacleides (*Ath.*, xii, 512*e* ; *FHG.*, iv, 443) blames the poets for laying too much stress upon the labours and privations of his earthly career in the life of Heracles, the Greek national hero. He rather points to the fact that Heracles, in his association with mankind, took the

[1] Sminidurides was famous in antiquity for his luxury. In the time of Athenæus (xii, 518*c*) the inhabitants of Sybaris in lower Italy were still proverbial gluttons, fond of eating and drinking. Sardanaplus, the last King of Assyria, is the typical debauchee.

greatest pleasure in sensuality, wedded many women, and begat children with many maidens. His numerous intrigues with boys—Iolaus, Hylas, Admetus, and others, are not mentioned.[1] Further, Heracleides reminds us that Heracles during his lifetime greatly enjoyed the pleasures of the table; that throughout Greece bubbling warm springs were called Baths of Heracles, and, indeed, that specially soft and voluptuous beds bore the trade mark Heracles. What, he thinks, could be the origin of all this, if Heracles had despised voluptuousness? It was very bad taste on the part of the poets—following Homer and Hesiod, to represent Heracles, this pronounced gourmand and voluptuary, as if he ran about all his life long with his tree-trunk club, his bow, and lion's skin.[2]

In the twelfth book of his *Banquet of the Learned*, Athenæus gives a detailed account of the luxury and sensual manner of life of antiquity. After some theoretical observations on feasting and debauchery, beginning with the Persians, he discusses the individual peoples of ancient times, informing us how each of them knew how to fill life with luxury and voluptuousness; he then enumerates an imposing list of men in Greek history who had led a specially refined sensual life. It is not uninteresting to find that not a few of these are known to us as leaders and heroes of the Greek people. Much will be said later on this subject; here we may mention some points specially characteristic of the Greek conception of sensual life.

According to Heracleides (*Ath.*, xii, 514*b*; *FHG.*, ii, 95), the Persian King had a harem of three hundred women. "They slept during the day, that they might be awake during the night, which

[1] Greek mythology gives the names of fourteen of his boy-loves cf. R. Byer, *Fabulæ Graecæ quatenus quave aetate puerorum amore commutatæ sint*, Leipziger Doktorarbeit, 1910, pp. 9–24).

[2] The worthy Megacleides was perhaps not so far wrong; at least in comedy Heracles appears only as the typical voluptuary who enjoys every imaginable kind of sensual pleasure. The oldest poet who describes him only as the sorely tried sufferer and man of sorrows was Stesichorus.

was spent by lamplight with singing and music, and in cohabiting with the king. These women of the harem also accompanied him when he went hunting."

Of the Lydians Xanthus (*Ath.*, xii, 515*d*; *FHG.*, i, 39) had informed us that it was their custom to castrate not only boys but also girls, to be employed as eunuchs in the palaces of the great (see *infra*, ch. vii. § 2, pp. 507-12).

As Timæus (*Ath.*, xii, 517*d*; *FHG.*, i, 196) attests, it was the custom among the Tyrrhenians that maidservants should wait upon the men naked. This is confirmed by Theopompus (*Ath.*, xii, 517*d*; *FHG.*, i, 315), who adds: " It was a law amongst the Tyrrhenians that the women were common property. They took the greatest care of their bodies, and often practised gymnastic exercises together with men and often among themselves; for they considered it no disgrace to show themselves naked. They did not take meals with their husbands, but with any men who happened to be present, and drank with anyone they liked; they were very fond of drinking, and very beautiful. The Tyrrhenians bring up all the children who are born, often without knowing who their father is. When they are grown up, they live in the same manner as those who reared them, often arrange drinking bouts and have connection with all the women they meet. It is not considered objectionable among the Tyrrhenians to have to do with boys openly, whether actively or passively, for pæderasty is a custom of the country. And they have so little shame in regard to sexual matters that when the master of the house is enjoying the society of his wife, and anyone comes and asks for him, they say quite calmly that he is engaged in this or that, at the same time mentioning each act of indecency by its name.

" When they are with friends or relatives their custom is the following. When they have stopped drinking and are going to bed, servants bring in to them courtesans, beautiful boys, or women, while the lamps are still burning. When they have enjoyed themselves sufficiently with these, they fetch young men in their prime, and let them enjoy themselves with these courtesans, boys, or women. They pay homage to love and sexual intercourse, sometimes looking on at one another, but generally letting down curtains from poles fastened on the beds. They are very fond of women, but find more pleasure with boys and young men. These are very beautiful, since they take the greatest care of their persons and remove all troublesome hairs from their body. Among the Tyrrhenians there are many shops for this purpose and well-trained staffs, as in our barbers' shops. Persons enter these shops and let themselves be treated in any way on any part of the body without troubling about the looks of passers-by."[1]

According to Athenæus (*Ath.*, xii, 519*e*) the inhabitants of Sybaris were the first who introduced hot baths. At drinking-bouts they made use of chamber-pots, a somewhat disgusting innovation, which, according to a fragment of the comedies of Eupolis (Frag. 351 in *Ath.*, i, 17*d*; *CAF.*, i, 350), no less a person than Alcibiades is said to have transferred to Athens.

Of the luxury of the inhabitants of the well-known city of Tarentum, in lower Italy, Clearchus (*Ath.*, xii, 522*d*; *FHG.*, ii, 306) relates that "they removed every hair from their body and went about in transparent, purple-bordered garments. After they had destroyed the town of Carbina in Apulia, they dragged all the boys, girls, and young women into the temples and exposed them naked to the

[1] To understand the passage, we must remember that the shops in ancient times, as even to-day, often in the south, were open to the street. We shall have to deal at greater length with the "depilation" here described, that is the removal of an undesirable growth of hair. We will only here observe that it is less a question of the removal of the hair over the private parts (which was certainly regarded as ugly in the case of the female sex, but was considered a special charm in the males) than of the ugly hairiness of the legs of Greek boys.

gaze of visitors. Any one who liked might rush upon this unfortunate herd, and satisfy his lust upon the naked beauty of those exposed to view, before the eyes of all, and certainly of the gods, which they least suspected. But the gods punished this crime, for soon after all these debauchees were struck by lightning. Even at the present day every house in Tarentum has as many memorial stones before the door as the dead who came to it; and when the day of their death returns, the people neither lament the dead, nor pay them the usual honours, but offer sacrifice to Zeus Kataibates" (Zeus who descends in thunder and lightning).

The city of Massalia (i.e. Marseilles), according to the testimony of several witnesses, was one of the chief seats of homosexuality, whence the proverb, "Ship to Marseilles!" (*'Ες Μασσαλίαν πλεύσειας*).

What Athenæus (*Ath.*, xii, 526*b*) tells us of the inhabitants of Colophon in Asia Minor is interesting, although perhaps not to be taken literally: that many of them had never seen sunset or sunrise in their lives, since when it rose they were still drunk, and when it set they were drunk again. This is in agreement with the law which, according to the same authority, was still in existence during his time, that flute-players, dancers, and similar ladies of the demi-monde might only be paid for from early morning to midday, and after that only till "the lamps were lighted", since during the rest of the day everyone was drunk.

We will also give a few specimens of the luxury of individuals in ancient history. First, the epitaph written on himself by the Assyrian king Sardanapalus, already mentioned, if we may believe the testimony of Amyntas (*Ath.*, xii, 529*f*): "I have been a king and as long as I saw the light of the sun; I have eaten, drunk, and done homage to the joys of love, knowing that the lifetime of men is only short and subject to much change and misfortune, and that others will reap the benefit of the possessions that I leave behind me. For this reason I let no day pass without living in this manner."[1]

Aristobulus (*Ath.*, xii, 530*a*) also knew of a monument to Sardanapalus in Anchiale, one of his subject cities; on the stone statue of the king the right hand was so formed as if it wanted to snap off something valueless with the finger. The Assyrian inscription was as follows: "Sardanapalus, the son of Anacyndaraxes, who conquered Anchiale and Tarsus on a single day. Eat! drink! love! For all else is naught." This seems to be the meaning of the gesture of the finger.

Clearchus (*Ath.*, xii, 530*c*; *FHG.*, ii, 307) told several remarkable things of Sagaris, an effeminate person from the Bithynian people of the Maryandini: In consequence of his effeminacy he ate nothing until he reached old age unless his nurse had chewed it for him, so that he himself might be relieved of the trouble. Also he was too indolent to reach further than his navel with his hand. Hence Aristotle, jesting about the fact that, when making water, he never grasped his member, quoted the verse of Euripides: "The hand is pure, but the thought has some pollution" (Eurip. *Hippol.* 317).

The orator Lysias (frag. 4 in *Ath.*, xii, 534) tells the following story of Alcibiades. "He was once travelling with his friend Axiochus to the Hellespont. In Abydos they wedded a girl in common named Medontis, and lived with her in turns. Afterwards she bore a daughter, of whom they said that they did not know who was the father. When the daughter grew up they also lived with her, and when she was with Alcibiades in bed with her he said she was the daughter of Axiochus, and when she was with Axiochus he said she was the daughter of Alcibiades."

In comedy also Alcibiades was soundly criticized for his love adventures, of which Athenæus gives several examples. It was not without reason that

[1] This inscription is also given in hexameter form (*Ath.*, viii, 335*e*).

the youth, admired by all for his beauty, bore on his coat of arms (*Ath.*, xii, 534*e*) an Eros hurling the lightning. Diogenes Laërtius (iv, 49) said of Alcibiades that "when a young man he separated men from their wives, and, later, wives from their husbands"; and, similarly, the comedian Pherecrates (frag. 155; *CAF.*, i, 194): "Alcibiades, who was formerly no man, is now the man of all women."[1]

In Sparta he had committed adultery with Timæa, the wife of King Agis, which, indeed, according to Athenæus (xii, 535*b*), he explained as not being due to lustful, but to political motives. According to the same author, he was accompanied on his campaigns by two of the most famous courtesans at that time.

The historian Clearchus (*Ath.*, xii, 541*c*; *FHG.*, ii, 307), in his *Biographies*, wrote of Dionysius the Younger, the tyrant of Sicily: "When Dionysius reached his mother-city Locris, he had the largest house in the city filled with wild thyme and roses, then sent for the young women of Locris one after the other, stripped himself and them naked, and rolled on the bed with them, practising every kind of obscenity imaginable. Shortly afterwards, when the insulted fathers and husbands had got the wife and children of Dionysius in their power, they forced them to commit indecencies before the eyes of all, and abandoned themselves to every kind of conceivable debauchery. After they had satisfied their desires they drove needles under their finger-nails and put them to death." Strabo (vi, 259; cf. Aelian, *Var. hist.*, ix, 8), with a few alterations, tells the same story, adding that Dionysius set doves with clipped wings flying about the banqueting-hall, which had to be caught by the naked girls, some of whom were obliged to wear sandals that were not pairs, on one foot a low, on

[1] According to Suetonius (*Julius Cæsar*, 52) Curio had said the same of Cæsar; cf. also Cicero, *Verres II*, 78, 192.

the other a high one. Duris (*Ath.*, xii, 542*c* ; *FHG.*, ii, 475) had told of the debaucheries of Demetrius of Phalerum, governor of Athens for many years ; he mentions the luxurious drinking-bouts arranged by him, " his secret orgies with women, and nightly amours with young men ; the man who gave other people laws and acted as the guardian of their lives claimed for himself the greatest licence. He also took great pride in his personal appearance, dyed his hair blond, and painted his face. He wanted to be beautiful, and to make himself agreeable to everyone who met him."

A life of pleasure as the true object of life, which alone indicates happiness, had been also made the motto of an entire philosophical school. It had been founded by Aristippus, who, according to the testimony of Athenæus (xii, 544*b* ; see also C. M. Wieland's romance, *Aristipp*), beautified his life " by luxurious clothing and the enjoyment of love ". His favourite mistress was the famous courtesan Lais.

Of special significance for the Greek conception of sensual enjoyments are the ideas which the great savant and musical theorist Aristoxenus (*Ath.*, xii, 545*a* ; *FHG.*, ii, 276), in his *Life of Archytas*, put into the mouth of Polyarchus, who was notorious for his luxurious mode of life and was one of the ambassadors who had been sent by the younger Dionysius to Tarentum. In conversation with Archytas and his pupils, sensual enjoyment in the widest sense of the word was talked about. Polyarchus delivers a long lecture, in whch he endeavours to prove that the entire edifice of virtue erected by the ethical philosophers is contrary to human nature ; that Nature herself demands that we should make pleasure the maxim of our life. The greatest possible exaltation of the feeling of pleasure is the aim of every intelligent man, but to suppress the desire for pleasure means neither intelligence nor happiness, but only shows that the man who acts in such a way is ignorant of the character and needs of human nature. Hence it was a very intelligent act on the part of the Persians to reward those who had invented any new kind of pleasure. Indeed, that was the only reason why the Persians had deprived the Medes of their empire, that, as their power was enlarged and their prosperity increased, they might also be able to widen the scope of their sensual pleasures.

Although these views of Polyarchus are certainly exaggerated, yet it must be admitted that they contain a kernel of truth, as is clear from these introductory remarks. In any case the reader will now have learnt enough of the Greek gospel of *Hedone* (sensual pleasure) to be able to consider in the following chapters the most important manifestations of Greek culture from this point of view. He will then make the acquaintance of a people which, certainly like no other, made sensuality the basis of life, but which knew also how to combine this sensuality with higher ethics and thereby created a culture of life which mankind will admire until the end of all time.

CHAPTER I

Marriage and the Life of Women

1. The Greek Woman

It is hardly necessary nowadays to emphasize the fact that the assertion, one often heard, that the position of the Greek married woman was an unworthy one, is fundamentally wrong. This erroneous opinion was bound to arise, since it originated in an incorrect assumption—a perverted estimate of women. However inferior as politicians the Greeks were throughout their short history, they were always admirable artists of life. Hence they assigned to woman as a whole the limits which nature had prescribed for them. The modern idea that there are two types of women, the mother and the courtesan, was recognized by the Greeks in the earliest times of their civilization; and they acted in accordance with it. Of the latter type, we will speak later, but no greater honour could be paid to a woman than the Greeks assigned to the mother type. When the Greek woman had become a mother she had attained the object of her life. Then two tasks were allotted to her, which she considered the highest imaginable—the management of domestic affairs and the bringing up of her children, of the girls, until they were married, of the boys until the awakening of the spiritual individuality of the soul. Thus marriage became for the Greeks a means to an end, the means of acquiring a legitimate generation to come after them, and an organized and trustworthy management of household affairs. The kingdom of the wife involved the complete control of domestic affairs, in which she was absolute mistress. If we please we can call such a marriage dull; indeed, we must do so, if we think of the part played by the modern woman in social life. But, on the other hand, it was free from the unnaturalness and falsehood which is frequently attached to modern society. It is not by accident that the Greek language has no equivalent for the ideas of "flirt", "gallantry", and "coquetry".

The modern man might feel inclined to ask the question whether the Greek girls and women did not feel desperately unhappy in a life of such retirement. But the answer must be in the negative. It must never be forgotten that what one does not know cannot be missed; then, also, the Greek women took the strictly limited (but for that reason no less noble) tasks which resulted from their household duties so seriously, that they had no time for detailed or painful thoughts about their existence.

But the foolishness of the talk about the unworthy position of the Greek woman is indisputably shown by the fact that in the oldest literary records marriage, and with it the woman, is described in a manner more intimate and charming than can be imagined. Where in all literature is the parting of a husband and wife represented with greater depth of feeling than in the famous scene in the *Iliad* (vi, 392–496),[1] in which Hector takes leave of Andromache?

"When now he was come to the gate, as he passed through the great city, the Scaean gate, whereby he was minded to go forth to the plain, there came running to meet him his bounteous wife, Andromache, daughter of great-hearted Eëtion, Eëtion that dwelt beneath wooded Placus, in Thebe under Placus, and was lord over the men of Cilicia; for it was his daughter that bronze-harnessed Hector had to wife. She now met him and with her came a handmaid bearing in her bosom the tender boy, a mere babe, the well-loved son of Hector, like to a fair star. Him Hector was wont to call Scamandrius, but other men Astyanax; for only

[1] Dr. A. T. Murray's translation, in the Loeb Classical Library, is used by kind permission of the Editors and Publisher.

Hector guarded Ilios. Then Hector smiled, as he glanced at his boy in silence, but Andromache came close to his side weeping, and clasped his hand and spake to him, saying: 'Ah, my husband, this prowess of thine will be thy doom, neither hast thou any pity for thine infant child nor for hapless me that shall soon be thy widow; for soon will the Achaeans all set upon thee and slay thee. But for me it were better to go down to the grave if I lose thee, for nevermore shall any comfort be mine, when thou hast met thy fate, but only woes. Neither father have I nor queenly mother. My father verily goodly Achilles slew, for utterly laid he waste the well-peopled city of the Cilicians, even Thebe of lofty gates. He slew Eëtion, yet he despoiled him not, for his soul had awe of that; but he burnt him in his armour, richly dight, and heaped over him a barrow; and all about were elm-trees planted by nymphs of the mountain, daughters of Zeus that beareth the aegis. And the seven brothers that were mine in our halls, all these on the selfsame day entered into the house of Hades, for all were slain of swift-footed, goodly Achilles, amid their kine of shambling gait and their white-fleeced sheep. And my mother, that was queen beneath wooded Placus, her brought he hither with the rest of the spoil, but thereafter set her free, when he had taken ransom past counting; and in her father's halls Artemis the archer slew her. Nay, Hector, thou art to me father and queenly mother, thou art brother and thou art my stalwart husband. Come, now, have pity and remain here on the wall, lest thou make thy child an orphan and thy wife a widow. And for thy host, stay it by the wild fig-tree, where the city may best be scaled, and the wall is open to assault. For thrice at this point came the most valiant in company with the twain Aiantes and glorious Idomeneus and the sons of Atreus and the valiant son of Tydeus, and made essay to enter; whether it be that one well skilled in soothsaying told them, or haply their own spirit urgeth and biddeth them thereto.'

"Then spake to her great Hector of the flashing helm: 'Woman, I too take thought of all this, but wondrously have I shame of the Trojans, and the Trojans' wives, with trailing robes, if like a coward I skulk apart from the battle. Nor doth mine own heart suffer it, seeing I have learnt to be valiant always and to fight amid the foremost Trojans, striving to win my father's great glory and mine own. For of a surety know I this in heart and soul: the day shall come when sacred Ilios shall be laid low, and Priam and the people of Priam with goodly spear of ash. Yet not so much doth the grief of the Trojans that shall be in the aftertime move me, neither Hecabe's own, nor King Priam's, nor my brethren's, many and brave, who then shall fall in the dust beneath the hands of their foemen, as doth thy grief, when some brazen-coated Achæan shall lead thee away weeping and rob thee of thy day of freedom. Then haply in Argos shalt thou ply the loom at another's bidding, or bear water from Messeïs or Hypereia, sorely against thy will, and strong necessity shall be laid upon thee. And some man shall say as he beholdeth thee weeping: Lo, the wife of Hector, that was pre-eminent in war above all the horse-training Trojans, in the day when men fought about Ilios. So shall one say: and to thee shall come fresh grief in thy lack of a man like me to ward off the day of bondage. But let me be dead, and let the heaped-up earth cover me, ere I hear thy cries as they hale thee into captivity.'

"So saying, glorious Hector stretched out his arms to his boy, but back into the bosom of his fair-girdled nurse shrank the child crying, affrighted at the aspect of his dear father, and seized with dread of the bronze and the crest of horsehair, as he marked it waving dreadfully from the topmost helm. Aloud then laughed his dear father and queenly mother;

and forthwith glorious Hector took the helm from his head and laid it all gleaming upon the ground. But he kissed his dear son and fondled him in his arms, and spake in prayer to Zeus and the other gods: 'Zeus and ye other gods, grant that this my child may likewise prove, even as I, preeminent amid the Trojans, and as valiant in might, and that he rule mightily over Ilios. And some day may some man say of him as he cometh back from war: He is better than his father; and may he bear the bloodstained spoils of the foeman he hath slain, and may his mother's heart wax glad.'

"So saying, he laid his child in his dear wife's arms, and she took him to her fragrant bosom, smiling through her tears, and her husband was touched with pity at sight of her, and he stroked her with his hand, and spake to her, saying: 'Dear wife, in no wise I pray thee, grieve overmuch at heart; no man beyond my fate shall send me forth to Hades; only his doom, methinks, no man hath ever escaped, be he coward or valiant, when once he hath been born. Nay, go thou to the house and busy thyself with thine own tasks, the loom and the distaff, and bid thy handmaids ply their work: but war shall be for men, for all, but most of all for me, of them that dwell in Ilios.'

"So spake glorious Hector, and took up his helm with horsehair crest; and his dear wife went forthwith to her house, oft turning back, and shedding big tears."

Can one think of the woman to whom Homer devotes so touching, indeed, so lofty a scene of parting, as a miserably neglected, vegetating creature? If anyone is dissatisfied with this example, let him afterwards read in the *Odyssey* the part played by Penelope, the wife of Odysseus. How loyally she waits for her husband during his absence of many weary years! With what displeasure is she conscious of her weakness in the face of the uncouth, turbulent, and disorderly suitors! Full of nobility, every inch a queen, insulted in her woman's honour by the riotous behaviour of her insolent admirers, she appears amongst their band flinging them back into their boundaries with words which only true womanhood can invent. How amazed she is at the change in her son Telemachus, who is ripening from a boy into a young man; she is amazed, but resigns herself, when her son calls to her (*Odyssey*, i, 356–60): "Now go to thy chamber and busy thyself with thine own tasks, the loom and the distaff, and bid thy handmaids ply their tasks; but speech shall be for men, for all, but most of all for me; since mine is the authority in the house."

Would Homer have been able to create so charming an idyll as the Nausicaa scenes, if the Greek "young girls" had felt unhappy in the confinement of their domestic duties? We need only point out these facts, since the readers of this book should be sufficiently acquainted with the poems of Homer to remember the scenes of woman's life that are given there and to correct their judgment on the position of the Greek woman of that time and on marriage. Now Aristotle (*De republ.*, ii, 8, 1260) refers to the fact that, in Homer, the man, as it were, purchases the bride from her parents; he pays for the *hedena* (ἕδνα), the bridal presents, which consisted of natural products, mostly in cattle, which perhaps might be felt unworthy by the modern man. Yet we must point out that this custom arises from the view, current among the old Teutons and Hebrews, that the unmarried daughters are a valuable possession of the household for whom an indemnity must be demanded if they are given up. Further, many passages from Homer (*Odyssey*, i, 277, ii, 196; *Iliad*, vi, 395, ix, 144, etc.) show us how, just at the time when the handing over was completed, it was customary to give the daughters a dowry. Critical people might consider this custom, which is also usual at the present day, to be in the circumstances even more unworthy, especially as the object is at any price to find a husband for the daughter. It is very remarkable that even in Homer (*Odyssey*, ii, 132), in cases of a separation, the dowry reverts to the father or a relatively heavy fine must be paid. Certainly as early as Homer's time (*Odyssey*, iv, 535) the wife's unfaithfulness plays an important part; indeed, the Trojan war is entirely founded upon the supposition that Helen is unfaithful to her husband Menelaus, and follows the beautiful Phrygian King's son, Paris, into a foreign land; and Clymtæmnestra, the wife of Agamemnon, the shepherd of his people, allows herself to be seduced by Ægisthus during the many years' absence of her husband, and with the help of her paramour, after a treacherously affectionate reception, slays Agamemnon on his return, in the bath, " like a bull in his stall." The poet—or what is the same in this case, the naïve popular view—is certainly amiable enough to exculpate the adulteresses from the guilt of these two errors of married life, and to put them down to infatuation (*Odyssey*, xxiii, 218; *Iliad*, iii, 164, 399) caused by Aphrodite, more particularly due to the action of the powers of destiny (*Odyssey*, iii, 265) that secretly govern the house of the Tantalidæ; but this in no way alters the fact that both the commanders-in-chief in the mighty struggle of the people, the poetical expression of which is preserved in Homer's *Iliad* and *Odyssey*, are deceived husbands in the traditional account reproduced by the poet (*Odyssey*, xi, 424). Thus it is easy to understand why the shade of Agamemnon, murdered by the base cunning of a woman, bitterly abuses the female sex, thereby opening the list of women-haters so numerous in Greek culture, of which we shall speak later. " But she, the shameless one, turned her back upon me and, even though I was going to the house of Hades, deigned neither to draw down my eyelids with her fingers nor to close my mouth. So true is it that there is nothing more dread or more shameless than a woman who puts into her heart such deeds, even as she too devised a monstrous thing, contriving death for her wedded husband. Verily I thought that I should come home welcome to my children and to my slaves ; but she, with her heart set upon utter wickedness, has shed shame on herself and on women yet to be, even upon her that doeth uprightly."

Menelaus takes the matter less tragically. After the fall of Troy he becomes reconciled to his runaway wife, and in the *Odyssey* we find him living peacefully and highly honoured in his ancestral kingdom of Sparta by the side of Helen, who by no means feels any embarrassment in speaking about the " misery " which Aphrodite has caused her (*Odyssey*, iv, 261).

" I groaned for the blindness that Aphrodite gave me, when she led me thither from my dear native land, forsaking my child and my bridal chamber, and my husband, a man who lacked nothing, whether in wisdom or in comeliness."

Not in Homer, but in the poets of the so-called Epic Cycle (especially Lesches, frag. 16), we find the story that Menelaus, after the conquest of Troy, wanted satisfaction for his insulted honour and threatened Helen with drawn sword. Then she bared " the apples of her bosom " and so enchanted Menelaus, that he repented and threw away the sword and folded the beautiful woman in his arms in token of reconciliation—an agreeable story, which later writers, such as Euripides (*Andromache*, 628) and the lyric writer Ibycus (*PLG*., frag. 35) were fond of repeating. It was eagerly seized upon by comedy (Aristoph., *Lysistr*., 155 ; Scholiast on *Wasps*, 714), and also became a favourite subject in vase-paintings (see Roscher *Lexikon der Mythologie*, i, 1970).

It must not be forgotten that everything that has hitherto been said concerning marriage in Homeric times only refers to the lives of great men, the kings and nobles, and that we know little or nothing of the position of women of the lower classes. But if we consider that the Homeric epos gives us complete information on the life of the lesser people—peasants, cattle-breeders, huntsmen, shepherds, fishermen—the fact that nothing is said about the women can certainly be regarded as a proof that the life of the woman was restricted to house and home, and that as early as that time the saying of Pericles (*Thucydides*, ii, 45), afterwards so famous, can be applied to the women—that " those women are the best, of whom one speaks least in the society of men, either well or ill."

What the Boeotian poet Hesiod, in his poetical shepherds' calendar entitled *Works and Days* (519 ff., 701 ff.), tells us of the life of the Greek women only confirms this view. The poet finds nice words for the girl still unmarried, " who still remains at home by her dear mother's side, as yet inexperienced in the works of the gold-adorned Aphrodite." While outside the furious winter storm rages, throws down the high-topped oaks and pines, and benumbs men and cattle with cold, she takes a warm bath in her room comfortably heated throughout, increases the suppleness of her maiden limbs by rubbing them with oil of balsam, and then snugly slips between the sheets. Certainly the poet, who was himself a peasant, cannot rise above everyday commonplaces, and his precepts—that the simple man of the neighbourhood may marry somewhere about the age of thirty, while his choice should be about nineteen and, of course, still a virgin—clearly show that marriage at that time had not much to do with poetry. But this narrow-minded, commonplace idea of the woman in such early times as those, and even among these simple men of the lower classes, cannot have been a matter of course, otherwise Hesiod would not so impressively admonish them, that the " clever man tests everything and retains the best, to avoid marrying to the malicious joy of his friends", as he expresses it both wittily and with psychological truth. For, as he goes on to say: "a good wife is a very precious possession, but a bad one is the worst torment, who as it were is only a parasite in the house and even exhausts the resources of a well-to-do husband and hands him over to a needy old age."

It is very significant that already this still entirely naïve and simple peasant had looked very deeply into the nature of woman. It is a matter of less importance that he also attributed all the evil in the world to a woman, the silly and vain Pandora (*Works and Days*, 47), who, having been amicably received by Epimetheus opens her box and pours out from it all evil upon humanity, for here the poet was under the spell of mythological tradition; but it is of great weight and of extraordinary interest for the history of morals that he feels obliged to warn female vanity in impressive words against coquetry, against such girls as seek to increase the charms of their hinder parts by coquettish movements (*Works and Days*, 373), and consequently do their utmost to lure the man with that part of the body which the Greeks especially prized in the young man, so that Lucian (*Amores*, 14, τὰ παιδικὰ μέρη) can venture to call the posteriors generally by the name of "parts of the youth". That such a method of charming her husband being employed by a wife should be found in the naïvely simple poet of the shepherd's calendar is worthy of notice, and proves that even in those early times, as generally at all times, the woman was conscious of possessing the means which seldom, if ever, failed in their effect upon the sensuality of the man. Hesiod (*Works and Days*, 582) also knows that the season of the year and temperature are not without influence on sexual life: "When the artichoke flowers and the chirping cicada, perched upon a tree, pours down its shrill song continuously from beneath its wings in the season of tiring summer, then kids are fattest and wine is most mellow, and women are most lustful, but men are feeblest, for the skin is dry through the heat"—but, he continues, a good meal and good wine soon restore their vigour.

As time went on, Hellenic culture became more and more occupied with the male sex, as is shown by the fact that an actual education is only spoken of in the case of boys. The most necessary elementary knowledge in reading and writing, and likewise skill in female handiwork, the most important of which were spinning and weaving, was taught girls by their mothers.

If a little instruction in music is included female education is substantially exhausted; we hear nothing of scientific culture, indeed, we hear often enough that the married woman ought not to be cleverer than befits a woman, as, for instance, Hippolytus in Euripides (*Hippolytus*, 635) expressly says. The Greek was penetrated with the conviction that the proper place for girls and women was the women's quarters, where they had no need of book learning. At that time social intercourse with women was unknown, but it is false to assert that this was the result of the retired life led by them. Rather it was the knowledge that conversation with men, such as highly cultivated Athenians demanded as their daily bread, was impossible for women, considering their entirely different psychological conditions and their completely different interests—it was this that banished the woman to the seclusion of the woman's chamber. That " young girls ", especially up to the time they were married, led a very retired and according to our ideas a joyless existence, might generally have been the rule, perhaps with the exception of those of Sparta. Only on special occasions, perhaps the spectacle of a festal procession or taking part in such or at funerals, girls were to be seen in larger numbers in the streets and then certainly some kind of communication between the sexes might take place. Thus, in a charming idyll of Theocritus (*Idyll*, ii), the story is told of a a girl how, during a festal procession in the grove of Artemis, at which, " among great numbers of other animals " a lioness was brought on, she was fetched away by a female friend and on this occasion sees the beautiful Daphnis and falls in love with him.

Marriage brought the wife a somewhat greater freedom of movement, yet the house was, and remained, the kingdom to which she was assigned. How persistently the maxim, which in Euripides (*Troades*, 642) is clothed in the words " just that brings blame upon a woman, if she will not remain at home ", was carried through during life is exemplified by the fact that, even at the news of the fearful defeat of Chaeronea, the women of Athens only ventured as far as the house-doors (Lycurgus, *Leocrates*, 40), where, half senseless with sorrow, they inquired after husbands, fathers, and brothers—but " even that was considered unworthy of them and their city ".

Indeed, from a passage in *Hypereides* (Stobæus, lxxiv, 33) it may be conjectured that women were not free to go out until they were of such an age that a man who saw her in the street did not ask whose wife, but whose mother, that was. Hence the tortoise, on which the foot of the Aphrodite Urania of Pheidias in Elis rested (Plutarch, *Isis and Osiris*, 76) was regarded as the symbol of the woman's life shut up in the narrow limits of the house, " that unmarried girls in particular need to be guarded, and that housekeeping and silence befit married women." At least the good custom forbade women showing themselves in public unless they were accompanied by a gynaekonomus (γυναικονόμος), that is, by some older confidential male person of the household, and generally followed by a female slave. It touches us peculiarly that even Solon (Plutarch, *Solon*, 21) deemed such things worth regulating by law, when he ordered that women, when they went out for funeral or festivals, "might take with them no more than three pieces of clothing ; further, no more than an obol's worth (about 1½*d.*) of food and drink," and at night time should only go out in a carriage with a lighted lantern—rules which appear to have been still in existence in Plutarch's days. But Solon, not unjustly called "the wise" by the men of ancient times, certainly knew very well what he meant by such apparently unimportant orders—it is nothing else but the expression of the "principle of the male", which dominates the whole of ancient culture.

It would, of course, be absurd to assume that these and similar regulations prevailed everywhere, and always in Greece to the same extent ; our only concern is to sketch the picture of culture in its broad outlines, in which we consider Greece as a unity held together by language and custom, without going painfully into the differences on every occasion, as they are conditioned by place and time, thus taking up a position which is fundamentally that of the whole book, in so far as it is not expressly contradicted. If Euripides (*Andromache*, 925) emphatically requires from sensible married men that they should not allow their wives to be visited by other women, since they are "teachers of everything that is bad", he certainly does not stand alone in this view, but practice contradicted him. Thus we know that women, certainly unaccompanied by their husbands, visited the studio of Pheidias, and the court of Pyrilampes, a friend of Pericles (Plutarch, *Pericles*, 13), in order to admire the magnificent peacocks kept there. If the women greet Pericles after his funeral oration and heap flowers upon him (ibid., 28), it seems to follow from this that the offence which, as already mentioned, was caused by the attitude of the Athenian women after the news of the battle of Chaeronea, was mainly due to the fact that late in the evening they questioned the men who passed by.

Here, if ever, the saying holds good, that extremes meet. Many shut up their women in the *gynaekonitis* (women's room) well guarded, sealed and bolted, on the threshold of which a rough Molossian hound (Aristoph., *Thesmoph.*, 414) was made to keep watch, while on the contrary, according to Herodotus (i, 93), in Lydia it was thought nothing of if the girls paid for their clothes by prostitution. While the Spartan girls appeared in the costume often derided by the rest of Greece, which slit the dress to the hips, so that the thigh was bared while walking along, in Athens, according to Aristophanes (*Thesmoph.*, 797) himself, even the married woman was obliged to retire into the interior of the house, to avoid being seen through the window by a male passer-by.

It has been asserted that the great retirement in which the Greek woman in general certainly lived led to a simplicity of character and mental narrowness, and in support of this appeal is made to anecdotes and stories something like that related of the wife of King Hiero (Plutarch, *De inimicorum utilitate*, 7). Having been ridiculed by an opponent for the bad smell of his mouth, the king ran home in a rage and asked his wife why she had not drawn his attention to it. The wife is said to have answered, as an honest and modest wife should: "I thought that all men smelt like that." Certainly several anecdotes of the kind could be quoted, but their conclusiveness, assuming their correctness generally, is slight, not so much since the Greeks were a people who were fond of anecdotes, but rather since the universally high respect which Greek men had for their wives, and of which numerous indisputable instances have been handed down to us, cannot possibly have concerned only the sexual and child-bearing function of the wife. One thing certainly we must not expect to find in the Greek husband—

what we usually call "gallantry". In Greek antiquity, such differences as those between "woman" and "wife" were excluded. There *gyne* (γυνή) designated the woman without reference to age, no matter whether she were married or not; and to be addressed as *gynai* (γύναι) was no disgrace to the queen or the simple woman of the people. At the same time, it is to be observed that linguistically the word means "bearer of children",[1] and the etymology also shows that the Greek chiefly honoured the mother of his children in the woman. Not until Roman imperial times do we meet with the word *domina* (lady, mistress) as the address of women of the imperial house (whence the French *dame*). The Greeks reserved the word *despoina* (meaning the same as *domina*) for actual ladies, that is, for the wives of kings, without lowering it to a merely conventional term, or in opposition to domestic servants; for in the house the women were mistresses in everything which constitutes her particular domain, as Plato expressly calls attention to in a well-known passage (*Laws*, vii, 808*a*). From the modern point of view the Greek separation of women into three classes, though certainly not "gallant" is very significant, as given by the author of the speech against Neaera: "We have courtesans for our pleasure, concubines for daily personal service, and married women to bear us children and manage our house faithfully" (§ 122).

The position of the concubine was very different. We hear of such who were entirely the property of their master, who could also sell them (Antiphon, *De Veneficio*, 14), e.g. to a brothel; yet from a law referred to by Demosthenes (*In Aristocratem*, 55; see also *Ath.*, xiii, 555), in which mother, wife, sister, daughter, concubine, are named in one breath, we may conjecture that the relations between a man and his concubine may have been like those of husband and wife. Besides, it was only in the heroic

[1] Plato, *Cratylus*, 414*a*: γυνὴ δὲ γονὴ μοι φαίνεται βούλεσθαι εἶναι.

age described by Homer that the possession of one or several concubines was universally common, indeed, a matter of course, at least among the nobles. In historic times, however, the admissibility of such a relationship is by no means certain; indeed, there is much to be said against it, and probably it was only in times of need (such as increased mortality owing to war and epidemics) that a concubine was allowed by the side of the wife for the purpose of bearing children.

That men took wives mainly for the sake of begetting children, not only follows from the official formula of betrothal, "for the procreation of a legitimate offspring," (Ἐπὶ παίδων γνησίων 'αρότῳ; cf. Lucian, *Tim.*, 17; Clem. Alex., *Stromata*, ii, 421; Plutarch,. *Comparatio Lycurgi cum Numa*, 4), but is also frankly admitted by several Greek authors (Xenophon, *Memor.*, ii, 2, 4; Demosthenes, *Phormio*, 30; Plutarch, as above). In Sparta matters went much further, where according to Plutarch it was nothing unusual for the husband "to transfer his conjugal rights temporarily to one sexually stronger, from which he could expect especially beautiful and vigorous children, without the marriage being thereby upset". We must agree with Plutarch (*Lyc.*, 15), when he compares Spartan marriage with a stud, in which the only matter of consequence is to obtain an issue as numerous as possible and of excellent race. In another passage (*De audiendis poetis*, 8) he speaks of a certain Polyagnus, who played the pander for his own wife, wherefore he was ridiculed in comedy, because he kept a goat who brought him in much money.

Also Stephanus, well-known from the speech against Neaera (§ 41), was a cunning procurer who enticed strangers, whom he supposed had money, with the charms of his young wife. If the stranger fell into the snare he knew how to arrange matters so that he caught the loving couple in a compromising situation, after which he extorted a considerable sum of money from the young man who was surprised *in flagrante delicto*. In the same way Stephanus played the pimp for his daughter: from a certain Epænetus, whom he found in bed with her, he extracted 30 *minae* (about £120). We frequently hear of similar cases in ancient literature, and it may often have first taken place in cases of which written authorities tell us nothing. That those who were disturbed in their amorous enjoyment were glad if they could get out of it by so large a payment is explained by the heavy fines which were fixed for the seduction of a married woman or a girl of irreproachable character. We shall speak later of these penalties.

In a place so sensitive as Athens, and, indeed, in the rest of Greece, marriage was regarded, at least if we may believe Plato (*Laws*, vi, 773), as the fulfilment of a duty to the gods; the citizen was meant to leave behind in his children servants and worshippers of the gods. It was also held to be a moral duty to ensure the continued existence of the state by the procreation of descendants. We have no certainly attested information concerning laws which made marriage a duty, except in Sparta; indeed, Solon is said to have refused to introduce such laws with words that are not improbable in view of his own position with regard to sexual relations, that woman is like a dead weight on a man's life (Stobæus, *Sermones*, 68, 33). If Plato elevates marriage to a legal demand (*Laws*, iv, 721; vi, 774), and would like to have a single life punished by fines and loss of civil rights, he takes, as he often does in the *Laws*, quite the same point of view as the Spartans, among whom, according to Ariston (Stobæus, *Sermones*, 67, 16), not only single men, but also those who married late were punished, those who concluded a bad marriage, that is one of unequal birth or that proved unfruitful, being punished most severely. The law by which the great law-giver Lycurgus punished unmarried men makes a singular impression upon us (Plutarch, *Lycurg*, 15): "The civil rights of unmarried men were curtailed; thus they were not allowed to take part in the festival of the naked boys (*gymnopædia*); in the winter they were ordered to go round the market, while they sang a song of ridicule attacking themselves, declaring that they deserved what had happened to them, as they had disobeyed the laws of their country; and they were also deprived of the respect and attention which was usually shown by young people to their elders."

When a young man did not get up from his place before the famous but unmarried Spartan general Dercyllidas, and said impudently: "You have begotten no one who will later make way for me" the attitude of the youth was generally approved. These punishments and mortifications do not seem to have done much good even in Sparta; rather the number of unmarried men in Greece appears to have been fairly large, whether it was that entering into the married state was forbidden by the desire for a peaceful life, unimpaired by anxieties about wife and child, or even by a natural dislike for women generally. The conversation of Periplectomenus with Palaestrio in the *Miles Gloriosus* (iii, i, 677–702) of Plautus (adapted from a Greek original) is instructive in this respect:

"PERIPLECTOMENUS: Thank God, I have the means to entertain you in my home agreeably; eat, drink, do as you please in my company, and enjoy yourself to the full. This is Liberty Hall, and I have my own liberty, too. I like to live my own life. Why—thank God I may say so—I'm a rich man and could have taken a wife of wealth and station; but I have no desire to admit a she-yapper into my house.

"PALÆSTRIO: Why not, sir? Getting children is a delightful duty, you know.

"PER.: I'll take my oath that getting the joys of freedom is more delightful.

"PAL.: You, sir, are a man who can give good counsel to another, and to yourself as well.

"PER.: Yes, sir, it's all very pleasant to marry a good wife—if there were any spot on earth where you could find one; but am I to bring home a woman who'd never say to me: 'Husband mine, do buy me some wool to make a soft, warm cloak for you, and some nice, heavy tunics so that you won't be cold this winter.' Nothing like that would you ever hear from a wife, but before cockcrow she'd wake me up with: 'Husband mine, give me some money for a present for mother at the Matrons' Festival; give me some money to make preserves; give me some money to give to the sorceress at the festival of Minerva, and to the dream-interpreter, and the clairvoyant and the soothsayer. It's a shame if I don't send something to that woman that tells your fortune from your eyebrows. And then the modiste—I must tip her, in common decency. And oh, for ever so long the cateress has been angry at getting nothing. The midwife, too—she protested to me for sending her so little. What? Will you send nothing to the nurse that cares for the slaves born under your own roof?' These ruinous outlays of the women, and a lot more like 'em, keep me from taking a wife to torment me with talk like that.

"PAL.: The gods are kind to you, sir, for, by gad, once you let go of that liberty of yours, you won't readily restore it to its old place."

As many certainly had such ideas, on the other hand, the well-known majority of young girls in Greece was a special phenomenon, owing to the eternal struggles of the individual states amongst themselves, which cost much and just the best male blood. We may conjecture that the woman who never marries, the "old maid", may have been no rarity in Greece, although our authorities certainly do not trouble themselves in special detail about this regrettable type of the female sex, but only for the very reason that in Greek literature the woman generally only plays a subordinate part and particularly " the old maid ". But in Aristophanes (*Lysistr.*, 596) we already read the complaint of Lysistrata: " But the woman's time is short, and if she do not take advantage of it no one is willing to marry her, but she sits looking for omens."

The counterpart of the old maid is to a certain extent the childless married man; in both cases the object which is implied in the nature of the case is not attained. It is hence quite natural that in Greece recourse was had often enough to adoption, only that at that time there was an additional reason, namely, the wish to leave someone behind who might bring sacrifices and gifts of affection to the tombs.

Plutarch (*Lycurg.*, 16) tells us that according to the law of Lycurgus in Sparta it was usual to expose feeble and deformed children in a gorge on mount Taygetus. Even in Athens this was not unheard of, especially in the case of girls (Moeris Atticista, 102; Aristoph., *Frogs*, 1288 (1305), with the Scholiast; as to the girls, see Stobæus, *Sermones*, 77, 7 and 8). The children were exposed in large clay vessels, yet generally in such a manner that the helpless little wretches could be found by other people, who were perhaps childless or specially fond of children, and brought up. It also happened that people sold their children, especially, as Dion Chrysostom says (*Oratio*, xv, 8), to such women as had not had any, but did not want to lose their husbands. The newer comedy, in which the motive of the supposititious child frequently recurs, proves that this was not at all rare. Neck-chains, rings, or other distinctive marks (Euripides, *Ion*, 1430; Longus, i, 2; Aristænetus, *Epistulæ*, i, 1; Heliodorus, ii, 31; iv, 8) were also given to exposed children, by which they could later be identified according to circumstances; such identification plays also an important part in comedy.

Before we describe the details of a Greek marriage

feast, we would remind the reader of the conversation of Ischmachus in Xenophon (*Œconomicus*, vii, 10) with his recently wedded wife, in which he explains to her in detail the duties of a Greek housewife with an enviable naïveté. The pith of these admonitions is that the housewife should be chaste and sober-minded ; she must know how to make clothes, be experienced in the preparation of wool, and give every maidservant the task suited to her. The money and property acquired by her husband's labour she must keep together and make an intelligent use of it. Her chief task is the nourishment and bringing up of the little children ; like the queen bee, she has not only to distribute amongst the slaves, both male and female, the tasks which suit them, but also to attend to the health and welfare of the domestics. She must instruct those belonging to the family in everything worth learning and govern them wisely and uprightly. Also Plutarch's treatise, small but well worth reading, called *Gamika Paranggelmata* ("Advice to the Married"), dedicated by him to a newly-wedded couple who were friends of his, contains admirable lessons that might well be taken to heart at the present day.

2. MARRIAGE CUSTOMS

Let us now accompany a Greek youth from the day of his betrothal to the nuptial chamber. The Greeks were, and still are, clever calculators ; the poetry of a lengthy engagement was foreign to them ; family and dowry played a larger part than the personal qualities of the bride. But it would be wrong to assume that the dowry could be by no means large enough ; on the contrary, it was considered of far more importance that, if it were anyhow possible external conditions, should be in some measure equal. Hence fathers of daughters with a small dowry were by no means always happy if a rich man had become smitten with the pretty little face of the poor girl, as Euclio in the *Aulularia* (ii, 2) of Plautus expresses it in coarse comedy: "Now here's the way it strikes me, Megadorus: you're a rich man, a man of position, but as for me, I'm poor, awfully poor. Now if I was to marry off my daughter to you, it strikes me you'd be the ox and I'd be the donkey. When I was hitched up with you and couldn't pull my share of the load, down I'd drop, I, the donkey, in the mud, and you, the ox, wouldn't pay any more attention to me than if I'd never been born at all. You would be too much for me; and my own kind would haw-haw at me; and if there should be a falling out, neither party would let me have stable quarters; the donkeys would chew me up and the oxen would run me through. It is a very hazardous business for donkeys to climb into the ox set."

That young people before betrothal saw much of each other or became more intimately acquainted, is very improbable, which is already shown by the fact that Plato,[1] in order to prevent mutual deception as far as possible, speaks in favour of a freer intercourse between the two contracting parties, a demand which would be superfluous if such had already existed in practice. So, then, it is easy to understand that the husband very soon regarded marriage as a heavy fetter, and that the young wife was only too rapidly disappointed, as Sophocles (*Tereus*, frag. 524; *TGF*., Nauck) once touchingly expresses it: "Now I am nothing and left alone; I have often observed that such is the lot of womankind—that we are a mere nothing. When we are young, in our father's house, I think we live the sweetest life of all; for ignorance ever brings us up delightfully. But when we have reached a mature age and know more, we are driven out of doors and sold, away from the gods of our fathers and our

[1] *Laws VI*, 771. Plato even demands that young people before betrothal should see each other naked, "so far at least as decency permits". This may have happened here and there in individual cases, but can hardly have become a publicly recognized custom.

parents, some to foreigners, some to barbarians, some to strange houses, others to such as deserve reproach. And in such a lot, after a single night has united us, we have to acquiesce and think that it is well."

In general one took account of the law of nature, according to which the woman fades more rapidly than the man, by taking care that the bride was substantially younger than the bridegroom. Thus Euripides (frag. 24, *TGF.*, Nauck) expressly says: "It is highly wrong to join together two young persons of the same age; for the strength of man lasts far longer, while the beauty of the female body passes away more rapidly."

Hence, if a father could not soon find a husband for his daughter after she was of marriageable age, he had recourse to one of those obliging women who made a trade of match-making and were called *Promnestriæ* or *Promnestrides*. That their chief cleverness consisted in putting the excellent qualities of the girl in the clearest possible light is a matter of course, and it is the subject of special remark by Xenophon (*Memorab.*, ii, 6, 36) and Plato (*Theætetus*, 150).

It appears from the latter that their trade did not enjoy the highest reputation and might in many cases be combined with procuration. In the *Sorceresses* the splendid second idyll of Theocritus, the girl, aflame with love, sends her confidential maid to fetch the beautiful Daphnis, with whom she had fallen in love. She brings the longed-for swain, who after a love scene, wonderfully described with all the glow of sensual beauty, "made me unhappy, only a bad woman instead of a wife, and made me lose my virginity."

If, then, with or without the assistance of a matchmaker, the suitable man was found, the betrothal (ἐγγύησις) could take place. By this act of civil law we must only understand the public ratification of the wish of the two contracting parties to marry, which was required to make the ceremony legally valid. As a rule the amount of the dowry was settled at the same time. On these occasions it sometimes happened that charitable people equipped the daughters or sisters of those without means at their own expense (Lysias, *De bonis Aristoph.*, 59), and, indeed, that the daughters of poor but deserving citizens received their dowry from the State; for instance, we are told that the two daughters of Aristeides (Plutarch, *Aristeides*, 27) each received 3,000 *drachmæ*, i.e., about £112. We need hardly mention that, besides money, the dowry consisted of linen, clothing, finery, household goods and furniture; slaves are occasionally also mentioned as an additional contribution. It was asserted that there was a law of Solon (Plutarch, *Solon*, 20) that "ready money as part of the dowry should be excluded, in order that marriage, which is intended for the procreation of children and the bond of love between man and woman, might not become a matter of money", a law which like so many others probably only existed on paper, although Plato (*Laws*, vi, 774*d*) again advances it to a demand. Besides, this law may have sprung from an originally intelligent reflection, for, as it is very correctly remarked in the *Amatorius* (7; see also *De educ. puer.*, 19) of Plutarch, it is far better to wear chains than to be the slave of one's wife's dowry, wherefore in another passage he gives an emphatic warning against too wealthy a marriage.

When the legal formalities were complied with a family feast took place in the father-in-law's house, as might be gathered from a beautiful passage in Pindar (*Olympia*, vii, 1): "As one taking a goblet in his wealthy hand, foaming with the dew of wine, presents it to his young son-in-law for a draught welcoming him from one home to another, a goblet all of gold, chief of his possessions, for the sake of good cheer and in honour of the alliance, and if friends are present makes him envied for this love-match ; so I send to the prize-winners my liquid nectar, the gift of the Muses, the sweet fruit of my fancy, and pour a libation in honour of the victors at Olympia and Pytho (Delphi) ".

However, this family feast does not appear to have been the custom throughout Greece.

We are several times informed that winter was considered the most suitable season for marriage, without any reasons being given ; indeed, the first month took its name *Gamelion* from *gamos* (wedding) ; pious superstition appears to have prevented the time of the waning moon being chosen for the conclusion of a marriage.

Customs of various kinds were usual before the act of marriage proper, above all, of course, sacrifices to the divinities who protected marriage, consequently in particular to Hera and Zeus ; that the gall of the sacrificial victim might not be used is a symbol easy to understand, for the marriage must be free from " gall and anger " (Plutarch, *Præcepta conjugalia*, 27). Also Athene, Artemis, and other divinities were sometimes thought of by those who were going to marry ; as a rule sacrifice was only offered to Aphrodite on the wedding-day, and in the little town of Thespiæ (Plutarch, *Amatorius*, 26) in Boeotia the beautiful custom existed that the newly wedded repaired to the temple of Eros, to entreat happiness and blessing for the marriage before the glorious statue of Eros by Praxiteles. In many places it was usual for the bride to offer some locks of her hair or her girdle or both (Pausanias, ii, 33, 1 ; Eurip., *Hippol.*, 1416, and elsewhere) on the altar, in which the offering of the hair symbolized the taking leave of youth, of the girdle the resignation of virginity.

The sacrifice was followed or preceded by the bath of the bride, the water for which was fetched by a boy of the neighbourhood from a spring or river which has special importance for the place in question, as in Athens the fountain of Kallirrhoe

(Thucydides ii, 15), and in Thebes the river Ismenus (Eurip., *Phoenissae*, 347). In the so-called tenth letter of Aeschines we read the interesting note : " In the district of Troas it is the custom for brides to go to the Scamander and bathe in it, and utter the words sanctified by tradition : 'Take, O Scamander, my virginity ' ". In regard to this naïve custom it once happened that a young man represented himself to the bathing maiden as the god Scamander and literally fulfilled her prayer to take away her virginity. Four days later, when the pair, who had in the meantime married, were proceeding in the marriage procession to the temple of Aphrodite, she caught sight of the young man among the spectators, and cried out in alarm : " There is Scamander to whom I gave my virginity ! " To quiet her, she was told that the same thing had happened in the Mæander in Magnesia, which at least shows the fact, interesting for the history of culture, that the custom of brides bathing in the river before the eyes of all must have existed in several places.

We are reminded of the fact that in primitive times the bride was carried off by the ceremony which, certainly, was customary only in Sparta. There an apparent rape of the bride was carried out, apparent since her father and mother were informed of it beforehand. Plutarch (*Lycurgus*, 15) gives us the following account : " The wedding itself took place in this manner. Every man carried off a maiden, but not a young one nor one under age for marriage, but one who was fully grown up and marriageable. The so-called bridesmaid received the maiden who had been carried off, shaved her head close, and put on her a man's dress and shoes, laid her on a bed of straw, and left her alone in the dark. The bridegroom then crept in secretly, neither drunk nor weakened by dissipation, but quite sober, and after he had, as always, taken a meal with his table-companions, loosed her girdle and lifted her on to the bed. After he had spent a short time with her, he went away again quietly, to sleep in the usual place in the company of the other young men. He did the same thing again and again ; he spent the day with his comrades, slept with them at night, and visited his bride only secretly and with circumspection, feeling ashamed and being afraid that someone in her house might see him.

"Yet the bride herself assisted in this, and always knew how to arrange that they might be able to come together at the right time and without being seen. They did this not merely for a short time, but many of them had children born to them, before they had seen their wife by day. Such meetings served not only to make them practise restraint and moderation, but also promoted the birth of children and caused them to embrace with ever fresh and rejuvenated love, so that, instead of becoming sated or weakened by too frequent enjoyment, they left behind as it were a provocative and fuel of mutual love and inclination."

If this custom as described by Plutarch must be regarded as a specifically Dorian phenomenon, the habit of the wedding-banquet was certainly customary throughout Greece. It was generally given in the house of the bride's father. While at other times women kept away from men's feasts, they were present at marriage banquets, but certainly had their place at separate tables (Evangelius, in Ath., xiv, 644*d*). The expenditure at this meal and the nature of the entertainment were, of course, quite different according to financial conditions and the taste of the time being. Sesame cakes, to which according to Menander (frag., 938, *CAF*) a fructifying influence was ascribed, were a common dainty. It had an equally symbolical meaning, when during the meal a beautiful naked boy (Zenobius, *Proverbs*, iii, 38), adorned with thorns and oak-leaves, carried round a plate with pastry and offered to the guests, crying out at the same time: "I have avoided the bad, and found what is better" (ἔφυγον κακόν, ηὗρον ἄμεινον).

After the meal, at which naturally toasts were drunk and healths proposed (Sappho, frag., 51 (*PLG*), the bride was driven in a carriage drawn by oxen, mules or horses to the bridegroom's house. She sat in the middle between the bridegroom and his *parochos* (πάροχος) (Photius, *Lexikon*, 52; Pollux, iii, 40), his best friend or nearest relative. The custom of putting oxen to the carriage was explained by a myth, which is thus related by Pausanias (ix, 3): "Once Hera quarrelled with Zeus, and in her anger betook herself to Euboea: not knowing what to do, since he was unable to make it up with her, Zeus asked Cithæron, the ruler of Platæa at the time, who was famous for his wisdom, for his advice. He told Zeus to make a wooden image of a woman, to drive it round covered with a wrapper on a cart drawn by a team of oxen and to say that he is taking home his young bride, Platæa. Zeus did so. Hera, stung with jealousy, hurried up, but when, after the veil had been lifted and she saw that it was no young woman of flesh and blood but only a wooden image, she rejoiced greatly and was reconciled to Zeus."

The axle of the carriage was sometimes burnt (e.g. in Boeotia) after the arrival at the bridegroom's house. This was said to be an omen (Plutarch, *Quaest. Roman.*, 29) that the young wife might never have the wish to leave her husband's house again.

In case a widower married again, he took no part himself in the marriage procession, but waited at home for the bride, who was brought to him by a friend, now called not *parochos*, but *nymphagogus* (Pollux, iii, 40).

Wedding torches were indispensable in the procession; they were lighted by the mothers of the bride and bridegroom and carried by those who accompanied the procession on foot (Eurip.,

Phoenissae, 344; *Iphig. Aul.*, 722; Aristoph., *Peace*, 1318 and elsewhere). All those who took part in the procession were festively adorned, as we should assume considering the pronounced Greek sense of beauty, if it were not already attested by Homer (*Odyssey*, vi, 27). The bride's dress appears as a rule to have been particoloured, that of the bridegroom (which is very characteristic) not black, as is usual with us, but white and of the finest wool, like that of the male escort of the procession. Bride and bridegroom were crowned and adorned with particoloured bands (*taeniae*); the bride had not been sparing of costly perfumes, and from her head fluttered the flaming veil customarily worn by brides.

Many congratulations and jesting exhortations were offered to the marriage procession by those who met it as it moved through the streets of the city to the accompaniment of flutes, while those who took part in it sang the Hymenæus, the wedding-song named after Hymen, the god of marriage.

A Hymenæus is already mentioned by Homer (*Iliad*, xviii, 491; cf. Plutarch, *Mor.*, 667*a*); on the shield of Achilles (Hesiod, *Shield*, 272) a wedding-feast was also represented. "They conducted the bride through the city beneath the brilliant light of torches; the wedding-song resounded loudly, young men turned round in the dance, and above them floated the strains of flutes and lyres; but the women stepped to the door and in astonishment looked at the procession."

The Hymenæus is also sung in the wedding-procession, which was represented on the shield of Heracles and is described by Hesiod in detail. Perhaps Hesiod himself had composed an Epithalamium on the marriage of Peleus and Thetis, from which Tzetzes (*Prol. ad Lycophronem* = Hesiod, frag. lxxi) (Goettling)) (twelfth century) quotes two lines, containing a eulogy by Peleus of the noble bride who has fallen to his lot. But we know nothing more of the contents of these older hymenæi. They were artistically developed and thereby introduced into literature by Alcman in the second half of the seventh century; he seems to have elevated this class of poetry to high perfection, at least Leonidas of Tarentum calls him "the singing swan of wedding songs" (Anth. Pal., vii, 19: ὑμνητῆρ ὑμεναίων κύκνον). Further progress in their history is perhaps indicated by the name of Stesichorus (about 640–555), to whom an Epithalamium of Helen is attributed (Stesichorus, frag. 31, *PLG*). Yet nothing more is known about this, indeed the notice itself is so doubtful that we cannot even say with certainty that Stesichorus ever composed such an epithalamium.

Thus the oldest marriage-songs of the Greeks have disappeared, except for a bare mention. No information of their contents is given us, and even of the epithalamia of Sappho, who brought this class of poetry to its highest perfection, only miserable fragments are preserved. This is the more regrettable as, according to the testimony of antiquity, it is just the epithalamia that are the pearls of Sapphic poetry; Himerius (*Orationes*, 14; 16; 19), the sophist, describes in particular the beauties of this branch of Sapphic composition with glowing enthusiasm: "She enters the bridal chamber, prepares the bed for the bridegroom, praises the beauty of the maidens, makes Aphrodite, sitting in the car of the Graces, descend from heaven surrounded by a host of Loves to play with her; she twines the bride's hair with hyacinth blossoms, and lets it wave freely round her temples, a sport of the winds, while the Loves with gold-bedecked wings and tresses guide the car, swinging over their head the wedding torches."

These are evidently all allusions to passages occurring in the Epithalamia of Sappho, which Himerius puts forward as specially characteristic.

Köchly (*Akademische Vorträge*, 1859, vol. i, p. 195), beautifully describes these Epithalamia as " lyrical dramas, which, as it were, are divided into several sets, and in which the characteristic parts of the marriage celebration were described in song and accompanied by rhythmical action indicating their content ".

In ancient times it was the custom for the husband himself to adorn the nuptial chamber with cunning hand. Thus Odysseus had done (*Odyssey*, xxiii, 190), and boasts of it on his return from Ilium with justifiable pride before his wife, in order to overcome her last doubts, whether he himself is really the husband who has so long been thought dead. From the importance of the building of the nuptial chamber we may certainly conclude that the following words are from the beginning of an epithalamium of Sappho (frag. 89–90 (91–92), in Köchly's text): " Raise high, ye workmen, the bridal chamber; Hymenæus! the bridegroom draws near, like Ares to behold! No, not like Ares, yet greater than one of the great ones, gloriously tall, as when the Lesbian bard outsings all others.[1]

" Then was issued the appeal to arrange the nuptial couch and to adorn it with flowers. Young men and women are exhorted to take part in the feast for the glorification of which, considering the unusual beauty of the bride and the brilliant qualities of the bridegroom, the goddess of love herself comes down from heaven, beaming in beauty and accompanied by the charming Graces and love-gods, as we have learnt from the words of Himerius. Nor was the appeal in vain. The robust companions of the bridegroom and the blooming playmates of the bride are already assembled in the brilliantly lighted and festally adorned house of the former, waiting for nightfall and the arrival of the bride at

[1] The passage from here to " . . . conclusion of the entertainment " (p. 53) is from Köchly, *Akademische Vorträge*, vol. i, p. 196

the joyful meal, the singing of *Skolia* (drinking-songs) and the ringing sound of goblets. Already it is night, already the glow of torches flames from afar, and already is heard the sound of the old and yet eternally young song 'Hymen, O Hymenæus!' The noisy, excited procession, as we know of it from Homer and Hesiod, moves on, brings the bride home, high up in the carriage, to the bride-groom's house, before which young men and women have already arranged themselves in two separate choirs and are drawn up to contend in a zealous and joyful contest of song, while above in the heavens shines peaceful Hesperus, the star of love, which long ago the bridegroom's impatient, yearning desire has conjured up, while the bride quivers in sweet anxiety before its appearance. To him the maidens at first turn with their complaint:[1] 'Hesperus, worst of all the stars that shine forth in heaven, Hesperus, thou robbest all that loving care doth not protect; therefore, when thou appearest, loving care is ever on the watch; by night thieves skulk around and do not depart until thou returnest as the morning star at rosy dawn. Hymen, O Hymenæus, O Hymen, come, Hymenæus!'

"But the young men, although they have thought of other things at the drinking-bout, have not jumped up to no purpose and are resolved not to allow the palm of victory to escape them so cheaply. Immediately the counter-song resounds: 'Hesperus, most beautiful of all the stars that shine in heaven, Hesperus, thou bringest all, which the dawn hath driven afar; thou bringest the sheep and bringest the goat, and the little son to the mother; thou bringest the maid to the man. Indeed, the maidens say: I remain always a maiden. Yet they think in silence: Ah! if I were only a little wife! Hymen, O Hymenæus, Hymen, come O Hymenæus!'

[1] This and the two following pieces of verse are after *Catullus*, 62.

"Then the contest of song begins. It is at first a matter of discussing the question whether the class of maidens or that of the married housewife deserves the preference. The maidens begin; they see in the lot of the wife and mistress of the house only anxiety, only burdens[1]:

> Look how a flower in some close garden grows,
> Hid from rude cattle, bruiséd by no plows,
> Wind-stroked, sun-strengthened, nurtured by the rain:
> To pluck it many a youth and maid is fain!
> But once 'tis culled, its beauty fades away:
> No youth, no maid, desires it from that day.
> So is a virgin loved, while she is chaste:
> But if within a lover's arms embraced
> She lets her body's flower be gathered, then
> No longer is she dear to maids or men.
> Hymen alone is our defence and shield;
> To Hymen Hymenæus all must yield.

"The young men on the other hand describe the happy lot of the married man, which finds support in the husband who is beloved:

> Look how a vine unwedded never bears
> Ripe grapes, but with a headlong heaviness wears
> Her tender body, and her highest sprout
> Is quickly levelled with her fading root!
> For her no hinds, no lusty younglings care;
> But if by chance she shall be married there
> To the elm her husband, then all love her well
> And by her side full many a hind will dwell.
> Yea, as the vine untended, even such
> The maid who ne'er has felt a lover's touch.
> But when she gains a husband for her own
> No more upon her will her parents frown!

"Thus, and perhaps in several similar comparisons the state of the unmarried girl and that of the married housewife are weighed one against the other; who shall sink the scale is self-evident, while now the bridegroom comes in the carriage to fetch away and greet the bride. He accompanies her into the festally adorned hall, glittering with torches; in full tones the welcome to them resounds from

[1] This, and the next extract in verse, is from Mr. F. A. Wright's translation of Catullus, 62, in his *Catullus, the Complete Poems* (Broadway Translations, Geo. Routledge & Sons, Ltd.).

both choruses (after Sappho, frag. 99 (193); cf. 101 (105)): 'Hail to thee, O bride; hail to the bridegroom!' They have taken a seat side by side, and a new contest of song begins. First the young men praise the bride: 'She blooms like a rose, much brighter than gold her beauty beams, only comparable to golden Aphrodite, more melodious than the music of the lyre sounds her voice: a gentle charm flows o'er her gracious face.'[1]

"Therefore, she is long and often assailed with all kinds of wooing, but in vain:

As a sweet apple—rosy, O maid, art thou
At the uttermost tip of the uttermost bough,
Unseen in the autumn by gatherers—
Nay, seen, but only to tantalize.

"So also the bride: she has remained pure, inaccessible to all attempts; none of the many who desired to win her hand, can boast that he has ever touched her even with the tip of his finger. But at length he has approached her; he it is who has attained the highest goal. Naturally, he is worthy of his great happiness. And thus the bride's playmates need have no scruples for her sake about praising the bridegroom on their own part:

Dear bridegroom, in what likeness were it well
Thy praise in song to tell?
To the fresh tender sapling of a tree
I best may liken thee.

"But he is not simply young and beautiful, he is also strong and bold; girls may compare him to an Achilles, the eternal ideal of flourishing heroic strength. Both are worthy of each other; in this mutual admission peace is concluded, upon which

[1] These two lines and the five next passages are from the fragments of Sappho.

the seal is set by the marriage feast which now formally begins. To glorify it, to crown the newly-wedded with her blessing, Aphrodite is invoked: 'Come, O Cypris, come and mix in the shimmering golden goblet for us the nectar for the festal carouse, come and fill the goblet full.' That she is ready to come with her train, Eros the charming boy and the Three Graces, we know already. If the other heavenly ones do not come and fill the earthly hall, yet above, in the hall of the gods, they celebrate the festival of happy men; as the song of an inspired guest who, in his ecstasy, sees the heavens open and the gods carousing and drinking the health of the bridal pair, paints the scene in quite a lively manner: 'The mixing-jar was full of ambrosial drink; Hermes took the ladle and poured in the drink to the gods; then all held each his goblet up, and poured drink-offerings, and wished much that was good and beautiful for the bridegroom and the charming bride together.'

"Thus with song and games night comes on darker and darker. The long-yearned for hour has come. The bridegroom has rapidly got up, with bold grasp embraced the modestly resisting bride and, after an old custom of the heroic age, rapidly carried away his beautiful prize, followed by his most confidential friend, a youth 'of high stature and strong arm', capable of protecting the door of the nuptial chamber even against a more dangerous enemy than the girls—who rise up in haste and in well-imitated terror rush after the robber to rescue their playmate from his hands; they are as powerless as fowls in pursuit of a hawk which has carried off one of their number in its talons. When, breathless, they reach the nuptial chamber, then the door is slammed; at the same time they hear the bridegroom, now in concealment, push forward the mighty bolt and in a mocking voice call out to them the old saying, 'Back, here there are girls enough!' while outside, in front of the shut door, the trusty protector lifts up his gigantic body ready in position for battle, by no means disinclined for a merry struggle with the 'sturdy harlots'.

"Yet the girls do not oblige him, they know his weak side and know how to work him up. Instead of forcing the entrance, which he would have been only too glad to have defended, amidst merry surprise and general laughter they make the satirical song resound, which with its prosaic expressions forms a droll contrast to the highly poetical songs previously heard: 'Seven fathoms the feet of the door-keeper, five ox-hides used for the soles, and ten cobblers have made them!'

"But the merry banter lasts only for a moment. Yet it still remains to offer the last demonstration of affection, the last congratulations, the last farewell, to their playmate who, on her entry into the nuptial chamber 'has already become a mistress of a household'. The young maidens have rapidly arranged themselves anew and now sing the nuptial chamber song, the Epithalamium in the narrower sense, which forms the last act of the whole ceremony, even if this should be followed on the next day by a song of awakening as a conclusion of the entertainment."

Several Epithalamia have been preserved, not indeed from ancient times, but certainly the most beautiful is the highly artistic imitation of Theocritus (*Idylls*, xviii), which is the more valuable to us, since, as is expressly attested, it has turned to account corresponding poems of Stesichorus and Sappho, and for this reason may be quoted as a specimen of this kind of wedding poetry.

After a few introductory lines, the epithalamium in the narrower sense begins, the song sung before the door of the nuptial chamber in praise of the newly wedded pair.

Marriage and the Life of Women

THE EPITHALAMY OF HELEN

(The Eighteenth Idyll of Theocritus) [1]

It seems that once upon a time at the house of flaxen-haired Menelaus in Sparta, the first twelve maidens of the town, fine pieces all of Laconian womanhood, came crowned with fresh flowering luces, and before a new-painted chamber took up the dance, when the younger child of Atreus shut the wedding door upon the girl of his wooing, upon the daughter of Tyndareüs, to wit the beloved Helen. There with their pretty feet criss-crossing all to the time of one tune they sang till the place rang again with the echoes of this wedding-song :—

What Bridegroom ! dear Bridegroom ! thus early abed and asleep ?
Wast born a man of sluggardye,
Or is thy pillow sweet to thee,
Or ere thou cam'st to bed maybe
Didst drink a little deep ?
If thou wert so fain to sleep betimes, 'twere better sleep alone,
And leave a maid with maids to play
By a fond mother's side till dawn of day,
Sith for the morrow and its morn,
For this and all the years unborn,
This sweet bride is thine own.

When thou like others of high degree cam'st here thy suit a-pressing,
Sure some good body, well is thee, sneezed thee a proper blessing ;
For of all these lordings, there's but one shall be son of the High Godhead,
Aye, 'neath one coverlet with thee
Great Zeus his daughter is come to be,
A lady whose like is not to see
Where Grecian women tread.
And if she bring a mother's bairn 'twill be of a wondrous grace ;
For sure all we which her fellows be, that ran with her the race,
Anointed lasses like the lads, Eurótas' pools beside—
O' the four-times threescore maidens that were Sparta's flower and pride
There was none so fair as might compare with Meenlaüs' bride.

O Lady Night, 'tis passing bright the face o' the rising day ;
'Tis like the white spring o' the year
When winter is no longer here ;
But so shines golden Helen clear
Among our meinie so gay.
And the crops that upstand in a fat ploughland do make it fair to see,
And a cypress the garden where she grows,
And a Thessaly steed the chariot he knows ;
But so doth Helen red as the rose
Make fair her dear countrye.
And never doth women on bobbin wind such thread as her baskets teem,

[1] The translation is reproduced, by kind permission of the Editors and Publishers, from Mr. J. M. Edmonds' *The Greek Bucolic Poets*, in the Loeb Classical Library (Heinemann, 1912).

Nor shuttle work so close and fine cuts from the weaver's beam,
Nor none hath skill to ply the quill to the Gods of Women above
As the maiden wise in whose bright eyes dwells all desire and love.

O maid of beauty, maid of grace, thou art a huswife now;
But we shall betimes to the running-place i' the meads where flowers
do blow,
And cropping garlands sweet and sweet about our brows to do,
Like lambs athirst for the mother's teat shall long, dear Helen, for you.
For you afore all shall a coronal of the gay groundling trefoil
Hang to a shady platan-tree, and a vial of running oil
His offering drip from a silver lip beneath the same platan-tree,
And a Doric rede be writ i' the bark
For him that passeth by to mark,
'I am Helen's; worship me.'

And 'tis Bride farewell, and Groom farewell, that be son of a mighty
sire,
And Leto, great Nurse Leto, grant children at your desire,
And Cypris, holy Cypris, an equal love alway,
And Zeus, high Zeus, prosperitye
That drawn of parents of high degree
Shall pass to a noble progenye
For ever and a day.
Sleep on and rest, and on either breast may the love-breath playing go
Sleep now, but when the day shall break
Forget not from your sleep to wake;
For we shall come wi' the dawn along
Soon as the first-waked master o' song
Lift feathery neck to crow.

*Sing Hey for the Wedding, sing Ho for the Wedder, and thanks to him
that made it!*

Let one picture to himself the poem; how, accompanied by the song of female friends and by the soft tones of flutes, the youthful pair taste the inconceivable delights of the first night together; let him draw the parallel with the custom (still generally common amongst us) of degrading this night by spending it in an indifferent room in an hotel; let him hear, that the idyll may not lack farce, how the Scholiast, the ancient commentator on Theocritus, consequently a kind of dry-as-dust learned soul, "explains" the wonderfully beautiful custom of the Epithalamium. He says: "The epithalamium is sung, in order that the cries of the young bride, while she is offered violence to by her husband, may not be heard, but may be drowned in the song of the girls." So the scholiast explains "the exulting nuptial full chord of the festal song, which is struck up caressingly and banteringly at eventide by the maiden companions ," as Pindar, who was certainly a poet, once so beautifully said (*Pythia*, iii, 17).

But even the sweetest wedding night, or, as the Greeks so beautifully and sensibly put it, "the night of secrets," comes to an end, for that is not allowed to mortals which Zeus, the father of gods and men, allowed himself, when he lay with Alcmēnē. He had ordered the sun-god not to shine for three days, so that the bridal night lasted 72 hours; it was in this night that Zeus begat Heracles (Lucian, *Dialog. Deorum*, 10).

The next morning the newly wedded pair were awakened by a serenade and gladdened with all kinds of presents from relatives. From now onwards the young wife showed herself without the bridal veil, which she dedicated to Hera, the goddess of marriage (Anth. Pal., vi, 133). On this day a meal (Ath., vi, 243, Plutarch, *Sympos*., iv, 3) took place in the house of the bridegroom's father or of the bridegroom himself, in which it is significant that women, consequently the newly-married wife, did not take part (Is., *Pyrrh. her*., 14); but it certainly appears to have been the custom that the culinary enjoyments of this banquet were prepared by her, who, therefore, here for the first time had the opportunity of showing her knowledge of the art of cookery. The meaning is clear. In the wedding night the young husband had given his wife what was her due, now he belonged provisionally again to his friends and male relatives while the young wife had to perform her duties in the kitchen. That there appears to have been a good deal of joviality at this meal does not prevent its being the last and solemn authentication of the legally completed marriage ceremony, for which reason it was customary to invite as many guests as possible as witnesses.

3. ADDITIONS AND SUPPLEMENTARY INFORMATION

We may give a brief account of the further life of the married pair. In general the wife now remained in the Gynækonitis, by which we understand all the rooms which formed the wife's kingdom. Henceforth only the bedroom and eating room were common to husband and wife, presuming that the master of the house had no friends as guests. Then the meal was unattended by women, and it would never have occurred to a Greek wife, unless she wanted to be considered a courtesan or paramour, to take part in the meals of her husband and his friends. We may call this one-sided, indeed, we may think it shows a want of tenderness; that the intellectual enjoyments of the table were immensely enhanced by this arrangement must be clear to everyone who, raised above the force of convention, thinks what is the nature of the conversation, as long as ladies are present in modern society, and how scandalous stories succeed conversation, when, after dining together, the gentlemen have retired into the smoking-room. Yes, it is even so: "gallantry" was an unknown idea to the ancient Greeks, but on the other hand the difficult art of the conduct of life was all the more familiar to them.

If it was thought incompatible with the natural gifts of the woman to allow her to have an interest in the conversation of the men that possessed intellectual value, on the other hand an incomparably higher task was allowed her, namely, bringing up the boys until the time when they are exposed to the stronger wind of a man's education, and the girls until their marriage. To show how greatly the husband respected this activity of the wife, we will cite from the vast amount of evidence only the beautiful sentiment of Alexis (frag. 267 (Kock), in Stobæus' *Florilegium*, 79, 13): "God reveals himself to us in the mother more than in anything else."

It is not the task of this book to speak in detail on the further duties of the wife—the supervision of the movable and immovable property of the house, of the male and female slaves, the kitchen, the nursing of the sick, and whatever else still constitutes the domain of the wife.

The view that the Greek wife was always the miserable Cinderella condemned to the monotony of the kitchen, while the husband was the absolute master of the house, would be far from the truth. "You cannot drive out human nature with a pitchfork," says Horace in a well-known passage (*Epist.*, i, 10, 24), and this also holds good of the Greek woman. The nature of woman can never deny itself—in any people or at any time. There were three factors especially which assisted the woman in the happier times of Hellenism in sometimes obtaining physical and moral superiority over the man: occasional intellectual superiority, or inborn lust of power supported by feminine refinement, or a too extravagant dowry. As an example of this we may perhaps quote Xanthippe, the wife of Socrates, whose name has unjustly become proverbial—for she was an excellent housewife and never overstepped the limits appointed for her; and yet shrews can have been by no means rare, as is clear from the fact that in mythology, the truest mirror of the soul of the people, a prototype was created for her in the Lydian queen Omphale, who degrades Heracles, the greatest and most glorious of the Greek heroes, to the humiliating position of a vassal, so that he, dressed in woman's attire, does female handiwork at her feet while she wears the lion's skin and swings the club over the hero cowering at her side, placing her slippered foot upon his mighty neck (Aristoph., *Lysistr.*, 657; Anth. Pal., x, 55; Lucian, *Dial. Deor.*, 13, 2). Thus the slipper became a symbol of the deplorable condition of the married man, who is under "petticoat-government". The slipper, indeed, became the instrument which furious married women made use of to teach their husbands manners. This method was the more practical, since slippers at all times were at the disposal of the woman shuffling along in sandals, while had she wanted to use a stout stick she would have been obliged to hunt for one, for the Greek wand was merely the light, pithy *narthex* (parsley) stalk, the tropics not having at that time imported bamboo canes.

Thus it is understandable that married women were often called *empusae* (Aristoph., *Frogs*, 293, and Scholiast, *Eccles.*, 1056; Demosthenes, xviii, 130, and Scholiast) or *lamiae* (Apuleius, *Metamorph.*, i, 17, v, 11), by which names, as is well known, phantoms like vampires were intended (one of whose legs was of bronze, the other of asses' dung), or ugly old women—hags.

In Greek public opinion no kind of reason could be found for blaming a man who, tired of the eternal monotony of living with his wife, sought a welcome change in the arms of an intellectually stimulating and agreeable courtesan, or knew how to improve the triviality of every-day life with the small-talk of a beautiful boy. Infidelity, as we call it, can never have been spoken of by an ancient Greek, for in his day it had never occurred to a husband that the idea of marriage connoted the renunciation of æsthetic enjoyment, and still less would the wife have expected such a sacrifice from him. The Greeks are, therefore, not more immoral, but more moral, than we are, since they recognized the polygamous tendency of the man and acted accordingly, and also passed judgment on the action of others in the same way, while we, in spite of possessing the same knowledge, are too cowardly to draw the conclusions, and, satisfied if only the outer appearance is preserved, sin in secret so much the more. At the same time it ought not to be forgotten that there were also some among the Greeks, certainly very few and far between, who demanded a like morality for both sexes in marriage, somewhat like the homely Isocrates (*Nicocles*, 40); and Aristotle (*Repub.*, vii, 16, 1335) in certain definite cases demands *Atimia*, that is, loss of civil rights by the married man who "has intercourse with another woman or man"; but, in the first place, as observed, such voices are few and far between, and next, we nowhere hear that anyone in practice acted so; rather it remained a matter of circumstances, as the eighty-four year old slave Syra in the *Mercator* (iv, 6) of Plautus complains with comic indignation: "My, my! women do live under hard conditions, so much more unfair, poor things, than the men's. Why, if a husband has brought home some strumpet, unbeknown to his wife, and she finds it out, the husband goes scot free. But once a wife steps out of the house unbeknown to her husband, he has his ground and she's divorced. Oh, I wish there was the same rule for the husband as for the wife! Now a wife, a good wife, is content with just her husband; why should a husband be less content with just his wife? Mercy me, if husbands too were taken to task for wenching on the sly, the same way as wanton wives are divorced, I warrant there'd be more lone men about than there are now women!"

We may mention as a curiosity what we are told by the romance writer Achilles Tatius (viii, 6), (fifth century A.D.), about the so-called test of virginity. He says that in Ephesus there was a grotto, dedicated by Pan to the maiden Artemis in which he had hung up his flute, with the intention that only pure virgins might enter it. If any suspicion of unchastity arose against a young girl, she was shut up in the grotto. If she was innocent, the flute was heard to sound loudly, the door opened automatically and the girl came out with a clear character. If she was not, the flute was silent and a long-drawn moan was heard, the door was then opened, but the girl had disappeared.[1]

We cannot any longer verify how far the story told by Plutarch (*Lycurg.*, 15) in which the purity of Spartan marriages is praised, is based upon truth, but it may be given here as very characteristic: "Geradas, one of the old Spartans, being asked by a guest, how the Spartans punished adulterers, replied: 'There are no adulterers amongst us.' 'But if there should be?' insisted the guest. 'Then, as a punishment, he will have to give a bull large enough to stretch out his head over mount Taygetus and to drink from the river Eurotas.' When the guest in amazement asked: 'Wherever in the world could so big a bull be found?' Geradas laughed and said: 'How could there be an adulterer in Sparta?'"

Although Plutarch expressly puts forward the statement that in this case it was a question of old times, yet the same writer informs us, concerning the same Spartans, that a man unhesitatingly allowed another man to fill his nuptial bed, if he thought him better fitted for begetting descendants.

At least in Athens, as it appears, there was nothing extraordinary in the insulted husband killing the adulterer. This, for instance, was done by Euphiletus, who had surprised Eratosthenes in bed with his wife. We quote the following passage from Lysias: "When I had thrust open the door of the bedroom those who entered first saw a man still lying beside my wife, those who came afterwards saw him standing naked on the bed. I, gentlemen, knocked him down, bound both his arms behind him and asked him why he had insulted the honour of my house. He admitted that he had done wrong, but begged and prayed me not to kill him, but to take from him a sum of money. To this I answered, 'I will not kill you, but the

[1] Aelian in his *Var. Hist.* (xi, 6) tells a similar story of the dragon's cave near Lanuvium.

law of the State will kill you'." (Lysias, *De Caede Eratosthenis*, 24.)

If a girl of irreproachable character was seduced in ancient Athens severe, indeed barbarous, punishments were possible. We read in Æschines (*Contra Timarchum*, 182, 183): "Our forefathers were so severe where their honour was affected, and valued the purity of their children's morals so highly, that one of the citizens, becoming aware that his daughter had been violated and that she had not preserved her maidenhood until her marriage, shut her up with a horse in a lonely house, so that she died of hunger. The site of the house is still to be seen in our city, and the place is called 'The Horse and Girl'." According to the Scholiast it was a wild horse, which first ate the girl from hunger and then died itself. It is hard to say whether the frightful story is true. Probably it arose from the name of the place, when the latter was no longer understood.

Also in regard to the punishment of a woman caught in the act of adultery Æschines expresses himself as follows: "The woman may put on no ornaments and may not visit the public temples, lest she should corrupt women who were beyond reproach; but if she does so or adorns herself, then the first man who meets her may tear her clothes from her body, take her ornaments from her and beat her; but he may not kill her or make her a cripple, if only he makes her a dishonoured woman and deprives her of all pleasure in life. But pimps (male and female) are accused and, if they are convicted, are punished with death, since, while those who are greedy for lust are shy of coming together, they in addition practise their own shamelessness for recompense and finally make the attempt and come to an agreement."

Of course here and there many kinds of local customs were in existence. Thus Plutarch relates (*Quæstiones Græcæ*, 2) that in Cymē the adulteress was dragged to the market-place and exposed on a certain stone in the sight of all.. Afterwards she was made to ride on an ass through the city. The ride ended with a second exposure on the stone, and the dishonouring name " Rider on the Ass " stuck to the woman ever afterwards. At Lepreum (Heracleides Ponticus, *Pol.*, 14) in Elis adulterers were led through the city for three days bound, and were deprived of their civil rights for the rest of their life; the woman was obliged to stand for eleven days in the market without a girdle and in transparent vest and remained disgraced.

The way for adulterous intercourse was, of course, paved by willing maidservants and greedy chambermaids, a class that took a special interest in such matters. They attended to the notes and little presents, flowers and fruit, especially the favourite apples (Alciphron, *Epist.*, iii, 62; Lucian, *Tox.*, 13, *Dial. Meretr.*, 12, 1; Theocritus, xi, 10) even those that had been bitten—it is remarkable how here also the apple plays a similar part as in the case of Eve; in short, they performed all matters by which secret love-affairs were arranged, as is described so vividly and with great refinement by Ovid in his *Art of Love* (i, 351 ff.; ii, 251 ff.). The nurse of Phaedra, who had fallen madly in love with her beautiful stepson, Hippolytas, attempted similar arts of the pander with infernal cunning, as Euripides describes in a masterly manner in his *Hippolytus*. With the help of obliging servants ladders were procured and set up, by means of which the amorous friend could get into the women's room through the window or a dormer-window (Xenarchus, frag. 4 (*Kock*); Ath., xiii, 569), and all the other tricks were practised by which adulterous love attained its object. That the readiness of the go-betweens to oblige was enhanced by cash presents (Dion Chrysost., vii, 144) may be conjectured, although not many passages expressly confirm it. The universally-known myth of the beautiful Danaë, whose father, worried by an oracle, shut her away from the outer world in a double and triple brazen " tower-like room " (and yet she was visited by Zeus), attests this and nothing else, for the rain, in the form in which he came, was of gold.

Of course the adjustment of the forbidden joys of love did not remain confined to nurses, servants, or lady's maids; rather, a special class of " opportunity-makers ", procuresses [1] at all times ready to oblige for love or money, was gradually formed. With perfect plastic art and in a highly realistic manner Herondas (third century B.C.) has sketched such a person in the first of his *mimiambi* (discovered in 1891). He takes us into the room of the highly respectable madam Metriche, who is sitting alone with her maid at her needlework; her husband has gone to Egypt on business, and ten months have passed without her having heard anything of him. Then there is a knock at the door; she jumps up, full of joyful expectation, that it may be the husband whom she has missed so long; but it is not he who stands without, but Gyllis, in whom the poet introduces us to one of those dismal and cowardly, but obtrusive and extremely cunning " opportunity-makers ". After a few unimportant words of greeting the two ladies carry on the following conversation:

Metriche: Threissa, someone's knocking at the door; go and see if anyone has come from our friends in the country.

Threissa: Who's knocking?

Gyllis: It's I.

Thr.: Who are you? are you afraid to come nearer?

Gy.: Look, I am nearer.

Thr.: But who are you?

Gy.: Gyllis, Philænion's mother. Go in and tell Metriche that I am here.

[1] Προκυκλίς, προμνήστρια, προαγωγός and other names.

Met.: Ask her to come in. Who is it?

Thr.: Gyllis.

Met.: Mother Gyllis? Take yourself off, girl. [*Threissa goes out.*] What destiny persuaded you to visit me, Gyllis? Why have you come like a god to men? For I think it is about five months since anyone has seen you coming to my door, even in a dream.

Gy.: I live a long way off, my child, and in the streets the mud comes up to one's knees. I am no more good than a fly, for old age is dragging me down and the shadow of death is near.

Met.: Hush! don't tell lies about your age, for you are still able, Gyllis, to hug some more men.

Gy.: Jeer as much as you like, it is the nature of you young women to do so; but don't get excited. But, my child, what a lonely life yours must be, wearing yourself away on a solitary couch. For since Mandris started for Egypt it is ten months, and he has not even written to you; he has forgotten you and has drunk anew of the cup of love. There is the home of Aphrodite; for anything—all that there is or has been anywhere—is in Egypt: wealth, palaestrae, power, peace, glory, goddesses, philosophers, gold plate, young court favourites, the sacred precincts of the two deified brothers, the good king, the museum, wine, every good thing you can want, and women—what numbers of them! By the queen of Hades, the sky cannot boast of having as many stars, women to look at like the goddesses who once hurried to Paris to be judged in beauty—may I not be heard to mention their names. How does it feel warming your empty couch? You will waste away unseen and the ashes of decay will consume your ripe beauty. Look somewhere else and for two or three days change your course, and be happy with another friend; a ship moored with a single anchor is unsafe. If Mandris goes below, he is dead and done, for no one can rouse us from the grave, dear lady. You know a violent storm can arise from a calm, and none of us knows the future. For the time of our youth is uncertain—but there's nobody near? [*Looks at the door.*]

Met.: Not a soul.

Gy.: Listen then to what I came to tell you. Gryllos, the son of Matalīnē, the daughter of Pataekion, the winner of five victories—once when a boy at Pytho, twice at Corinth where he defeated youths with the first bloom upon their cheeks, and twice at Pisa where he overcame men in boxing—he is gloriously wealthy, so quiet that he doesn't even move a straw from the ground, heart-whole, as secure as a seal for secrecy. He saw you at the feast of the descent of Mise [1] and his vitals swelled with passion and his heart was goaded to madness; and he never leaves my house day and night, my dear, but bewails loudly to me and calls me "little mother", and is dying in his desire for you. Now, my dear child Metriche, grant me this one sin; attach yourself to the goddess, lest old age steal over you before you know. You will gain two advantages; you will live in pleasure and you will also secure greater rewards than you think. Think it over, listen to me. I love you, by the Fates I do.

Met.: Gyllis, your grey hairs are dulling your wits. For, as I hope to see Mandris return safely, by our lady Demeter, I would not have listened quietly to such words as these from any other woman —I would have taught her to come here with her crooked advice and made her go limping away, hating my very doorstep. Never come again to see me with a single proposal of the kind. Tell young women words which befit wearers of the girdle, but leave Metriche the daughter of Pytheës

[1] Mise's descent: a festival of the religious sacred cult of that time. Mise is a mystical female divinity, belonging to the cult of Eleusis. A similar cult existed on the island of Cos, the home of Herondas. See *Roscher, Lexikon der Mythologie*, ii, 3025.

to warm her lonely couch; no one can ever laugh in Mandris's face because of his wife. But this is not the kind of talk that Gyllis wants. Threissa, wipe that pitcher and pour out three measures of unmixed wine, and drop in water, and give her a bumper.

Thr.: There, Gyllis, drink.

Gy.: Give it me. I didn't come with the intention of persuading you to go astray, but to tell you about the festival.

Met.: And for this reason, Gyllis, you have enjoyed a drink.

Gy.: May you always have plenty of it in your press, my dear. It's sweet, by Demeter; Gyllis has never drunk sweeter wine than Metriche's. Well, good luck to you, my dear. Take care of yourself. I hope my girls Myrtale and Sime will remain young, as long as Gyllis has breath in her body.

In this case the procuress certainly had no luck; with unmistakable clearness she is sent home by Metriche, who is, however, good-natured enough to offer her a parting drink; for she knows the weak side of women of that kind, whose fondness for wine is again and again made prominent by authors and in comedy especially formed a motive that was always applauded.

If the woman was too timid, the pander (of whichever sex) put his or her own home at her disposal or procured a third neutral love-nest (brothel).[1]

The frequent mention of these amorous shelters in ancient authors and the numerous expressions for them, prove how widespread such arrangements were, and how often they were called into requisition, for the offer and demand for them are always in direct correlation.

A friend might also lend his own home to the furtherance of illegal amours; we are made

[1] Called μα(σ)τρυλεῖα (diminutive μα(α)τρύλλια).

acquainted with the best-known example through the poet Catullus (lxviii, 67) who cannot thank his friend Allius sufficiently for his readiness to oblige: "He opened a broad track across the fenced field, he gave me access to a house and its mistress, under whose roof we should together enjoy each his own love. Thither my fair goddess delicately stepped, and set the sole of her shining foot on the smooth threshold, as she pressed on her slender sandal."

Of course, it also happened that the married man had knowledge of the amorous dodges of his wife and endured them silently; indeed, that he gained material advantage from them, as in the speech against Neaera (wrongly ascribed to Demosthenes) the wife is obliged to defray the expenses of the housekeeping by her bodily charms. But, in the case of his wife's being unfaithful, the husband may have obtained a divorce. It cannot be our task to enter into the legal provisions of such divorce, but it may be mentioned that separation might also take place for other reasons. Among them was incompatibility of temperament, for which Plato (*Laws*, vi, 784) would have liked a court of arbitration to be established; further, childlessness, which seems quite logical, since the Greek regarded the begetting of legitimate descendants as the chief object of marriage. For this reason wives who had no children had recourse to the device of supposititious children, since, as Dion Chrysostom says (xv, 8): "Every wife would be very glad to keep her husband." A quite natural consequence of this was that the idea of "marriage on trial" offered no impossibility. It is reported of Crates the Cynic (Diog. Laërt., vi, 93) that "according to his own confession he had handed over his daughter to be married for thirty days on trial".

What has been hitherto said concerning Greek marriage is an attempt to combine systematically in a general picture, which might contain everything of importance, all the scattered passages in different authors in which marriage and the wife are spoken of. The results so obtained may now be further supplemented by various details and greater light thrown upon them by anecdotes, *bons mots*, and the like. A collection of such had already been made in ancient times, and much of it has come down to us. Thus, in the philosophical writings of Plutarch, problems concerning marriage are frequently examined. An inexhaustible mine of information about antiquity is the *Banquet of the Learned* in 15 books by Athenaeus of Naucratis in Egypt, who lived in the time of Marcus Aurelius. The dinner took place in the house of Larensius, a distinguished and highly educated Roman; twenty-nine guests from all branches of learning were invited—philosophers, rhetoricians, poets, musicians, physicians, and jurists, amongst them Athenæus, who in the work (completely preserved except for the beginning and end) recounts to his friend Timocrates everything that was discussed at the banquet. At the beginning of the 13th book the conversation turns upon marriage and married women: "In Sparta it was customary to shut all marriageable girls in a dark room and the unmarried young men with them; every young man carried off without a dowry any girl he caught hold of." According to Clearchus of Soli, on a certain festival, the women drag the unmarried men round the altar and beat them with rods, in order that, to avoid such disgrace, they may turn to love and approach marriage in due time. In Athens Cecrops first introduced the practice of monogamy, whereas hitherto sexual intercourse was unrestrained and marriages in common prevailed. According to a widespread opinion, which was said to go back to Aristotle, Socrates also had two lawful wives, Xanthippe and a certain Myrto, a great-granddaughter of the well-known Aristeides. At that time possibly this was legally permitted owing to the deficiency of population. Among the Persians the king's wife is treated with reverence and respect by the rest of the concubines, who prostrate themselves before her. Priam (*Iliad*, xxiv, 496) also has a number of concubines without his wife Hecuba being annoyed. " Fifty sons I had when the sons of the Achæans came ; nineteen were born to me of the self-same womb, and the others women of the palace bare."

As Aristotle (frag. 162) remarks, we might be surprised that Homer in the *Iliad* never mentions a concubine as sleeping with Menelaus, although he allows more than one wife to the rest. For there slept by him even old men like Nestor and Phœnix with their wives. They had not weakened themselves in their youth by drunkenness, sexual excesses, or gluttony, so that quite naturally in their old age they were still vigorous. If then Menelaus renounces a subsidiary wife, he evidently does so out of regard for Helen, who is his wedded wife, and for whose sake he has assembled an army. But Agamemnon is abused by Thersites (*Iliad*, ii, 226) as a man of many wives : " Filled are thy huts with bronze, and women full many are in thy huts, chosen spoils that we Achæans give thee first of all, whenso'er we take a citadel." " Of course," says Aristotle further, " these many women are only a gift of honour, not for use ; since he was not supplied with much wine to get drunk." But Heracles, who is reputed to have had the greatest number of wives (for he was very fond of women), only had them one after another, when he was on a campaign and travelled in different countries.

The 50 daughters of Thestius he certainly deflowered in seven days, as we are told by Herodorus (*FHG* II, 30). Istrus in his *Attic Stories* (*FHG* I, 420) enumerates the different wives of Theseus, and says that some he married for love, others he carried off as booty, while one was his lawful wife.

Philip of Macedon took no women with him on his campaigns, but Darius, who was overthrown by Alexander, although he was fighting for his very existence dragged round with him 360 concubines, as Dicæarchus tells us in his *Life in Hellas* (*FHG* II, 240).

The poet Euripides was also fond of women. Hieronymus (frag. 6) in his *Historic Memoranda* tells us that, when someone said to Sophocles that Euripides was a woman-hater, " Yes, in his tragedies," said Sophocles, " but in bed he was very fond of them."

Married women came off very badly in the comedy *The Dealers in Garlands*, by Eubulus (frag. 98, Kock), wherein is said of them: " If you go out during the summer, two streams of dark paint flow from your eyes, and from your cheeks the sweat makes a red furrow down to your neck, and the hair on your forehead is grey, full of white lead."

From *The Seers*, a comedy of Alexis (frag. 146, Kock), one of the guests quotes the following lines: " Unhappy that we are, we who have sold freedom of living and luxury; we live as slaves to our wives instead of being free. Then must we put up with it for nothing, and get no equivalent? Except the dowry, which is bitter and full of woman's gall, compared with which the gall of men is like honey. For they when injured by their wives forgive them, but the wives, when they do wrong, reproach us as well. They begin what they should not, and what they should begin they neglect, perjure themselves, and when they suffer no evil they complain that they are always suffering."

Xenarchus (frag. 14, Kock) praises the grasshoppers as happy, since their females have no voice; and Eubulus (frag. 116, 117, Kock) as well as Aristophon (frag. 5, Kock) give expression to the idea that a man who marries for the first time is not to be blamed since he does not yet know the " rotten swindle " ; but he who marries the second time is beyond help.

In the same play one of the characters wants to take wives under his protection, " the most excellent of all blessings." He is also successful in confronting the notorious mischief-makers with some examples of good wives—Medea with a Penelope, Clytæmnestra with an Alcestis. " But perhaps someone will speak ill of Phædra ; but, by Zeus, who indeed was a good woman ? unhappy man that I am, good women will soon fail me, but I have still many bad women to mention."

Antiphanes (frag. 221, Kock) quotes the words: " He has married. What do you say? Is he really married, whom I left walking about yesterday."

The following two passages are from Menander (frag. 65, 154, Kock), " You will not marry, if you've any sense, and leave this life of yours. For I who speak to you have married. Therefore I advise you: 'Do not wed.' The matter's voted and decreed. Be cast the dice! Well then, go on! But heaven send you come off safe. On a real sea of troubles you're embarking now, No Libyan nor Ægean nor Sicilian sea where three boats out of thirty may escape from wreck—there is no married man at all who has been saved ! "

" Now may he perish, root and branch, whoever was the first to marry, and then the second one, and next the third, and then the fourth, and then the last one on the list."

A tragedy of the poet Carcinus (frag. 3, Nauck) contains the words : " O Zeus, what need is there to abuse women ? It would be enough if you only said the word 'woman' ".

We might supplement these extracts by some others, but if we desired to collect all the passages in which Greek authors, more or less cleverly, turn their attention towards the female sex, this alone would fill an imposing volume. From the tragedians, especially Euripides, hundreds of attacks on the female sex could be got together, which can all more or less be included under the motto: "To bury a woman is better than to marry her."

Not to weary the reader, we will content ourselves with a small selection from comedy. It is certainly more than a remarkable coincidence that the very first fragment of all, which is preserved to us among the remains of the old Attic comedy, contains an attack on women.

With comic pathos Susarion of Megara, who in the first half of the sixth century had transplanted comedy to the deme of Icaria in Attica, appears before the public, to which he exclaims that it is misery with women, but an evil hardly to be avoided, so that he comes to the startling result: "To marry and not to marry are both equally bad" (*CAF*, p. 3, Kock). We may quote from Aristophanes (*Lysistr.*, 368, 1014, 1018):—

"There's no poet wiser than Euripides; for there's no creature so shameless as women . . . There is no wild beast more unconquerable than a woman, nor fire nor any panther so shameless . . . Why, are you aware of this, and then make war upon me, when it is in your power, you wretch, to have me as a firm friend . . . For I will never cease to hate woman."

Aristophanes often makes the women themselves announce their baseness very amusingly. We quote a specially characteristic passage from the *Thesmophoriazusae* (383 ff.): "O ladies, it is not love of ostentation that has made me get up to speak, but it is because I have indeed been a vexed, unhappy woman now for a long time, seeing you treated with contumely by Euripides, the son of the herb-woman, and abused with much abuse of every kind. For what abuse does he not smear upon us, and where has he not calumniated us? I don't believe there is a single theatre or stage where he has not called us adulteresses in disposition, lovers of men, wine-bibbers, traitresses, gossips, masses of wickedness, great pests to men. So that, as soon as they come home from the theatre-benches, they look askance at us, and straightway search, lest any paramour be concealed in the closet. And we are no longer able to do any of those things we used to—such suspicion has Euripides taught our husbands, so that, if any woman even weave a crown she is thought to be in love, and if she let fall any vessel while roaming about the house her husband asks her in whose honour is the pot broken ?—it must be for the Corinthian stranger ! Is any girl sick ? straightway her brother says, 'This colour in the girl does not please me.' Well, does any woman, lacking children, wish to substitute a child, it is not possible even for this to go undiscovered ; for now their husbands sit on their very beds ! And Euripides has calumniated us to the old men who heretofore used to marry girls, and now no rich old man is willing to marry us—all through his verse : 'An old man weds a tyrant, not a wife' (*Phœnix*). In the next place, through him they now put seals and bolts upon the women's apartments, guarding us ; and, moreover, they keep Molossian dogs—a terror to lovers ! We might, my friends, put up with all this, but now our little perquisites—our right as housewives to pick out and take barley meal, oil, and wine—even this is no longer permitted us ! "

The objection certainly suggests itself that all these passages prove nothing or only very little concerning the Greek conception of marriage and women generally, since they are for the most part taken from comedy, which, as is well known, does not represent actual life, but its grotesquely distorted reflection. Certainly ; yet comedy does not create any completely new views, but caricatures and exaggerates only what is ready to hand, so that comedy also may very well be considered as a mirror of the time; it is further to be remarked, that such attacks upon marriage and the female sex are by no means to be found only in the comic poets, but run through the whole of literature like a red thread. Unfortunately, considerations of space compels us to limit our selection to a definite class of literature; but, as early as the times when an artistic comedy was not yet thought of, there is an echo of voices which refuse to allow women to possess a single good quality. As early as the first quarter of the seventh century B.C., Simonides of Amorgos (*PLG.*, ii, 446) had given vent to his feelings in a long satirical poem which is still preserved, and expressed and confirmed his conviction of the physiological as well as the moral weakmindedness of women with startling clearness and frankness. The poet affirms that of ten women nine are worthless, a phenomenon which he endeavours to explain by their origin. The uncleanly woman comes from the sow, the exceedingly clever from the fox, the curious from the dog, the intellectually dull, who knows nothing about anything except eating, from the insensible earth; the changeable and capricious is like the ever-shifting sea, that can never be reckoned with; the idle must put up with the ass as her ancestor, and the spiteful with the cat; she who has a passion for dress and finery, who is ever on the look-out for fashionable novelties is derived from the horse, and lastly, the ugly from monkeys.

"The ninth descends from the ape; this is decidedly the worst evil that Zeus hath given to men. In appearance most ugly; when such a woman shows herself in the street, people laugh at her. She is short in the neck, hardly moves, has no buttocks, is withered of limb; unhappy a man who embraces such a pest. And she knows all intrigues and tricks like an ape, nor does she ever care to laugh. Nor will she ever do a good turn to anyone, but it is her aim which she plans every day how she may do him the greatest injury."

After this systematic compilation of female vices in no fewer than 82 lines there follows in only nine lines the praise of a true wife, the industrious mistress of the house and mother, who descends from the bee and who " loved and loving, grows old with her husband, the mother of a beautiful and famous race ".

Naturally, voices are not wanting to announce the praise of the wife. In the bulky Anthology of Stobæus, iv, 22 (No. 4), several chapters deal in great detail with marriage; numerous quotations from poets and philosophers are advanced, amongst which are to be found a mixture of very spiteful and also very eulogistic and admiring expressions. Thus the comedian Alexandrus, *CAF.*, iii, 373 (No. 5), says: " A noble wife is the storehouse of virtue," and even Theognis (1225) commits himself to the opinion that " there is nothing sweeter than an honest wife ".

According to Euripides (*TGF.*, 566) it is a mistake to blame all women alike: " for as there are many women, so will one find many a one bad, but also many good ". Certainly, it would be easy to quote several judgments of this kind, but they are more or less scanty and the praise of women is hardly ever expressed without reservation. It is also significant that in this chapter of Stobæus there is a section entitled " Blame of Women ", without a parallel on the praise of women.

We possess an excellent pamphlet by Plutarch entitled "Advice to the Married" (see p. 38), dedicated to a newly wedded couple, with whom Plutarch was acquainted.

Plutarch also wrote an extant monograph " On Women's Virtues " (better translated " Heroism of Women "), a collection of examples with the well-known saying of Pericles in his funeral oration, that those women are the best of whom one speaks least in society, either for good or ill, and treats the subject often discussed in the philosophical schools since the time of the sophists—whether the virtues of women can be compared with those of men. The conclusion reached is that the sexes are morally equivalent, which is illustrated by historical examples of distinguished women.

CHAPTER II

The Human Figure

1. Clothing

The question whether the men's clothing is a result of the awakened sense of shame or whether the sense of shame developed after the use of clothing, as to which there was formerly a lively dispute, is decided in the latter sense. This is no longer a theory, but can be regarded as a proved fact; hence it is superfluous to repeat the proofs that have often been stated. The most primitive art of clothing grew out of the desire to protect oneself against the inclemency of the weather; the skin of animals that were slain for food was made use of, and the covering of the body that followed only very slowly produced, on the one hand, the feeling that one had something to conceal, on the other hand, the wish to adorn oneself or to bring into prominence individual parts of the body and thereby to accentuate one's sensual charms. The adornment of the body is at the present day the chief object of "clothing" among the people living in a state of nature in the torrid zone; it remained the object of dress, even after the progress of culture had developed the so-called feeling of shame, to cover the body entirely or some parts of it, according as the feeling of shame that had become the property of individuals or the whole people (which is now called "morals") demanded it. It cannot therefore be a question for us to describe the dress of the Greeks with the detail required by a history of costume; our task will be limited to showing how far the feeling of shame on the one hand, and the need of adornment on the other dominated the fashion. Since, at the time of the most highly developed culture as it is displayed in the spirit of the Greeks, the two factors of the feeling of shame and the need for protection against the weather cannot be separated in reference to clothing, it appears that we shall not have much to say of men's clothing; but even women's clothing can be treated with comparative brevity, since, considering the seclusion of Greek women and the very small part played by them in public, there was hardly any opportunity to wear specially splendid dress when walking, so that the fashion could not have had nearly the same importance in the life of Greek women as at the present day.

The Greek boy, in his short chlamys, which, however, did not show the forms of the youthful body, was disadvantageously dressed. The chlamys was a kind of shawl which was fastened on the right shoulder or on the breast by a button or clasp, and was worn till the lad reached the status of the ephebi (that is, about sixteen years). Smaller boys wore, at least in Athens and until the time of the Peloponnesian war, only a short chiton, a kind of thin shirt. Aristophanes praises the hardening effect and simplicity of the old times in the words (*Clouds*, 964): "I will, therefore, describe the ancient system of education, how it was ordered, when I flourished in the advocacy of justice and temperance was in the fashion. In the first place, it was incumbent that no one should hear the voice of a boy uttering a syllable; and next, that those from the same quarter of the town should march in good order through the streets to the school of the Harpmaster, naked, and in a body, even if it were to snow as thick as meal."

And it is well-known that Lycurgus (*Lycurg.*, 16) also endeavoured to harden the boys of Sparta by making them wear in summer and winter one and the same wretched garment, as long as they were little, up to about 12, the chiton, and later the tribon, a short wrapper of coarse stuff.

The question arises, why the Greeks, who yet had such understanding of boyish beauty, did not contrive some more advantageous dress for their young ones, since they continually had the opportunity to see boys and young men in the most beautiful dress, in the nakedness of paradise. Yet the boys were in the baths and palaestrae, the gymnasia and wrestling-schools, for three-quarters of the day and were consequently seen naked, indeed quite naked, that is, without the hideous swimming-drawers, of which we will speak later.

The clothing of the men consisted essentially of the chiton, the woollen or linen under-garment (shirt) and the himation thrown over it. This may be described as a large four-cornered piece of cloth which was thrown over the left shoulder and, held firmly with the arm, was then drawn away on the back towards the right side over or under the right arm, and then again thrown over the left shoulder or the left arm. From the more or less clever way in which a man put on this article of clothing one was able to recognize the general culture of the wearer. The mild climate often enough permitted him to dispense with the himation, and to go out in the simple chiton. Conversely, many dispensed with the chiton and went out only wearing the himation, as Socrates nearly always did (Xenophon, *Memor.*, i, 6, 2); so did Agesilaus (Aelian, *Var. hist.*, vii, 13), the excellent king of Sparta, who even in severe cold weather and when he was old found the chiton superfluous; and Gelon (Diod. Sic., xi, 26), the ruler of Syracuse, and many others. It is also specially told of Phocion (Duris in Plutarch, *Phocion*, 4), that he "always went along without shoes and without a chiton, unless the weather was bitterly cold, so that the soldiers used to say jokingly that it was a sign of intense cold when Phocion wore the chiton". The word *gymnos*, usually meaning "naked", was also applied to those who went without the chiton. The himation generally reached to the knee, or a little lower ; to wear it too long was considered a sign of extravagance or pride ; for instance, Alcibiades (Plato, *Alcib.*, i, 122 ; Plutarch, *Alcib.*, 1), when a young man, often gave offence by this, while those whose himation ended above the knee were considered indecent (Theophrastus, *Charact.*, 4) ; especially to sit down so that the himation slipped up above the knee was regarded as directly barefaced, which is intelligible considering that drawers were not worn. Thus we must understand what Lucian tells us of the cynic, Alcidamas (*Sympos.*, 14), who at a meal lies down half-naked (that is, with his himation slipped up high above the knee), leaning on his elbow, holding the cup in his right hand, just as Heracles is shown by painters in the cave of the centaur Pholus. This was considered indecent, since here there is no motive for the exposure of the person ; but if the same Alcidamas, in order to show the pure white of his body, bares himself to the extreme limit, that only excited the laughter of the guests.

What was said here of the clothing of men holds good for the whole time Greece lasted, a few unessential modifications excepted. In the case of the women's clothing, we must dwell upon this somewhat longer and distinguish different epochs. It is extraordinarily interesting that women's clothing at no time in Greece developed with greater luxuriance and refinement than during Hellenic prehistoric times, which are usually called " Ægæan Civilization ". Thanks to several monuments, paintings, and small examples of plastic art from the palace of Cnossus in Crete we are well informed as to the fashion of upper-class women of these very ancient times, from which no literary testimony has come down to us. We see the ladies of the royal court of the first half of the second millennium B.C. appearing in a costume, which modern times would certainly stigmatize as immodest. From the hips to the feet they wore a skirt which consisted of numerous pieces laid one over the other, as if made of several skirts. The upper part of the body was covered by a fairly tight-fitting garment, like a jacket, provided with sleeves. From this garment the breasts protruded, totally bare in their full roundness ; like two ripe love-apples they laughed at the spectator.

We shall return again to this costume, when we speak of nakedness and denudation in connection with each other. In any case, the Cretan finds prove that the artful way of leaving the neck and shoulders uncovered and indeed, as we saw, in its most defiant form, is not foreign to the oldest Greek civilization ; further that probably, and as a matter of course, it continued to be a right reserved for the upper-class lady.

It is quite logical and easy to show that with the further development of Greek civilization the bare neck and shoulders, which in Crete had begun by promising so much, again disappears from female fashion. The magnificent court banquets, at which the ladies could shine with the dazzling nakedness of their bosom, gradually became forgotten, since, except during the short period of the Greek "tyrants", republics were formed everywhere ; and further since, as is frequently indicated, civilization developed more and more on the male side, which led to the disappearance of women from public life, so that they no longer had the opportunity of charming the senses of men with their cunningly refined dress—or, more correctly, their undress.

We certainly find here and there among those of the Greek female statues that are robed a rather bashful and usually pointed *décolletage*, though it cannot be said that such became the favourite fashion ; later—favoured again by the climate—there seems to have come into vogue the alternative custom of wearing upper garments so thin that the forms of the breasts could be clearly seen through, as we can observe even at the present day in numerous monuments of plastic art—for instance, in the two magnificent female forms on the east pediment of the Parthenon.

For completeness we may remark that a *décolletage* of the reverse side was nothing unheard of; at any rate a passage in the *Satires* of Varro [1] cannot well be differently explained, where in describing the costume of a huntress with her dress tucked up, *à la* Atalanta, he says that she walks along with her dress gathered up so high that one could see, not only her calves, but almost her buttocks as well.

In the times that followed the Aegaean period the dress of the Greek women assumed a comparatively simple form. On the bare body the shirt-like chiton was worn, the form of which was throughout Greece essentially the same, except in Sparta (on the short chiton of Spartan girls, cf. Clem. Alex. *Pædag.*, ii, 10, p. 258 (Potter)). There, girls usually wore no other article of clothing except this chiton, which ended above the knee and at the side was slit up high, so that in stepping along the entire thigh was exposed (φαινομηρίδες: showing the thigh; cf. Pollux, vii, 55). Not only did several authors agree in stating this, so that its truth cannot be disputed, but it is also confirmed by vase-paintings and other memorials of pictorial art; it also becomes a positive certainty that elsewhere, although in Greece generally people were sufficiently used to the sight of nakedness, this costume of the Spartan girls was ridiculed. Hence they were called "thigh-showers", "those with bare thighs", and the expression "to dress in Doric fashion" (δωριάςειν: Eustathius on *Iliad*, xiv, 175) was used of those "who liberally bared a great part of their body". In gymnastic and bodily exercises Spartan girls also put off this single piece of clothing and appeared completely naked.

[1] Varro in Petronius (ed. Bücheler, 1895, p. 193, frag. ix): *non modo suris apertis, sed paene natibus apertis ambulans.*

In the rest of Greece the chiton as a single article of dress was only worn in the house; in public the himation was indispensable for women; this, with the exception of the somewhat modified cut required by the differently conditioned build of the female body, was not essentially different from the man's himation, although it is not improbable that slight variations were due to time, fashion, and locality.

We need not go into such details, as the question of dress in this book only belongs to the subject so far as it plays any kind of part in the morals and sexual life of the Greeks.

The girdle that surrounds the hips and keeps up the dress had an erotic meaning so far as it was the symbol of virginity, so that the turn that often occurs in Homer "to loose the maiden's girdle" is easy to explain.

Greek women and girls knew nothing of stays or corsets, but they wore breast-bands, or "bust-supporters", which may be compared to the *brassière* of to-day. The object of this band, worn as it was round the breast, usually under the chiton and therefore on the bare skin, was to raise the bosom and thereby not only to prevent the unsightly hanging of the breasts, but also to emphasize them or to cover any defect in their beauty (Ovid, *Remedia Amoris*, 337); and it also served to limit excessive development of the bosom, that "there may be something for our hand to encompass and cover" (Martial, xiv, 134.) All this would consequently agree with the functions of the modern stays; but the ancient breast-band differs from the modern corset in that it did not include any lacing-up of the waist.[1]

For the rest, a number of toilet-secrets were already known to the ladies of classical antiquity, by which charms which they lacked could be imitated so as to appear real or at least those which were defective

[1] A covering for the private parts (χοιροκομεῖον) is often mentioned: Aristoph., *Wasps*, 844, Lysist. 1073.

could be increased, although it is certainly not improbable, that such devices were employed less by respectable housewives than by the ever obliging ladies of the demi-monde, who at that time were distinguished by the amiable name of *hetaerae*, that is, companions. Thus we hear of a bandage, which was intended to confine a too stout body, and thus to appear to get rid of an approaching pregnancy (περίζωστρα or περίζωμα; cf. Pollux, vii, 65). A fragment from a comedy of Alexis (Frag. 98 (Kock), in *Ath.* xiii, 568*a*) gives us further information concerning such means of beautifying oneself: "When a girl is small, she stitches cork soles in her shoes, when tall, she wears quite thin slippers and goes out with her head between her shoulders; one who lacks hips puts on under her clothes some material as a substitute, so that all who see her praise aloud her *eupygia* (beautiful buttocks).

Of the materials of which women's clothing was made, only flax and silk need be considered in the framework of our statement. Fine flax grew best on the island of Amorgos, hence clothes made from it were called "Amorgina" (Pollux, vii, 74). They were extraordinarily thin and transparent and hence a very favourite costume among beautiful women. Still more attractive were the famous Coan dresses, with the invention of which Erotic reached its highest point. They are the fabrics of silk which were made in the island of Cos in such perfection that an old writer (Dionysius Periegetes, 753, 242) could say of them that they were like the colours of a meadow sown over with flowers and that no cobweb could rival them in thinness. The silkworm cocoons were imported to the island of Cos, later the silkworm also was reared; yet many ready-made silken garments were imported to Greece, expecially from Assyria, whence the Latin expression *bombycinae vestes* (from *bombyx*, silkworm), which perhaps indicates that this importation did not take place until Roman times. The effect of these dresses can be seen, *e.g.*, from a passage in Hippolochus (*Ath.*, iv, 129*a*), who tells us of a wedding-feast at which Rhodian flute-players entered who appeared to him completely naked until the other guests informed him that they wore Coan garments. Lucian even says (*Amores*, 41) that these " clothes of a tissue as fine as a spider's web are only pretence, so as to prevent the appearance of complete nakedness ". Petronius (§ 55) calls them " woven stuff light as air ", and the somewhat pedantic Seneca gives vent to his indignation at this fondness of women for display in the following words (*De Beneficiis*, 7, 9): " I see silken clothes, if those can be called clothes, with which the body or only the private parts could be covered; dressed in them, the woman can hardly swear with a good conscience that she is not naked. These clothes are imported at considerable expense from most distant countries, only that our women may have no more to show their lovers in the bedroom than in the street ". The frequent mention of these Coan dresses in old authors shows how very popular they were; the Tarentine veils often mentioned were very similar.

If by preference the hetaerae made use of this costume, which was more than generous in displaying their charms, yet we see, *e.g.* from a passage in Theocritus (*Idyll* xxviii: ὑδάτινα βράκη), that respectable women also were not afraid to appear in such attire. In Theocritus they are called " wet garments ", an expression easy to understand, and one which is still used by modern artists when speaking of clothes that allow the outline of the body to show through.

2. NAKEDNESS

The Coan dresses, which as we saw did but pretend to be clothing, and not only did not cover but erotically accentuated the form of the body, leads us to a discussion of the part which nakedness played in the life of the Greeks. We have already said something about this in the description of the costume of Spartan girls, the question of *décolletage*, and elsewhere.

It is a tolerably widespread opinion, which is found even among well-educated people who know many things about antiquity without having consulted the best authorities, that among the Greeks nakedness was quite common. But this assumption requires essential limitation. In order to get to the bottom of the question we must distinguish between natural and erotically emphasized nakedness.

It is certainly correct to say that the Greeks showed themselves entirely or partly naked in public far more frequently than would be possible amongst ourselves; and Wieland is doubtless right when he says in his *Essay on the Ideals of the Greek Artists*, that Greek art obtained the mastery in the treatment of the naked, since the sight of it was an almost everyday occurrence. He goes on to say: " The Greeks had more opportunity and were more at liberty to contemplate, study, and copy the beauty represented to them by nature and their times than is the case with modern artists. The gymnasia, the public national games, the contests for the prize of beauty at Lesbos, at Tenedos, in the Temple of Ceres at Basilis in Arcadia, the wrestling matches between naked boys and girls in Sparta, in Crete, etc., the notorious temple of Venus at Corinth, whose young priestesses even Pindar does not blush to celebrate in song, the Thessalian dancers, who danced naked at the banquets of the great—all these opportunities of seeing the most beautiful forms uncovered and in most lively movement, beautified by emulation, in the most varied positions and groupings, were bound to fill the imagination of artists with a quantity of beautiful forms, and by comparing the beautiful with the more beautiful to prepare their minds for rising to the idea of the most beautiful."

One might also think, and has often thought, that nakedness gave no offence to the Greeks in any circumstances. But important testimony proves this to be erroneous. Plato says expressly (*Repub.*, v, 452): " It is not long ago since it was ridiculous amongst the Greeks, as it still is among most of the non-Greeks, for men to allow themselves to be seen naked," and Herodotus (i, 10) gives the same as the opinion of " Lydians and other non-Greeks "; indeed, he affirms that it was considered " a great shame by them ". In confirmation of this view one may refer to the example of Odysseus (*Odyssey*, vi, 126) who is washed ashore, shipwrecked, and naked in the land of the Phæacians, and, when he hears the laughter of maidens in the neighbourhood, " breaks off from the thick bush a leafy branch with his strong hand to cover his nakedness." In the national games at Olympia, from about 720 B.C., it was the custom for the runner to appear, not completely naked, but with an apron round his hips, as Thucydides expressly attests in a well-known and much discussed passage (*Thuc.* i, 6). Only we must beware of tracing back this partial covering to " moral " reasons; it is rather the remains of an opinion influenced by the East, as is clear from the passages quoted from Plato and Herodotus. This also follows from the fact that the Greeks freed themselves from the Oriental point of view and from 720 onwards allowed runners and indeed all the other contestants to appear quite naked. Consequently the Greeks, the healthiest and most æsthetically perfect people hitherto known to the world, soon felt a covering of the sexual parts, while the body was otherwise uncovered, to be unnatural, and recognized that such a covering only had any meaning if one had ascribed a moral and inferior value to their functions. But just the opposite was indeed the case, so that far from being ashamed of these organs, the Greeks rather regarded them with pious awe and treated them with an almost religious reverence as the mystical instruments of propagation, as the symbols of nature, life-producing and inexhaustibly fruitful. Hence we must understand the terms αἰδοῖον and αἰδώς, not as "parts of shame," "privy parts," of which one should be ashamed, but as those which arouse the feeling of αἰδώς, that is, awe and pious adoration of the incomprehensible secret of the power of propagation belonging to nature, that ever renews itself, and of the preservation of the human race that is thereby rendered possible. Thus the phallus [1] became a religious symbol; the worship of the phallus in its most various forms is the naïve adoration of the inexhaustible fruitfulness of nature and the thanks of the naturally sensitive human being for the propagation of the human race.

We shall have to speak of the phallus-cult elsewhere: here it is enough to emphasize that it does not, as ignorance or malice affirms, represent a gross immorality, but just the opposite, since it is nothing else but the view of the divine nature of the process of generation carried to its last extreme and depending upon the natural, and consequently in the highest degree moral, conception of the sexual. The further consequence of the conception was that the Greeks, on all occasions when clothing was felt to be unnecessary, burdensome, or impossible, went over to complete nakedness, without making use of any kind of apron or piece of stuff that concealed the private parts.

There was no such lack of taste in ancient Greece. As is shown by the word *Gymnasion* (from *gumnos*,

[1] The phallus (φαλλός) was the Greek name for the male member, especially when artistically imitated for any purpose in horn, more frequently in wood, especially of the fig-tree. Linguistically the word is connected with φάλης (post, pillar), which is also used in the sense of penis: cf. Aristoph., *Thesmoph.*, 291; *Lysistrata*, 771; *Anthol. Pal.*, ix, 437. It corresponds to the Indian *lingam.*

naked), all clothing was thrown off in bodily exercises. There is certainly nothing new in this, and it is hence superfluous to confirm this generally known fact by passages from ancient literatures which might be quoted in vast numbers. Also the countless representations in pictorial art, which have scenes from the gymnasium for their subject, especially vase paintings, attest complete nakedness and hardly ever cause any such offence as the humdrum Romans of old times felt at this complete denudation, as is shown by a verse of Ennius, preserved by Cicero (*Tusc. Disp.*, iv, 33, 70): "Shame has its beginning in public nakedness."

Yet the Romans went so far that they did not consider it decent for growing boys to bathe with their fathers, or sons-in-law with their fathers-in-law (Cicero, *De Officiis*, i, 35, 129). Plutarch (*Cato Minor*, 20) confirms this, but adds that they had very soon learnt the perception of the naked from the Greeks and then on their part the Greeks introduced the custom of men and women bathing together.

3. GYMNASTICS

If then, to return to our subject, nakedness in the gymnasia might be regarded as a fact well-known to most people, it will perhaps not be superfluous to say a few words on the gymnasia in general, of which many, influenced by the modern meaning of the word, might form a wrong idea. The normal arrangements of a Greek *gymnasion* is in the main described as follows by Vitruvius (v, 11) who lived in the time of the Emperor Augustus and has left a valuable work on architecture. The gymnasium (the Latin equivalent) in the first place contains a large peristyle, that is, a space surrounded by columns, in extent about two stadia (1,200 feet), enclosed on three sides by simple colonnades, and towards the south by a double colonnade within which was the *ephebeion*, the exercise ground of the ephebi, that is, young men declared of full age and independent citizens after they were entered in the register of their deme, which as a rule took place at Athens at the age of 18. At the sides baths, halls and other spaces were allotted, where philosophers, rhetoricians, poets, and all the numerous friends of manly beauty were accustomed to meet together. Further colonnades adjoined the peristyle, amongst them the xystus, which appears to have chiefly been used for the exercises of the men. With the gymnasium was generally combined the palaestra, the chief arena for bodily exercises and games of the boys. It need hardly be emphasized that all the spaces were adorned with works of art of every kind, with altars and statues of Hermes, Heracles, and especially of Eros, but also of the Muses and other divinities. Thus to the beauty of the bodies of boys, youths, and men, most harmoniously developed by regular bodily exercises, was added the daily sight of numerous marvels of art; and it is easy to understand how and why the Greeks developed into the most beauty-loving people that ever walked on earth. One can also understand how it was that no gymnasium or palaestra of the Greeks was ever without an altar or statue of Eros: yet the daily sight of the highest manly beauty was bound to lead to the homosexual love that animated the entire people.

Goethe in his *Italian Journey* once described a ball-game, which he had seen in the arena at Verona: "The most beautiful attitudes, worth imitation in marble, appear therein. As they are merely well-grown, sturdy young people in short, scanty, white clothes, the sides are distinguished only by a coloured badge. Especially beautiful is the position into which the striker falls while he runs down from the slanting surface and lifts his arm to strike the ball." Now let anyone imagine an Athenian or

Spartan palaestra, full of the joyous, boyish laughter of the youths bustling about in the naked splendour of their supple limbs, the whole beneath the delightful blue of the Greek sky, and he will at least admit that it was there that earthly beauty celebrated its highest triumphs.

Thus the Greek gymnasium and palæstra, originally the places where young men hardened themselves in bodily exercises of every kind and developed their bodies to a condition of perfect harmony, became places which were sought for to linger in for many hours of the day and to gossip within sight of the highest beauty; the extensive colonnaded halls were regularly used for walks where philosophers and itinerant teachers gathered their hosts of pupils and hearers round them. It was not until later, in the second century B.C., that the institution of the ephebi in Athens was reorganized and the bodily and intellectual education of youths was combined in the Diogeneum and Ptolenæum which, by the side of numerous schoolrooms, also contained an extensive library; and it is not until the fifth century A.D. that we hear of a gymnasium—and that in Carthage—which is expressly called a linguistic institute and a place of education (Salvianus, *De gubernatione dei*, vii, 275; vel linguarum gymnasia vel morum).

According to the consistent testimony of all the authorities, the Greeks kept their gymnasia free from women; that is, no female creature might ever set her foot in any of these places intended for the education of the male—even at the popular festivals of the great national games women were excluded as spectators. Pausanias (v, 6, 7) says expressly, in mentioning the rock Typaeum at Olympia, that it was the custom to throw those women down from it who were caught in the act of stealing in as spectators at the Olympic games, or even those who, on the days forbidden them (consequently during the festal time), had crossed the river Alpheus, which separated the site of the festival from the rest of the ground. Only on one occasion was this neglected, when the mother of Peisirrhodus had stolen in in order to be present, with a mother's joy easy to understand, at the hoped-for victory of her son. The case is not without a certain tragi-comedy. To avoid the danger of discovery she had disguised herself as a trainer; but, unfortunately, when trying to leap over the barrier that shut off the trainers from the arena in order to congratulate her son on his victory, her scanty garments exposed her person and it was seen that she was a woman. Possibly as a recognition of her mother-love, but chiefly out of regard for her family which had produced several Olympic victors, she was not punished; but, to avoid similar incidents in the future, it was ordered that henceforth the trainers should enter the lists naked.

Of course, the prohibition which excluded women from viewing the public games did not prevail with equal strictness throughout Greece; at least Böckh on Pindar, *Pythia*, ix, p. 328, has made it probable that in the contests of the African Greek colony of Cyrene women were allowed to be spectators, and Pausanias says (vi, 20, 9) that unmarried girls were not forbidden to look upon the contestants at Olympia. According to the same author, the priestess of Demeter had the vested right of looking on; she even had a definite seat for the purpose on the steps of her white marble altar. Classical scholars have racked their brains to discover why the right to look on at the contests of naked boys and youths was permitted to maids but not to married women. The problem seems very easy to solve, if we remember that the Greeks felt the greatest enjoyment of beauty more than any people that ever existed. They desired at their national festivals to surround themselves only with beauty, hence they allowed young girls to look on, while they made the married women remain at home.

Besides, what has been said will only hold good for the Doric stock, of whose freer conception of such things we have already spoken at some length; among the somewhat pedantic inhabitants of Attica girls may certainly have been forbidden to look on at the competitive exercises of young men.

The Dorians, and especially Sparta, were freer from prejudice in this respect. When Plato demands (*Laws*, vii, 804) that young men and young women should carry on gymnastic exercises without discrimination as between the sexes, and indeed, as was a matter of course at that time, with naked bodies, we recognize in this the Spartan point of view; but we can also understand why the pedantic narrow-mindedness, which certainly at that time existed though it did not hold sway, felt that his proposals were unseemly. Nevertheless, his demand was carried out among the non-Dorian states, at least by the inhabitants of the island of Chios, where, according to the express testimony of Athenæus (xiii, 566*e*), no person took offence if he happened to be present at the running and racing contests of naked boys and girls in the gymnasia.

Of Sparta we know perfectly well that the girls there carried on gymnastic exercises as earnestly as did the young men; but whether on these occasions they were completely naked or were only lightly clad has been discussed in detail by learned men of both ancient and modern times. The question cannot, however, be decided with absolute certainty, since the word *gymnos* (as remarked before) means both " naked " and also " only clad in the chiton ", and, moreover, it does not seem of such importance that it is worth while to waste much time over it. In any case it is certain that the Spartan girls, although not completely naked, yet at all events carried on their bodily exercises so lightly clad that the moral heroes of our time would not have got out of it without a shock or, more precisely, without sensual excitement; and it is also more than probable that custom in such matters may have varied more or less from time to time. If the fairly numerous passages of old writers, where information is given on the point, be examined impartially, we can only think that they were completely naked; and such is the opinion also of Roman authors when they speak of the *nuda palæstra*, the naked wrestling place of Spartan girls, as Propertius, Ovid, and Martial (Prop. iii, 14; Ovid, *Heroides*, xvi, 149; Martial, iv, 55) do, not without a delighted smirk and tacit acquiescence. This explains how the expression "to behave in Dorian fashion" became synonymous with "to strip oneself", which would also agree if the girls wore in their bodily exercises the light everyday clothing (already described), thanks to which they were not infrequently bantered by the rest of the Greeks as "thigh-showers". Also the question, whether male spectators were admitted to the exercises of the girls dressed (or more correctly undressed) in such a manner cannot be settled convincingly, since on this point our information appears to be contradictory. When, for instance, Plutarch (*Lyc.*, 15) against Plato (*Rep.* v, 458—against this *Theætetus*, 169)) [1] affirms that these exercises of undressed girls took place before the eyes of young men, and with the express addition (an attack on Plato) that there were sexual reasons for this, namely, to encourage young men capable of marrying to do so; this contradicts Plato's express statement that in the Spartan gymnasia the principle held good—"Undress and practise gymnastics together, or get away," which consequently excluded the hanging about of idly gaping spectators which was so offensive to the Romans (Seneca, *De brevitate vitæ*, 12, 2). That,

[1] According to Stobæus (*Sermones*, 44, 41), the exercises of boys and girls were separate; according to Eurip. (*Andromache*, 591) in common.

in spite of complete undress, regard was had to decency and modesty in the gymnasia, is clear from a passage in Aristophanes (*Clouds*, 973): " And it behoved the boys, while sitting in the school of the gymnastic-master, to cover the thigh, so that they might exhibit nothing indecent to strangers; and then again, after rising from the ground, to smooth down the sand and to take care not to leave an impression of the person for their lovers. And no boy in those days anointed himself below the navel so that the first tender down bloomed on his privates as it were on fresh apples."

4. BEAUTY CONTESTS AND FURTHER REMARKS ON NAKEDNESS

It would not be easy to decide the question—" Did the Greeks, in the artistic representation of the naked human body, attain the most perfect mastery because they so often had an opportunity of seeing beautiful men perfectly naked, or did they feel such delight in the sight of naked men because their eye had been rendered impressionable and capable of understanding the marvel of the naked human body through art?" Between the two facts an harmonious reciprocal action may have existed; by art the joy in nakedness became elevated, and the numerous opportunities of seeing ideally beautiful men naked must have had a fruitful reaction upon art.

Certainly it will no longer appear surprising that this almost unbounded delight of the Greeks in bodily beauty led to the arrangement, everywhere popular, of beauty contests, some of which have been already mentioned. We know of most of them from Athenæus (xiii, 609*e*) who unfortunately only briefly mentions them, but expressly gives details of the prizes which were bestowed upon the victorious girls, with which we need not weary the reader. In any case, these contests were combined with a more or less complete undress of the girls contending for the prize.

Beauty Contests

The goddesses themselves had set a brilliant example for such beauty contests. Hera, Pallas Athene and Aphrodite disputed which of them was the most beautiful; but Zeus sagely shirked the decision for himself and left it to the Trojan prince Paris. This beauty contest has been represented times without number in both ancient and modern literature and art, most amusingly perhaps by Lucian in the twentieth of the *Dialogues of the Gods*.

It is probable enough that the Greeks also knew of beauty contests among young men, considering their attitude in regard to the male, and it is at least expressly attested by Athenæus (xiii, 565, 609) for Elis: those who gained prizes were amongst other things also distinguished by being allotted certain functions belonging to the service of the gods. Also at the festival of the Panathenæa (to be afterwards mentioned) young men from the different phylae (tribes) were selected according to their beauty and dexterity for the torch race.

If, therefore, delight in the naked was a general peculiarity of the Greeks as well as of the southern peoples, it is almost as a matter of course that there also existed, or were created in the ordinary lives of individuals, many opportunities of gladdening the eye with the sight of naked beauty of the body. This delight is stronger than any moral (more correctly, conventional) consideration that exists elsewhere. We may assume that the example of the Lydian King Candaules did not remain unique; and likewise that among the Hellenes who exulted in beauty the painful consequences—which could not fail to appear elsewhere considering the prudery, for example, of the Lydians, who were blinded by prejudice on this point—were lacking.

Candaules was very much in love with his wife and very proud of her beauty. He boasted of this beauty before others, and had no rest until his favourite, Gyges, had seen his wife naked. Gyges resisted with all his might, since, as he thought, a woman in undress divested herself of her sense of shame. But Candaules did not give way, and knew how to manage so that Gyges remained concealed in the nuptial chamber and was able to spy upon the queen in the evening when she was undressed.

This is the story told by Herodotus (i, 8) who further informs us that the queen, though aware of the presence of Gyges, was at first unable to say anything for shame. Later, she put the choice before him : " Either slay Candaules and become my lord and gain the kingdom of Lydia, or be content to die at once yourself where you are ". Gyges thereupon slays Candaules, and thus gets possession both of the wife and of the kingdom.

That flute-players appeared at private festivals naked or in Coan garments to strengthen the sexual effect of nakedness was stated earlier by Hippolochus (*Ath.*, iv, 129*d*) in his description of a wedding feast. Thus naked girls, or, according to circumstances, also naked boys were drawn to feasting and drinking bouts in order to strengthen the effects of alcohol and to do homage not only to Bacchus but also to the god of love. Anaxarchus, the favourite of Alexander the Great, was fond of having his wine poured out for him by a beautiful, naked young girl (*Ath.*, xii, 548*b*). As the Stoic philosopher Persæus, the confidant of King Antigonus, relates (*Ath.*, xiii, 607*c*), there was once a banquet given by the king at which the conversation was at first very serious and scientific. " But as the drinking increased among other amusements Thessalian dancers entered the dining-hall and danced stark naked except for a girdle ; which pleased the guests so exceedingly that, enchanted, they expressed their approval, sprang up from their seats and declared the king happy in that he could always enjoy such delight for his eyes." At the wedding of which Hippolochus tells us, " naked female acrobats also appeared, who with naked swords performed dangerous tricks and spat fire." Numerous vase-paintings, on which such female artistes are represented either quite naked or only wearing an apron, prove that such exhibitions were not rare, but, especially in the Hellenistic period, enjoyed general popularity.

That, considering the freedom from prejudice of the attitude of the Greeks towards nakedness, the naked were not excluded in acts that concerned the worship of the gods is self-intelligible and hence need only be illustrated by a single example. From artistic representations it is familiar to us that at the processions at the Dionysiac festivals naked youths and women exposed their beauty for show. It would be perverse to see in that only the whim of the freely creative artist, for of such a procession Lucian expressly says (*De Baccho* 1): "For they had heard strange reports from their spies concerning his army: that his phalanx and bodies of troops consisted of mad and raging women, crowned with ivy, clad in fawn-skins, carrying short spears, not of iron, but also made of ivy; they bore small shields, which gave forth a booming noise if one so much as touched them—for their drums resembled shields. There were also, it was said, a few rustic youths among them, naked, dancing the cordax, having tails and horns."

5. Bathing

We may briefly refer to an occasion on which it was not possible for the Greeks to see human bodies naked—at the public baths.

As early as Homeric times it was generally the custom to swim and bathe in the sea or rivers; yet even then the luxury of warm baths—for these were regarded as a luxury by nearly the whole of Greece—was quite common. Similarly, it was a matter of course for a warm bath to be the first thing prepared for a guest after he alighted.

In the bath he was attended to by one or more girls, who poured lukewarm water over him and "anointed him with oil": that is, they massaged him vigorously with hands moistened with oil in order to make his skin supple. Later it was preferred to have a boy to wait upon one in the bath (*Odyssey*, vi, 224; x, 358; girl-attendants, *Odyssey*, viii, 454; boy-attendants, Lucian, *Lexiphanes*, 2).

The better families in the earlier times had their private baths, besides which there were nearly everywhere public ones (δημόσια: cf. Xen., *Resp. Atheniensium*, ii, 10); and, in the rare cases where these did not exist, the baths of the gymnasia and palæstræ were at the disposal of the public, as, according to Pausanias (x, 36, 9), at Anticyra in Phocis. We cannot say with certainty whether the public baths in old times were separated according to the sexes, as one might conjecture from a passage in Hesiod (*Works and Days*, 753), since the expression "women's bath" (γυναικεῖον λουτρόν), which is forbidden to men by the poet, may refer both to a "women's bath" and "a bath after the manner of women", by which, if the latter be correct, a bath of warmer temperature and more agreeable to women may be meant. It would agree with this conception that the Spartans at least, of whose ruder customs we have already spoken, forbade the use of warm baths as effeminacy, and kept to their cold baths in the Eurotas.[1] According to a fragment of Hermippus (*Ath.* i, 18), warm bathing was forbidden to the well-born youth just as much as drunkenness; and it appears that when baths are spoken of in ancient writings as a rule warm baths are meant. Plutarch expressly informs us that Phocion had never been seen in the public baths (*Phocion*, 4), and Demosthenes considers it as a great lack of

[1] On the cold baths of the Spartans (ψυχρολουτεῖν), cf. Scholiast on Thucydides, ii, 36; Plutarch, *Alcibiades*, 23.

discipline on the part of sailors to visit the baths (Demosthenes, *Adv. Polycl.*, 35); and it is in agreement with this that Aristophanes (*Clouds*, 991, 1045) warns young men against them, since " they make a man slack and effeminate ", that in earlier times they were not allowed inside the city walls, and that Plato in his ideal state (*Laws*, vi, 761) approves of them only for old and sickly people—harsh judgments undoubtedly according to our modern ideas, but easily explainable by the nature of the southern climate. That opinion on this point altered in the course of time, and that after the Peloponnesian war warm baths became an everyday custom, is clear from numerous passages in ancient written works.

Besides the regular opportunities for bathing, there were also sweat-baths and vapour-baths, which are already mentioned by Herodotus (iv, 75) as a matter of course. However, a detailed description cf the ancient baths with their different cells, rooms, halls, etc., does not come within the scope of the present work. That people bathed perfectly naked, without our silly bathing-drawers, needs no special mention. If several notices (see Becker-Göll, *Charicles*, iii, p. 109) seem to point to the fact (by no means certain) that in the public baths men and women were kept separate, this is not to be explained by the hypocritical prudery of our own days but from the fact (already frequently mentioned) that the Greeks excluded the " fair sex " from public life, and that boys and young men, who represented it, completely satisfied their need for companionship. Besides, women bathed in their baths completely naked, as is shown by numerous vase-paintings; only quite isolated instances are found amongst them in which girls are wearing an extremely exiguous shift as thin as a spider's web. In time, however, the custom developed of both sexes bathing together; yet, apart from the lexicographer Pollux (who lived in the reign of the

Emperor Commodus), who makes the highly questionable assertion that both sexes, as well as the bath attendants, used bathing-drawers, there is no proof elsewhere.[1] He quotes at the same time two lines from a comedy of Theopompus[2] that have a bearing on the subject.

If we understand rightly the general sense of the passage torn from its context, which is at least doubtful, it is certain that it refers to a quite late period. Besides this passage and a mention in the comedian Pherecrates (Pollux, x, 181: *ἤδη μὲν ᾠὰν λούμενος προζώννυται* (Kock., *CAF.*, i, 161), I cannot bring forward any literary evidence for the use of drawers over the private parts during the bath among the Greeks.

[1] Pollux, vii, 66: *τὸ δὲ περὶ τοῖς αἰδοίοις οὐ μόνον γυναικῶν ἀλλὰ καὶ ἀνδρῶν, ὁπότε σὺν ταῖς γυναιξὶ λούοιντο, ᾤαν λουτρίδα ἔοικε Θεοπομπος ὁ κωμικὸς ἐν παισὶ καλεῖν ειπών. τηνδὶ περιζωσαμενος ᾤαν λουτρίδα κατάδεσμον ἥβης προπέτασον* (girding round you these bathing drawers, spread them before you as a bandage for your private parts).

[2] Pollux, x, 181: *τὸ μέντοι δέρμα ᾧ ὑποζώννυνται αἱ γυναῖκες λουόμεναι ἢ οἱ λούοντες αὐτάς, ᾤαν λουτρίδα ἔξεστι καλεῖν* (Kock., *CAF.*, i, 743).

CHAPTER III

Festivals

I. National Festivals

Even at the present day we admire and shall always admire Greek civilization, and live on the remembrance of it, since our own civilization is indissolubly connected with the spirit of antiquity. How greatly Greek science and art have fructified modern life and continue still to do so is, perhaps, not quite so obvious at the moment merely because it has become a commonplace in the passing of the centuries. But there is no perfection on this earth; even the Greeks were not perfect; indeed, politically, they were great blunderers, and their internal distraction, their petty party-politics, their continually jealous squabbles perhaps find their counterpart in the internal political history of Germany. In a word, the Greeks lacked the political or national centre. Even the famous athletic sports in Elis, the north-western district of Peloponnesus, were not such a centre, although they certainly in course of time had lost their local character and became the possession of the whole nation, so that time was reckoned by olympiads, the interval of four years between festival and festival, throughout Hellas from 776 B.C. These and other games are certainly called national, but only because the whole nation (more correctly all the tribes) took part in them; nevertheless, they were unable to realize a national union, though as long as the *Ekecheiria* (the truce of God) lasted, that is, during the five festal days, a certain unity existed.

But as in these athletic sports the praiseworthy emulation of cities and districts was the driving impulse, so also the particularistic discord due to jealousy was only deferred to burst forth anew and with less restraint. But certainly the life the scene of which was laid during the festal week on the banks of the Alpheus was an incomparable one, rejoicing in colour, fresh and stirring.

An exhaustive description of the festival of Olympia and the other national games does not come within the limits of this book, whose task is the description of the morals, that is the sexual life, of the Greeks. Only what is most important may be mentioned to give the reader his bearings or to freshen his memory. As the cult of Zeus at Olympia was very old it was believed that Heracles or Pelops had founded these games; after having been for a time forgotten, they were revived about 800 B.C. by Iphitus, king of Elis. The festival was celebrated every fifth year, at the time of the first full moon after the summer solstice, consequently at the beginning of July. During the games all weapons were to remain unused; the land of Elis, in which the national sanctuary was situated, was placed for all time under the protection of the god as inviolable.

The contests (or *agōnes*) were partly gymnic, that is, those in which the strength and agility of the naked body decided the result, such as running, wrestling, boxing, throwing the discus, etc.—and partly hippic (from *hippos*, horse) that is, races with horses or mules, with teams of two or four horses, or with race-horses. The Olympiad was named after the victor, *i.e.*, the recipient of the first prize for running, in pious remembrance of earlier times when contests took place only in that branch of athletics.

If in oldest times the prize of victory had been any object of value, later, by command of the Delphian oracle, the victor was presented with only a simple crown from branches of the olive-tree, which—characteristic of the sentiment of the Greeks—a handsome boy, whose parents were still living, for whom the Greek invented the beautiful word "blooming on both sides" (ἀμφιθαλής), was obliged to cut with a golden knife from the sacred tree of the garland of fame. Men fought simply for honour and fame, and "an Olympian victor", in the words of Cicero, "was honoured amongst the Greeks almost more than a triumphant general at Rome." "The crowns were exhibited on a table made of gold and ivory in the temple of Zeus before the image of the god. Here, at the feet of the god who bestowed victory, also stood the seats of the Hellanodikæ, who distributed the prizes. The victors appeared, accompanied by friends, relatives, and a crowd of people, which, so far as space permitted, pressed into the halls and galleries of the temple. Then the name and birth-place of every victor was again called out by the herald, a woollen bandage (*tænia*) was wound round his head by one of the Hellanodikæ and the crown of victory placed upon it.

Sacred hymns, says Pindar (*Olympia*, iii, 10), are wafted over the world in honour of any man for whom the strict Ætolian umpire, in accordance with the olden ordinances of Heracles, 'flingeth o'er his brow and on his hair the grey-hued adornment of the olive-spray.' After this, those who had been crowned proceeded with their friends to offer sacrifice there: at the same time songs of victory burst forth from the choirs that accompanied them; these were sometimes prepared by a friendly poet for the particular occasion, but, in the absence of such, an old song of Archilochus in celebration of the victorious Heracles and his companion Iolaus was usually sung :—

Hail to thee in the garland of victory, mighty Heracles,
Hail, Iolaus, hail to the noble pair of fighters,
Tra-la-la, hail to the victor.

Then followed a banquet, which the Eleans arranged in honour of the victors in the dining-hall of the Prytaneum, at the hearth of the sanctuary. Loud joy prevailed inside and outside the Prytaneum through the whole festive assembly. Pindar says: 'When the beloved evening light of the beautiful moon shines, then the whole floor re-echoes with songs of victory at festive banquets.'

"An Olympian victory was almost more highly thought of by the Hellenes than a triumph by a Roman general; the man who had attained it, according to Pindar's expression, had reached the pillars of Heracles; he had achieved the greatest earthly happiness, and the wise poet warns him against trying to mount higher and striving to become equal to the gods. Chilo of Sparta, one of the Seven Wise Men, died for joy at his son's victory. Diagoras of Rhodes, belonging to a family descended from Heracles and distinguished for boxing, had been victorious twice at Olympia and several times at the other national games. When he saw his two sons victorious at Olympia, a Spartan cried out to him: 'Die, O Diagoras, for thou shalt not ascend to heaven!' And he died when the two young men embraced him and placed their crowns upon his head. The friends and relatives of the victor had the right to erect a statue of him in the Altis (the sacred grove of Zeus); but one who had been victorious three times may have his statue set up life-size and as lifelike as possible.

"A victor was usually represented as a contestant in the game in which he had distinguished himself, and often at the moment when he gained the victory. The Altis must have possessed a remarkably large number of such statues, for Pausanias, who only mentions the most distinguished, enumerates more than 200. Rich victors in the knightly contests had themselves, their charioteers, horses, and chariots, set up in bronze.

"Great honours awaited the Olympian victor in his native town, which the fame of his victory also glorified. Sitting in a purple dress in a carriage drawn by four white horses, accompanied by friends and relatives on horseback and in carriages, he entered the town amidst the applause of the people. Part of the town wall and gate was pulled down to make a wide path for his carriage; a town which possessed such men believed, says Plutarch, that it needed no walls. The festal procession moved through the main street to the temple of the chief god, where the victor laid down his crown as a votive offering. After this a great banquet was held in honour of the victory. Solemn choral songs resounded during the procession and also at the banquet. It was considered a great piece of good fortune if a distinguished poet, like Pindar, composed a song of triumph for a victor at such a festival, for then he was sure of lasting fame. The feast of victory, together with the song, was usually repeated in succeeding years. Other rewards also fell to the lot of the victor; statues of honour were erected to him in the gymnasia and palæstræ, in the market-place, or at the entrance to a temple. At Athens, according to a law of Solon, the Olympian victor received a present of 500 drachmæ (about £20) as well as the right of a seat of honour at all public spectacles; he also had the privilege of being entertained in the Prytaneum. In Sparta, besides similar distinctions, a victor also had the honour of fighting in battle at the side of the king."[1]

Many states sent special ambassadors (θεωροί) to the games, who often appeared with great pomp, to glorify the common festival and to let their home be seen in special brilliancy. A great fair was also held in combination with the festival,

[1] This passage from "The crowns were exhibited (p. 105) . . . of the king" is a quotation from H. W. Stoll, *Bilder aus dem altgriechischen Leben* (1875, p. 230).

to which travellers of all kinds, and girls and boys who were ready to make friends, rushed in vast numbers. There all dialects of the Greek language were to be heard; friends foregathered who had not met for years; acquaintance was made with the great men of the age; new friendships, business and family relations were formed. After the middle of the fifth century, lectures by rhetoricians, sophists, historians, and poets were also heard at Olympia, and, as time went on, the hold of the sensational on Olympia may have been firmer. Thus in A.D. 165 the half-mad itinerant philosopher, Peregrinus Proteus, in order to increase his fame, proclaimed that he would publicly burn himself to death at the Olympian festival. He actually carried out his intention, under the pressure of the multitude, however greatly he may have repented of his over-hasty resolution.

In connection with our description, the costume worn by the contestants at Olympia is also interesting. On this point we learn from an important, but certainly much disputed passage in the historical work of Thucydides (i, 6; cf. Herodotus, i, 10) that in the oldest times the competitors entered the arena naked, except for an apron round their hips. This is quite probable, but we must be careful not to attribute this covering of the private parts to moral scruples in accordance with our modern code, regarding it rather as a relic of Oriental opinion, by which the older spirit of the Greeks was very strongly influenced. The Asiatics, as before mentioned, considered it disgraceful to bare the body, and if we connect this dread of the sight of the naked with the very old belief in spirits we shall not be far wrong. Anyhow, it is a fact that the Greek athletes at Olympia, at least the runners after the fifteenth olympiad, that is, after 720 B.C., gave up wearing this apron, and from that time entered the arena completely naked.

The Pythia, the festival of the Pythian Apollo at Delphi, was originally held every nine years, with musical contests, that is, the contest of singers with the accompaniment of the cithara, who were hence called *citharœdi*. But after 586 the festival took place every five years, each time in the third year of the olympiad, and the musical agön was enlarged, *auletæ* (flute-players) and *aulōdæ* (singers accompanied by flutes) entering the contest; gymnic and hippic games were also added, in which the laurel sacred to Apollo was used as the crown of victory.

The Isthmia and Nemea were also national games, the former being held on the isthmus of Corinth near the sanctuary of Poseidon, the latter in the grove of Zeus at Nemea, both taking place every third year. Beside these there was a number of local games which could not compare with the four great games, especially the Olympian, of which we need only mention two in the framework of our description. In Corinth, besides the great Isthmian games, the Hellotia in honour of Pallas were celebrated; and in them a race of beautiful youths, who carried torches in their hands (Pindar, *Olympia*, xiii, 40; with Scholiast), took place. In Megara, at the beginning of spring, were celebrated the Diocleia games in honour of the national hero Diocles. Different accounts are given of Diocles; of his death it is related that he fought in battle by the side of his favourite and in the moment of danger covered with him his shield and saved his life, but lost his own. These games were instituted to keep green the memory of the Athenian stranger and his sacrifice of his life, and at them a kissing contest of youths took place, as described by Theocritus (xii, 30): "About his tomb, so surely as Spring comes round, your children vie in a kissing-match, and whoso sweetliest presses lip upon lip, returns laden with garlands to his mother." This kissing contest of beautiful boys, certainly embellished after the style of a novel, but vividly and on the whole quite in the spirit of the antique, is described in the romance of *Antinous* by Aimé Giron and Albert Tozza, which represents a similar festival in Egyptian Thebes, the locale of the romance.

Gymnic contests, popular games, song and dance, later also theatrical performances, were combined with the Eleusinian festival, to be spoken of later. If the Eleusinia, in spite of their sanctity or rather because of it, did not dispense with the erotic undercurrent, so this was in a yet higher degree the case at the five-days' festival of the Thesmophoria, celebrated only by women in honour of the two *thesmophoroi*, that is, law-bringing goddesses, Demeter and Persephone. Although some of the details are very obscure, yet it may be said in general that the deeper idea at the bottom of the festival was the memory of Demeter, who as the inventress of agriculture first made generally possible a settlement of human life, and in particular decidedly influenced the life of women and married life. " Sowing " and " begetting children " are identical among the Greeks in conception and linguistic usage ; hence the festival was celebrated in the month of sowing, called in Crete and Sicily *Thesmophorios*, in Bœotia *Damatrios*, in Attica *Pyanepsion*, corresponding more or less to our October. If we may believe Herodotus (ii, 71), this cult had already been widespread among the Pelasgian original population of Greece. In any case it was common throughout Hellas and extended to the most distant colonies in Thrace, Sicily, Asia Minor, and on the shores of the Black Sea.

In Attica Thesmophoria, which have become partly known to us by the merry comedy of Aristophanes, the *Thesmophoriazusæ* (that is, the women at the festival of the Thesmophoria) were celebrated from the ninth to the thirteenth day of the month Pyanepsion. All the women who desired to take part in the festival were obliged to abstain from sexual intercourse for nine days before; the cleverness of the priests demanded this as an act of piety, the real reason of course being that the women, whipped up by their long abstinence, might be able to take part in erotic orgies with less restraint. To strengthen themselves in this chastity that was demanded of them, which they probably found hard enough to preserve, women laid cooling herbs and leaves in their bed, especially agnus castus (λύγος ἄγνος = ἄγονος: making non-productive) and other plants (such as κνέωρον, κόνυζα). But, according to Photius (ii, 228 (ed. Naber)), at this time women ate garlic, in order to frighten men away by the unappetizing smell of their mouth.

2. OTHER FESTIVALS

At the country Dionysia a gigantic phallus, or several, was carried round in solemn procession. At the same time all kinds of rustic amusements were usual, grotesque dances and jesting banter, in which there was no lack of more or less coarse indecencies, On the second day of the festival, the Askolia [1] caused special amusement. In this, naked boys hopped about on one leg on a wine-skin or sack filled full and well-greased with oil, the effort to hold themselves up and to avoid slipping off doubtless leading to highly laughable postures, although the gracefulness of the young " wine-skin hoppers " also led to many beautiful pictures. According to Virgil (*Georgica*, ii, 384), this pastime was popular in Italy.

Soon after the country Dionysia the Lenæa, the feast of winepresses, was celebrated in Athens itself; the chief part of the programme being a great banquet—for which the State supplied the meat—and a dance through the city with the more

[1] Possibly derived from ἀσκός wine-skin, bladder.

or less practical jokes common at festivals of Dionysus. Many who took part in this procession (which may be compared to the modern masked ball) appeared in costume, with special preference as Nymphs, Hours, Bacchantes, and Satyrs; and it is evident that the light clothing prescribed by mythological tradition invited all kinds of erotic jokes. There was of course no lack of wanton dances, as they are described vividly and beautifully by Longus (ii, 36) in his graceful narrative of the love of Daphnis and Chloe. We read there: "The spectators lay there in silence and enjoyed themselves. But Dryas got up and ordered him to play a song to Dionysus on the pipe, and afterwards danced a measure to celebrate the vintage. In the dance he at one time imitated the gathering of the grapes, at another the bringing of the baskets, then treading the grapes, filling the casks, and lastly, tasting the must. Dryas represented all this in his dance so cleverly and clearly that the spectators believed that they saw the vines, winepresses, and casks, and Dryas really drinking." Many who took part in the festival drove there in carriages, from which they played all kinds of foolish tricks and jokes, so the "jokes from the carriage" (ἐξ ἁμάξης ὑβρίζειν) became a proverbial expression. We may see in this the original of the drives up and down the Corso in Rome with throwing of confetti and similar pranks. It does not require special mention that the new wine flowed in streams, as at all the festivals of Dionysus, but it deserves notice that contests in singing solemn dithyrambs took place, as was already the custom at the country Dionysia, and that dramatic performances were given, the scene of which was the Lenæum, whence the feast took its name. The Lenæum was a district sacred to Dionysus on the south of the Acropolis, with two temples and a theatre.

In the next month, *Anthesterion*, the *Anthesteria* were celebrated; on the first day the fermented wine was broached. On the second day, the Feast of Pitchers, the new wine was drunk at a public meal for a wager, and by a secret sacrifice which the wife of the Archon Basileus, the second highest government official, offered to Dionysus, her wedding with the god was symbolized. The third day was called the Feast of Pots, since pots with boiled vegetables were set out as a gift to Hermes Chthonios (' of the underworld ') and the souls of the dead.

Lastly, in the month of *Elaphebolion* (March-April) followed the great or city Dionysia, which lasted several days and by its magnificence attracted many people from the country and from foreign parts. In this also a brilliant procession was an object of admiration, at which choruses sang joyful dithyrambs in honour of Dionysus, the choruses, which then also executed beautiful dances, being furnished by boys. We still possess a document (*Corpus Inscriptionum Atticarum*, ii, i, 203, No. 420) in which recognition is paid to the boys and to the teacher who trained them in singing and dancing. When the sun went down the procession returned, in connection with which in the streets (Philostratus, *Vitæ Sophistarum*, II, i, 235) people drank heavily on improvised couches and one or several phalli played their part in the entertainment. The two or three days, on which tragedies and comedies were performed at great expense before a huge crowd of spectators, formed the culmination of the festival.

It may at least be mentioned that, in many parts of Greece, especially on Cithæron and Parnassus, on the islands, and in Asia Minor every two years a festival of Dionysus took place at night time, shared only by women and girls. The women wearing Bacchic costume, goat-skins, and with dishevelled hair, and carrying in their hands the thyrsus and tambourine, performed on the heights near their abode all kinds of sacrifices and dances, which, thanks to the wine which was otherwise only rarely drunk, very soon degenerated into wild orgies, of which we can get a clear idea from numerous pictorial representations and descriptions in the poets.

It does not belong to the task of this book to enter more closely into the other very numerous festivals which were celebrated in the most different places in Greece; instead of this, we give a concise survey of those Greek festivals in which the sexual impulse plays a part.

In the month of *Hekatombaion* (July-August) the *Hyacinthia* was celebrated in honour of Hyacinthus. He was the favourite of Apollo; but Zephyrus, the wind-god, also loved the boy; wherefore, out of jealousy, when Apollo was amusing himself in a game of discus with his favourite, Zephyrus directed the heavy ring of the discus against the head of Hyacinthus, so that he died. The festival lasted three days: on the first, sacrifices were offered to the dead in solemn melancholy in memory of the beautiful youth; on the two days following joyous processions and contests took place in honour of Apollo Carneus. Athenæus (iv, 139*d*) gives a detailed description of the Hyacinthia: "The Spartans keep the sacrificial festival Hyacinthia for three days; owing to their sorrow for the death of Hyacinthus they neither crown themselves at their meals, nor set on table bread nor cakes nor any kind of other pastry; they sing no pæan to the god, nor do anything else of the kind such as is usual in the other sacrifices, but after they have taken their meal in a most orderly manner they depart. On the second day a varied spectacle takes place and an assembly that is well worth seeing and magnificent. For boys come on, playing the cithara with their chiton girt high, and, singing to the flute, run over all the strings at once with the plectrum, and praise the god in anapæstic rhythm and with shrill voices. Others, well-equipped, ride on horseback through the place of meeting; then numerous choruses of young men come on, singing some of the native songs: and dancers mingle with them and perform an old-fashioned kind of dance to the accompaniment of flute and song. Some of the maidens are borne along in basket carriages, or wooden carved chariots expensively made; others, as if they were engaged in circus contests, lead the procession with chariots close together, and the whole city is in a state of agitation and delight at the spectacle. Very many sacrifices are made on this day, and the citizens give entertainment to all their acquaintances and also to their own slaves. No one is absent from the sacred festival and the whole city seems to be empty, since every one has gone to see the spectacle."

Gymnopædia (literally " the naked boys' dance ") was a gymnastic festival which, after 670 B.C. was held at Sparta every year, later arranged in honour of the Spartans who had fallen at Thyrea (544 B.C.), and was celebrated with dances and bodily exercises of naked boys. It is characteristic that this festival, which served for the glorification of the beauty of boys and lasted from six to ten days, was so highly thought of among the Spartans, that not even the most disturbing events were allowed to keep them away from it.[1]

There is considerable uncertainty about the gymnopædia, but the following notices cannot be disputed. Bekker (*Anecdota*, i, 234) tells us that at the gymnopædia in Sparta naked boys sang pæans and danced in honour of the Carnean Apollo; and in Hesychius (s.v. γυμνοπαίδια) we read: " According to some this is a Spartan festival, at which boys run round the altar in Amyklaion, at the same time striking one another on the back. But this is false, for they celebrate their festival in the market-place; also, no blows are given, but there are processions and choral songs of naked boys. " Cf. also Pausanias, iii, 17, 9, Suïdas, s.v., Athenæus, xv, 678b. This

[1] For a description of the dance of boys, see *Athenæus*, xiv, 631*b*.

is in agreement with the discovery of a bronze statuette of a naked leader of the chorus with the characteristic garland found in the sanctuary at Amyclæ (see Wolters, *Archäologie*, vol. i, 11, 96, 70).

In *Boedromion* (September–October) the long-famous and highly sacred Eleusinia were celebrated. The special peculiarities of the festival, which lasted over nine days, are difficult to define, but need not be discussed in connection with this book. The original country festival came later, when to the idea of the dying away and subsequent revival of the seed-grain, which had its mythical counterpart in the story of Persephone carried off by Hades to live six months in the underworld, and six months in the light of the sun, deeper ideas of immortality were attached, of a strangely religious, esoteric character. These developed into a secret cult, into which persons were initiated by special mysterious usages, the secrets of which no one was allowed to reveal. As early as those times, bread, wine, and blood played a mysterious part in the sufferings, death, and resurrection of a divinity.

In the first days of the festival sacrifices, purifications, and washings were undertaken on a festal procession to the sea, sometimes accompanied by noisy proceedings. On the sixth day the great festal procession started on the Sacred Way from Athens to Eleusis (about 9 miles), the leader of which was supposed to be Iacchus, the name by which Dionysus was known in the Eleusinian mysteries. Thousands took part in it, crowned with ivy and myrtle, carrying in their hands torches, agricultural implements, and ears of corn. Iacchus, like a bright star, led the *mystæ* (the initiated) to the holy ceremony on the bay of Eleusis, where for successive nights the mountains re-echoed with enthusiastic songs and the waves of the sea reflected the brilliancy of the torches.

In *Pyanepsion* (November–December) the

Pyanepsia were celebrated in Athens, Sparta, Cyzicus, and elsewhere. It took its name from *pyanos*, a dish of pulse or hulled barley, a harvest-home in honour of Apollo and Artemis. At this it was the custom for boys to carry the *eiresiōnē*,[1] an olive-branch wound round with wool and made into a crown, from house to house, at the same time singing popular songs and begging kindly gifts.

In the same month the *Oschophoria* [2] was celebrated at Athens. It was named from the *oschoi*, the vine-branches with grapes on them, which were partly carried before a procession by two beautiful boys dressed as women [3] both of whose parents were alive, chosen from every tribe; and were partly brought by exquisitely beautiful and active ephebi, who raced from the temple of Dionysus to that of Athene Skiras in the harbour of Phalerum. The victor received as a prize a bowl containing a drink (called πενταπλόα: "with five ingredients"; *Ath.*, xi, 495*f*) composed of the five products of the year—wine, honey, cheese, meal, and oil—and gave a joyful popular dance with a chorus of other boys.

Of the disguise of the two boys, which appears strange to us, Plutarch (*Theseus*, 23) who refers the establishment of the festival to Theseus, gives the following account: "For he is said not to have selected all the maidens chosen by lot at the time to accompany him, but two youths, intimate friends of his, who combined a bold and undaunted courage with a womanish and delicate appearance. By the use of warm baths, keeping them from the sun and fresh air, oiling their hair and skin, and by feminine adornment, he gave them quite a different

[1] This was also the name of the begging-song: cf. the swallows' song of the Rhodian boys in Ath. viii, 360.

[2] The name of the festival gave rise to all kinds of jokes, for ὀσχοφορικοί (carriers of vine-branches) sounded to the Greek ear like ὄσχεος (scrotum).

[3] That is, they wore the old Ionic dress which gave the impression that they were girls (see Böttiger, *Baunkult*, p. 339, fig. 42; many details of the festival are obscure; cf. also Proclus, *Chrestom.*, 28).

appearance. He accustomed them to imitate, as well as possible, the voice, walk and gestures of young girls, and put them amongst other girls, without their being different from them or being recognized by any one as boys. After his return, he held a solemn procession, accompanied by those youths, who were dressed just like those who now carry the vine-branches, at the festival. According to the story, this was said to be done in honour of Bacchus and Ariadne, or, what is more probable, since Theseus returned at the time of the gathering, of the fruit of the vine ".

That the most beautiful boys were selected to carry the vine-branches is clear from a letter of Alciphron (iii, 1) in which a girl, who had come to Athens to see the festival, thus describes it to her mother: " I cannot contain myself, mother, I cannot endure now to marry that stripling from Methymna, the pilot's son, whom my father told me the other day was to be my husband. I have seen someone else, a youth at Athens who was carrying the vine-branch in the procession on the day you sent me to the city to watch the festival. He is beautiful, mother, so beautiful and such a darling. His curls are more crisp than hazel blossoms, his smile is more charming than the summer sea. When he looks at you his eyes gleam with a dark radiance, even as the ocean gleams beneath the rays of the sun. And his whole face! You would say that on his cheeks dance all the Graces; and as for his lips—he has filched the roses from Aphrodite's bosom and made them bloom again upon their surface."

A genuine boy's festival was the *Theseia*, held at Athens on the day after the Oschophoria. The chief event was a parade of the Athenian youth, accompanied by gymnic contests. Here there was a swarm of boys of every age, about four times as numerous as youths or men, for Theseus was the ideal type of boys, to whom they looked up and whom they strove to emulate. Any one who as a gymnast showed efficiency, proudly called himself a Theside and also, as a dutiful son and pupil Theseus, was a model for the boys of Attica. Even at the *Epitaphia*, the festivals of the dead, races and gymnastic contests of large numbers of boys and ephebi were common.

In *Munychion* (April–May) the *Adonia* was celebrated in various parts of the ancient world. According to the originally Oriental myth Adonis, a youth whose beauty has become proverbial, the favourite of Aphrodite, was slain by a boar while hunting; as he was passionately mourned by the goddess Zeus consented to his returning to her from the shades for a short time once a year. This was symbolized by the Adonis festival, on the first day of which his disappearance was lamented, while on the second joy and exultation at his return prevailed. The festival was especially celebrated with great magnificence by women. Images of Adonis and Aphrodite were exhibited or carried round; lamentations for his death and rejoicings for his return were sung, of which beautiful specimens are preserved in the poems of Theocritus and Bion (Theocritus, xv; Bion, i).

In *Thargelion* (May–June) every nine years the *Daphnephoria* was celebrated. The name means "the festival of bearing the laurel", and is explained by the fact that, in the solemn procession, a boy, both of whose parents were alive, a beautiful boy, the so-called *daphnephorus* (laurel-bearer) carried the so-called *kopo* (see Proclus in Photius, *Bibliotheca*, cod. 239), a piece of olive-wood, adorned with laurel, flowers, and wound round with wool, to the temple of Apollo Ismenius. It was furnished with a bronze globe above, from which smaller globes were suspended, and below with a similar, smaller globe; these globes were supposed to represent the heavenly bodies.

At the festival of *Munychia*, held in memory of

the glorious victory of Salamis, Athenian ephebi proceeded to Salamis where a regatta, a festal procession, sacrifices, and gymnic games took place. We also hear of a running match, in which the ephebi competed with youths from Salamis, and of a procession by torchlight.

At the *Thargelia*, in honour of Artemis and Apollo, choruses of men and boys appeared, and to all appearances the boys' choruses were especial favourites.

At the Thargelia held at Colophon, in the event of an expiation of the city being necessary after famine, pestilence, or some such catastrophe, the so-called *pharmakos*—that is, a man sacrificed as an atonement for others, a scapegoat, for which purpose characteristically the most universally hated inhabitant was sought out—was conducted through the city to take upon himself contamination, and was then driven out. Outside the city bread, cheese, and figs were put into his hands, and, according to Hipponax (*PLG*., frag. 4–9; Tzetzes, *Chiliades*, 5, 726), his genitals were whipped with branches of wild fig and sea-onions, while a special melody was played on the flute.

It is quite astonishing, how many wanton dances meet us in old writers. Thus in Elis there was a dance in honour of Artemis Cordaka, whose name sufficiently indicates its indecent character (cf. Pausanias, vi, 22, 1).

Other erotic dances are enumerated by Nilsson, who observes: "Thus these indecent dances, sometimes also songs and dumb-show in the service of the maiden-goddess, are attested for a great part of the Greek world—Laconia, Elis, Sicily, Italy. Sexual life is introduced into the cult, coarse and undisguised. The phallic equipment here plays a part at a sacrifice to Artemis, which we otherwise are accustomed to find only in the cult of Dionysus and Demeter."

The retinue of Dionysus consists of ithyphallic

spirits, spirits of fruitfulness and vegetation. Their dances were imitated by their human worshippers; performances in dumb-show, which appear to accompany these spirits everywhere, were also given.

Now there is nothing remarkable in finding something of this kind in the cult of a goddess of fruitfulness, such as Artemis was. Her retinue is of course female, except in one uncertain case. The female spirits which correspond to the satyrs and the like, have become so ennobled that the kinship can hardly be recognized any longer; but we must remember the Homeric hymns to Aphrodite (v, 262) ("the Sileni united in love with the Nymphs") and the illustrations on vases, which museums cannot exhibit publicly.

Such dances belonged to the cult of Artemis Corythalia; but her festival, the *Tithenidia*, is called a "Festival of Nurses". It is possible that the dances were performed at another festival of the same goddess; but nothing prevents us from claiming them as part of the Tithenidia, for the cult of the goddess extended far more widely than the name of the festival suggests. There is a trace of this in the fact that the Tithenidia was also a festival of fruitfulness of general importance. While the nurses carried the little boys to Artemis Corythalia, in the city a kind of "feast of tabernacles" was held (called κοπίς; cf. Ath., iv, 138*e*, 139*a*) as at the Hyacinthia. These huts also occur outside Greece at the festivals of gods of fruitfulness, especially harvest festivals; and the huts at the Carnea (σκιάδες) may also be compared (see Ath., iv, 141*e*). Why only male children were carried out to the goddess, and by their nurses, not by their mothers, we do not know, but it creates the impression that the festival had somewhat deteriorated. In any case it was believed that the goddess would bestow her blessing upon the little ones and that they would prosper more under her protection.

Orgiastic dances were also common in many other festivals of Artemis, but to go more into detail would only be a repetition of what has been already said.

We need not here refer again to the wild boisterousness of the mænads, since this is sufficiently well known; that the phallus played a great part in it has already been said. On a red-figured vase from the Acropolis we see a completely naked mænad, swinging a phallus in an ecstatically enraptured attitude of dancing. Phalli of stone or other material, as well as figures and figurines have been found in large quantities in the course of excavations. If the Dionysiac orgies originally held good for the god of fruitfulness, they became gradually a symbol of something higher, especially of the union with the divine that is hoped for and attained by ecstasy, an impulse which is deeply rooted in man's heart and owes to Dionysus its victorious march through the Greek world.[1]

From a certainly very mutilated inscription (*Corpus Inscriptionum Græcarum*, ii, 321) we learn that measures were taken, even in war, to secure that the phallus procession should be led safely into the city. That the colonies were obliged to send phalli to the great Dionysia at Athens has already been mentioned; and it is interesting to note that we still possess an account from the island of Delos, according to which a gigantic phallus which was once prepared for this purpose and made of wood cost 43 drachmæ; it was cut by a certain Caicus and painted by Sostratus (*Bulletin de Correspondance Hellénique*, xxix, 1905, p. 450).

Unfortunately Pausanias, when speaking of the mysteries celebrated in honour of Dionysus and

[1] On the phallus cf. Plutarch, *De Cupiditate divitiarum*, 527*d*: "The festival of the Dionysia was in old times celebrated in a popular and cheerful manner; a wine-jar was carried round and a vine-branch; then someone brought a goat, another a basket full of figs; and over all the phallus." In the magnificent procession, arranged by Ptolemy Philadelphus in Alexandria, "a gigantic phallus accompanied it" (Callixenus, in Ath., v, 196).

Demeter, says " it is considered impious to impart to the general public the rites performed yearly by night in honour of Dionysus ". In another passage he tells us that at the festival of the Scieria in Arcadia women were scourged—the female counterpart of the scourging of Spartan boys and young men (Pausanias, ii, 37, 6 ; viii, 23, 1).

As at the Thesmophoria, so also at the festival of Demeter Mysia, not far from Pellene in Peloponnesus, the entry of men was forbidden ; indeed, not even a male dog was allowed (Pausanias, vii, 27, 10). The festival lasted seven days ; in the night after the third day was the principal celebration, and on the day following both sexes indulged in much coarse banter and grossness.

That the male sex was excluded from the festivals of Demeter, at least for a time, is frequently attested : e.g., for the festival of Ægila in Laconia (Pausanias, iv, 17, 1), for the mysteries of Demeter in the island of Cos (Paton-Hicks, *Inscriptions of Cos*, No. 386), and many others, which we need not mention, since nothing essentially new could be said about them.

Aphrodite also, the great dispenser of love, was originally a goddess of vegetation and fruitfulness ; in Greece she was hardly honoured anywhere so much as in the island of Cyprus.

We know of a festal gathering, which was held every year at Paphos in Cyprus, to which men and women from the whole island flocked together ; both sexes went in company to Palaipaphos which was no great distance away, where all kinds of erotic mysteries took place, of which we chiefly hear from the Fathers of the Church (Clem. Alex., *Protrepticon*, p. 13 ; Arnobius, *Adversus Gentes*, 5, 19 ; Firmicus Maternus, *Err. Prof. Rel.*, 10), who certainly in their Christian wrath snarl rather than give us an intelligent and connected account of them. The initiated were handed salt and a phallus, after which they presented a coin as a return gift to the goddess. With this was continued the custom of religious prostitution, which according to Herodotus (i, 198; ii, 64) was usual, not only in Paphos, but throughout the whole island of Cyprus generally. Comparing it with the similar custom in Babylon, we must conclude that the girls once in their life repaired to the sanctuary of Aphrodite (Melitta) and surrendered to the first friend who presented himself (see the romance of Nitocris, priestess of Ishtar: H. V. Schumacher, Berlin, 1922).

3. THE ANDROGYNOUS IDEA OF LIFE

We shall have to deal in a later chapter with Greek homosexuality in greater detail. However, in this place we must anticipate the fact that the Greeks possessed a really astonishing notion of the double sexual (hermaphroditic) nature of the human being in the embryonic condition and of the androgynous idea of life generally. Hence, in the history of Greek civilization, we meet with not a few ideas and usages which have their origin in the conception of the double natural arrangement of the human being or of individual gods.

In Amathus on the island of Cyprus a male-female divinity was worshipped, in whose cult a youth once a year was obliged to lie in childbed and to imitate a woman in the pains of labour. This took place in honour of Ariadne, who landed with Theseus on Cyprus and was said to have died there in childbed, without having borne a child, as is told by the historian Pæon (Plutarch, *Theseus*, 20; and Hesychius, s.v. *'Αφρόδιτος*), who also mentions the hermaphrodite god Aphroditos. According to Macrobius (*Saturnalia*, iii, 8, 2) his statue was bearded, with the bodily form and dress of a female, but with male sexual organs; at sacrifices men wore female, and women male clothing. To understand these usages, we shall first have to deal with the form of Hermaphroditos.

According to the most detailed story told by Ovid (*Metamorphoses*, iv, 285), Hermaphroditos grew up a dazzingly beautiful boy, who at the age of fifteen kindled the love of Salmacis, the nymph of a spring of the same name in Caria ; against his will he was enticed by her down into the water and forced to have connection with her ; desiring never to be separated from her lover, the gods united them into a single being of two sexes. According to the desire of Hermaphroditos, Hermes and Aphrodite bestowed upon the spring the property that every man who bathed in it came out as *semivir* (half-man, half-woman) and effeminate in character.[1] With this it is very probable that, in the subconsciousness of the people ideas of the androgynous origin of life, and also contact with Oriental androgynous cults, may have cooperated. Such dissemination of the views of the Orient are frequently attested in Greece ; we may remember the change of clothing at marriage. Thus in Sparta the bride wore male clothing, on the island of Cos the bridegroom (Plutarch, *Lycurgus*, 15 ; on Cos, *Moralia*, 394), just as the priests of Heracles and he himself, wore female dress. In Argos a festival was celebrated every year, in which both men and women wore the dress of the opposite sex, the feast called Hybristika, to be spoken of later.

Mythological investigation has proved that the conception of androgynous divinities had already arisen in ancient times and was not a product of the so-called decadence, although the name Hermaphroditos does not occur in Homer and Hesiod, but is for the first time met with in

[1] There are no essential variations of the story : cf. Hyginus, *Fabulæ*, 271 ; Martial, vi, 68, 9 ; x, 4, 6 ; xiv, 174 : *masculus intravit fontes, emersit utrumque ; pars est una patris, cetera matris habet.* Ausonius, *Epigrammata*, 76, 11 ; Statius, *Silvæ*, i, 5, 21 ; Diodorus Siculus, iv, 6 ; *Anthol. Pal.*, ix, 317, 783 ; ii, 101 ; Hans Licht, *Untersuchungen zur Geschichte der antiken Erotik in der Bearbeitung von Lukians Erotes*, München, 1920.

Theophrastus (*Characters*, 16). From this passage it is clear that one or more images of Hermaphroditos, which were set up inside the house, were crowned on the fifth and seventh days of the month, in reference to which we may notice that the fourth day was sacred to Hermes and Aphrodite and, according to Proclus (*On Hesiod*, 800), was considered specially favourable to sexual enjoyment. Thus we may see in Hermaphroditos a being that has its root in the dim consciousness of the androgynous idea of life, artistically perfected by sensually æsthetic longings, who was worshipped as the good spirit of the house and private life, more than as a divinity who was the object of public worship. Hence we hear nothing of special sanctuaries or even of temples of Hermaphroditos; only for the Attic deme of Alopeke is anything of the kind, perhaps only a chapel, attested (Alciphron, *Epist.*, iii, 37). But the importance of Hermaphroditos for plastic and pictorial art is much greater. After the fourth century B.C. rooms in private houses, gymnasia, and baths were adorned with statues or pictures representing Hermaphroditos (Anth. Pal., ix, 783; Martial, xiv, 174), mostly as a blooming, beautiful youth with female luxuriantly developed hip-muscles and male genitals. Especially beautiful are the numerous sleeping hermaphrodites that have come down to us; resting comfortably in a graceful attitude, which brings into full relief all the charms of the male-female body, the hermaphrodite lies half on his side on a couch adorned with a magnificent covering, the arms crossed beneath the head. This type was especially popular, as the numerous replicas show: the most beautiful are to be seen in the Uffizi at Florence, and the Villa Borghese in Rome, others in the Thermæ museum at Rome, the Louvre in Paris, and the Hermitage in Petrograd. For this reason already mentioned cult-images of Hermaphroditos are rare; one had been carved by the elder Polycles in Rome (Pliny, *Hist. Nat.*, xxxiv, 80), of which there is a copy in the beautiful statue of the Berlin Museum (No. 192). Much more common are the representations of Hermaphroditos, which were executed only for the sake of their sensual charm. We may mention hermaphroditic forms of Eros, Dionysus, and satyrs and often of Priapus. In Rome and Athens reliefs are to be seen with hermaphroditic dancers. Hermaphroditos frequently appears in statues and herms, lifting up the garment to draw attention to the erect member. A beautiful wall-painting of Pompeii [1] shows how Hermaphroditos is adorned with festal attire, while Priapus holds a mirror in front of him.

More sensual and, according to modern ideas, extremely obscene, is the effect of the representations exhibiting Hermaphroditos in sexual connection with Pan or with Satyrs. Now an Eros wantonly pulls away his garment, now Satyrs lustfully handle his charms, or are entangled with him in an embrace near completion or completed.

Another hermaphroditic divinity was Leucippus (Antoninus Liberalis, 17), in whose honour the festival *Apodysia* (the " Festival of Undressing ") was celebrated at Phæstus in Crete. Leucippus had originally been a girl, who at her mother's entreaty was changed by Leto into a young man. This is the story told by Antoninus Liberalis, who adds that sacrifice was offered in Phæstus to Leto Phytia (the creator), since she had created for the girl male genitals; and that, before the wedding night, brides were put to bed by the side of a wooden

[1] On the Pompeian wall-painting, cf. W. Helbig, *Wandgemälde der vom Vesuv verschütteten Städte Campaniens*, with several pictures of Hermaphroditos. On the form of Hermaphroditos, cf. Herrman in Roscher's *Mythologisches Lexikon*, vol. i, p. 2319; Reinach, *Cultes, mythes et religions*, vol. ii, p. 319; Clarac, *Musée de Sculpture*, plate 666 (Paris, 1836). There are no monographs on the subject later than the work, now in great part out of date, by C. F. Heinrich (1805), which may be supplemented by the works of Pauly Wissowa-Kroll and Roscher, and the important work of L.S.A.M. von Römer, " Uber die androgynische Idee des Lebens," in Hirschfeld's *Jahrbuch fur sexuelle Zwischenstufen* (5th year, vol. ii, Leipzig, 1903).

image of Leucippus, which had female form and clothing, but male genitals. The name of the festival may be derived from the habit of undressing the wooden image at this ceremony; it is not difficult to guess what more the young bride-to-be had to do, if we remember what we know of prostitution in the temple.

These strange customs appear to have found their expression also in comedy. Only miserable fragments of Menander's *Androgynos or the Cretans* are preserved, but the double title allows us to conclude *a posteriori* that it contained hermaphroditic scenes, the more so as in the fragment a bride in the bath played a certain part (*CAF*., iii, pp. 18, 19 (frag. 57)). Cæcilius Statius also wrote an *Androgynos* (Ribbeck, Com. Rom., frag. 37). When the Argives were defeated by the Spartan King Cleomenes, the women, led by Telesilla, took up arms and saved the city. To commemorate this, the festival of *Hybristika* (Plutarch, *De mulierum virtute*, 245*e*) was celebrated in which the sexes changed clothes. To increase the population, marriages had been permitted between full female citizens and *periœci* (a subject class of freemen who had no political rights). But since the latter were not considered of equal birth, according to Plutarch the women had to put on false beards, before they slept with their husbands. There was a similar custom on the island of Cos (Plutarch, *Quæst. Græcæ*, 304*e*) where young married men received their wives in female attire; the priests there also offered sacrifices to Heracles dressed as women. In Sparta (Plutarch, *Lycurgus*, 15) the bride waited for her husband in male attire, that is, wearing the himation and shoes, and with her hair cut short.

All attempts at explaining these and similar usages seem to me erroneous. I am myself convinced that they afford us a new proof of the conception of the androgynous idea of life that has its root in the subconsciousness of the Greek people (Plutarch, *An seni*, 875*e*; *Non posse suaviter vivi secundum Epicurum*, 1097*e*).

4. Further Remarks on the Popular Festivals

The *Aphrodisia*, celebrated everywhere on Greek soil, certainly did not enjoy recognition by the State, but so much greater was its popularity. As the name shows, they were originally festivals held in honour of Aphrodite, from which obliging servants of Aphrodite, prostitutes and hetairæ, might not be absent. Indeed, it is clear from Plutarch that at least in later times the name Aphrodisia denoted the excesses in which sailors indulged after the long privations of a journey by sea without women's society.

A genuine festival of the hetairæ was the Aphrodisia on the island of Ægina, which formed the conclusion of the festival of Poseidon. There Phryne played the famous scene described by Athenæus (xiii, 590*f*): "But it was really Phryne who was more beautiful in her private parts. Wherefore it was not easy to get sight of her naked; for she wore round her body a tight-fitting small chiton and did not make use of the public baths. But at the festival of the Eleusinia and the Poseidonia, in the sight of all the Hellenes, she used to put off her *himation*, let down her hair, and go into the sea; and Apelles made her the model of his Aphrodite Anadyomene."

The Aphrodisia, as can be understood, were celebrated in a most sensual and lascivious manner at the noisy harbour of Corinth, with its babel of tongues, where according to Alexis (Ath., xiii, 574*b*, (Kock, ii, 389, frag. 253)), the numerous prostitutes even had their own festivals of Aphrodite. Of course, such festivals lasted into the night, even until morning, during which the hetairæ, "the foals of Aphrodite," poured through the streets in wanton bands. Such a nightly festival was called *Pannychis*, which then also became a favourite name for hetairæ. The latter, " almost naked in fine-spun attire in long array," to quote the words of Eubulus (Ath., xiii, 568*e* (Kock, ii, 193, frag. 84)), " sold their favours for a small fee, which everyone might enjoy safely and without danger."

The festival of Aphrodite Anosia (Ath., xiii, 589*a* ; Scholiast on Aristoph., *Plutus*, 179 ; Plutarch, *Amatorius*, 767*f*), celebrated in Thessaly, may have had a homosexual background, since men were excluded, although details are wanting—the only thing we know is that erotic flagellations also played a part.

The amiable, friendly god Hermes, who is nearly always in love, had comparatively but few festivals in Greece ; but, on the other hand, his memory is kept alive almost at every step by the remarkable arrangement of the so-called Hermes columns, or, more correctly, Hermes pillars. By these are meant stone pillars with elaborate head, which at first represented Hermes, and then other divinities, and a phallus.

After what has already been described it is easy to understand that the few festivals that belong to the god Hermes do not lack an erotic background. But Hermes was regarded by the Greeks as the type of the bloom of man's beauty, as it is represented with the greatest purity in the transition from the boy to the young man. Remember the lines of Homer (*Od.*, x, 277 ; also Aristoph., *Clouds*, 978 ; Plato, *Protagoras*, beginning), in which it is told how Odysseus, arrived at the land of Circe, sets out to explore the country and to find out whether it is inhabited, and by what kind of men. On the way he is met by Hermes, who is of course unknown to him, " in the form of a young man, whose lips are covered by the first down, whose youthful bloom is especially charming." Hence it is not by mere chance that, at the festival of Hermes at

Tanagra, the most exquisitely beautiful and brightest of the ephebi was obliged to carry a ram on his shoulders round the city wall. So Pausanias tells us (ix, 22, 1), who adds that this custom was intended to preserve the memory of Hermes himself having once averted a plague from the city in this manner. The ram carried round, which was then presumably sacrificed or chased beyond the city boundaries, was supposed to take the sins of the whole city upon itself and thereby to expiate them. This is a custom known to us elsewhere, the characteristic point being that the most beautiful boy in the city was chosen to perform this service.

On the island of Crete (Ath., xiv, 639*b*; vi, 263*f*.) a Hermes festival was held, which reminds us of the Roman Saturnalia. The relation between master and servant was reversed; the master waited on the slave who even was allowed the right to beat him, and on this day every sexual licence was permitted.

We further hear of Hermes festivals with which were combined gymnic contests of boys and young men; no more exact details have been handed down, yet they can hardly have been different from other usual gymnic games. That Hermes, together with Heracles, Apollo, and the Muses was the patron god of the gymnasia, hardly needs mention, any more than that images of Eros were to be seen in all the gymnasia, where special reverence was paid him. On the island of Samos the Eleutheria were held in his honour, in memory of a political act of liberation, which originated in a bond of love between man and man, and often led to heroism and genuine patriotism in Greece (*Eleutheria*, Ath., xiii, 561).[1] Nothing further is known of the festival in honour of Hylas, held by the inhabitants of Kios-Prusias on the Black Sea (Antoninus Liberalis, 26;

[1] On gymnic Hermes festivals in Pheneus, cf. Pausanias, viii, 14, 10; in Arcadia, Pindar, *Olympia*, vi, 77, and Scholiast on vii, 153; in Pellene, Schol. on Pindar, *Olympia*, vii, 156; ix, 146; Aristoph., *Birds*, 1421; in Sparta, Pindar, *Nemea*, x, 52.

Strabo, xii, 564); but we know that this festival also had its root originally in homoerotic. Hylas was a beautiful boy, whom Heracles loved beyond everything.[1] He accompanied the hero on the voyage of the Argonauts; but, while drinking from a spring, was carried down into the water by the nymphs, who were seized with a violent passion for him.

This much may be said of the festivals celebrated in the land of the Hellenes. Out of the abundant material available we have selected what appeared specially characteristic for the purpose of the present work. Completeness has neither been achieved, nor attempted. We are acquainted with yet other festivals, the mention of which would, however, only be a repetition of what has been already said.

[1] On the love of Heracles for Hylas, see the wonderful description by Theocritus, *Idyll*, xiii.

CHAPTER IV

The Theatre

Side by side with the festivals and festal customs public performances are of the greatest importance for the knowledge of the manners of a people. Obviously, our description of Greek theatrical affairs has to be limited to emphasizing what is characteristic of the sexual life of the Greeks, and we must assume the knowledge of Greek dramatic art, at least of the extant drama, as a self-evident postulate of general culture. Our task will therefore be essentially limited to showing what erotic motives were brought before the spectators on the Greek stage, and what performances with erotic background could be publicly seen in Greece. At the same time the fact will become manifest, which appears singular to many but a matter of course to the one who knows, that also on the Greek stage the homosexual components of the life of love are by no means ignored or suppressed for any reason, but on the contrary play a very important, indeed an almost preponderating part; hence, much which in strict sequence belongs to a later chapter will be mentioned here or described in detail.

I. Attic Tragedy

Of Æschylus and Sophocles seven dramatic works of each are completely preserved, of Euripides nineteen. These will not at first be discussed, but only those Attic tragedies which are preserved in fragments. The works completely preserved are so much better known than the fragments, that it seemed to me of more importance to give some account of the latter.

The Theatre

1. Æschylus

Of the dramas of Æschylus which we know only from incidental quotations, we may here mention the *Laïus* by reason of the love of boys shown by its content. It was the first piece of a tetralogy, with which the poet won the first prize in the 78th Olympiad (467 B.C.) under the archon Theagenides; the other pieces were *Œdipus*, the *Seven against Thebes*, and the Satyric drama *Sphinx*.

Of the *Laïus* unfortunately only two unimportant glosses of words are preserved; yet we are in a position to state something in regard to the plot. There is much to be said for the conjecture that the love of Laïus for the boy Chrysippus, the beautiful son of Pelops, formed the background for the further tragic destiny of the unhappy king. Indeed, according to many traditions, Laïus was considered by the Greeks to be the founder of the love of boys. We may also add the information according to which Pelops, the father robbed of his boy, pronounced that fearful curse upon the robber, which then, descending gloomily from generation to generation, dominated the son and grandchildren of Laïus, until it found its end in the death of Œdipus, who after a long life full of sorrow was cleared from sin by the powers of heaven. Here one must avoid a grave error, into which in fact many, otherwise well acquainted with antiquity, have fallen. The father is not driven to the curse because Laïus loved a boy and was intimate with him, consequently not by the "unnatural nature" of his passion, as might be assumed considering the modern views upon pæderasty; but simply and solely because Laïus steals the boy, and abducts him against his father's wish: it is not the perverted direction of his impulse that makes Laïus guilty, but the violence employed by him. Certainly, rape is generally the usual beginning of all sexual intercourse in primitive ages, and we know that the abduction of women and boys as a religious ceremony has frequently lasted into most highly civilized times; but we likewise find everywhere that the rape must remain an apparent one, and that the employment of actual violence is equally condemned by public opinion and by the law. That this view of the guilt of Laïus is the correct one we are taught by a comparison of the usual form of abduction in Crete, of which we shall speak later.

Thus we may say that the tragedy of Æschylus found its special theme in the fact that the royal hero Laïus became a curse-laden man in consequence of an offence against conventional form; he thought he might be allowed to abduct the boy, when he could have sued for the beautiful prize freely and openly. The curse pronounced over his head contains a fearful irony: what in his youth formed his greatest delight, a lovely boy, is denied to him, the married man; his marriage remains childless, and when he nevertheless forces a son from fate, he is destined to fall, through disastrous links in the chain of destiny, by the hand of the son he had so eagerly longed for. The murderous hand of the son, led by blindly raging destiny, avenges the sinful encroachment which the father formerly permitted himself upon the free will of a free-born boy. But the murder by his own son has its beginning first of all with the appearance of the fearful Sphinx; for Laïus, in order to free the land from this plague, journeys to Delphi to implore help or advice from the god of light; on his return he is met by his son, unknown to him, to whom he falls a bloody victim. Suddenly light now also falls on the deeper meaning of the well-known riddle of the Sphinx: "Man," so ran the answer, "in the morning of life fresh and of joyful hope, in the evening a weak and broken creature." Laïus was the type of this pitiable creature, and the son, who has just slain his father, was the only man clever enough to solve the riddle. Anyone who is not affected by such tragic art but, according to the modern view, founds the guilt of Laïus upon the love for the son of Pelops—for him the poet has not written.

In another passage I have spoken of the wide-spread opinion that in the Homeric poems no trace of pæderasty is found, and that it was not until a late, degenerate age that people believed in the occurrence of it in the works of Homer. Now Æschylus, in his drama the *Myrmidons*, shows that the bond of affection between Achilles and Patroclus was explained as nothing but sexual, not for the first time in the period of the decadence, but as early as the time of the most beautiful spring-tide of Hellenic civilization. The piece contained the episode in which Achilles, sorely offended by Agamemnon, in his wrath retires from the battle and consoles himself in his tent with Patroclus. The chorus of the tragedy was represented by his Myrmidons, who finally persuade him to allow them to take part in the battle under the command of Patroclus. The drama ended with the death of the latter, and the despairing sorrow of Achilles.

2. SOPHOCLES

In the fragments of the dramatic works of Sophocles that have been preserved, the love of boys and young men is often spoken of.

That does not appear surprising to anyone who is acquainted with the life of the poet. The great tragedian, of whose beauty as a man the glorious statue in the Lateran even to-day gives eloquent testimony above all other monuments, was already as a boy endowed with remarkable grace and comeliness. In dancing, music, and gymnic arts he had become so proficient that the crown of victory was often placed upon his dark hair. And when the Greeks prepared to celebrate the glorious fight at Salamis with a festival, the youthful Sophocles appeared to be so perfect an embodiment of boyishness, that they made him leader of the dances of the boys, naked and with the lyre in his hand (see the γένος Σοφοκλέους, and Ath., i, 20).

Achilles, the dazzling hero of the *Iliad*, meets us as a beautiful boy in the piece called the *Lovers of Achilles*, which was probably a satyric drama. It seems probable that the scene of this drama, of which only a few scanty fragments are preserved, was the summit of Pelion or the cave of Cheiron, the famous centaur and tutor of the heroes. The beauty of the boy can be judged by the line: " He hurls glances from his eyes, which wound like spears " (Sophocles, frag. 161). A longer fragment (Soph., frag. 153) of nine lines compares love to a snowball, which melts in the hand of the boys at play. It may be conjectured that Cheiron thereby alludes to his uncertain longing for the boy. Lastly, Thetis fetches her son away from his tutor (Soph., frag. 157, where τα παιδικὰ is used in an erotic sense), and the satyrs endeavour to console Cheiron for the loss of the loved one. Probably also the satyrs, who formed the Chorus, appeared as lovers of the boy; it has been conjectured that they finally had to withdraw " deceived and tamed ".

Troilus, known from the *Iliad* (xxiv, 257), the delicate son of Priam about whose youthful beauty the tragedian Phrynichus has already waxed enthusiastic, appears as the favourite of Achilles in a drama by Sophocles of the same name. All we know of the subject of this piece is that Achilles killed his favourite by mistake during some gymnastic exercises. He was consequently as unfortunate as Apollo, who killed Hyancinthus, the boy whom he dearly loved, by an unlucky accident when hurling the discus. Achilles lamented his death; a single verse has been preserved from his lament, in which Troilus is called ἀνδρόπαις, that is, a boy whose intelligence equals that of a man (Soph., frag. 562).

There is no doubt moreover that obscene

expressions occurred even in the dramas of Sophocles (e.g. frag. 388 ἀναστῦφαι; frag. 390 ἀποσκόλυπτε; frag. 974 οὐράν).

3. EURIPIDES

The story of Chrysippus, the young favourite of Laïus, was also made the subject of a drama by Euripides. The drama, called after its hero Chrysippus, was prompted by a personal experience of the poet himself. Among the most beautiful boys, who at that time of Hellenic sensual enjoyment attracted attention in the streets of Athens, was Agathon, the son of Tisamenus. It is the same Agathon, of whom Aristophanes in the *Thesmophoriazusæ* gives the well-known witty characterization and who plays an important part in Plato's *Symposion*, the same Agathon who is highly praised by Aristotle as a tragic poet. To his contemporaries he seemed a god come down from heaven and wandering among men in earthly form. But many were eager to gain the love of this ephebus; his beauty lead to the scene of jealousy between Socrates and Alcibiades, so delightfully described by Plato. We are now told that even the cynical Euripides allowed himself to be overcome by the unusual charms of this wonderful phenomenon; indeed, that for his sake he wrote his *Chrysippus* and put it on the stage. If this statement is correct, and there seems no reason to doubt it, we may conjecture that the hero of the piece, in fact Chrysippus, was created by the poet from his beautiful prototype Agathon, and that the poet imagined himself to be playing the part of Laïus. But now we find a note in Cicero (*Tusc. Disp.*, iv, 33, 71), from which it is evident that the foundation of the piece was longing sensuality and that the wishes of Laïus who courted the favour of the boy stood out plainly and distinctly. We must make it clear that it is a question of a drama performed in public, at which of course Euripides and the beautiful Agathon were present.

Thus, about the end of the fifth century, in Athens, a famous poet courted the favour of a distinguished youth equally celebrated for his beauty and refined culture.

Certainly the few fragments give no detailed information as to the content of the drama. Euripides also shares the opinion, elsewhere often expressed, that Laïus was the first who introduced pæderasty into Greece. Laïus also appears to have struggled against his passion, especially in view of the opinion of the Greeks who, at that time, regarded love generally as a disease, since it disturbs the tranquillity of the mind and must therefore be combated with the weapons of understanding. Just as Medea struggles against her love for Jason (Ovid, *Metam.*, 720) so also Laïus complains (Eurip., frag. 841) that one knows what is right, but does what is wrong. It is probable that the drama ended with the death of Chrysippus, since it is a tragedy; it is impossible to say more owing to the discrepancies of tradition.

II. Attic Comedy

The comedy of the Greeks is the result of the exuberant humour of piety elevated by wine, which has its root in gratitude to Dionysus, the great banisher of care and bringer of joy, the eternally youthful god of the fruitfulness of luxuriant nature that ever renews itself. Hence comedy is saturated with obscenities, which are inseparably united with the cult of the spirits of fruitfulness. As comedy is the mirror of life grotesquely caricatured, so sexual life meets us everywhere in Greek comedy in its dominating importance, a bubbling witches' cauldron, a monstrous orgy, in which the infinitely complicated machinery of all sexual practices and of all erotic varieties are whirled round the towering axis of a grotesque gigantic phallus in a manner calculated to bewilder the senses. As now in the sexual life of the Greeks the love of boys has at least the same importance as the love of the wife, we may hazard the conjecture that we shall be able to find its expression also everywhere in Greek comedy. As a matter of fact, also, Greek comedy, like all other kinds of poetry, is simply unthinkable without the love of boys; and this is certainly not only in some way the reverse of the grotesque wit of Dionysian wantonness, but it is one of the focuses round which the ellipse of Greek, especially Attic, comedy turns. But, as already said, we have to do with caricatures. Hence tender tones are silent here, for the modest Eros-boy has become the coarse Priapus. Charis certainly hides her face for shame, but science may not pass them by.

1. PHERECRATES

From an unknown drama of Pherecrates (frag. 135) comes the bitter saying, which as it reproached Alcibiades with being too obliging to men, also taunts him with his dangerousness to the female sex: "Alcibiades who formerly, as it seems, was no man, is now every woman's husband."[1]

2. EUPOLIS

Eupolis of Athens offers us a more abundant source of profit. He flourished during the Peloponnesian war and about 411 met his death in the Hellespont when fighting for his country. He was one of the finest intellects of the Old Comedy and long after his death his cheerful muse was a universal favourite for its grace and wit. No fewer than seven of his comedies, the number of which is variously given as fourteen or seventeen, were distinguished by the first prize. In the fourth

[1] Cf. Suetonius, *Cæsar*, 52; Curio pater eum (i.e. Cæsar) omnium mulierum virum et omnium virorum mulierem appellat; Cicero, *Verres*, ii, 78, 192; at homo . . . magis vir inter mulieres, impura inter viros muliercula proferri non potest.

year of the 89th Olympiad (421 B.C.) Eupolis brought on the stage his comedy *Autolycus*, which was revised some ten years later and was performed for the second time. Autolycus was the son of Lycon and Rhodia, a youth of such beauty that Xenophon (*Symposion*, i, 9) says of him in admiration: "As a light flashes up in the night and draws the eyes of all upon it, so the clear beauty of Autolycus turned the gaze of all upon him. And no one who saw him went away without a wound in his heart." Now this Autolycus was the favourite of Callias, known for his wealth and his frivolous life, who, after he had gained the victory in the pancratium in 422 at the great Panathenæa, gave the beautiful youth that banquet described by Xenophon in his well-known *Symposion*. The end of Autolycus was a sad one, for after the conquest of Athens by Lysander he was put to death by order of the Thirty. As for the content of the piece all that can be said with certainty seems to be that the love of Callias and Autolycus was represented in a very unfavourable light, and that even the parents of the young man, who took part in the banquet, were pelted with scorn and dirt, just as the banquet itself was derided (Ath., v. 216*e*; Eupolis, frag. 56: *εὐτρήσιος παρὰ τὸ τετρῆσθαι τὸν Αὐτόλυκον ὁ Εὔπολις σκώπτει*; frag. 61: *ἀναφλασμος* (onanism).

In 415 Eupolis brought on the *Baptæ* (the "Baptizers"), a sportive piece, in which the private life of Alcibiades was severely criticized. Among these baptæ we might understand the comrades of Alcibiades, who carried on nightly orgies in honour of Cotytto, the goddess of lewdness, at which they imitated female dances and in which lascivious baths and purifications played a part. That the piece reeked with indecency, is clear from Lucian (*Adv. Ind.*, 27), who says: "And did you not blush to read this piece?"

The *Flatterers* (performed in 423) was evidently devoted entirely to pæderasty. Demos himself is represented offering himself for sale, and in frag. 265 we read his complaint: "By Poseidon, the door will never rest," that is, because of the number of visitors, who are pressing to see him. Demos, the son of Pyrilampes, a rich Athenian friend of Pericles, appears in Aristophanes as a celebrated favourite (*Wasps*, 97; cf. the play on words in Plato's *Gorgias*, 481*d*). In the play there also occurred a conversation of Alcibiades with B., an unknown person, in which Alcibiades is ridiculed for some blameable innovations, the more so as he still boasts of them. By λακωνίζειν the simplicity of Spartan meals would be meant, while "to roast in the pan" points to something more luxurious, such as Alcibiades was fond of. But B. seems to give the word a sensual meaning; λακωίζειν, according to Suïdas, means "to be fond of boys" (παιδικοῖς χρῆσθαι), so that Alcibiades comes out with a further one of his merits: he has taught people to drink, quite early (that is, modestly).[1] Now the Athenians considered a drink begun too early as certainly objectionable; interesting on this account is a passage of Baton, in which a father complains bitterly that his son was tempted by a lover to indulge in this bad habit, so that he can never give it up. Pliny also mentions Alcibiades as the inventor of this innovation.

3. ARISTOPHANES

We cannot discuss the importance of the poet Aristophanes and his prominent position in the history of Greek comedy beyond a brief consideration

[1] Frag. 351.—*ΑΛΚΙΒ.* μισῶ λακωνίζειν, ταγηνίζειν δὲ κἂν πριαίμην.
B. πολλὰς δ' . . . οἶμαι νῦν βεβινῆσθαι . . .
A. . . . ὃς δὲ πρῶτος ἐξεῦρεν τὸ πρῷ 'πιπίνειν;
B. πολλήν γε λακκοπρωκτίαν ἡμῖν ἐπιστασ' εὑρών.
A. εἶεν. τίς εἶπεν 'ἀμίδα παῖ' πρῶτος μεταξὺ πίνων;
B. Παλαμηδικόν γε τοῦτο τοὐξεύρημα καὶ σοφόν σου.
On early drinking cf. Baton in Ath., iii, 103*c*; also the commentators on Aristoph., *Birds*, 131; Pliny, *Nat. Hist.*, xiv, 143; Ath., xii, 519*e*.

of the historical premises of the individual comedies and their connection, from which the following passages are taken :—

(*a*) *Acharnians* (performed 425 B.C.)

We find a Phallus-song in 262 ff. :—

Proceed, O Phales, companion of Bacchus, fellow-reveller, roaming by night, friend of love and lechery; in the sixth year I address you, having come with delight to my township, having made for myself a peace, and being freed from troubles and battles and Lamachi.

(*b*) *Ecclesiazusæ* (performed 389 or 392 B.C.)

Lines 877 ff. A grotesque scene of the amœbæan (alternately answering) singing match of old and young prostitutes, the only one existing in any literature.

Old Woman: Why in the world are the men not come? It has been time this long while; for I am standing idle, decked out with grease-paint and clad in a saffron-coloured robe, humming an amorous tune to myself and sportively playing meanwhile, in order that I may catch one of them as he passes by. Ye Muses, come hither to my lips, ready with some soft Ionian ditty!

Girl: This once then, you ugly old woman, you've forestalled me, and peeped out first; thinking to steal my grapes as I was not here; aye, and singing to attract a lover! Well, go on singing, and I'll sing against you, for this, even though it would be tiresome to the audience, has yet something amusing in it and a comic flavour.

[*An ugly old man goes across the stage.*]

Old Woman: Here, talk to this thing, and vanish: but do you, my little darling of a flute-player, take your instrument and play a tune that's worthy of you and worthy of me. (*Singing*) 'If anyone wants to experience bliss he should sleep with me, for knowledge is not in young women but in the ripe ones. Would *she* be as faithful and true, and constant and loving as I? No, she would fly off to another—would fly, would fly, would fly, would fly; and off to another would fly.'

Girl: Do not be envious of the young women. For pleasure is in their tender limbs, and blossoms on their bosoms; while you, old woman, have had your eyebrows polled and your face painted, and you look like a darling for—the embracement of death!

Old Woman: May your teeth drop out and the cords of your bedstead break, and when you wish to be caressed, I hope you will find him a snake—a snake, a snake, a snake; I hope you will find him a snake!

Girl: O dear, what will become of me? my friend is not come, as for the rest, I think nothing of them. Mother is out, she has gone and deserted me, she has left me alone. Nurse, nurse, pity and comfort me; fetch me Orthagoras, I pray; so may it always be happy and well with thee; oh, I beseech thee, obey!

Old Woman: These, these are the prurient tricks of Ionian harlotry, and you seem to me a labda after the Lesbian fashion.

Girl: But you shall never steal away my darling, you shall not disturb nor filch my little hour!

Old Woman: Sing as much as you please, and peep out like a weasel! They will all come first to me!

Girl: What, to your funeral? A new joke, hey?

Old Woman: No! Not in the least new!

Girl: How could there be anything new in such an old crone?

Old Woman: My age won't trouble *you*.

Girl: Then what will? Your rouge and white lead, perchance.

Old Woman: Why talk to me?

Girl: Why peep out?

Old Woman: I? I'm only singing under my breath to my dear Epigenes.

Girl: I thought old Geres was your only friend.

Old Woman: You will soon see; he'll be here presently; he'll come to *me*! See, here he comes himself!

[*A youth is seen in the distance.*]

Girl: He doesn't want anything of you, you pest.

Old Woman: O yes, you skinny jade!

Girl: His acts will show. I'll get away unseen.

[*Leaves the Window.*]

Old Woman: And so will I, that you may know that I'm right and you wrong!

Youth [*entering crowned with flowers and carrying a torch*]: Would that I might sleep with the young girl, nor first be doomed to have to do with an old, snub-nosed hag! This is unbearable for a free-born lad.

Old Woman [*aside, peeping out*]: Then, by Zeus, you'll wench to your cost, for these are not the times of Charixena! Under a democratic government you must obey the laws! I'll run and watch what next you're going to do. [*Withdraws again.*]

Youth: O might I find, dear gods, my fair one alone, to whom I might hasten, flushed with wine and overcome with longing for her!

Girl [*looking out above*]: That vile old hag, I neatly deceived her. She thinks I'm remaining within, so off she's gone. But here's the very lad of whom we were speaking. (*Singing*) This way, this way, come hither, my beloved! O come to my arms, my love, my own, see that you be my bedfellow this night. For the sight of your curls excites me exceedingly, and the wondrous desire which assails me has worn me away! O God of Love, I cry to thee; in mercy and in pity for me! grant that he may come to my bed.

Youth [*singing under the Girl's window*]: Hither, O hither, my love, I pray. Run down from above and open the gate, I pray: else I shall surely fall down and swoon in the dust! My beloved, come, I would rest in thy bosom. O Cypris, why dost thou make me so madly rage for her? O God of Love,

I cry to thee, grant that she may come to my bed. I have said enough to prove my anguish, and do thou, my dearest, I beseech thee, descend and give me welcome! Through thee I suffer! O my beloved decked with golden light, child of Aphrodite, the Muses' bee, the nursling of the Graces, Beauty's face, open to me, embrace me! Sore pangs I undergo for thee!

Old Woman: Hallo there! why are you knocking? Are you seeking *me*?

Youth: Not exactly!

Old Woman: And yet you knocked furiously against my door!

Youth: May I die if I did!

Old Woman: Then why that lighted torch? What seek you here?

Youth: An Anaphlystian citizen.

Old Woman: What's his name?

Youth: No, not Sebinus, whom *you* perhaps expect!

Old Woman: By Aphrodite [*grabs him by the arm*], whether you like it or not.

Youth: Ah, but we're not now bringing cases over sixty years old—they've been adjourned till later! We're taking now those under twenty years.

Old Woman: Ah, but that was under the old régime, my duckie; *now* you must take us first!

Youth: Aye, to take or pass at choice, so runs the Pætian law![1]

Old Woman: You didn't, did you, dine by Pætian law?

Youth: Don't understand you; I must knock at this door.

Old Woman: Aye, but you must first knock at my little door!

Youth: O we don't want a musty bolting-sieve now!

Old Woman: I know I'm loved; but you wonder, don't you, to see me out of doors; come, kiss me—do!

[1] That is, after the manner of the law of draughts.

Youth: No, no, I am afraid of your lover.

Old Woman: Whom do you mean?

Youth: That best of painters.

Old Woman: Who is he, I wonder?

Youth: Who paints the vases for the dead [i.e., *the undertaker*]. Be off—he'll see you at the door!

Old Woman: I know, I know your wishes.

Youth: And I yours.

Old Woman: I vow by Aphrodite, whose own I am, I'll never let you go.

Youth: You're mad, old woman.

Old Woman: Nonsense! I'll *drag* you to my bed!

Youth: Why then need we buy hooks to raise our buckets, when an old hag like this, let down by the heels, could draw up all the buckets from our wells with her nails?

Old Woman: No more jokes, my dear, but follow me at once.

Youth: But I need not do so, unless you've paid the tax—one-fifth per cent on all your years!

Old Woman: O yes, you must, by Aphrodite, because I love to sleep with lads like you!

Youth: But *I* don't love to sleep with hags like *you*, nor will I ever do so!

Old Woman: O yes, you will. *This* will compel you!

Youth: What in the world is "this"?

Old Woman: "This" is a decree which bids you follow me.

Youth: Let's hear what it says.

Old Woman: O yes, my dear, I will. *Be it enacted*, please to listen, you, *by us the ladies*: *if a youth desire a maiden he shall not have to do with her before he has first lain with some old woman; if the youth refuse, then may the old women be allowed to use violence and drag him in, laying hold of him by the middle.*

Youth: A crusty law! a Procrustean law!

Old Woman: Well, anyhow, you must obey the law!

Youth: What if some man, a friend or fellow-citizen, should come and set me free?

Old Woman: A man, forsooth? No man is liable beyond a bushel now!

Youth: But can't I swear off?

Old Woman: Nay! no tricks allowed now!

Youth: I'll pretend to be a merchant!

Old Woman: You may, but to your cost!

Youth: What—must I come?

Old Woman: You must—follow me to my house.

Youth: Is it a stern necessity?

Old Woman: Yes, quite Diomedean.

Youth: Then strew the couch with dittany, and break off and place four well-crushed branches of the vine beneath; bind the fillets on your head; set the oil beside, and at the entrance the water-vessel [*trappings, etc., of a bier*].

Old Woman: Now, of course you'll buy me a garland yet!

Youth: A *waxen* garland, so by Zeus, I will! You'll fall to pieces, I think, within!

Girl [*coming from her house*]: Where are you dragging him?

Old Woman: I'm taking my husband home.

Girl: Not wisely then: for he is not of the age for sleeping with you, such a young thing as that! You are fitter to be his mother rather than his wife! If thus you carry out this law you'll soon have an Œdipus in every house.

Old Woman: You nasty spiteful girl, you said that out of sheer envy, but I'll be revenged! [*Exit.*]

Youth: Now, by Zeus the preserver, my sweetest darling, you have done me a great service in having frightened off that old hag, for which this night I'll make you what return I can.

4. ALEXIS

Alexis came from Thurii in Lower Italy, lived about 392–288, and, according to Suïdas, left 245 comedies.

The first of these which interests us is *Agonis*

(the name of a hetaira). The scanty fragments give us no information as to the subject-matter, but it is certain that Misgolas of the Attic deme Collytus played some part in it. His passion for beautiful boys, especially those who could play the lute, is confirmed by several passages: e.g. in Æschines (*Tim.*, i, 41): "It is this Misgolas, son of Naucrates, of Collytus, in other respects a man of beautiful body and soul; but he has always been fond of boys and is constantly in the habit of having about him players on the lute, both male and female." Antiphanes (frag. 26, 14–18) had already alluded to him in the *Fishermen* and Timocles (frag. 30) in *Sappho*. In the *Agonis* of Alexis (frag. 3) a girl said to her mother: "O mother dear, do not give me, I beg, to Misgolas, for I do not play the lute."

Frag. 242 (from *Hypnos*, Sleep): "The young man does not eat chives, to avoid disgusting his lover when he kisses him."

5. Timocles

In his comedy *Orestautocleides* the amours of Autocleides played a certain part. Autocleides of Hagnus is meant, to whom the orator Æschines refers in his well-known speech against Timarchus (1, 52). The situation was perhaps thought of as one in which, as Orestes was once pursued by the Furies, so the pæderast Autocleides is pursued by a host of hetairæ; at least, frag. 25 seems to point to this, in which it is described how a number of hetairæ, no fewer than eleven, keep watch over the unhappy man even when he is asleep.

6. Menander

Menander of Athens, the son of Diopeithes and Hegesistrate, who lived from 342 to 291, was a nephew of Alexis already spoken of, a poet of the Middle Comedy who introduced Menander into the technique of comedy. As early as the age of 21 he won a victory, yet if this success became his seven times more, he belongs to those poets on whom posterity bestowed greater admiration and affection than his contemporaries. We have already spoken of his *Androgynos or the Cretans*.

In frag. 363 the behaviour of a *cinædus* (lewd fellow) is described, with a sly hit at Ctesippus,[1] son of Chabrias, of whom it is said that he even sold the stones from his father's grave, to be able to indulge his life of pleasure: "And yet, wife, I too was once a young man, but then I did not bathe five times a day. But now I do. Nor did I even have a fine over-cloak. But now I have. Nor even scented oil. But now I have. And I will dye my hair, and I will pluck me smooth, and in short shrift will turn into a Ctesippus."

Retrospect and Supplementary Remarks on Tragic and Comic Poetry

The tragedy of the older period rarely employs erotic motives; and with the exception of the *Agamemnon* of Æschylus, the subject of which is the murder of Agamemnon by an adulterous wife seized with raging jealousy, we can hardly quote any tragedy the nucleus of which is love, apart from homosexual motives, of which we have already spoken. At first, love stories with a tragic ending were not regarded as adapted to allow men to feel the sublime in tragic destiny at the feast of the god of the highest enthusiasm.

Sophocles employed the passion of love much more frequently, but only as a subsidiary motive, e.g. the love of Medea for Jason in the *Women of Colchis*, of Hippodameia for Pelops in the *Œnomaus*. As the essential and only subject the passion of love appears in only one of his dramas, the *Phædra*, in which the irresistible love of Phædra for her

[1] On Ctesippus, see Diphilus, frag. 38 (ii, 552, Kock), and Timocles, frag. 5 (ii, 452, Kock); frag. 480: *πόσθων*, *penis*, and a caressing word for a little boy. Cf. Hesychius, s.v. *σμόρδωνες*: *ὑποκοριστικῶς ἀπὸ τῶν μορίων, ὡς πόσθωνες*; Apollodorus, frag. 13, 8; *τὴν γὰρ αἰσχύνην πάλαι πᾶσαν ἀπολωλέκασι καθ' ἑτέρας θύρας*. Further sexual allusions witticisms, and obscenities from Attic comedy have been collected by myself in Anthropophyteia, vol. vii, 1910, pp. 173, 495.

beautiful stepson Hippolytus that rises to a crime is the axis round which the whole play turns. It is the oldest example of a Greek love-tragedy in the proper sense of the expression. We may assume that the brilliant representation of the frenzied love-passion made a powerful impression upon the spectators and became a strong stimulus for the later treatment of erotic stories. Not only did Euripides employ the same motif in two dramas, one of which is preserved, but according to Pausanias (i, 22, 1), it was the very same story of Phædra and Hippolytus that later became everywhere known "even to non-Greeks, if only they had learnt the Greek language". Euripides turned his attention by preference to erotic material, and thereby transferred heroic tragedy into a kind of bourgeois play with an unhappy ending; for although he frequently enough kept the names and characters of the heroic age, yet the men were men of his own time, and the feelings and passions represented by the poet are the common possession of all humanity, no longer connected with a definite period.

Erotic had now taken possession of the Greek stage, and Euripides and the later tragedians were never tired of describing, in constantly renewed variations, the almighty power of love—the highest bliss and the most burning passion—and allowing the spectators to explore all the depths and abysses of this greatest of all riddles which men call love.[1] Euripides was also the first who ventured to represent the motif of incest on the stage, in the *Æolus* (fragments in Nauck, *TGF*², p. 365), which had for its subject the love of Canace and her brother Macareus with its tragic consequences. Similar motifs were then more frequently employed by the tragedians of later times; and in connection with

[1] For erotic motives in the Greek tragedians see E. Rohde, *Der Griechische Roman* (1900, p. 31), although he does not take into account the numerous homosexual motives.

this we must remember that not only the love of Byblis for her brother Caunus, but also that of Myrrha for her father Cinyras, of Harpalyce for her father Clymenus, were brought forward on the stage. Certainly Ovid (*Tristia*, ii, 381–408) did not exaggerate when, after giving a long list of erotic tragedies, he says that time did not allow him to mention all of them by name—indeed, that a list of the titles alone would be enough to fill his book.[1]

While Aristophanes (*Clouds*, 1372; *Frogs*, 850, 1043 *ff*., 1081), thus the chief representative of the Old Comedy, attacked the conquest of the stage by the representation of the passion of love brought in by Euripides, that is, as the centre and driving impulse of a drama—for his own pieces, as we saw, are also filled with erotic—this also was altered by the advent of the New Comedy. As the women in their life emancipated themselves more and more from the retirement imposed upon them in ancient times, so also in comedy the love of man for a woman occupied an increasingly greater space. Gradually love-intrigues and the sentimental life of love formed the chief subject of comedies. Hence Plutarch (in Stobæus, *Florilegium*, 63, 64) rightly says that "the poetry of Menander was held together by a single bond—by love, which breaks forth in all his comedies like a single breath of life". Yet even now the sensual side of love remains the chief thing, for all the young women of the New Comedy, whom the young men court in longing passion, are hetairæ. Man still remained convinced that marriage was a fulfilment of duty, relation with an hetaira an affair of love.

It may be taken for granted as well known that the ancient stage managed with few actors and that the female parts also were taken by men.

By the side of the strange masks, mad inventions and jokes, ancient comedy is still characterized by

[1] Cf. his *Ars Amatoria*, i, 283–340; Propertius, iii, 19; Virgil, *Æneid*, vi, 442 ff.

the wearing of the phallus, mostly made of leather, by the actors as servants of the fertilizing god. After what we have already said about the phallus cult, this custom will at least no longer appear unintelligible; comedy had grown up from the songs of the phallus-processions.

If a part were to be played naked the actor wore a close-fitting bodice with, usually, a false breast and false belly on which the nipples and navel were clearly marked. The phallus appears to have fallen more and more into disuse in the course of time; at least, not a few vase-pictures with scenic representations in which it is missing are known to us. It clearly belonged to the Old Comedy, in which, in scenes where mythological motives were comically made use of, it emphasized the grotesqueness and strengthened the comedy of the situation. The chorus of the satyric drama wore an apron of goat's skin in front of the phallus, behind which the little tail of the satyr appeared.

The modern man will perhaps ask whether comedy, with its strongly erotic, often highly obscene performance, was also visited by women and children. Certainly it was not forbidden; it is possible that comedy was frequented more by hetairæ than by respectable wives of citizens, but the presence of boys is sufficiently attested. Anyone who finds this singular or even offensive, must again be reminded that the ancients faced the sexual quite naively; that, as being a matter of course, they did not surround it with a veil of mystery, but paid it religious homage as the preliminary condition of all existence, whose last offshoots in comedy, although distorted into the grotesque, are yet not difficult to recognize.

III. *Satyric Drama. Pantomime. Ballet*

As may be generally known, the performance of serious tragedies was followed by the so-called satyric drama, which, recalling the cheerfulness of the earlier festivals of Dionysus, satisfied the desire of the public for coarser fare and, with jest and joke, restored the balance after the mental shocks of tragic destinies. Such satyric dramas, of which only one has been preserved, the *Cyclops* of Euripides, enjoyed great popularity until the Alexandrine period, although we can say little that is definite about their subjects. The Old Attic comedy also long found imitators; it lived again through the " Dionysian artists ", who from their chief seat on the island of Teos everywhere spread the " Dionysian practices " at the courts of princes, in military garrisons, in all the larger, and often in the smaller cities.

By the side of this the farce continually extended its range, and, if we may believe Polybius (xxxii, 25; cf. Ath., x, 440), as we probably can, with this countless throng of actors, singers, dancers, and the like, " Ionic licentiousness and immorality " everywhere found an entrance. In Roman imperial times the dialogue parts of tragedies and comedies were still performed, until gradually, from about the third century A.D., they were driven out by the pantomime, the effect of which depended almost entirely upon sensual charms.[1] By incessant practice and a strictly regulated mode of life the pantomimists had secured an absolute mastery over their bodies, and were able to carry out every movement with perfect grace owing to their suppleness. Of course only the most beautiful and graceful forms appeared as pantomimists. " In the lewd scenes, which were the spice of this drama, seductive grace combined with luxury and shamelessness knew no limits. When Bathyllus, a beautiful boy, was dancing, Leda, the most impudent actress of mimes, felt like a mere country novice on seeing such mastership in the art of refined sensuality." (L.

[1] On the continuous life of dramatic performances cf. Dion Chrysostom, xix, p. 487; Lucian, *De Saltat.*, 27.

Friedländer: *Roman Life and Manners*, English trans., ii, p. 106.)

Representations from mythology were especially in favour; a detailed description of such a mythological ballet can be read in the *Metamorphoses* of Apuleius (x, 30–34). The stage represents the mountains of Ida, built up high of wood, planted with shrubs and living trees, from which springs flow down; goats can be seen grazing, tended by Paris, a beautiful youth in Phrygian dress. Now a boy, beautiful as a picture, enters, naked, except for a short cloak fluttering round his left shoulder. Fair hair, from which two golden wings, united by a golden band, stand out, crowns his head and waves over his naked back. It is Mercury; in a dancing attitude he glides around, hands a golden apple to Paris, and indicates by gestures the commission of Jupiter, after which he gracefully withdraws.

Now Juno enters, a beautiful woman with diadem and sceptre; then Minerva rushes in, with shining helmet and shield, brandishing her lance. Afterwards appears a third. Inexpressible grace is spread over her whole being, and the colour of love blooms on her face. It is Venus; no garment enviously conceals the irreproachable beauty of her body, she walks along naked, only a transparent, silken veil covers her nakedness. Now wanton winds lift up the light veil, and the bloom of youth shines uncovered; now the hot breath of the wind presses the veil firmly against her body, and beneath the airy covering every voluptuous outline stands out in relief.

Each of the three women, who represent the goddesses, has a special retinue. With Juno appears Castor and Pollux; to the delightful sound of the flutes Juno strides along in quiet majesty and by serious gestures promises the shepherd the Kingdom of Asia, if he awards her the prize of beauty. Minerva, in warlike attire, is accompanied by her usual companions and shield-bearers, the spirits of Terror and Fear, who perform a dance over naked swords.

Round Venus flutters a crowd of little Cupids. Smiling sweetly, she stands with her own bodily charms amidst them, to the general delight of the spectators. One would have thought the round, milk-white, tender boys were all of them true Cupids; they carry flaming torches before the goddess, as if going to a wedding feast; also charming Graces and beautiful Hours surround the goddess in dazzling nakedness. Roguishly they pelt Venus with bouquets and flowers and glide along in an artistic dance, after they have paid homage to the great goddess of sensuality with the firstfruits of spring.

Now the flutes sweetly give forth Lydian measures, and every heart is moved with joy. Now Venus, more charming than any music, begins to move. Slowly she lifts up her foot; her body bends gracefully with her head gently nodding; every enchanting position is in harmony with the soft sound of the flutes. Paris, entranced, hands her the apple as the prize of victory.

Juno and Minerva leave the stage, discontented and wrathful, but Venus manifests her joy at the victory she has won by a concluding dance with all her retinue. After that, from the summit of Mount Ida a fountain with saffron and wine spouts on high and fills the whole theatre with a sweet fragrance; then the mountain sinks and disappears.

On the pantomime and its favourite dances Lucian has written a very readable monograph, from which it is clear (*De Saltat.*, 2 and 5; see also Libanius, *De Saltat.*, ch. 15) that, of the numerous mythological subjects, it is just the erotic that enjoyed special popularity. Naturally also, at that time a reaction set in owing to the pedants who concealed themselves under the mask of philosophy, a representative of whom, a certain Craton, is made to speak as follows: "But, most excellent sir, how can one forgive you, and what must anyone think of you, who have enjoyed a learned education, and have a moderate knowledge of philosophy, when one sees you abandon the noblest studies and the company of the wise men of old, sitting down and letting your ears be soothed with the pipes, while you are looking at an effeminate man, who swaggers about in a soft female dress, and with most lustful songs and movements represents the most notorious women of antiquity, the Phædras, Parthenopes, Rhodopes, and whatever may be the names of such wanton wretches, at the same time piping and trilling, and beating time with his feet." And later: "Truly, it only wanted that—that I with my long beard and grey hairs should find myself amongst a heap of foolish women and insane men, applauding the wanton contortions of the limbs of a wretched good-for-nothing fellow, and that I should have shouted 'Bravo! Bravissimo!' with indecent transports of delight."

Among the subjects here mentioned by Lucian also occur those dealing with incest, such as the love-affair of Demophon (called Acamas wrongly by Lucian) and his sister Phyllis; of Phædra with her step-son Hippolytus; of Scylla with her father Minos. Of course, in Greece homosexual motives were not lacking; of intrigues with boys, which were danced upon the stage, Lucian names the story of Apollo and Hyacinthus. The enumeration of the scenes, which were presented in pantomime, fills several pages in Lucian; we see that nearly all the erotic motives of Greek mythology (of which there is an astonishingly large number) were employed in pantomime.

Under the cloak of mythology even love-scenes with animals were represented. The best-known is the pantomimus *Pasiphaë* (Lucian, *De Saltat.*, 49; Suetonius, *Nero*, 12; Martial, *Spectacula*, 5; Bährens, *Poetæ Latini Minores*, v, p. 108). As the story tells us, Poseidon, angry at the neglect of an offering, had inspired Pasiphaë, the wife of King Minos of Crete, with violent passion for a specially beautiful bull. The famous architect Dædalus came to her assistance, made a cow of wood, and dressed it in a natural skin. Pasiphaë concealed herself in the empty body of this cow and was thus coupled with the bull, by whom she had the Minotaur, the well-known monster, half-bull, half-man. (Ovid, *Ars Amatoria*, ii, 24; *Semibovemque virum semivirumque bovem*.)

That such scenes were not unheard of in Greek theatres in imperial times is shown by the fact that the mythological motive and the disguise with the animal's skin was given up, and scenes of weddings between a human being and an animal were put on the stage *in puris naturalibus*. The subject of Lucian's *Lucius or the Ass*, as is well known, is that Lucius is changed by enchantment into an ass, which, however, keeps its human power of thought and feeling. The end of the adventure of the human ass is formed by the love-story of the distinguished lady of Thessalonica. Lucian tells this adventure in sufficient detail; we can only here briefly sketch an episode that is very readable in itself and must refer the curious reader to the original text (*Asinus*, 50 ff.).

This distinguished and very rich lady has heard of the wonderful qualities of the ass, whom certainly no one supposes to be an enchanted man. She comes, sees, and falls in love with him. She buys it, and henceforth treats him quite like her lover. But the singular loving couple is watched, and it is resolved to make the rare abilities of the ass a public show. It is to be exhibited for all to see, how the ass consummates the marriage nuptials with a woman who has been sentenced to death.

"And when the day arrived on which my master was going to give his show it was decided to exhibit me in the theatre. I made my entrance in the following manner. I was laid upon a great bed, made of Indian tortoiseshell and fastened with golden nails; the woman also was ordered to lie beside me. Then, as we were, we were placed upon a machine, carried down to the theatre, and set down in the midst of the theatre. When I appeared, loud shouts of applause and clapping of hands burst forth. Then a table was put before us, containing dishes with which those who fare sumptuously regale themselves. At our side beautiful boys stood as cupbearers, serving us with wine in golden cups. My master, standing up behind me, ordered me to eat; but I was ashamed at being in such a position in the theatre, and at the same time I was afraid that some bear or lion might suddenly jump out upon me.

"At this moment, a man went by carrying flowers. I noticed that among them there were some leaves of freshly cut roses; at once, without hesitating a moment, I jumped off the bed. The audience thought that I was getting up to dance; but I, running over each bunch, chose the roses from among the rest, and devoured them. Then, to the great astonishment of the spectators, the apparition of the animal disappeared, and he who had formerly been an ass, Lucius himself, stood naked and upright in the theatre."

Only gradually does the cheated public calm itself. But Lucius, pleased at becoming a man again, considers it a duty that etiquette requires to pay a farewell visit to the distinguished lady, who had loved him so as an ass. He is received by her in friendly fashion and invited to dine with her in the evening.

"However, thinking it my duty to go and pay my respects to the lady who had been enamoured of me when I was an ass, I said to myself that she would think me more beautiful now that I was a man. In fact, she appeared delighted to see me, and was highly amused at the singular affair; she even invited me to supper, and to spend the night with her. I accepted her invitation, thinking that it would be unworthy of me, if, now that I was a man, I were to despise one who had loved me so much when I bore the form of an animal. I supped with her, rubbed myself with perfumes and put on a crown of that dear flower which had made me a man again. When the night was far advanced and it was time to retire, I got up from the table, and, thinking that I was doing something grand, I stripped and stood quite naked, thinking that I should please her more, in comparison with what she had done with the ass. But when she saw that I was a man from head to foot, she spat at me and said: 'Away with you! get out of my house, go and sleep somewhere else.' When I asked what enormous crime I had committed, she replied: 'Really, I was not in love with you, but with the ass; it was not with you, but with the ass that I spent such pleasant nights; I thought that you now also would certainly preserve the great sign of the ass and drag it along, but you have come to me changed from that beautiful and useful animal into a ridiculous little ape.' Then she called her servants, and ordered them to take me by the shoulders and put me outside. Thus thrust out of the house, there I was in the street, in the open air, naked, beautifully crowned and perfumed, forced to embrace the bare earth and to sleep on its bosom. At daybreak, I ran naked to the vessel, where, laughing heartily, I told my brother what had happened to me. Then, as a favourable wind sprang up, we set sail, and in a few days reached my country. There I offered sacrifice to the protecting gods and consecrated votive gifts to them for having brought me home safe and sound, and for having saved me, after a long time and with difficulty, not from the dog's mouth, as the proverb says, but from the curiosity which had made me take the shape of an ass."

CHAPTER V

DANCES, GAMES, MEALS, ETC.

DANCE AND BALL-GAMES. MEALS AND DRINKING-BOUTS. RIGHTS OF HOSPITALITY

Dances, which in ancient times were always an exhibition, may be regarded as theatrical productions in the wider sense. Antiquity is ignorant of the modern society dance, in the form in which couples of male and female dancers move to the sound of music for their own amusement. The dance of the Hellenes is the science of rhythm and mimic art; that is, it is the bodily expression of an internal idea and works through movement as poetry through the word. Hence the Greek dance was a real art, no aimless turning round, but always the rhythmical representation of internal processes, in the expression of which all parts of the body, not least the hands and arms, participated. Hence the Greeks, rejoicing in beauty, took extraordinary delight in performances of the art of dancing, in which men diligently exercised their youth in order to make splendid their festivals and spectacles as also their banquets, drinking-bouts, and other private festivities. This was true even in oldest times; the finds in Crete still speak to us to-day of the beautiful female dancers of the prehistoric Ægæan period and their very free clothing; and Homer (*Od.*, viii, 263 ff.; 370 ff.; monographs by Lucian and Libanius: see also Ath., xiv, 628) several times mentions rhythmic dances, intended to amuse and give pleasure to the spectators. During the whole period of ancient civilization we find dances as the exhibition of bodily beauty and graceful movement throughout literature and in plastic and pictorial art; apart from the mention of them scattered everywhere through the writings of the ancients we still possess several monographs on the art, and still at the present day numerous wall-pictures from Pompeii and vase-paintings enchant us by their indescribable beauty and inimitable grace no less than by the nobility of nakedness, partial or complete, of the youthful dancers, male and female.

A survey of the history of the Greek art of dancing, if only half complete, would make a book in itself. In accordance with the object of our sketch, we have to limit ourselves to those degenerate varieties of Greek dances, in which a sexual impulse shows itself more or less.

When we said that the Greeks were not acquainted with the society dance in our sense of the word, this remark needs to be supplemented by the statement that Plato (*Laws*, vi, 771*e*) appears to mean something at least resembling it, when he declares it to be desirable that on festive occasions young men and women should dance together, in order to get to know one another before marriage. This is the same passage in which he demands that the sexes should have more opportunity to see each other naked, " so far at least as regard for modesty permits " ; yet it is very questionable whether by Plato's demand we are to understand the modern dance in couples, or whether, which at least seems more probable, it means that young men should perform their dances before the eyes of girls and *vice versa*. Yet even if he had demanded society dances such as are fashionable amongst ourselves, it is clear from the passage that they were not usual, at least in Attica ; and it is nowhere handed down to us that they were common at a later date. No more does the well-known description on the shield of Achilles in the *Iliad* (xviii, 593 ff.) correspond to a modern society dance ; it is rather round dances of young men and women, who perform them, not separately, as is generally the case, but together : " There youths and maidens worth many oxen were dancing, holding each other's hands by the wrist. Of these some wore delicate linen dresses, and others were clad in well-spun tunics, with oil soft shining; some had beautiful garlands, and others golden swords hanging from silver belts. At one time they moved rapidly in a circle with cunning feet, right easily, just as when a potter, seated, tries the wheel fitted to the hand, to see whether it runs; at another time they moved rapidly in file. And a great crowd stood round the charming dance, enjoying the spectacle; and amongst them a divine bard sang to the cithara; and two tumblers, when he began his song, whirled about in the middle."

The same holds good of what Lucian (*De Saltat.*, 10) tells us of the dance of the ephebi at Sparta: "Even now you can see their young men learning to dance as eagerly as they learn the use of weapons. When they have done struggling at arm's length, beaten and being beaten by another, then they rest in turns, and the contest ends in a dance. The piper sits in the middle of them, plays his instrument, and beats time with his feet. The others follow in order, and, observing the measure, take up all kinds of attitudes—sometimes warlike, sometimes suited for the dance—which please Dionysus or Aphrodite. Wherefore the song which they sing while dancing is an invitation to Aphrodite and the Loves to join them in revelling and to dance with them. One of these songs (for they sing two) contains a lesson on the way to dance. 'Forward, young people,' they say, 'put your feet one after the other and enjoy yourselves as much as you can,' that is, dance as well as possible. They do the same thing in the dance called *hormus*.

"The *hormus* is a dance of young men and maidens together, who perform it one by the side of the other, while forming a figure very like a necklace. The chorus is led, on one side by a young man, who dances with the vigour of youth, and takes steps such as he will afterwards make use of in war;

on the other side, a young girl follows him, teaching her sex how to dance, so that the whole performance is as it were the union of strength and modesty. The *gymnopædia* is a similar dance among the Lacedæmonians."

That in Greece dances of boys and young men everywhere enjoyed popularity, need not be expressly confirmed by the testimony of authors. From the overwhelming supply of evidence we can only give a small selection. Thus we read in Lucian (*De Saltat.*, 16): "At Delos no sacrifices are offered without dancing, all being accompanied by music and dance. Choruses of boys assemble together, to the sound of flute and cithara; some of them dance together, and the most expert selected from among them dance in character alone. Therefore the songs composed for these choruses are called *hyporchemata*, that is to say, dances with songs, of which lyric poetry is full."

He then enumerates an imposing number of dances, without, however, giving any more detailed account of their nature, so that they are mere names, with which we will not trouble the reader.[1] Although the dances hitherto discussed are not without the erotic undertone, yet the oldest mention known to me of a dance with a decided erotic element first appears in Herodotus (vi, 126 ff.): Cleisthenes, the mighty ruler of Sicyon, had a daughter as lovely as a picture, named Agariste, for the wooing of whom the most distinguished young men from the whole of Greece and Italy came crowding together. The suitors stayed for a year at the court of Cleisthenes, who during that time tested them thoroughly. Finally, the Athenian Hippocleides, through his wealth and beauty, had the best chance. When the decisive day had arrived, Cleisthenes, after offering sacrifice, prepared a magnificent feast, after

[1] A few more of them may be noticed: the Tray of Sacrifice, the Tongs, Flowers, Mortar, Kneading-Trough, etc. (named from figures evolved), Flight, Boisterousness, Spilling the Meal, etc., etc.

which the suitors displayed their musical and social talents. Hippocleides, who had drunk heavily of wine, enchanted all by the fullness and wit of his whimsicalities. Rendered insolent thereby, he executed a lascivious dance to the accompaniment of flutes. Yet Cleisthenes, although he looked on with a gloomy air, kept his temper. But when Hippocleides mounted the table, and there performed yet more audacious dances, standing finally on his head, and gesticulating indecently with bare legs, his hoped-for father-in-law indignantly addressed him as follows: "O son of Teisander, you have danced away your bride," to which he replied: "Hippocleides cares not," and so left the hall laughing.

Even though the shamelessness here described took place so to say in private company, yet the dance was well enough known, and certainly would, according to our ideas, have been called indecent, and it was danced in full publicity. Of the same character were the earlier indecent dances at the festivals of Artemis and the dance of the Callabides, and further the notorious Sicinnis.[1] The ancients were uncertain about the meaning of the name, but at least we know that the satyrs in the satyric drama were in the habit of dancing it, and that its grotesque movements and the defiant stripping off the clothes made it a dance that according to our ideas was one of positive indecency. The soft sounds of the flutes greatly contributed to the stimulating effect.

Equally indecent, or rather erotic, was the Cordax (Dion Cassius, lix, 27; Alciphron, iii, 18; Dem., ii, 18; Bekker, *Anecdota*, 101, 17, 267; Ath., xiv, 630*e*; Pausanias, vi, 22; Aristoph., *Clouds*, 532, 547; Lucian, *Bacch.*, 1; Theophrastus, *Characters*, vi), which consisted chiefly of reeling backwards and

[1] See Ath., xiv, 630*b*, for attempted explanations of the name. The most important passages that deal with it are: Dion. Halic., vii, 72, 1*d*; Clement Alexand., *Paed.*, i, 7; Eurip., *Cyclops*, 37; Ath., i, 20; xiv, 629*d*., 630; Pollux, iv, 99; Scholiast on Aristoph., *Clouds*, 540.

forwards, as though representing drunkenness ; and to this was added a series of grotesque and unseemly movements that ostentatiously and prominently exhibited movements of the body, and apparently unintentional denudation, so that " Cordax " finally became the typical name for an indecent dance.

Summing up, we may say that the Cordax was the embodiment of what the modern science of sexual psychopathy calls " exhibitionism ", but with the fundamental difference, that the Hellenes enjoyed such exhibitions as were occasionally offered them and cleverly avoided public scandal by the formal permission of such extravagances from time to time.

Ball-games are closely connected with the dance as an artistic performance. Their harmonious movements, which set the beauty of bodily forms in the clearest light, can be almost calle a dance in the ancient sense. Homer (*Od.*, viii, 370 ff.) introduces the Phæacians as delighting their guest, Odysseus, with such a game : " And Alcinous bade Halius and Laòdamas dance alone, since no one contended with them. And after they had taken the beautiful purple ball in their hand, which the wise Polybus had made for them, the one hurled it into the shadow of the clouds, bending back ; but the other, lifting himself up from the ground, easily caught it in turn before he reached the ground with his feet. And after they had tried their skill in throwing the ball straight upwards, they then proceeded to dance on the all-nourishing earth, in turn and repeatedly ; and the rest of the youths shouted in applause, standing in the crowd ; and a great din arose."

Athenæus describes various kinds of ball-games, and gives very learned explanations as to the name and origin of these games, quoting the following lines from a comedy of Damoxenus (Ath., i, 14*d* ; Damoxenus, frag. 3 in Kock, *CAF.*, III, 353, from Ath., i, 15*b*) : " A boy, who might be about seventeen years of age, was playing at ball. He came from Cos, which island, as it appears, produces gods. Whenever he looked at the spectators, as he threw or caught his ball, we shouted loudly in applause: 'How beautiful the boy is! The grace and harmony of his limbs in movement!' or, when he spoke, 'A marvel of beauty! I have never heard of nor seen such enchanting grace! Something worse would have befallen me, had I remained longer; and ah! already my heart aches with love.'"[1]

Besides the public festivals, banquets and drinking-bouts in particular afforded the opportunity of enjoying the spectacle of the dance, accompanied by the insinuating sounds of music, especially the sensual flutes. Greek drinking-bouts or, as the Hellenes called them, *Symposia*, have been so often described in the generally well-known representations of Greek life (Becker, *Charicles*, 1840; Stoll, *Bilder aus dem altgriechischen Leben*, 2nd edn., 1875), that a detailed account of them would be superfluous. Finally we may refer to two writings of antiquity, the perusal of which cannot be sufficiently recommended to everyone who wishes to make himself acquainted with the spirit of ancient Greece. They are the writings of Plato and Xenophon,[2] that have come down to us under the same title *Symposia*. If the graceful narrative of Xenophon, by its living truth and freshness, transplants us into the social conditions of his time, the intellectual and at the same time easily intelligible philosophy of Plato, with its conversations that exhale a fragrance illuminated by poetry, on the nature of love, will always enchant the reader, unless he is completely overwhelmed by the triviality of everyday life, and fill him with bitter-sweet longing

[1] Cf. Goethe's description of a game of ball, seen at Verona (p. 91).

[2] In addition to these, two others may be mentioned, neither of which deserves to be spoken of contemptuously: Plutarch's *Symposium* or *Banquet of the Seven Wise Men*, and the *Banquet of Learned Men* by Athenæus. Both are priceless and rich sources for the knowledge of ancient life, although certainly they are anything but poetical. The *Feast of the Lapithæ* in Lucian may be strongly recommended to those who like coarsely satirical characterization.

for the blooming age of humanity—he will, as Goethe says, " seek the land of the Greeks with his soul."

It may be briefly mentioned that wine in ancient Greece was so cheap, that even slaves and labourers could obtain their daily full measure; that too much wine was often taken; that the female sex especially did homage to wine, that in many places, such as Massalia and Miletus, women were forbidden to drink wine, and were directed to be satisfied with sober water.[1]

The drinking all round, consequently the *Symposion* proper, did not begin till eating was finished. Generally, a president was chosen by throwing the dice, the so-called *Symposiarchos* or *Basileus*, to whose arrangements the carousers had to submit. He decided the proportion of wine and water to be mixed. Of course the arrangements were made according to the intellectual level of those who took part in the company. Among men who were intellectually stimulated it was customary to season and ennoble the joys of wine with excited conversation, of which Plato, Xenophon, Plutarch and others give us wonderful specimens in the writings mentioned above. But also full scope was allowed to jest and joke, and the more so, naturally, as the gift of Bacchus exercised its stimulating effect, or more correctly, eliminated all obstacles.

We should not look at such jests through critical spectacles. Plutarch indeed quotes many which can certainly be called stupid, but which no doubt afforded much amusement to the guests in their jolly, merry mood caused by intoxication (Plutarch, *Sympos.*, i, 4, 3). " The symposiarch ordered a stammerer to sing, a bald man to comb his hair,

[1] Cheapness of wine: Böckh, *Staatshaushaltung der Athener*, i, 87, 137 (there is an Eng. trans.). Public economy of Athens; slaves and labourers, Demosth., *Lacritus*, 32; Plutarch., *Comparison of Cato and Aristeides*, 4. Women's fondness for wine: Ath., x, 440; Anth. Pal., ix, 298; Aristoph., *Eccles.*, 227, etc. Women forbidden to drink wine: Ælian, *Var. hist.*, ii, 38; on the different kinds of wine see Becker's *Charicles*.

and a lame man to dance. The philosopher Agapestor, who was very weak on his legs, was ordered to stand on his right leg and to empty his glass or to pay a forfeit. But when it came to his turn to settle the conditions, he demanded that they should all drink in such a manner that they saw his foot. Then he sent for an empty vessel, got into it with his lame foot and drank up his glass; but the guests, since they could not see his foot, paid the penalty agreed upon."

According to Lucian (*Saturnalia*, 4), it was a favourite "punishment" to be made to dance round naked or to carry the flute-player three times round the room.

The guests were served at the Symposion chiefly by young slaves, whose special dexterity was shown in the graceful presentation of the full drinking goblets. In the enchanting fourth *Dialogue of the Gods* by Lucian, in which is described the abduction of the Trojan royal child Ganymede and his installation in office as cupbearer and favourite of Zeus, prominence is given to the manner in which the boy must first learn to hand the goblet. If we may believe Xenophon (*Cyrop.*, i, 3, 8), Persian cupbearers, who offered the goblets very charmingly with three fingers, best understood this graceful attitude. In any case, as Pollux (vi, 95; cf. Heliodorus, *Æthiopica*, vii, 27) expressly observes, etiquette demanded that boys who served should balance the drinking-cups on the tips of their fingers. The boy in waiting went from guest to guest, filling their drinking-cups or offering them jugs of wine and water freshly filled. Anyone who knows the Greek spirit would conjecture that, while he went round, the guests touched the cupbearer tenderly and gently, even if this is not expressly confirmed by different literary authorities and plastic and pictorial representations. Thus Lucian (*Symposium Lapith.*, 15, 26, 29, 39) tells us: "Here I must in passing mention a trifling incident, which is only to be regarded as an episode, but yet contributed its part in making the banquet more interesting. I had seen a beautiful young slave, who was appointed to act as cupbearer and stood behind Cleodemus, smiling, and I was interested to know the reason. I therefore watched him closely, and as the beautiful Ganymede soon drew near again to take back the drinking-cup from Cleodemus I noticed that the latter stroked his finger and, as it seemed to me, together with the cup pressed a couple of drachmæ into his hand. The boy smiled again at his finger being stroked, but I thought he did not notice the money. Consequently the two drachmæ fell rattling on the floor, at which the philosopher and the boy became very red. His nearest neighbours asked to whom the money belonged; but it remained uncertain, for the boy denied that it had fallen out of his hand, and Cleodemus, near whom the rattling was heard, did nothing to show that he was interested in the matter. Consequently, nothing more was done and the matter was allowed to rest, since only a few persons had noticed what had taken place. Yet I believe that Aristænetus was one of these. For soon afterwards he took the opportunity to remove the boy from the hall, without its being noticed, and beckoned to one of the strong lads, who had passed the dangerous age, a mule-driver or groom, to take his place behind Cleodemus instead of the boy. So this little incident passed, which might have turned out much to Cleodemus' disgrace,[1] if it had become known, and had not been suppressed on the spot by the cleverness of Aristænetus, who attributed what had happened to the wine."

During the drinking-bout a letter is handed to the host from the philosopher Hetæmocles, which

[1] Seeing that Cleodemus had forgotten his dignity as a philosopher, since he was, or should have been, able to control his passions; above all, it was beneath his dignity to have anything to do with a slave.

contains amongst other matters: "I have told you these few things out of many others, that you may see what a man you have passed over, to play the host to a Diphilus and to hand over even your son to him. He is well adapted for it; for he is pleasant to the boy and strives to gain his favour. If it were not indecent for a man like myself, I could tell you more about such things, but if you wish to find out the truth, you need only ask his tutor Zopyrus. Far from it being my wish to destroy his joy in his marriage or to accuse the informers of such shameful charges; although Diphilus has deserved nothing better from me, since he has already taken away two of my pupils; but for the honour of philosophy I would rather say nothing." Lucian goes on to say: "When the servant ceased reading, all the guests cast their eyes on young Zeno and his tutor Diphilus, whose astounded countenance, paleness and evident embarrassment only too fully confirmed the accusation of Hetæmocles. Aristænetus became restless, and had difficulty in keeping back his internal agitation, although he invited us to drink and endeavoured to put the best appearance upon what had happened, while he sent back the philosopher's servant with the usual answer that it should be attended to. Soon afterwards Zeno secretly got up, after his valet, at his father's orders, had given him a hint that he might retire."

According to Pausanias (i, 20, 1; cf. Ath., ii, 39*a*, x, 423*b*; Plutarch, *De Nob.*, 20), the "Satyr" of Praxiteles was represented as a youth handing the cup.

The assertion of the learned archbishop Eustathius, who lived in the twelfth century, that girls also were employed as cupbearers, must be an error, as anyone will know who has penetrated the psychology of Greek spirit even to a moderate extent, nor could I quote any Greek authorities for such a custom (Eustathius on Homer, *Od.*, i, 146, p. 1402, 41; his mistake may be due to a passage such as that in Ath., xiii, 576*a*). No doubt the merry mood of intoxication might sometimes entrust to the obliging hetairæ who stimulated the drinking-bout with their nakedness the business of pouring out wine and similar duties; but according to the entirely æsthetic opinion of the Hellenes this was a privilege of their young slaves. Certainly Micali (*L'Italia avanti il dominio dei Romani*, plate 107) describes a relief, on which a girl is filling the cups of the guests reclining on two couches from a jug, while three other girls are playing music, but this can certainly be only an exception.

How greatly the service of cupbearer was appreciated is clear from the fact that at public festivals this office was performed by boys and young men from the best families. Thus Athenæus (x, 424*e*) says: "Among the ancients one of the noblest boys poured out the wine, as in Homer the son of Menelaus; Euripides also was a cupbearer in his youth. At any rate Theophrastus in his treatise on drunkenness says: 'I hear that the poet Euripides at Athens also acted as cupbearer for the so-called dancers.' These danced in the temple of the Delian Apollo, were the best-born of the Athenians, and also wore garments made at Thera. And Sappho often praises her brother Larichus, since he was cupbearer in the Prytaneum (town-hall) at Mitylene. And also among the Romans the noblest boys had to perform the office of cupbearers at the public sacrifices, imitating the Æolians in every respect."

That the joys of the winecup were seasoned, according to taste and caprice, by many kinds of exhibitions of dancers, acrobats, and singers of both sexes, hardly needs special mention: we have already spoken of the female dancers, who danced at the banquets of Thessalian nobles. Song and dance in Homer (*Od.*, i, 152) were already inseparable from the drinking bout; and few pictorial representations are found in which flute or cithara-players are wanting. If serious men during the "drinking round" were accustomed to give themselves up to serious conversation, they sent the flute-players home, as Eryximachus did in Plato (*Sympos.*, 176; *Protagoras*, 347), remarking that the flute-player might play something to herself, if she liked, or to the women in the room; and Plato in the *Protagoras* declaims more vigorously against it: "Many are unable, owing to poverty of intellect, to converse with or amuse one another over their cups. Hence they raise the price of flute-girls, and hire for hard cash the foreign note of the flutes and converse through their voice. But where honest gentlemen and educated tipplers come together, we find among them no flute-girls, dancing girls, or harp-girls, but they are quite contented with each other's conversation, of which their own voices are the medium, without any farcical nonsense. They carry on by turns, and listen attentively, although they may have drunk heavily."

But such opinions may have formed the exception; the general taste would not like to renounce the female dancers, who, of course, later were employed for other purposes; indeed, according to Athenæus (xiii, 607*d*), they were often sold by auction, and vase-paintings leave no doubt as to the sexual functions of female dancers and flute-players. In a drama of Chæremon (frag. 14 (Nauck[2], p. 786) in Ath., xiii, 608*b*) it is said of such a girl who was always ready for friends: "The one lay there, and showed in the moonlight her naked breast, after she had thrown her garment off her shoulders; another, while dancing, had bared her left hip, naked in the sight of heaven she offered a living picture; another bared her well-rounded arms, while she flung them round the delicate neck of another. One of them exposed her thigh, as the slit in her dress with its folds opened, so that the charm of her radiant body unfolded itself beyond all expectation."

At the extravagantly luxurious wedding-feast of the Macedonian Caranus, described in detail by Athenæus (iv, 128*c* ff.), among its delights by the side of the flute-players *sambykistriæ* are named, that is, girls who played the *sambyke* (on the sambyke, see Ath., xiv, 633 ff., Aristot., *Pol.*, viii, 6, 11), a three-cornered stringed instrument. In this case they came from the island of Rhodes, and appeared in clothes as light as air, so that many of the guests thought them naked. Later in the feast *ithyphalli* appeared as dancers, who also sang phallic songs; in addition, jugglers, male and female, danced naked over swords fixed in the ground and spat fire. Later, a chorus of 100 singers came on, which recited the nuptial song, afterwards again female dancers, dressed as nereids and nymphs. While the bottle went the rounds of the guests, and twilight came on, a room was opened, lined with white cloths. In it youthful forms presented themselves in the costume of naiads, Eros, Artemis, Pan, Hermes, and other mythological forms, distributing light with silver candlesticks, in the most graceful attitudes of their more or less bare bodies (Becker-Göll, *Charicles*, i, p. 152, chiefly after Xenophon, *Sympos.*, 2, 1 ff.). The sambyke-players, owing to their ever ready willingness to oblige, enjoyed great popularity. In Plutarch they are once mentioned in the same breath with the *cinædi*.

From other passages of Greek authors it is clear that at drinking-bouts acrobatic tricks were greatly enjoyed, thus described by Becker: " A professional dancer, who exhibited his accomplishments for money brought in a charming girl and a beautiful boy, grown to a young man's size, and a female flute-player followed. The boy seized the cithara and beat the strings to the accompaniment of the flute. Then the sound of the cithara ceased; the girl had some hoops given her, which, while dancing to the tones of the flute, she skilfully whirled in the air and caught, one after the other, as they fell.

More and more were handed to her, until quite a dozen rose and fell between her hands and the ceiling, and the spectators loudly applauded the grace of her movements and her dexterity.

"Then a large hoop was brought in, set round with pointed knives, laid on the floor and fastened down. The girl began the dance again, threw a summersault into the middle of the hoop, and then out again, repeating the feat several times, so that the spectators were afraid that the beautiful girl might hurt herself. Then the boy also came on, and danced with a skill that gave greater and clearer effect to the symmetry of his youthful body. His entire form became an exhibition of most expressive movement; one could not distinguish whether his hands, heels, or feet had more share in producing the impression which the grace of his postures made upon the spectators. He also was noisily applauded, and several of those present were of opinion that they preferred the boy's performance to the girl's."

Carousals and drinking-bouts in ancient times took place in private houses, restaurants and hotels being unknown. Certainly there were, at least in later Athens, many sorts of places, where people met to play dice, drink, and enjoy sociable conversations, as it is said in Æschines (*Timarchus*, 53): "He spent his days in the gaming-house, where cocks and quails are set fighting, and dice-playing goes on"; yet places of that kind cannot be called restaurants in the modern sense.

It was also impossible to dispense with hotels in ancient times, for as early as the time described by Homer the right of hospitality was so far developed that travellers in foreign parts could be sure of a friendly reception. This was also still the case in historical times. The story in Herodotus (vi, 35) is well known—that Miltiades, when sitting before his house and seeing people whom he recognized as friends by their dress pass by, got up and offered them the shelter of hospitality. Indeed, we know of laws which, in memory of Zeus Xenios, the protector of the rights of hospitality, regulated and made a duty of the friendly treatment of strangers and their hospitable reception (Law of Charondas in Stobæus, *Sermones*, 44, 40). Even among non-Greek peoples we find this high respect for the rights of hospitality: thus a law of the Lucanians (Ælian, *Var. hist.*, iv, 1; cf. Heracleides Ponticus, *Politika*, 18; Plato, *Menexenus*, 91), a people of lower Italy, forbade anyone to refuse a stranger, who asked for admission after sunset, and fixed a severe punishment for any who did so.

Naturally, as social intercourse developed, private hospitality did not keep pace with it; and so institutions gradually grew up corresponding to our hotels. We can catch a glimpse of the first beginnings of such in the *leschē* [1] already mentioned in Homer and Hesiod; this was a common hall, which served homeless and needy people as a nightly shelter. Here also in severe weather people sought refuge or met in idle conversation; and at such times the smithy also would serve the same purpose. It is interesting nevertheless to note that Hesiod warns people from both places as abodes of idleness, in which man, "to protect himself from the cold of winter, warms himself comfortably and idles away his time, while at home much work remains undone." Also, later, staying in the *leschæ*, of which there were certainly several everywhere, at least in Athens and Boeotia, was not considered respectable and was avoided by the better class of people. This did not apply to the famous *leschē* at Delphi, which was built at the expense of the people of Cnidus and served to support and shelter the countless swarms who thronged to Delphi. According to the detailed description of Pausanias (x, 25, 1) the two long sides of the building were

[1] On the leschē and smithy, see Homer, *Od.*, xviii, 328 ff.; Hesiod., *W. and D.*, 493, 501; Etym. Magnum, λέσχαι παρὰ Βοιωτοῖς τὰ κοινὰ δειπνητήρια.

adorned with large-scale pictures rich in figures by Polygnotus, one of which represented the conquest of Troy and the departure of the Greeks, the other a visit of Odysseus to the underworld.

In course of time there was in every fairly large place a *pandokeion* (an inn); and in most frequented places, such as Olympia or Cnidus (Olympia: Schol. Pindar, *Olympia*, xi, 55; Ælian, *Var. hist.*, iv, 9; Cnidus: Lucian, *Amores*, 12), where every year strangers thronged in vast crowds to see the famous temple and the statue of Aphrodite by Praxiteles, and not last of all, on account of the joys of love that were to be enjoyed there, such places of shelter were maintained at the public expense. When Thucydides (iii, 68) also relates that the inn erected by the Spartans in Platæa near the temple of Hera was 200 feet long and contained plenty of rooms for strangers, we must still regard these strangers' courts as being as primitive as possible. Thus one had to bring his own bedclothes, for which reason nobody ever travelled without one or more slaves to carry his baggage (cf. Xenoph., *Memorab.*, iii, 13, 6).

Of course these inns were entirely different according to their class; some of them, as everywhere at all times, were regular dens of thieves, where the stranger could not be sure of his life. Thus Cicero (*Divin.*, i, 27, 57; the second story in *Invent.*, ii, 4, 14) tells us: "When two friends, Arcadians, were travelling together and had reached Megara, one put up with an innkeeper, another with a friendly host. When they had had supper and retired to rest, in their first sleep the one who was staying with his friend dreamed that the other begged him to help him, because the innkeeper was preparing to kill him. At first he woke up terrified; then, when he had composed himself, he lay down again, thinking that what he had seen was nothing. Then, after he had gone to sleep, his friend again appeared and begged him, since he had not come to his aid when he was alive, at least not allow his death to go unavenged ; he said that he had been killed by the innkeeper, put in a cart and covered with dung ; and begged him to come to the city gate in the morning before the cart left the town. Roused by this dream in the morning when the ploughman was near the gate, he asked him what was in the cart. The ploughman fled in affright ; the dead man was pulled from under the dung, and the innkeeper, having confessed, paid the penalty."

A Greek inn may also have been the scene of the story, also told by Cicero, in which the host murders a stranger from avarice and, to divert suspicion from himself, assigns ownership of the bloody sword to another traveller.

That the inns very often swarmed with bugs we could believe even were they not particularly mentioned, e.g. by Aristophanes (*Frogs*, 114, 549). From the same writer we learn that inns were often carried on by women. Since, besides, certainly in most of them a number of obliging girls met the most intimate desires of travellers, it is easy to explain why Theophrastus (*Characters*, 6) mentions inn and brothel in the same breath, and why female innkeepers had a poor reputation (e.g. Plato, *Laws*, xi, 918).

Strabo (xii, 578) professes to know that in an inn in a Phrygian village during an earthquake by night a keeper of girls and a great number of girls were killed, a notice which is interesting, since it appears from this that not only the host himself kept women ready to meet the wishes of his customers, but also that capable and businesslike procurers had their quarters in the inns with their living merchandise, in order to exchange the girls' flesh for ready money by letting them out for a longer or shorter time to the guests for payment. Conversely, distinguished and especially wealthy guests brought their women with them ; if they did not wish to abandon their accustomed harem, they made them come to the inn after their arrival. This, according to Plutarch (*Demetrius*, 26), was what Demetrius, for many years ruler of Athens, did when he quartered himself in the Parthenon on the Acropolis; and the fact was thrown in his teeth in a satirical song often sung at the time: "He made the Acropolis his hotel, and brought hetairæ into the temple of the Maiden."

The more as time went on, communication by travelling developed, the more the number of guests increased, of course in all gradations, so that, as Plutarch (*De Vitioso Pudore*, 8) says, there was ample choice; later, we hear also of very comfortably arranged hotels, in which, according to Epictetus (*Dissert.*, ii, 23, 36; Strabo, 801*a*), one might like to stay even longer than was absolutely necessary. This is especially true of the north African city of Canopus in the Nile delta, whose inhabitants were well known for their luxury, which expressed itself in numerous noisy festivities. Strabo tells us: "On the canal, which runs between Alexandria and Canopus, the traffic of the ships journeying backwards and forwards never ceases by night and day. Men and women dance, totally unembarrassed, with the utmost licentiousness, some of them on the ships, others in the inns on the side of the canal, which seem to be made for such riotous and voluptuous proceedings."

CHAPTER VI

Religion and Erotic [1]

Any one who is entirely a biased supporter of the Jewish-Christian view that the moral ideal of man consists in the " mortification of the flesh ", that a lasting communion in eternal blessedness, with the angels imagined as sexless, beckons to the pious as the highest reward after earthly death, will only with difficulty be able to understand the idea that there exists any connection at all between erotics and religion. And yet this connection exists, and is certainly a very intimate one. The Protestant church with its dull, foggy-grey northern frame of mind has indeed in its external forms known how to separate sensuality and religion. That the majority of those who profess the Protestant religion are no longer conscious in any way of the erotic undertone of their religiosity does not at all mean that in their subconsciousness erotic vibrations are altogether absent, or that these vibrations, though not easily observable, are any less effective on that account. But anyone who has familiarized himself with Catholic usages in Catholic countries, can see that many of these usages, if not indeed most of them, are based upon the natural and therefore sound sense of man, are indeed rooted in great part in erotics : which certainly does not enter the consciousness of most of those who profess the Catholic religion, but yet catches the eye of the expert observer much more easily than in the case of Protestantism. One may affirm, without exaggeration, that religious need and the

[1] For the connection between Religion and Erotic, see W. Achelis, *Die Deutung Augustins*, analyse seines geistigen Schaffens auf Grund seiner erotischen Struktur ; James, *The Varieties of Religious Experience* (1902) ; Starbuck, *Psychology of Religion* (1899).

fulfilment of religious desire is for the great part displaced sexuality, in single instances also conscious. The Catholic church reckons with this fact, and this in great part is the explanation of its unexampled success. Think of auricular confession!

Erotic conceptions meet us already in the manifold stories of the beginnings of the world. According to the opinion of Hesiod (*Theogony*, 116 ff.), not *one* God created the earth, but after Chaos, the infinite, empty, yawning space, arose the broad-breasted earth and Eros, " the most beautiful of all immortals, who governs the mind and thoughtful counsel of all gods and men." But already love, that divine natural law of Becoming, which separates male and female, rouses himself to bring them together again and couple them, and therefrom by coupling and procreation to cause one generation to arise after another.

The Greeks called the sky Uranus, understanding by the name the generative power of the sky which penetrates the earth with warmth and moisture, and through which the earth brings forth every living thing. In the *Danaïdes* of Æschylus (frag. 44 (Nauck [2]) in Ath., xiii, 600*b*) we read: " The pure sky desires to penetrate the earth, and love seizes the earth and longs for union with it; the rain falling from the fair-flowing sky fructifies the earth, which bears for mortals fodder for flocks and the sustenance of Demeter."

The fruit of the embrace of Uranus and Gæa are the Titans, whose number is variously given and who represent many kinds of phenomena of sky, earth, and sea. Further, the three Cyclopes (not to be confused with those in Homer), representatives of mighty powers of nature, and also the Hekatoncheires, hundred-armed giants. Cyclopes and Hekatoncheires gradually become too powerful for their own father, and now Greek fancy thinks of a truly grandiose myth. The father thrusts the monsters into the bosom of the earth.

But she calls her sons, the Titans, and demands that they avenge her wounded maternal honour on the father ; thus fervent love has become hate that yearns for revenge. But the sons do not venture to lift their hand against the father, and only the wily Cronos declares himself ready. The mother gives him a huge, very sharp sickle. Cronos conceals himself, and when Uranus sinks down to Gæa for a nightly embrace of love, Cronos springs towards him from his hiding-place and cuts off his mighty organ of generation, and throws it behind him. From the drops of blood that trickle down, the earth bears the Erinyes, Giants, and Melian nymphs, spirits of revenge, violence, and bloody deeds. The cut-off member itself falls into the sea, and from its white foam, Aphrodite, the charming goddess of love, is born.[1]

Although religious reformers, like Xenophanes (in Sextus Empiricus, *Adv. Mathem.*, i, 289, ix, 193 ; Clem. Alex., *Stromata*, v, 601) and Pythagoras, again and again pointed out that there was far too much of the human that adhered to the Greek conception of their world of gods, yet this does not appear to have had overmuch success. The people had now once become accustomed to the coarsely sensual conception of its gods, and imagined them to be as its poets described them and as its artists represented them.

The nature of the Greek gods is not the moral, but the æsthetic idea carried through to its extreme consequence, and their peculiar happiness is nothing else but the possibility, clouded by no sickness, no age, and no death, of enjoying to the full a

[1] In many handbooks Aphrodite is said to have been born from the foam of the sea ; this is, of course, sheer nonsense. In the oldest source of the myth it is stated quite clearly (Hesiod, *Theogony*, 190) : " The member was borne a long time over the sea and round it was white foam, which came from the immortal member, and in it the maiden was nourished. The member, which was cut off immediately before the act, was already full of sperm ; this now gushes out, and in and with the sea produces Aphrodite." There is no allusion to the foam or froth of the sea.

refined sensuality, beauty, grace, and joy to the bottom of the cup. Schiller's words "At that time nothing was sacred but the Beautiful" are in fact the key to the understanding of Greek mythology and at the same time of Greek life generally.

One must hold fast to this conception of the nature of the godlike, if we desire to face the countless erotic adventures of these gods with impartiality; further, one ought not to forget that the land of Greece was divided into many small lands each of which had its own local stories. Obviously, it is not the task of our book even to try to mention all these local stories; we put together the most important erotic motives of the Greek mythology, without even making an attempt to attain completeness.

We begin with Zeus, the supreme god of light, the father of gods and men. At the bottom of the numerous marriages and amours of the god, lies the idea of the fructifying moisture of the sky, which was naturally forgotten in course of time; in addition many distinguished families traced back their origin to him with intelligible vanity. Finally, of all this only the erotic kernel remained, and thus Zeus appears as the suitor and benefactor of a simply incalculable number of mortal and immortal women and girls, which again not only gives innumerable poets and artists ever new motives for floridly sensual inventions, but also lays the foundation of the continually renewed jealousy of his wife and sister, Hera; and all the more when Zeus, by carrying off the beautiful Trojan royal boy, Ganymede, sanctioned the love of boys in the airy heights of Olympus. We have spoken before of the jealousy of Hera, and if we regard the countless amours of Zeus from the moral standpoint as acts of adultery, we can hardly reproach her for it. Neither does poetry become tired of glorifying the marriage of Zeus and Hera with all the enchantment of poetry. In religious cults this wedding was celebrated in spring, as "the sacred wedding", the wedding, rich in blessing, of two heavenly powers, whom earth has to thank for all its fertility. A reminiscence of the first consummation of the marriage in the blessed countries of the Ocean, where according to Euripides (*Hippolytus*, 743 ff.) ambrosia flows and where the earth had made the tree of life grow with the golden apples of the Hesperides, is the wonderful narrative in the *Iliad* (xiv, 152 ff.), in which Hera, after she had adorned her immortal body with all the charms of youth and beauty, draws near to her husband. Aphrodite had given her the wonderfully precious girdle, "the charm of love and longing, which subdues all the hearts of the immortal gods and mortal men." Thus the goddess of the lily-white arms appears before her husband, who is looking at the battle between the Greeks and Trojans on the high mountain, but, infatuated by her bodily charm, forgets everything around him and, full of ardour, embraces his wife.

In memory of the sacred marriage, besides, in many places in Greece spring-time festivals were celebrated with flowers and garlands; the image of Hera was carried round, dressed in bridal attire, a bridal bed woven with flowers was prepared for her, in short, everything was arranged as for a human marriage, since, indeed, that heavenly marriage was usually regarded as the model and origin of marriage generally.

But even this divine marriage did not pass off without storm and tempest, which cosmologically is only the logical consequence of the significance of the two divinities as powers of nature. As it is just in Greece that atmospheric phenomena, such as rain, storm, and tempest, develop with special violence and suddenness, so the idea of wedded strife between the two heavenly powers lay tolerably close at hand. With the naivety and vividness peculiar to them, the Greek poets have also humanized this. Thus, as early as Homer, in the great quarrel-scene at the end of the first book of the *Iliad*, where Zeus ends the quarrel with the words: " 'Sit then quietly and obey my command! Otherwise all the other immortals in Olympus will hardly protect thee, when I come near, and whenever I lay my invincible hands upon thee.' Thus he spake, and majestic-looking Hera was afraid, and sat silent curbing her stubborn soul" (*Il.*, i, 565 ff.).

Of the further scenes of wedded discord between Zeus and Hera described by Homer (*Il.*, xv, 18 ff.), we may mention the one in which Zeus suspends his wife in the sky, so that she hovers freely in universal space, with a heavy anvil on each foot. Probus (*Ecl.*, 6, 31) had already explained this singular scene cosmologically, in that in the anvils he saw earth and sea and in the whole a picture of the highest god, who keeps the air and everything that exists in a state of suspension.

As she herself is faithful to her husband, she expects the same from all married men, and becomes the patron-goddess of marriage.

As fire had come down to men from heaven, so Hephæstus, the god of fire, was regarded as the son of Zeus and Hera. His lameness, in which men thought they recognized " the shaking, flickering flame ", was explained in a story told us by Homer: that Zeus, when Hephæstus once took his mother's part in a quarrel, seized him by the foot and flung him down from Olympus. Hence his legs remained weak; to support them, he made two girls of gold (*Il.*, xviii, 410 ff.), " like youthful living maidens," which, however, were endowed with life and animation. The nape of his neck is sinewy, and his breast, which he keeps bare like a smith, is covered with shaggy hairs.

In the Lemnian story his wife is Aphrodite, but as, according to another story, she is the wife of Ares, that story easily arose which the bard Demodocus (*Od.*, viii, 266 ff.) recites to the Phæacians with gleeful satisfaction and abundant raciness, and which recurs in a continually new version as an extremely favourite motive in the literature and graphic art of ancient and modern times. Helios, the all-seeing sun-god, had revealed to Hephæstus that Aphrodite, in the absence of her sooty husband, gave herself up to the joys of love with the imposing and handsome Ares. Full of wrath, he hastens to his workshop, and forges a net with chains so fine, that they are not visible either to mortal or immortal eye. This net he secretly attaches to the nuptial couch, and then apparently takes leave of his wife. The lovers enter the trap set for them. When they are revelling in the sweetest intoxication of love, they suddenly feel themselves ensnared by the cleverly made bonds of the net, so that they are unable to move (Ovid, *Ars Amatoria*, 583). In this painful position they are surprised by Hephæstus, who in great haste calls all the gods of the sky together as witnesses of this base infidelity, and he demands from the father the return of the wedding presents, which he gave him " for his shameless daughter."

This story, which is not without humour and piquancy, has often been handled in ancient and also in modern literature and has served as a subject for many graceful painters. With justice Ovid could say that no tale was better known in all Olympus than this (Ovid, *Amores*, 9, 40 : *notior in cælo fabula nulla fuit*). Ovid himself, in his *Art of Love* (ii, 561 ff.), has depicted the painful adventure of Ares and Aphrodite with visible satisfaction as an episode, not without adding several comic features to it : e.g. that Aphrodite made merry with her paramour over the hands and feet of her husband the smith, and mimicked his limping walk.

It has already been mentioned that the cult of the maiden goddess Pallas Athene also was not without an erotic undertone. There is something comic attached to the originally very profound story that Athene was born from the head of Zeus, which had been split by Hephæstus with an axe. This story, which is told by older poets such as Hesiod (*Theogony*, 886 ff.) and Pindar (*Olympia*, vii, 34 ff.; *Homeric Hymns*, 28) with religious seriousness, and meets us on numberless vase paintings, gave later times occasion for fun and jest. Thus Lucian, in his eighth *Dialogue of the Gods*, wittily parodies the story as follows :—

Hephæstus : What must I do, Zeus? for I have come as you ordered, with the sharpest axe I have, sharp enough even if it were necessary to cut a stone with a single blow.

Zeus : Good, Hephæstus! Cleave my head and divide it into two parts with a downward blow.

Heph. : Are you testing me, to see whether I am mad? Come now, tell me only what you want done to you.

Zeus : Just this—divide my skull. Obey at once, or you will make me angry, and not for the first time! But mind you strike with all your might, without delay; for I am dying with the pains which distract my brain.

Heph. : Mind, Zeus, that we do no harm; for the axe is sharp, and will not play the midwife without bloodshed, in the gentle manner of Eilythyia.

Zeus : Come, strike down boldly; for I know what is best!

Heph. : I will do so, but unwillingly; for who can resist when you give an order? [*Strikes*] What is this? A maiden in full armour! You had a great evil in your head, O Zeus, so naturally you were ill-tempered when producing so mighty a virgin beneath the membrane of your brain, and one in full armour too; forsooth, you had a camp and not a head, without us knowing it. Already she leaps and dances the Pyrrhic dance, shakes her shield and brandishes her spear and is roused to fury; and most wonderful of all, she is very beautiful and has attained maturity in a few moments! She is bright-eyed, somewhat like a cat, but her helmet becomes her not amiss! Now, I beg you, O Zeus, betroth her to me in lieu of my midwife's fee.

Zeus: You ask what is impossible, Hephæstus, for she will always wish to remain a virgin. Nevertheless, as far as I am concerned, I have no objection.

Heph.: That's what I wanted; I will attend to the rest. And now I will snatch her up and carry her off.

Zeus: If you think it easy, do so; but I know that you won't get much out of your bargain!

With these last words Zeus was said to be right after all; we read in Apollodorus (iii, 188), "Athena once more came to Hephæstus, wanting him to forge some arms for her. He, having been forsaken by Aphrodite, fell in love with her and began to pursue her, but she fled. And when he got near her after a great effort (for he was lame), he endeavoured to do violence to her, but she, being modest and a maiden, could not allow it, and Hephæstus discharged his seed on her leg. The disgusted goddess wiped the seed away with some wool and threw it on the ground. And when she fled and the seed fell to the ground Erichthonius was born; and Athena reared him unknown to the other gods, since she desired to make him an immortal."

With the birth of Phœbus Apollo, the god of the sun and the light, is connected the story of the furious jealously of Hera, who drives Leto (Latona), who is with child by Zeus, over half the earth until she finds a modest refuge in Delos, a little rocky island at that time, still tossed about unsteadily in the sea. The god of light, the saviour of the world, was born in most modest surroundings by his mother pursued by hate. The parallel with the birth of Christ forces itself upon us. But the enormous difference between the two opinions, the Jewish-Christian and the ancient, is at once apparent. If it says in Luke: "And she brought forth her first-born son and wrapped him in swaddling-clothes, and laid him in a manger; because there was no room for them in the inn," that is certainly a touching picture, simple and intimate, which in particular has given to art countless incitements to wonderful representations. But the Greek poetical account celebrates true orgies of beauty in describing the birth of its god of light (*Homeric Hymns*, iii, 89 ff.; *Theognis*, 5 ff.).

Thus the Greek saviour entered into life, to begin the fight with the powers of darkness, who were conceived of as horrible dragons, and afterwards to fulfil his own special mission, that is, to bless men with light, sun and joy in life. When his mother Leto is handled by the uncouth giant Tityus (Homer, *Od.*, xi, 576) with lustful grip, he lays the monster low with his unerring arrows and banishes him to the underworld, there to be punished eternally as a symbol of illicit sexual greed.

As god of light and joy he selects as his charming favourite and playmate, Hyacinthus. But all that is beautiful flourishes only for a short while; an unlucky accident or, according to another version, the jealousy of the wind-god Zephyrus, who had fallen in love with the beautiful boy, directs the orb of the discus when hurled while they were playing together, so that it hurtled down upon the head of Hyacinthus, and he dies in tenderest youthful beauty; and the earth afterwards causes the flower named after him to spring from his blood, an ingenious symbol—that soon found its way into popular song—of the quickly passing transitory time of youthful bloom and the sweet spring, whose flowers speedily wither under the glowing orb of the sun (to which the discus points), and in the fiery heat of the dogstar of summer. In memory of the beautiful favourite of Apollo, who died so early, the festival of the Hyacinthia was celebrated in July (p. 114).

Among the most charming stories related of Apollo in mythology, are those of his life as a herdsman. Homer (*Il.*, xxi, 448; ii, 766) already knows how he tended the oxen of Laomedon in the gorges of the tree-clad mountain range of Ida and performed the same service for his friend Admetus in Thessaly (Eurip., *Alcestis*, 569 ff.). When he drove the herds on before him Apollo played and sang so wonderfully that the wild animals came forth from their hiding-places on the mountains and listened; but the dappled hind, Apollo's favourite animal, danced gracefully to the music, as is said in a beautiful choral song of Euripides. But he is still ever the god of shining beauty and irresistible lovableness, now solitary, rejoicing in the shepherd's pipe, now chasing with the Nymphs or playing tenderly with the beautiful boys. Among the maidens loved by Apollo, the beautiful but prudish Daphne is best known; she refuses to sacrifice her virginity, and, in order to escape persecution by Apollo, is changed at her wish by the gods into a laurel-tree, which henceforth is sacred to Apollo. Individual local stories enumerate an imposing number of Apollo's darlings, which the Fathers of the Church (Clem. Alex., *Protrept.*, p. 27 (ed. Potter); Arnobius, iv, 26; Julius Firmicus, *De Erroribus*, 16) in their lack of understanding enter in their lists with moral indignation, which almost amounts to falsification, even though they gather together local traditions throughout Greece into a single uniform story and thereby make it appear as though large numbers of love-affairs could be correctly attributed to the god. This point, which holds good for other amours of the gods still to be mentioned ought to be settled once for all.

Less known, but illuminated by Pindar (*Olympia*, vi, 36) with the gold of genuine poetry, is the love of Apollo for Evadne, the foster-daughter of the Arcadian king Æpytus. When she can no longer avoid her pregnancy her foster-father repairs to Delphi to question the oracle. Meantime, the pains of labour come upon the king's daughter, as she is going to draw water, after the simple custom of ancient times; she secretly bears a child in the forest, a boy, whom in her sore need she is obliged to leave lying there; but two snakes come and feed him with honey. The foster-father returns from Delphi with the answer that the new-born boy is Apollo's son, and is destined to become the ancestor of an immortal family of seers. He now inquires everywhere, yet no one knows anything of the boy; but the mother fetches him out of the wood, where he lay covered with violets, wherefore she named him Iamos, that is, "the son of violets" (from *ion*, a violet).

The story further told that Apollo had forced the love of Cyrene, the daughter of the Thessalian King Hypseus. This story also Pindar has illuminated wonderfully in his own manner; it was inconsistent with his high conception of the gods that Apollo should have obtained the love of Cyrene by force, therefore the poet describes how in the heart of Apollo passion strives with the nobility of his soul, and transfers this conflict to a dialogue between Apollo and Cheiron, the wise centaur and tutor of the heroes. As Heinemann says, Apollo and Cheiron, that is, youthful impetuousness and the spirit of wisdom, are the twin souls in the breast of the god. Hence is to be explained Cheiron's humorous, indeed bantering tone: he gives his advice, but he knows that Apollo will not decide otherwise than he does (*Pythia*, ix, 18 ff.). "And Hypseus cherished his fair-armed daughter, Cyrene; she cared not for pacing to and fro before the loom, nor for merry banquets with stay-at-home maidens of her own age; but, using for the contest brazen darts and the falchion, she would slay the fierce beasts of prey, thus in very deed assuring deep and perfect rest for her father's kine, while she spent on her eyelids but a scanty store of that slumber which is so sweet a bed-fellow when dawn draweth near. Once did Apollo, the far-darting god of the wide quiver, find her without spears, wrestling alone with a monstrous lion; and forthwith he called Cheiron from out his halls and spake to him in this wise: 'Son of Philyra, leave thy hallowed cave and look with wonder at a woman's spirit and mighty power. See what a contest she is waging with undaunted head—this maiden with a heart which no toil can subdue, and a mind that no fear can overwhelm. From what mortal being was she born? From what race hath she been reft, that she should be dwelling in the hollows of the shadowy mountains? And she is putting to the test a strength that is inexhaustible. Is it right to lay an ennobling hand upon her? aye, and by consorting with her, to cull the honey-sweet flower of love?' Then did the inspired centaur, softly smiling with kindly brow, at once unfold his counsel in reply: 'Secret, O Phœbus, are the keys of wise Persuasion, that unlock the shrine of love; and, among gods and men alike, do they shun to enter for the first time the sweet bridal-bed in the light of day. Thou then, who canst not lawfully breathe a lie, hast been tempted by thy mood to dissemble in thy words. Dost thou ask, O King, of the maiden's birth? thou who knowst the end supreme of all things, and all the ways that lead thereto, the number of the leaves that the earth putteth forth in spring, the number of the sands that, in the sea and rivers, are driven before the waves and the rushing winds, and that which is to be, and whence it is to come—all this thou clearly seest. But if I must measure myself against one that is wise, I needs must speak. Thou camest to this glade to be her wedded lord, and thou shalt bear her over the sea to the choicest garden of Zeus, where thou shalt make her queen of a city, when thou hast gathered the island-folk around the plain-encircled hill: and soon shall queen Libya amid her broad meadows give in golden palaces a kindly welcome to thy glorious bride.'"

Even more frequently in Greek mythology are Apollo's amours with boys spoken of. Rudolph

Beyer, in his essay (*Fabulæ Græcæ quatenus quave aetate puerorum amore commutatæ sint : Diss. Inaug.*, Weida, 1910) on the homosexual fables of the Greeks, eumerates no fewer than nineteen favourites of Apollo, in which list he has omitted Ileus once mentioned by Hesiod (frag. 137 (Kinkel)). Hyacinthus has been already spoken of ; here it may be added that pictorial art also seized upon the motive of Hyacinthus loved by Apollo, otherwise by Zephyrus, with special partiality, as several vase paintings preserved to us attest. Also among the poets, especially of the Alexandrian period, the love of Apollo and Hyacinthus enjoyed great popularity.

That Apollo, as a lover of manly youth, was also worshipped as its ideal type and patron-god, is easy for anyone who has penetrated the nature of Greek homosexuality to only a moderate extent to understand. Hence his image was always to be found by the side of Hermes and Heracles in every Greek gymnasium.

Plastic art represented Apollo as a bright, beautiful, youthful form, and repeats this motive in countless variations, of which such numbers have come down to us that we need not speak of them here. But I should like briefly to discuss a representation, one of the most charming, since it does not appear to me to have been hitherto correctly interpreted.

We read in Pliny (*Nat. Hist.*, xxxiv, 70) in his list of the bronze works of Praxiteles : " He also created an Apollo between the ages of boyhood and youth, who is lying in wait, with a dart in his hand, for a lizard creeping up the branch of a tree ; he is called *Sauroktonos* (the lizard-killer)." Now several statues are preserved to us which represent a naked, delicate, somewhat girlishly formed boyish man, who is supporting his left hand on the trunk of a tree, up which the lizard is running, against which he is lifting up his right hand ; the best copies of these are in the Vatican and the Louvre. It is further known that the lizard, as an animal loved by the sun, is sympathetic to Apollo, and further that a special kind of prophecy was associated with this delicate little creature (Pausanias, vi, 2, 4; Cicero, *Div.*, i, 20, 39 (Galeotæ)). But why in the world should the god want to kill it? An unprejudiced examination will explain the motive to be that Apollo, the light and sun-god, with his warm beams, symbolized by the dart, entices the lizard from its hiding-place, in order to enjoy its brisk and gracious movements.

But I conjecture that the motive has also an erotic foundation. The Greek word for lizard means also especially the male member,[1] and by preference that of a boy or young man. Now we have an epigram of Martial, which runs: "Spare the lizard creeping towards you; it desires to fade away in your fingers." This is not far from the idea that the images of the lizard-killing Apollo are a symbol for the god who is the friend of boys, who does not desire to kill the little animal, but rather entices it out to play with it, until it perishes from desire and love under his coaxing finger.

It has been already mentioned that the cult of the maiden Artemis did not lack the erotic undertone. The Greeks imagined this goddess as maidenly, of severe beauty, of tall figure and prominent stature, so that she is always the most beautiful and tallest among her nymphs. She was always thought of as hunting or otherwise in rapid movement, lightly clad, with dress tucked up high, sometimes on horseback or in a car drawn by deer. In many places in Greece maidens on their marriage dedicated to her the maiden chiton or girdle, whence her name "girdle-looser"; and it was to her that after their confinement married women dedicated their girdle and garment. As Artemis herself is a goddess of severe modesty, so all chaste young men and maidens are her especial favourites, which is

[1] Often in Anth. Pal., e.g. xii, 3, 207, 242; cf. Martial, xiv, 172, *Ad te reptanti, puer insidiose, lacertæ parce; cupit digitis illa perire tuis*, where *perire* = to pass away in love, to be madly in love.

particularly represented in the story of the beautiful Hippolytus spoken of before; we have also mentioned Artemis Orthia and the scourging of boys at her altar.

The story of the beautiful hunter Actæon, who, having the doubtful good fortune of spying upon Artemis in the midst of her nymphs while bathing, was afterwards changed into a stag by the enraged goddess and torn to pieces by his own dogs, is well known. It is less known that for the same reason she changed Siprœtes (Antoninus Liberalis, 17) into a woman.

The cult of the famous Artemis of Ephesus is mixed with Asiatic ideas. Here she is not thought of as a maiden, but as a nurse and all-nourishing mother, as is indicated by the numerous breasts of her cult-image; among her numerous priests are also many *hieroduli* (temple-slaves) and eunuchs. According to Asiatic story the service of Ephesian Artemis was founded by the Amazons, whom the Greeks thought to be warlike women of foreign stock, who fight with the most famous heroes of antiquity; thus Penthesilea, queen of the Amazons of Thermodon (the north coast of Asia Minor), went to the aid of the Trojans and after fighting bravely was slain by Achilles. Heracles undertook a victorious campaign in the land of the Amazons.

Homer long ago called the Amazons "a match for men", but it was not until later that legend made of their state a perfect *gynaikokratia* (rule of women). Their superiority to men was based upon a severe defeat of the latter in a campaign, caused, according to some by climatic, according to others by astronomical, conditions. Boys were blinded or lamed after birth, or at least their bodily development was neglected; only the girls were trained for the chase and war by gymnastic exercises. Callimachus describes dances of the Amazons of a warlike character. From their name (ἀ, privative, and μαζός, breast) it was thought in later times that the girls had one or both breasts cut or burnt off, that they might not find themselves hampered when bending the bow or hurling the javelin. This etymology is improbable, but the final interpretation of the name is still unknown. They were clad like men in a short chiton, which often leaves the right breast bare. Thus they were represented by preference in plastic art, yet nothing is to be seen of the mutilation of one breast—for æsthetic reasons. They fought with the heavy arms of the heroes, but were especially fond of bow and arrow, and the dreaded one- or two-edged axe; they were splendid horsewomen, yet occasionally they also fought from war-chariots. If the Amazons are to be thought of as what the Latin designates by the name *virago* (man-woman), yet there is nowhere to be presumed in the authorities a reversal of the sexual impulse. Still it is to be observed that they were considered to be disinclined to love, and that the later poets by preference speak of their chastity. (On the Amazons, see *Iliad*, iii, 189; Steph. Byz., s.v. *Αμάζονες*; Callimachus, *Hymn to Diana*, 237 ff.; Ptol., *Astr. Jud.*, i, 2, p. 18.). In the plastic art of the ancients the Amazons are a favourite motive, yet without any sexual note. As the goddess of female fruitfulness, finally, Artemis was worshipped in Persia and the other parts of Asia, where she bore the name Anakitis and was honoured by the temple prostitution of numerous hieroduli.

The form of the war-god Ares, as known to all readers especially from the *Iliad*, affords little scope for the tender emotions of love and sensuality; but that nevertheless erotic fabulous stories weave their threads around him is shown by the tale of the illicit intercourse of Ares and Aphrodite (p. 186). Neither is this motive foreign to plastic art; the so-called Ares Ludovisi in Rome shows the god, with arms laid aside, in a comfortable resting position, while an Eros is playing with his weapons.

But those groups are especially popular which represent Ares with Aphrodite and of which many have come down to us, in marble, on gems, and in pictures from Pompeii. The latter in particular strike a strongly sensual note ; as a rule Ares voluptuously grasps the loved one's breast and draws aside the garment that conceals her charms.

If in these pictures Aphrodite is merely the woman that grants and asks for love, this is only the final gradation of her originally far more comprehensive functions. Aphrodite denotes at first the love of the sky for mother earth and the joy of seeing the growth of the Cosmos ; then the creative instinct of life generally, especially in sexual generation, which the religion of nature carries over from men—and animals also—to the gods. The cult of Aphrodite, originally of an Oriental character, unites the Beautiful and the Ugly, the Lofty and the Low, the Moral and (according to our view) the Immoral in a singular mixture.

The worship of Aphrodite conjecturally reached Greece through the Phœnicians, from that great Semitic family of peoples which spread from Asia Minor to Babylon and Arabia ; hence the two chief emporiums of Phœnician commerce, the islands of Cythera and Cyprus, were regarded as the oldest seats of her cult, indeed as her birthplace.

We have already spoken of the birth of the goddess from the generative member of Uranus that was hurled into the sea (p. 182). In the words of the Homeric Hymn to Aphrodite (*Homeric Hymns*, 6 ; Hesiod, *Theogony*, 194 ff.) we read : " Gentle west winds bore her in the soft foam of the waves in motion to the coast of Cyprus, where the Hours received her, clothed her in sumptuous garments and adorned her, and led her into the circle of the immortal gods. Eros also and beautiful Himeros (Desire) accompanied her ; and this honour is the portion allotted to her among men and the immortal gods—girlish caress and smile and roguery, sweet pleasure and love and gentle grace."

Greek poetry and plastic art never tired of representing the myth of the birth of Aphrodite and her reception amongst the gods in ever new variety and embellishing it with all the colours of sensual enjoyment. Indeed, the whole of ancient poetry and plastic art is really a single hymn on the almighty power of Aphrodite and Eros, and it would fill an imposing volume if one were to attempt to collect the relevant passages with only approximate completeness.

From Plato (*Sympos.*, 180*d*) onwards philosophical speculation distinguished an Aphrodite Urania, the goddess of pure and wedded love, from Aphrodite Pandemos, the goddess of free love and its purchasable joys. The subtlety can hardly have made its way into the popular consciousness; at least, it is clear from Lucian (*Dialogi meretr.*, 7, 1; cf. Ath., xiii, 572*d* ff.) that the hetæræ made offerings to both Urania and Pandemos.

The power of Aphrodite extends over the whole world. She is the heavenly Aphrodite in the narrower sense of the word, that is, she is the goddess of the atmosphere and of all the heavenly phenomena. But she also rules on the sea, whose waves she stills when excited by storms, and she bestows lucky voyages and joyful homecoming.

With these two sides in the nature of the goddess we have no need to deal more closely here, but may refer the reader to the mythological handbooks. But it is certainly our duty to speak of that Aphrodite who bestows upon gods and men the joys of love. Love and beauty are for the Greeks inseparable: therefore Aphrodite is the goddess of spring, of flowers and blossoms, especially of myrtles and roses, which thrive through her and with which she crowns and adorns herself. In and through her in early springtime love awakens; adorned with flowers she walks through the woods to the loved one, and where she shows herself the wild animals of the mountain ranges follow her and fawn upon her, and give themselves up to the sweet impulse, as the Homeric hymn says (iv, 69 ff.). In spring took place most of the festivals in honour of Aphrodite, which were held by night, in blooming gardens and bowers, with dances, music, and unbridled abandonment to love, " the sweet gifts of gold-adorned Aphrodite."

Especially luxurious were these love-feasts on the island of Cyprus, the incomparably charming island, breathing perfumes of flowers that bloomed there in luxuriant magnificence, myrtles, roses, anemones, pomegranates, etc., all of which owed their growth to Aphrodite.

The festival commemorated her birth from the sea and on the strand of Paphos, where she had first set foot on the blissful island, the people gathered together to receive the goddess and to escort her to her sacred gardens in festive jubilation. The image of the goddess was bathed by women and girls in the holy sea and afterwards bedecked, after which they themselves bathed in the river under myrtle bushes in preparation for the coming orgies of love. (Concerning this feast at the Cypriote Paphos, cf. Ath., iii, 84*c*; Strabo, xiv, 683; Ovid, *Metam.*, x, 270 and *Fasti*, iv, 133; Æschines, *ep.* 10.)

Such festivals of Venus were celebrated everywhere in sensuality-loving Greece, being especially luxurious at Cnidus on the coast of Asia Minor, where Aphrodite had a distant sanctuary, thus described by Lucian (*Amores*, 12): " No sooner had we approached the temple, than breezes of Aphrodite blew to meet us. The floor of the vestibule was not, as elsewhere, laid out with dead, smooth stone slabs, but—as was quite natural in the temple of Aphrodite—completely planted with living trees and shrubs, which with their magnificent leaves and flowers combined to form a luxuriant foliage, spreading its rare fragrance to a distance. Especially the myrtle, rich in fruits, made a show in the temple of its mistress in profuse abundance, like all the other trees which were distinguished by special beauty. Nowhere could be seen branches dried up or withered, but all blossomed out in overflowing plenty with fresh shoots. There was indeed, no lack of trees that bore no fruit, but their beauty made up for the absence of it, cypresses soaring heavens-high and plane-trees, and amongst them the tree which during its human existence would have nothing to do with Aphrodite, but fled before her—the laurel.[1] On all the trees the clinging ivy lifted and spread its tendrils in a tender embrace. Luxuriant vines could barely support the burden of their grapes. For more delightful is Aphrodite combined with Dionysus, and both together dispense more delicious pleasure ; but, separate, their enjoyment is less. Where the trees stood thicker and gave more abundant shade welcome seats were placed, whereon people could take their meals; the townspeople, certainly, seldom made much use of them, but the great crowd enjoyed itself there and there rejoiced in all kinds of love-toying."

But the bitter truth, which the Nibelungenlied expresses in one of its few really beautiful verses " wie liebe mit leide ze jungest lônen kann " was not spared to Aphrodite. The brief delight of spring is followed by the glowing heat of summer, which withers all the flowers and blossoms and robs the fields of their beauty. To symbolize this, Greek fancy invented a number of stories which, in their details, differ from one another according to the locality in which the scene is laid, but which have essentially the same meaning. A beautiful youth adorned with every charm is loved by Aphrodite but to her unutterable sorrow is obliged to part from her by an untimely death. It is the infinitely touching form of the beautiful Adonis (p. 119).

[1] An allusion to Daphne.

Aphrodite is best known as the goddess of female beauty and love. Poetry and plastic art revel in equipping the goddess with ever fresh charms. She is the gold-adorned, the smiling-sweetly; embellished with a costly diadem she wears the seductive girdle, in which all the enchantment of love is contained, devotion, longing, and infatuating passion. Homer already knows the famous girdle, which, he adds, even infatuates the mind of the wise. Especially glorious are her large, moistly gleaming eyes, her delicate neck and bosom, her sweet mouth, which the poets compare to a rosebud: in short, all imaginable charms are found united in their goddess of love by the Greeks. These charms are enhanced and emphasized by her magnificent raiment and brilliant adornment, and the poets are regularly intoxicated by the lovingly painted description of all those delights. In the goddess even that portion of the human back which, in present-day good society, is unnameable, is endowed with fabulous charm; a fact which—thanks to the lack of foolish prudery among the ancient Greeks—does not seem so very wonderful. Only in Greece could the idea have occurred to one to build temples and set up statues to a goddess in order to glorify that practically unmentionable part, but there, from one end of the country to the other, the Greeks worshipped their "Aphrodite Kallipygos", the goddess "with beautiful buttocks".

Any visitor to the famous Museo Nazionale in Naples who enters the little room named Veneri in the east wing of the ground floor, will see in the centre of the room, set up on a revolving pedestal, the statue of a Venus, exquisitely bare. Coquettishly she lifts up her dress and throws a backward glance over her shoulder at her charms, which she looks at almost caressingly with a mingled satisfaction of tenderness and pride. This position denotes the culminating point of refined erotic, without, however, causing a painful or even indecent effect. This at once depends upon the marvellous plastic art with which these forms of the body are worked out from the æsthetic point of view, and also to the naïve, one may say the entirely innocent, joy with which the goddess regards these charms.

A work of the most ardent, naked sensuality produces its effect as perfect beauty without causing any painful impression, since it combines with the plastically unsurpassable form the naïve joy at the possession of this beauty.

Among no other people has the æsthetic pleasure in the charms of *kallipygia* left so dominating an impression and found its expression in art and literature. We read in Athenæus (xii, 544*c*) of the two beautiful daughters of a countryman, who were chosen in marriage by two brothers on account of their beautiful buttocks, and were always called thereafter *Kallipygoi* ("with beautiful buttocks") by the citizens. Also, as Cercidas of Megalopolis says in his iambics, there was a pair of *Kallipygoi* at Syracuse; and they, having obtained considerable means by their marriage, set up a temple of Aphrodite, and called the goddess *Kallipygos*, as Archelaus also tells us in his iambics.[1]

The goddess of beauty is at the same time the goddess of love. She is the queen of souls, she subjects every element to her, she can unite that which is at variance. But she not only makes love worth craving for and institutes it amongst men and gods: she herself blesses many, both mortals and immortals, with her favour. She presents her favourites with every imaginable happiness, bestows upon them beauty and youth, riches and power, joy and charm. So Cinyras, already known to Homer (*Il.*, xi, 20) as first king of Cyprus, who was, according to Pindar (*Pythia*, ii, 15), when a boy the favourite of Apollo. He was also

[1] A similar but more detailed story is told of the dispute between two girls, Thryallis and Myrrhine, in the letters of Alciphron (i, 39). A similar subject occurs also in Anth. Pal. (v, 35–6, attributed to Rufinus; cf. v, 54, 55, 129).

the first priest of Aphrodite in Cyprus, and had introduced civilization into the island by teaching men to shear sheep and prepare wool, to dig the metal from the bowels of the earth, and work it up into artistic productions. Of an intoxicating beauty he combines with the manliness of the strong ruler and bringer of civilization the luxurious effeminacy of the Oriental prince of lovers.

Oriental influence also shows itself in the appearance of another favourite of Aphrodite—Paris, sufficiently well known from the story of the Trojan war. He also is a dazzlingly beautiful youth, adorned with every charm, brilliant in the exercise of music and elegant in the dance. But he is unwarlike and effeminate, quite an Oriental type, so that, to use Virgil's expression (*Æneid*, iv, 215), " half-men," that is, castrated associates, are given him as his retinue.

Aphrodite has given him an almost uncanny power over women, so that it is easy for him, when the guest-friend of King Menelaus in Sparta, to infatuate his wife Helen, who follows the beautiful stranger to Troy and thereby invokes the misery of the deplorable Trojan war. Aphrodite indeed, by promising him the most beautiful wife in the world, had known how to secure the victory in the judgment of Paris (p. 155*f.*) ; at the same time a symbol worth observing for the painful fact that it matters nothing to the woman, if she causes misery and sorrow, provided only that she can attain the object of her paltry vanity. How under the influence of Aphrodite and with her aid Paris captivates the heart of Helen, has been constantly represented by the poets and artists of antiquity. Of the old poets, perhaps none has painted the devilishly infatuating side of the character of Paris in more glowing colours than the great teacher of love, Ovid (*Heroides*, 15 and 16), the most elegant of all Roman poets.

The love of Aphrodite for Anchises, which is

described in the Homeric hymn to Aphrodite with great poetical beauty and sensual fire, also belongs to the Trojan circle of legends. The fruit of this bond of love is Æneas, who during his life, rich in happiness and unhappiness, enjoys the lasting protection of Aphrodite, until upon the fall of his native city, and after long wanderings and adventures, he finally becomes the ancestor of the Julian family in the land of Italy.

When Aphrodite makes herself mistress of the hearts of men and inflames them with love there is no resisting her, no choice is left them, and the goddess then becomes a she-devil who infatuates women, so that, though they are often conscious of doing wrong, they are powerless to resist and yield themselves to the sweet passion. Thus, in the *Iliad*, Helen already appears infatuated by her; so also Medea, who in her raging love for Jason, forgetting all duty to parents, brothers and sisters, home and her paternal roof, follows the handsome stranger to Greece; and finally, being scorned by him, becomes a fearful demon of hatred and revenge and sacrifices her two dear children. The devilish power of Aphrodite was next fated to be experienced by the three Cretan women Ariadne, Pasiphaë, and Phædra, whose fate with inexorable cruelty shows how far raging love can go and to what despair love can lead: Ariadne the type of the forsaken mistress, Pasiphaë the victim of unnatural lust, Phædra the typical example of despised love transformed into murderous hate. These women and many others were fated to learn from Aphrodite the meaning of that love which Euripides afterwards described in a long fragment of an unknown play,[1] in which among other things he said, that it is death and irresistible power, raging madness and hot desire, bitterness and torment, the greatest power of nature, but also the mother of all that is

[1] In Stobæus, *Flor.*, 63, 6, where the verses are attributed to Sophocles; but cf. Nauck[2] on Soph. Frag. 865.

beautiful. Yet even after death those who are seized by such devilish love still find no rest, since according to Virgil (*Æneid*, vi, 444 ff.) those who are unhappy in love wander restlessly on lonely paths in a myrtle grove in their own part of the underworld.

Such power is not only inherently founded in the character of Aphrodite, but she owes it also to the charm of love, whose inventor the Greeks considered her. As Pindar (*Pythia*, iv, 214 ff.) says, Aphrodite brought the iynx to Jason, " and taught him the lore of suppliant incantations, that so he might rob Medea of reverence for her parents, and that a longing for Hellas might lash her with the whip of compulsion while her heart was all aflame."

Also the forsaken girl in Theocritus (ii, 17 ff.) makes use of this love-charm to exorcise her faithless loved one. Iynx is the Greek name for the wry-neck (*iynx torquilla*, a woodpecker), and the restless play of colours on its shimmering neck symbolized the restless movement and undulations of the emotions of love. To make the charm effective the bird was " stretched upon a four-spoked coloured wheel ", that is, fastened by its feet and wings to a four-spoked wheel, after which the wheel was rapidly turned round.

Naturally, Aphrodite not merely awakens the desire of love, but brings it to fulfilment. The Greek was not even ashamed of " the sweet gifts of Aphrodite ", as their poets call it ; and so quite consistently the sensual enjoyment of love finds its expression in their opinion of the nature of the goddess and in her cult. Once we realize that sexual indulgence is a duty divinely ordained, the institution of religious prostitution—a custom at first difficult for us to understand—becomes intelligible. We need here only mention it, since it has been discussed in detail in the chapter dealing with purchasable love in Greece. The same holds good of Aphrodite as the goddess of hetairæ, while we have already spoken of her in her capacity of protectress of marriage (p. 198). In accordance with the frequently mentioned natural conception of the sexual it is only logical that Aphrodite Hetaira (the patron goddess of hetairæ) gradually developed into Aphrodite Pornē (literally, Aphrodite the Prostitute), which merely means that all varieties of sexual enjoyment, or, as we say, every imaginable form of immorality, were under her protection. This may be recognized at once in Sparta, where a number of surnames were invented for Aphrodite, which must, according to our ideas, be designated in the highest degree shameful. Thus we hear of an Aphrodite Peribaso, that is, who walks the street, and Trymalitis, that is, bored through. (On the names of Aphrodite, see Clem. Alex., *Protrept.*, p. 33*P* ; and Hesychius under the catchwords.)

In course of time the cult of the so-called Syrian Aphrodite also found an entrance into Greece, so that in the Hellenistic period she was worshipped in several places (Tacitus, *Annals*, iii, 63 ; *CIGr.*, Nr. 3137, 3156, 3157 ; Diod. Sic., v, 77 ; Pausanias, iv, 31, 2 ; vii, 26, 7). She is the same goddess who, according to Tacitus, was worshipped in Smyrna under the name of Aphrodite Stratonikis, by which it was intended to honour the memory of Stratonike, the wife of the Syrian king Antiochus Soter (280–261 B.C.). Lucian has written an essay, extremely interesting and relating to the history of civilization, in which phallus-worship and eunuchs play a great part, but which is too long to quote here.

As in the worship of the Syrian goddess the phallus has prominent significance, so in general in the cult of Aphrodite everything was important which reminds one of sexual life or arouses the idea of sensuality and luxuriant fruitfulness. First and foremost of course the sexual organs themselves, images or imitations of which were employed in different ways in the service of Aphrodite ; and many in earlier times attempted to associate the Homeric epithet *philommeides* (laughter-loving) with the preference of Aphrodite for *medea* (genitals).[1] In Paphos, according to Clement of Alexandria, at initiation into the cult of Aphrodite those initiated were handed salt and a phallus. Venus Fisica also, who was specially worshipped in Pompeii, can be most easily explained by the Greek word *physis* in the sense of genitals.

The myrtle and apple were sacred to Aphrodite; lovers brought apples as a present or threw them to their loved ones, to show their affection, as Plato tells us in an epigram.[2] Catullus (lxv, 19) draws a charming picture of a girl to whom her lover has sent an apple. Half glad, half anxious, she conceals it in her bosom; when her mother suddenly enters she springs up forgetting the apple, which now rolls down from her bosom and betrays her, while a lovely blush of shame colours the cheeks of the maiden confused by the betrayal of her secret. Thus the apple has a symbolical erotic meaning not only in the biblical legend of the apple of Eve. Among the Greeks this goes back to the story of Acontius (Ovid, *Heroides*, 20 and 21) who loved Cydippe without finding his love returned. To win her he wrote the words: "I swear by Artemis that I will wed Acontius" on an apple and threw it to her in the temple of Artemis. Cydippe read the words aloud, but then threw the apple away. Later she fell ill, and being instructed by the oracle that the cause of her illness was the wrath of the offended goddess, she listened to the wishes of Acontius. We may also mention the beautiful but prudish Atalanta (*Apollodorus*, iii, 106; Ovid, *Metam.*, x, 560 ff.), who consented to marry none but one

[1] Hesiod, *Theog.*, 200, explains the epithet as "since she was born from the genitals of Saturnus". But the verse is spurious, and the explanation due to the grammarians.

[2] The epigram of Plato is in Diog. Laërt., i, 23. On the apple as a symbol of love, cf. the commentators on Theocr., ii, 120; Propertius, i, 3, 24, and elsewhere; Aristoph., *Clouds*, 997.

who could defeat her in racing. Milanion, who loved her, spread golden apples on the racecourse, and as Atalanta lost time in picking them up, she was thus conquered by her lover. Milanion had received these apples as a present from Aphrodite.

In the animal world the goat, the ram, the hare, the dove, and the sparrow are sacred to Aphrodite because of their amorous nature. Hence the ram often appears on coins of Cyprus; an Aphrodite Epitragia, riding on a goat, was not only known in Athens, but in Elis an Aphrodite on a goat was seen from the master hand of Scopas (Pausanias, vi, 25, 2). Doves were kept in large flocks in many temples of the goddess, especially in Cyprus and Sicily, an Oriental custom the last traces of which we see to-day in the doves on the square of St. Mark in Venice, whither the cult of doves came from Constantinople. That married couples are especially fond of feeding the doves of St. Mark is the last, although somewhat faded, offshoot of the cult of Ishtar that was once so flourishing, as we can still recognize by the language, for the foreign word *peristera*, the Greek name for dove, means "the bird of Ishtar". In Apuleius (*Metam.*, vi, 6) Venus appears in a magnificent car drawn by four white doves, and accompanied by sparrows and other birds. Sappho (frag. 1, 10) makes the goddess ride along in a car drawn by sparrows, for the sparrow, owing to its amorously sensual nature, belongs to the escort of Aphrodite.

The lovable form of the god Hermes is also influenced by erotic ideas. Thus we have already had occasion to speak of the ithyphallic Hermes (p. 130 *f.*); and his image is often found together with that of Aphrodite, of which Pausanias (ii, 19, 6; vi, 26, 5; viii, 31, 6; cf. Plutarch, *Præcepta Conjugalia* (*ad init*)) gives several examples. Something originally naïve is attached to the god of flocks and herdsmen, which frequently rises more or less to coarseness in his continual intercourse with the nymphs of the forests and mountains. Already, when a little child in the cradle, he had behaved in an unmannerly fashion in the well-known quarrel with his brother Apollo, so wonderfully described in the Homeric hymn (iv, 295 ff.; cf. Dion Chrysostom, vi, 104) to Hermes, "while then, conceiving a plan, the mighty slayer of Argos, raising himself on his hands, broke wind against Apollo, sending forth an omen, a miserable servant of his belly, a presumptuous messenger."

We have already spoken of the meaning of the Hermes-pillars, as also of Hermes as manager and protector of the gymnasia and palæstræ and of the manly youth who met there. As such he has also inspired artists to continually new representations; they make him a mature, vigorous youth, his chlamys generally thrown open, so that the grace of the youthful form is most beautifully asserted. But also in amorous sport with the nymphs Hermes is a favourite subject of plastic art; perhaps most beautiful and characteristic is the famous group in the Villa Farnesina at Rome, which shows Hermes with tender looks inclining towards an almost naked nymph, while with one hand he caresses her bosom and with the other withdraws the scanty garment from it.

An ever amorous goddess is Eos (Aurora), the goddess of dawn, whom Homer calls rosy-fingered from the phenomenon often observed in the south, that the sun, before it rises, sends over the sky a rosy-coloured image of its beams like a fan, as an outspread hand.

According to Apollodorus (i, 27), this ever amorous nature in Eos was due to Aphrodite having had intercourse with Ares. She loves everything that is beautiful, especially young men, and she seizes forcibly anyone who inspires her heart with passion, thereby symbolizing the necessity of grasping without delay the delights of the short-lived mornings, fresh with dew. Thus she carries off Cleitus,

Cephalus, Orion, Tithonus (Tyrtæus frag., 12, 5; *Hom. Hymn.*, v, 218 ff.; Horace, *Odes*, ii, 16, 30). The last named, who was so beautiful that his beauty became a proverb, seems to have pleased her most, and for him she obtained by entreaty from Zeus the boon that he should be deathless and live eternally. But, unfortunately, the queenly Eos omitted to ask also that he should be endowed with eternal youth; so when, in her palace by the farthest floods of Ocean, grey hairs and decrepitude came upon Tithonus, Eos wearied of him and discarded him. The fable, almost modern in tone, is symbolical of the ever renewed young day and morning, which, at first fresh and beautiful, as it were dries up and becomes old under the increasing heat. The symbol is also repeated in the sun; Memnon (*Od.*, xi, 522), according to Homer the most beautiful of all who fought before Troy, falls by the hand of Achilles, whose dear friend Antilochus he had slain. Therefore still to-day (?) the pillars of Memnon, set up near Egyptian Thebes in honour of his memory, utter a note of melancholy when the tender mother Aurora ascends the sky and with her first beams gilds the image of her son.

That Selene (Luna), the moon-goddess, the " beaming eye of night ", was also of an amorous nature, hardly needs special mention. She had once rested in the arms of Zeus, to whom she bore the beautiful Pandia. In Arcadia Pan was regarded as her sweetheart who, according to Virgil (*Geor.* iii, 391), had won her love by the present of a flock of white lambs. But best known of all is her love for Endymion, the beautiful youth whom she surprised while he slept in the wooded hills of Latmos, and after that blessed him every night with her love. Some recognize in this the symbol of the sleep of death, into whose darkness the gentle light of love still penetrates. Licymnius (frag. 3 in Ath., xiii, 564*c*) of Chios had indeed written that Hypnos, the god of sleep, had fallen madly in love with Endymion: "He so dearly loved the eyes of Endymion, that not even when he was asleep did he cause them to shut, but let him keep them open when he put him to sleep, that he might ever enjoy the delight of gazing on them."

Of the origin of Orion,[1] the splendid constellation, fabled by the ancients to be either a giant who with brandished club or brilliant weapons at his side strides along the sky, or a mighty hunter, the following singular story is told. Zeus, Poseidon, and Hermes in their wanderings upon earth once came to the aged Hyrieus at Thebes, by whom in spite of his poverty they were received with great hospitality. By way of thanks, the gods granted the old man permission to ask the fulfilment of a prayer; he told them that he had long been a widower, and that while he did not want a second wife, he did want a son. The gods resolved to grant his prayer. The skin of a previously slaughtered bullock is brought forward and in it the three gods deposit their seed. Skin and all is then buried in the earth, and from it after nine months steps forth a boy, who later develops into the mighty Orion. The story, that no doubt arose from a false interpretation, is said to indicate that so mighty a giant as Orion needed not one, but three fathers, and that he, like nearly all the giants, came from the earth.

When grown up Orion shows his sensuality in an outrageous manner for, in a fit of drunkenness, he violates the daughter (or the wife) of his guest and friend, Œnopion, king of Chios (Parthenius, 20; Pindar, frag. 72). For this he is blinded by his father, but he gropes his way towards the rising sun and at last finds the light of his eyes restored by its beams. Later, he conceives a desire for Artemis, and seeks to lay violent hands on her: whereupon

[1] For the birth of Orion see Ovid, *Fasti*, v, 495 ff.; Nonnus, *Dionysiaca*, xiii, 96 ff.; Hyginus, *Fab.*, 195, and *Poet. astron.*, ii, 34, although, according to Strabo, ix, 404, Pindar had already spoken of it (frag. 73). False derivation from οὐρεῖν, which not only means to make water, but also to discharge semen (so e.g. in Anton. Liberalis, 41).

the goddess sends a scorpion which kills the giant with its poisonous sting (Aratus, *Phæn.*, 636 ff.; Nicander, *Ther.*, 13 ff.; Horace, *Odes*, iii, 4, 70). According to another story, told by Pindar (frag. 74), Pleïone with her daughter had excited the lust of Orion; he persecuted them for five years, after which Zeus placed the whole group among the stars—the oppressed women as the Pleiades, the giant as Orion, and his dog as the dog-star Sirius.

If beauty appeared the highest thing to the Greeks, and they continually paid homage to it, it is conceivable that there were some among the varied throng of their divinities who were thought of and revered as bestowers and dispensers of beauty. To enter in greater detail into the enchanting fables which Hellenic sensual joy and fancy has invented concerning these divinities would swell the extent of this book beyond all measure. In our brief selection, chosen for a definite purpose, it is only possible for us to touch lightly upon what is absolutely necessary. Hence we must be content with the bare mention of the Horæ, who were regarded as the symbols of the seasons of the year, in so far as they bring forth flowers, blossoms, and fruits, all at the right time. Poets and artists represented them as charming girlish forms, adorned with golden jewels, flowers, and fruits, but otherwise clad only lightly, in transparent attire. Especially graceful among the Horæ, who are generally thought of as three in number, is the goddess of spring, among the Greeks called Chloris, among the Romans Flora. Boreas, the mighty god of the north wind, and Zephyrus, the delightful west wind, had both fallen in love with her, but she gave her affection to Zephyrus, to whom she remains constant in her touching love. A beautiful picture in Pompeii, unfortunately partly destroyed, represents the lovely youthful Zephyrus crowned with myrtles, holding a branch in blossom in his left hand, and accompanied by two Erotes, drawing near to his sleeping loved one, from the upper part of whose body a third Eros is drawing away her dress (for a different explanation of the picture, see W. Helbig, *Wandgemälde Campaniens*, p. 194, No. 974). In course of time the Horæ became identified rather with the hours of the day, and the seasons were represented by male forms.

Perhaps even more enchanting forms than the Horæ are the Charities, or, as the Latins call them, the Graces. They also are generally regarded as three in number, and personify everything in life that is enchanting, cheerful, graceful, sensually beautiful. It is very significant of Hellenic civilization that such a glorification of the naked sensual charm does not belong to the later period of the decadence, as it is beautifully phrased, but that, long before the old original poets, meditating in the mist of prehistoric times—for instance, Pamphos (*Pausanias*, ix, 35, 4), the mythical singer of hymns—had sung of the Charities and their sensual charms. These goddesses are everywhere where it is a question of manifesting the more cheerful joys of life, at dance and game, at joyful meal, when stringed instruments and songs resound. According to Theognis (*Theognis*, 15; the proverb in Zenobius, i, 36; cf. Seneca, *De Benef.*, i, 3), in company with the Muses, they sang at the wedding of Cadmus and Harmonia the words: "What is beautiful is dear, what is not beautiful is not dear"—words which so correctly embody the nature of the Charities, indeed, affirm the quintessence of Greek worldly wisdom generally. They themselves are charming forms, ever laughing and dancing, singing and leaping. They bathe in springs and rivers, and crown themselves with the flowers of spring, especially roses. While the older artists represent them still clothed, in course of time their drapery becomes more and more diaphonous, until they generally appear completely naked, embracing each other in the well-known attitude, so that the expression "naked as the Graces" became proverbial.

With the Graces the Muses, the goddesses of the arts in the widest sense of the word, are often coupled; they are generally regarded as nine in number, and among them Erato, the Muse of erotic poetry, should especially be mentioned.

Among the poets and plastic artists Hebe appears as the personification of youthful bloom, who with the Hours, Charities, and nymphs belongs to the retinue of Aphrodite. It is known from Homer (*Il.*, v, 905; *Hymn. Apol.*, 17; *Il.*, iv, 2. Hebe in the train of Venus: Horace, *Odes*, i, 30, 7; *Hymn. Apol.*, 195) how she assists Ares in the bath, how while Apollo is playing she dances with the Muses for the gods and presents the winecups at their banquets. When Heracles, after a life full of never-ending troubles, was received amongst the gods he obtained Hebe as his wife. Her duty as cupbearer had in the meantime become superfluous, since Eros had stirred the heart of Zeus so that he carried away the beautiful Trojan royal boy, Ganymede, to his heaven, so that he might, as his page, offer him the cup filled with wine and, as his favourite, share his bed with him. We shall have occasion to speak more in detail of Eros and Ganymede when we come to discuss the love of boys.

Lastly, Hermaphroditos, of whom we have already spoken, is to be mentioned as one of the following of Aphrodite. It may be added that according to Pliny (*Hist. Nat.*, xxxvi, 33), plastic art also knew of Hermerotes.

Female sexual life, and especially confinement, according to the ideas of the ancients, stands in intimate relation to the moon; so that all the goddesses who are in any way connected with the moon, such as Hera, Artemis, Aphrodite, and Athene, are at the same time protectresses of women throughout their sexual life, but chiefly during childbirth. Yet a special goddess of childbirth was also known, Ilithyia, supposed to be the daughter of Hera, whose name expresses the pains of labour; hence Homer (*Il.*, xi, 270) already imagines several Ilithyiæ. There were sanctuaries of her in many places in Greece, the best known being that of the kneeling Ilithyia in Tegea. It was believed that childbirth took place most easily in a kneeling posture.

The great mother of the gods, who bore Zeus, Poseidon, and Hades, and thereby created the entire kingdom of the gods, is Rhea, who is generally given the epithet Cybele, pointing to the caves and cavernous sanctuaries of the mountain ranges of Phrygia, where, as well as in the island of Crete, she was chiefly worshipped. Her cult, corresponding to the nature of that range of wooded hills, shows a wild loftiness; panthers and lions are her companions, but in other respects she is akin to the Cyprian and Syrian Aphrodite, with whom she is often identified, especially in Lydia. Her priests and worshippers are fanatic enthusiasts who roam over forest and mountain with wild cries, with noisy music of horns and pipes, kettledrums and castanets, by the light of the blazing torches, and carry their orgiastic madness so far that they often wound themselves or one another—like the modern dervishes and fakirs—or even castrate themselves. This religious disorder, which finds its counterpart in the orgies of the flagellants of the Middle Ages, chiefly flourished in the district of the Phrygian city of Persinus on the river Sangarius. There, on the towering height of Dindymon, after which the goddess is often called Dindymene, was a sacred rock named Agdos, and a cave which was regarded as the oldest sanctuary of Rhea Cybele Agdistis. There also was shown the grave of her beloved Attis. Attis also, like Adonis and similar forms in Greek mythology, is a symbol of sweet beauty, but also of the painful shortness and frailty of life with its constant change of birth and death, spring and winter, joy and sorrow. Pausanias (vii, 17, 10;

Arnobius, *Adv. Nat.*, v, 5; Catullus, lxiii; Lucian, *Dial. Deorum*, 12) tells the story in the following form: "Zeus once had an emission of semen and his seed fell on the ground, which after an appointed time brought forth a spirit, that is, a divine being named Agdistis, possessing both male and female genital organs. But the gods bound Agdistis and cut off his male organs, since they were afraid that this being would otherwise become too powerful. From the cut-off organs an almond-tree grew up from the fruits of which, after they were ripe, the daughter of the river Sangarius took some and put them into her bosom, after which the almonds disappeared but the girl herself became pregnant. She bore a child, a boy, who grew up among the goats of the country fields and was always tended by a he-goat. As he grew in stature he became more wonderfully beautiful than any other man, so that the goddess Agdistis (Rhea Cybele) became hotly enamoured of the boy."

His spirit passes over into the fig-tree and violets spring from his blood that trickles down, and embrace the fig-tree in a tender wreath; a pretty idea, that the souls of the dead live again in flowers and trees. The sorrow of Agdistis is unspeakable; she cannot do without her beloved and implores Zeus to reunite them. But all he can do for her is to grant that the body of the beautiful young boy shall never be disfigured by unsightly decay, that his hair shall not wither, but that of his whole body his little finger alone shall live again. As this did not satisfy the goddess, who was eager for love, she takes the precious fig-tree and carries it into her cave, for ever to assuage her sorrow by contemplation of it.

Concerning the god Dionysus, the finely conceived symbol, glorified by poetry, of the inexhaustible fruitfulness of the earth and of the festivals held in his honour, we have little to add to what has been already said. Preller says as beautifully as correctly: "There is no other cult in which the pantheism and hylozoism that is spread throughout the whole of natural religion appears in so many-sided a manner or with such lively and appropriate traits. But, on the other hand, this service is also more rich in pictures, more inspired than any other. If we survey the abundant wealth of poetical compositions and pictorial creations which owe their origin to him, then, full of admiration, we shall renounce the idea of comprising them all in a short sketch. In poetry the dithyramb, comedy, and tragedy—with the satyric drama—sprang, entirely or for the most part, from the stimulus of the service of Dionysus. The livelier music and the homogeneous representation of ideal stories in allegorical dances and choruses has likewise been developed to the greatest extent in his circle. Let anyone who desires to have an idea of the abundance of motives which plastic art received from this service run through any museum, any collection of copies of ancient sculptures, vase-paintings, or other plastic works. Everywhere and always, among new and unexpected forms and in an equally abundant fullness and multiplicity of tones and groups he will be met by Dionysus and his inspired company."

In Thebes, Semele, one of the famous daughters of Cadmus, had enjoyed the love of Zeus but, being talked about by the jealous Hera, she demanded to see Zeus in his full majesty as the god of thunder and lightning. Human beings cannot, however, endure the sight of the divine majesty, and so the foolish woman dies in the flames, after she had brought forth a fœtus, which Zeus sews up in his thigh in order to give birth to it a second time after it had become mature (Lucian, *Dial. Deor.*, 9; see also Stephani, *Comptes Rendus*, 1861, pp. 12 ff.). This story also, whose deep meaning—the endless toil and care with which the vine must be handled—is easy to recognize, has given Lucian material for joke and jest, for he makes Hermes the midwife, "who has to fetch water for Zeus and attend to everything else which is usual amongst women in childbed."

Developing into a vigorous ephebus beautiful as the rays of the sun, Dionysus plants the vine, makes himself, his nurses and all the divinities and spirits of the woods and country fields drunk with the delicious newly-created liquor, and roves about with his following in noisy expeditions, somewhat weak, almost womanish to look at, and yet with the irresistible power of sweet desire and jovial inebriety.

The love of Dionysus for the beautiful Ariadne and her ascension to the stars has been so often treated by the poets that it may be assumed to be well known. As Seneca (*Œdipus*, 491) writes, at the nuptials of Dionysus with Ariadne the most delicious wine flowed from the hard rock. It is not so well known that the mystical side in the cult of Dionysus was developed especially in Argos, and that at Lerna were celebrated in honour of the god mysteries which may be considered an imitation of the Eleusinian but which, nevertheless, had a very obscene character. According to Herodotus (ii, 49), Melampus had introduced the phallus-procession that was common therewith, and Heracleitus (frag. 70) has recorded that very indecent songs were sung at the same time. According to our ideas also, the Dionysiac mysteries held in Thrace in honour of the goddess Cotytto, already mentioned in connection with the *Baptæ* of Eupolis (p. 141), were highly immodest.

A large number of the local stories, which in course of time were attached to Dionysus, have been represented by Nonnus (who lived in the fourth century A.D.) in his gigantic epic *Dionysiaca*, richly coloured and seasoned with numerous erotic episodes. The phallus, as has been often mentioned, naturally possessed great importance in the worship of Dionysus, and phallic processions were everywhere held in his honour. At Methymna in Lesbos a Dionysus Phallen was worshipped, according to Pausanias (x, 19, 3) and Athenæus (x, 445), mentions wanton phallophoria in Rhodes.

The animals of the Bacchic cult are the bull, panther, ass, and goat—the two last, of course, on account of their lustful nature.

The tenderer elementary spirits of springs and streams, flowers and trees, mountains and forests were named Nymphs. They are the friendly protecting spirits of nature, whose cheerful existence consists in singing and dancing, playing and jumping, hunting and roaming, loving and being loved. Apollo and Hermes are their specially favoured friends, in whose arms they love to cull the sweet gifts of Aphrodite; but this does not, however prevent them from enjoying the amorous caresses of many of the coarser satyrs, from whose ever lustful importunity they are, indeed, often obliged to save themselves by sly cunning and hasty flight. They are also fond of blessing men with their love, especially beautiful boys and youths, amongst them Hylas, who while drawing water was dragged down by the nymphs of the spring into the cold water.

The coarser elements of the spirits of mountain and forest are the Satyrs, who were imagined as possessing animal attributes, with pointed ears elongated upwards, and short little tails. Arch and cunning, sometimes also foolish, winebibbers, and above all ever longing for the flesh of women. Old writers frequently mention (e.g. Plutarch, *De Sanitate tuenda*, 381) a herb named *satyrion*, to which a stimulating effect was ascribed. Thus strong sensuality is their original and most peculiar character, as it is represented in the Sicinnis, a dance resembling the jumping of goats, which was danced by the satyrs in especial. How the Greek sense of beauty developed rapidly but with due precision can be recognized in the representation of the satyrs in plastic art. While older times showed them as still bearded, old, ugly, and often repulsive, they gradually became ever more youthful, pleasant, and beautiful, so that the satyrs of the classical period are included also among the male ideals of art forms, and are combined with nymphs and bacchantes into magnificent groups.

Silenus is often named as the earliest of the satyrs, and when the form was multiplied the older satyrs appear as Sileni. Sileni and satyrs are to be distinguished however, though common to them both is their delight in wine and their ever wakeful sensuality. The old Silenus is a highly amusing figure; originally the educator of Dionysus, he becomes his most enthusiastic worshipper: that is, he is generally drunk, so that he can hardly stand on his feet and hence always rides on an ass, ever in danger of falling under it; or he rides in a car drawn by goats, and the satyrs have trouble enough to hold him upright. The nature of the Sileni, who were originally the spirits of the flowing, fertilizing water, became gradually more and more sensualized, so that also in their special animal, the ass, only lasciviousness and strong sexual potency was recognized as the symbol of the Sileni. The old poets had many amusing little stories to relate concerning this animal. Thus we are told by Ovid[1] that preparations were once being made to celebrate the festival of Dionysus, which took place every other year at the time of the winter solstice and at which all the spirits who formed the retinue of the god—satyrs, nymphs, Pan, Priapus, Silenus, and others—took part. The festival is going on merrily. Dionysus pours out the wine, which flows in streams and is presented by charming half-naked naiads. The wine and the sight of the large supply of women's flesh sets free monstrous licentiousness on every side, and everyone rejoices at nightfall that, after the carousal is ended, they may let their passions

[1] *Fasti*, i, 391 ff.; also vi, 319 ff., where the story is told with trifling alterations. The festival is a festival of Ceres, and Vesta (not a nymph) excites the lust of Priapus; Hyginus, *Poet. astron.*, ii, 23; Lactantius, *Instit. Div.*, i, 21, 25.

have their fling. Priapus was especially struck with the beautiful but shy Lotis, who, however, refused to have anything to do with the god, who was assuredly not distinguished for his beauty. Yet the night drew on, and Lotis, overcome by wine and weariness, lay almost defenceless there on the soft grass under the shadow of a maple-tree. Priapus creeps up, gently, gently, holding his breath; already he fancies himself near the accomplishment of his wishes, the beautiful sleeper does not move, now he is pulling her clothes up high, when—the ass of Silenus brays "very inopportunely; Lotis wakes up alarmed, pushes the importunate Priapus away, and wakes up all the sleepers with her cries, who, by the light of the moon, stare at the disappointed lover amid general merriment". In his rage Priapus kills the guilty-innocent donkey, and that is the reason why from that time asses are sacrificed to him.

Priapus, who here plays such a regrettable part, is the personification of the sexual impulse in its most brutal form.

Priapus was generally regarded as a son of Dionysus and a nymph (or Aphrodite) and was the protecting spirit of meadows, gardens, and wine-plantations, of the rearing of goats, sheep, and bees. One may also say that he is the underlying, though coarse, principle of the form of Eros; indeed, Eros in the oldest times was worshipped at Thespiæ (Boeotia) in a form similar to that of Priapus. The sacrifice of the ass to him is, of course, not to be explained from the fabulous stories of Ovid; the real reason is that the ass [1] was regarded as specially possessed of generative power, and for the same reason the goose also was sacred to him. Priapus was worshipped at nearly all mysteries, not only the Dionysiac, according to Diodorus (Diod. Sic., iv,

[1] On the ass cf. Gruppe, *Griechische Mythologie*; on the goose, Petronius, 137; Keller, *Tiere des Altertums*, p. 288; and the constellation of the ass, Hyginus, *Poet. astron.*, ii, 23.

6, 4), "with coarse laughing and jokes." Still unknown to the older poetry of the Greeks, Priapus pops up in a comedy of Xenarchus (*CAF.*, II, 472), called *Priapus*, of which nothing more is known. That he also came on the stage on other occasions is shown by the indignation of Macrobius and Augustine (Macrobius, *Sat.*, vi, 5, 6; Augustine, *De Civitate Dei*, vi, 7). Priapus plays a great part afterwards in Alexandrine literature, especially in the Palatine Anthology and the Bucolic poets; a collection of Latin poems, in part strongly erotic and often of an obscene character, has been preserved under the name of *Carmina Priapea*.

Representations of Priapus in plastic art are numberless; even on coins, especially from Lampsacus on the Hellespont, on not a few of which—and this is very important for the conception of the sexual idea—he is shown with member erect. In Rome the cult of Priapus was introduced comparatively late (Prudentius, *Contra Symm.*, I, 102 ff.). He was worshipped in cities in special sanctuaries, and in the country (Pausanias, ix, 31, 2) wherever goats and sheep and bees are reared; sailors and fishermen also worshipped him. To Priapus was attributed not only the advancement of the fruits of the field, but he was also regarded as the warder off of thieves and birds. Thus the roughly made wooden figure, painted red, of a naked Priapus with a large erect member, was to be seen in fields and gardens, mostly with a sickle in his hand, not seldom a bundle of reeds on his head, intended to rustle in the wind and to scare away the birds. But as the phallus was also employed for the protection of graves, so Priapus likewise appears as the ornament of these memorials.

We need not go more closely into the question whether Dionysus and Priapus are identical (Ath., i, 30); in poetry Priapus is regarded as belonging to the retinue of Dionysus, so that Moschus (iii, 27) even spoke of several Priapi. Further, he was brought into close relations with Hermaphroditos, with whom indeed he actually has many points of similarity: e.g. in plastic art, in the way he lifts up his dress (Diod. Sic., iv, 6, 5. Bekker, *Anecdota Græca*, I, 472, 21; *FHG*., III, 155, 35) in order to exhibit his erotically strongly intensified charms; and frequently his breasts have the form of a woman's, so that in many representations it may be doubted whether a Hermaphroditos or a Priapus is intended; note also that Priapus is often represented by artists together with Hermaphroditos. (On Priapus and Hermaphroditos cf. W. Helbig, *Wandgemälde Campaniens*, No. 1369, Gerhardt, *Antike Bildwerke* (plate 306, 1)).

Since it was held that the principle of generation embodied in Priapus contained the conditions and origin of the nature of all existence he was also identified with those divinities in whom the men of antiquity saw the gods of life generally. It was believed at that time that sexual impulse and the principle of life are synonymous. Thus Priapus was identified with the sun-god Helios (Eustathius on *Iliad*, 691, 45) or with the Kosmos (Cornutus, 27); on a Dacian dedicatory inscription (*CIL*., III, 1139) Priapus is indicated as the universal god, Pantheus, and a plastic representation of the male organs of generation in the highest erotic power bears the subscription *ΣΩΤΗΡ ΚΟΣΜΟΥ*, "the saviour of the world" (E. Fuchs, *Geschichte der erotischen Kunst* (1908, p. 133)). The Greeks were acquainted with yet other ithyphallic divinities; thus Phanes (with the epithet *Protogonos*, the first-born) was one of the numerous names of the original principle of creation in the later Orphic mysticism (on Phanes, cf. *Orphica*, ed. Abel, frag. 62; 6, 9; 56, 4; 69, 1; also Stobæus, *Eclog*. I, 2, 11; Nonnus, *Dion*., xiv, 187). The story goes that Phanes came forth from the silver egg created by Chronos in the æther, double-sexed; we are again astonished to find how the results of modern natural science have been anticipated thousands of years before by Greek mythology. The other stories—some of them very complicated and profound—about Phanes do not concern us here; but it may be mentioned that Phanes was also identified with Priapus, and sometimes with Adonis, the beautiful favourite of Aphrodite, who, also, is often regarded as having been double-sexed.

Phanes is also the name of one of the twelve Centaurs of Helicon named by Nonnus, others of whom—namely Spargeus (lustful), Kepeus (gardener, like Priapus), and Orthaon (standing)—by their names allow us to infer ithyphallic characteristics. With these details the statement of Pausanias, that the cult of Priapus was native on mount Helicon, is in agreement.

Triphales (the man with three members) (*CAF.*, I, 528 ff.) was the title of a lost play by Aristophanes, in which probably the sexual life of Alcibiades was attacked. Varro also had named one of his satires *Triphallus*; it treated of manhood. Also according to Gellius (*Noct. Att.*, II, 19) it was the name of a comedy of Nævius. Tychon was the name of an ithyphallic spirit attached to the retinue of Aphrodite, who, according to Strabo (xiii, 588), was worshipped especially in Athens, and according to Diodorus Sicilus (iv, 6; cf. *Etym. Magnum*, 773, 1, Hesychius, s.v. τύχων), also among the Egyptians, as Priapus.

An amiable form is the god Pan, the friendly mountain-spirit, protector of flocks and symbol of peaceful nature, whom Cyllene bore to Hermes in the wooded mountains of Arcadia. Singular in appearance, with goat's feet, two horns and a long beard, he is especially the god of goats, which one sees feeding and jumping everywhere on the slopes of the Greek mountains. In his company the nymphs dance, sing, and play music, when they are not enjoying the sweets of love with him—for Pan is constantly in love. The singular voices and sounds, which one hears on lonely mountains, the echo of the towering rocks of Arcadia, had given birth to the beautiful story according to which Pan loves the nymph Echo, but she prefers the charming Narcissus and pines away in unfulfilled desire for him until her body gradually withers and of all her being only the voice is left (the story of Echo is variously told; cf. Moschus, 6; Longus, iii, 23). Narcissus, who had seen himself mirrored in a stream, fell madly in love with his own marvellous beauty, until in his unassuaged passion for himself he pines away—an ingenious and infinitely touching symbol of the spring flower, which, being reflected in the brook, dies after a short bloom. (For Narcissus, see Ovid, *Metam.*, III, 339 ff.; Pausanias, ix, 31, 7; Conon, 24. On the symbolism of the story, see Plutarch, *Conviv.*, 5, 7, 4; Artemidorus, ii, 7.) Similarly ingenious stories are attached by Greek poetry to the form of the nymph Syrinx (Ovid, *Metam.*, I, 690 ff.; Longus, ii, 34, 37), the personification of the shepherd's flute, or the Pitys, the personified pine-tree (Lucian, *Dial. Deorum*, 22, 4), with whose branches Pan is accustomed to adorn his head.

The most important feature in the character of Pan, for the purpose of the present work, is his continual lustfulness. As Longus says (ii, 39), no nymph has any rest from him, but he is not always fortunate in his adventures. Ovid (*Fasti*, ii, 303 ff.) tells a story about him, which he himself describes as exceedingly humorous. Pan once caught sight of the youthful Heracles together with Omphale, in compulsory service to whom destiny had compelled the hero to languish as a punishment for the murder, committed in madness, of his friend Iphitus, and in this service he degenerated till he became like a woman himself, spinning wool and wearing female attire, as poets and artists often represent him. No sooner had Pan seen Omphale than he fell madly in love with her. "Away with the nymphs of the mountain," said he, " I have nothing more to do with you, Omphale the beautiful, alone, is now my love." He was never tired of looking at her, with her unbound hair smelling of costly perfume and hanging down over her bare shoulders ; he admired her naked breasts, whose rosy buds were coloured with a tincture of gold.[1] Heracles and Omphale prepare a meal in an idyllic grotto by the side of a babbling brook which, as it rushes by invites to sweet dreams, and Omphale puts her own clothes on the hero ; she hands him the purple-coloured shift and the elegant girdle, which is too small for the hero's body ; she enlarges the tunic that is too cramped for him, neither will the bangles nor the tight shoes fit. Omphale herself puts on the dress of Heracles, wraps herself in the lion's skin, and proudly sees the conquered hero lying at her feet. After the meal they ascend their common bed.

About midnight, Pan sneaks along : already he has reached the bed, and, feeling carefully, stretches out his hand. Then he touches the lion's skin and starts back terrified, like some wayfarer who has incautiously trodden on a snake. Groping on the other side, he feels the softness of a woman's clothing, and so gets into bed and lies down by the supposed Omphale. With quaking hand he lifts up the light garment ; then he feels the hairs on the thighs of Heracles, who, while Pan is groping about further, wakes up and throws the impudent rascal with a mighty swing down from the bed, so that he can hardly lift himself from the ground for pain and is also heartily laughed at by Heracles and Omphale.

This brief survey of the erotic in the legends concerning the gods of Greece by no means exhausts the subject. We are unable, without extending the chapter to a disproportionate length, to treat

[1] Ovid is speaking of his own time, when such refinement may not have been unusual. In Juv., vi, 122, Messalina appears in the brothel " naked with gilded breasts " (i.e. " tinctured with gold ").

it fully, and so have been obliged to omit much and to refer only in brief to the rest. Hitherto we have spoken only of the Greek world of gods; but the legends and stories of the heroes also belong to mythology, and without them our description would show an important gap. We can, however, console ourselves with the thought that there is hardly a Greek legend of which erotic did not form the centre or at least the background. Consequently, we must limit ourselves to what is most important, otherwise the result would be a complete handbook of Greek legends. Also we may assume that the reader is acquainted with the majority of them at least, and shall therefore in what follows only mention what is either distinguished by special peculiarity or may be less known. Lastly, it may be noticed that all legends with a pæderastic character will be treated later.

Among the Lapithæ of Thessaly Cænis (Apoll., *Epit.*, 1, 22) grew up a maiden fair as a picture. She ventured to boast of the love of Poseidon, and as the reward for showing her favour she begged from the god that she might be changed into a man, which thing was granted her. This story perhaps treats of the idea of the woman with a man's soul, called by the Latins *virago*, that slumbers in the subconsciousness.

Ixion, also one of the Lapithæ, and their king, in his insolence lusted after Hera, the sublime queen of heaven, who apparently consents to his wishes and places by his side a cloud-form to represent her; and the fruit of this singular embrace was the centaurs. But Ixion is shameless enough, in a drunken fit, to boast of the favour he was supposed to have enjoyed, whereupon as a punishment he is tied to an eternally revolving wheel in the underworld (Soph., *Philoct.*, 676 ff.). Also the national hero of the Lapithæ, Peirithous, the son of Zeus, was obliged to pay dearly for his criminal love, since he attempted to carry off from Hades his wife

Persephone, for which he has to languish in the underworld in everlasting fetters (Horace, *Odes*, iii, 4, 79). In accordance with the outrageous lust of their origin the race of centaurs are of wildest sensuality, ever longing for woman's flesh and entering into the most extravagant adventures in a perpetual state of intoxication. Especially wild were the scenes in the poets and plastic artists at the frequently described wedding of Peirithous and Hippodameia (*Il.*, i, 262 ff.; *Od.*, xxi, 294; Hesiod, *Shield*, 178 ff.; Ovid, *Metam.*, xii, 146 ff.), when the guests got tipsy with wine and the sight of the beautiful bride. The wild centaur Eurytus grasps at the breasts of Hippodameia, and endeavours to handle her lustfully in other ways, whereupon, as the *Odyssey* relates, his nose and ears were cut off and he is thrown out, while according to the more usual version the fierce battle between the Lapithæ and centaurs begins, which ends with the victory of the Lapithæ.

We have already (pp. 150, 204) made the acquaintance of Phædra in circumstances recalling Potiphar's wife of the Old Testament. The story of Stheneboea, the wife of Proetus, the ruler of Tiryns, is similar. She fell madly in love with the beautiful young Bellerophon; but as she could not seduce him, her pretended love changed into a fierce thirst for revenge. "Either you must die," she said to her husband, "or else slay Bellerophon, who seeks the flower of my body." Proetus is weak enough to believe the slanders of his shameless wife, and sends the pure-minded lad to his brother-in-law in Lycia with a letter, written in secret characters, in which he asks him to put the bearer of it to death. But the wicked plot did not succeed; rather that journey to Lycia becomes for Bellerophon the beginning of great heroic deeds. It is interesting, that in many vase paintings the Uriah-letter is dedicated to the young hero in the presence of Stheneboea, who still strives to make love to him with languishing, lustful glances (for the story of Bellerophon see *Il.*, vi, 150 ff.). Two ideal forms of manly youth are the brothers Castor and Pollux (Polydeukes). Leda was considered to be their mother, with whom it was said that Zeus himself had cohabited in the guise of a swan. Poets and plastic artists of ancient and modern times never tired of representing this motive in ever renewed variations. Mythology gives different accounts as to the sequel; in the most common version Leda bore an egg, from which the two Dioskuroi (sons of Zeus) were born; they grew up to be a pair of brothers in whom everything that, according to Greek ideas, is an ornament to the young man, was united, so that one may say in a word that in them the ideal type of youth was to be seen.[1] Among the love adventures of the two brothers the rape of the daughter of Leucippus by Castor and Pollux is sufficiently well known from poetry and plastic art.[2] The same may be said of the abduction of the Phoenician king's beautiful daughter, Europa, by Zeus. Near Sidon he saw her gathering flowers in a blooming meadow, whereon, inflamed with love, he changed himself into a bull, entices her upon his back, and carries her away through the sea to Crete.

Less known, although also a frequent motif of poetical and plastic art, is the story of the sisters, Procne and Philomela, although its details are variously told. In the sobbing notes of the nightingale the Greek heard a melancholy lament; therefore the nightingale was to him originally a beautiful maiden, Philomela, who had suffered grievously and was changed by the compassionate gods into a bird. She was wedded to a man who longed for her sister, whom he, pretending that his wife was dead, violated. But Philomela learns the truth and threatens revenge, wherefore he cuts out her tongue

[1] For Zeus and Leda see especially Eurip., *Helena*; cf. Apollodorus, iii, 126 ff.; for sculptures, O. Jahn, *Archäologische Beiträge*, pp. 1–11.

[2] Theocritus, xxii, 137 ff.; Pindar, *Nemea*, x, 60 ff.; Ovid, *Fasti*, v, 699 ff. On representations in plastic art cf. Pausanias, iii, 17, 3; 18, 11.

and keeps her concealed. By means of an ingenious dress, in which she expresses her story by the aid of inwoven figures and signs, she is able to inform her sisters, after which in revenge they cut the little son Itys (Itylos) in pieces and set him before the father to eat. When he discovers the horrible truth he pursues the sisters with an axe, and they are all changed into birds—Tereus, the father, into a hoopoe, Procne into a swallow, Philomela into the nightingale (the story of Procne and Philomela in the version of Sophocles, *Tereus* (in Nauck, *TGF*[2], p. 257 ff.).

Less ghastly is the story of Ion, whom the Attic king's daughter Creusa had borne after a secret amour with Apollo. She exposes the babe in the same grotto where she had yielded to the god, but the latter has pity upon the helpless child and brings it to Delphi, where it is brought up by the priestess and grows to be a blooming youth. In Ion we have, once more, the ideal type of the wonderful youth, adorned with every gift of mind and body, in which Greek literature and art abounds. From a servant of the temple he becomes its superintendent, and guardian of its valuable treasures.

In the meantime, Creusa had married Xuthus, but they had no children; wherefore the disappointed couple consult the oracle, and receive the answer that he who first meets them when coming out of the temple shall be their son. After many complications all is beautifully cleared up, and Xuthus recognizes Ion as his son. The story was told by Sophocles in his lost *Creusa* (fragments in Nauck, *TGF*[2], pp. 199 and 207), and then by Euripides in the wonderful, still extant drama *Ion*. Greek heroic legend proper also abounds with erotic motifs, so that in this case also we must impose limitations upon ourselves.

The mightiest of all the Greek heroes is Heracles. When Alcmene is shortly to become the mother of Zeus's favourite son Hera, tortured by gnawing jealousy, is clever enough to extort an oath from Zeus that the son born on a certain day shall be the mightiest of rulers. She then hurries to Argos, where one of her friends was seven months gone with child, and, in her character of goddess of birth, hastens this birth and keeps back the labour pains of Alcmene, so that Eurystheus is born before Heracles.[1] Since Zeus, in spite of his rage, is obliged to keep his oath, the feeble coward Eurystheus becomes ruler of Argos and forces Heracles to become his servant. Heracles is persecuted all his life by Hera with such raging hatred as only the pitiful jealousy of a mean woman, untouched by any noble elevation of mind, can entertain, and, guiltless as he was, is obliged, through unspeakable troubles and labours, to atone for Zeus having, when he was born, lengthened the delights of love for three nights by not allowing the sun to rise one day. But cunning is met with cunning; Zeus succeeds in inducing Hera to lay the new-born child on her breast, which it sucks so vigorously, that she throws it from her, and the divine milk is spilled around in a wide arch, and thus the Milky Way in the firmament was formed (Diod. Sic., iv, 9; Pausan., ix, 25, 2). When he was 18 years old, according to a local story of Thespiæ, he slew a mighty lion. To lie in wait for the monster, he spent the night as the guest of king Thestius, who had fifty daughters, one of whom was more beautiful and more amative than the rest. But Heracles would not have been Heracles, if he had not blessed them all with his love in a single night. Although the fifty daughters of Thestius are properly the nymphs of the country, so that here also the allegory of the nature-myth is clearly recognizable, yet the older mythographers were satisfied to see in this night of love a conspicuous proof of the unusual vigour of

[1] For how Hera delayed the labour pains of Alcmene, see Ovid, *Metam.*, ix, 280. She sent the Pharmakides to her—evil spirits who had that power. According to Pausanias, ix, 11, 3, likenesses of them had been seen in Thebes.

Heracles, so that they indicated this fifty-fold love-contest as the hero's thirteenth labour (Diod. Sic., iv, 29; Pausan., ix, 27, 6).

The twelve labours, which Heracles was compelled to perform in the forced service of the feeble and cowardly king Eurystheus, thanks to the malice of his wicked stepmother Hera, are so generally known, that they can be passed over here, especially as they for the most part lack the erotic undertone; but a less well-known trifle may be mentioned.

When Heracles penetrates into the underworld to fetch up the horrible hell-hound, Cerberus, he finds there the famous pair of friends, Theseus and Peirithous, who as a punishment for their foolhardy attempt to carry off Persephone, the wife of Hades, were grown to a rock. The mighty hero succeeded in pulling Theseus away; but when he attempts to do the same with Peirithous, a violent earthquake warns him against further encroachment on the rights of the underground kingdom. The comic poets were accustomed to describe with much satisfaction how, when Theseus was being pulled away, his posteriors remained hanging to the stone to which they had become attached, so that he was obliged to run about *hypolispos*, that is, with hinder parts worn smooth, since they had been rubbed by the rock. We can easily imagine how the Athenians enjoyed applauding this piece of stage-wit, especially as it was known to them from their Aristophanes, that they themselves as seafaring people, who continually rubbed their hinder parts on the rowers' benches, were so called, and hence Aristophanes could speak of their "Salamis-arse". Anyone who is to some extent initiated in the language of Attic comedy, knows what obscene subordinate meaning the public, always ready to laugh, was intended to get out of it, and certainly did.[1]

[1] For Theseus see Suïdas s.v. λίσποι; Aristoph., *Knights*, 1368, and Schol. The story itself, without an erotic by-sense, is common: e.g. Apollodorus, ii, 124; Pausanias, x, 29, 9; Diod. Sic., iv, 26; Plutarch,

Through his twelve deeds, which in local poetry were increased by several others, Heracles had become the brilliant national hero of the Greeks and was looked up to with holy enthusiasm, especially by manly young men. Even more ignominious appears the state of servitude, far worse than with king Eurystheus, into which Heracles sank at the luxurious court of the Lydian queen, Omphale, where the glorious hero experienced the most insulting treatment imaginable according to Greek ideas, for he became, as we have seen, not only the slave of a woman but effeminate himself.

As Heracles is the hero of the whole Greek nation, so Theseus is the national hero of the Ionic stock. On the way from Trœzene, where he had spent his life as a boy, to Athens, he performs six mighty heroic deeds, which every reader should know from childhood. When going through the city to visit his father as a tender youth in trailing Ionic dress with hair elegantly tied up, the workmen engaged in building a temple ridicule this seeming girl who is roaming about alone; whereupon the hero hurls a wagon loaded with building material so high into the air that all are astounded and ridicule ceases.

When Theseus had delivered the seven Athenian boys and girls (p. 117) who were doomed to be sacrificed every ninth year to the Minotaur in the labyrinth at Crete by slaying the monster, great jubilation and nothing but rejoicing prevailed. To the sound of songs and lutes, adorned with garlands of joy and affection, Theseus dances with Ariadne, and the rescued boys and girls, in memory of the windings of the labyrinth, perform the artistically intricate "cranes' dance", the forms of which were preserved till the latest times in the island of Delos, where Theseus landed after he had abandoned the sleeping Ariadne on the island of Naxos (Lucian, *De Saltat.*,

Theseus, 35. The Athenians were hence called ἀπόγλουτοι (with small rump); cf. also Arsen., *Viol.*, 64. For the Salamis-arse cf. Aristoph., *Knights*, 785.

34; Plutarch, *Theseus*, 21; Schol. Homer, *Il.*, xviii, 590; *Od.*, xi, 321). That Theseus was more than susceptible to the love of women is sufficiently well known, so that we need not give the names of his numerous loves. (On his multitudinous amours, cf. Plutarch, *Theseus*, 29; Ath., xiii, 557*a*.) The historian Istrus (Ath., xiii, 557*a*), a pupil of Callimachus, in his *Attic Stories*, had spoken of the amours of Theseus, and distinguished three classes of them: some were due to " love ", others " since he had captured them for booty ", thirdly " legitimate marriages ".

The story of the Argonauts and other tales of the heroes, so as far as they are of an erotic character, can only be briefly recorded. First, it is not uninteresting to find that in Greek story a kind of rejuvenescence treatment was already known. (Cf. Argum. Eurip., *Medea*; Schol. Aristoph., *Knights*, 1321; *Clouds*, 749; Ovid, *Metam.*, vii, 242 ff.) When Medea came with Jason from the Argonautic expedition into Greece, she renewed the youth of her husband, who had become too old, by the fairly vigorous method of boiling him. She proposed a somewhat similar treatment for her very aged father Æson, who had become decrepit, boiling magic herbs in a golden kettle and giving him the liquor to drink; though in this case the decoction was too strong, so that the poor old man, according to some authorities at least, died after drinking it. Similarly, she rejuvenated the Nisæan nymphs, the nurses of Dionysus, by bringing them again together with their husbands, which proves that the clever Medea was acquainted with the last and most effective means of producing such a result.

How Medea later takes a fearful revenge on her supposedly faithless husband, and how, inflamed by boundless jealousy and inextinguishable hatred, she kills her two beloved children and succeeds in killing her rival by an infernal trick, is known from ancient and modern poetry and plastic art.

The same holds good of the forms and events of the Theban and Trojan cycle of legends. When Thetis, the immortal, was assigned in marriage to Peleus, a son of man, she struggled against her fate for long, for she was unwilling to lie in the arms of any mortal. Then a bitter struggle arose, and according to Pindar (*Nemea*, iii, 35) Peleus was obliged " to seize the woman of the sea with vigour " ; and Ovid (*Metam.*, xi, 229 ff.) depicts with great gusto how Thetis, who intends to give herself up to a sweet siesta in comfortable nakedness, changes herself into a thousand forms, to escape the desire of Peleus, until she is conquered by his cunning and at last surrenders herself to him and so conceives the great Achilles in this love-embrace—a highly erotic picture, which leaves nothing to the imagination. Then followed the wedding of Thetis with the mortal, with special preference glorified by the Greek poets, in which all the gods took part, which was also represented by plastic art in ever renewed, ever more beautiful variations. Certainly Eris (Strife) also appeared at the wedding-feast, and threw among the guests the notorious apple of strife, an action that brought in its train the devastating tragedy of the Trojan war. A deep-meaning symbol this, of the truth that a strong drop of bitterness is ever mixed with earthly happiness.

The story of Odysseus, full of cunning, the man of sorrows, the resolute sufferer, is known to everyone. But less familiar may be the story of how, in the district of Pellana, where Tyndareos and Icarius had once lived with their children, an image of Aidōs [1] was seen, dedicated by Icarius after the departure of his daughter. He had vainly attempted to induce Odysseus to change his abode

[1] The word *αἰδώς* does not mean " chastity ", but what the Latins call *pietas*, modest devotion to duty. The daughter of Icarius does not wish to grieve her father ; but neither does she desire to break faith with her beloved. Hence she veils her face, to conceal her mental conflict and to beg that she may not be further pressed (see Pausanias, iii, 20, 10, for the story of Penelope veiling her face).

from the rocky island of Ithaca to the charming valleys of Lacedæmon, and had in vain tried to persuade his daughter to remain there. In silence she had veiled her face and followed her beloved.

When throughout Greece men were recruited and gathered together to call up all the famous heroes for an expedition of revenge against Troy, whose prince, Paris, had offended all Greece by the rape of Helen and the robbery of boundless treasures, then Thetis took her son Achilles, the youthful distinguished ephebus, with maternal care to the island of Scyros, where he was to have been brought up among the daughters of Lycomedes so that he need not take part in the cruelties of war. (That, so far as I know, is certainly the oldest and perhaps a unique example of co-education in Greek antiquity—the Greeks were too intelligent to tolerate such mischief; they would have called it a yoking together of horse and ox.)[1] The natural consequences of this educational experiment did not fail to show themselves, for Achilles, though among the maidens, did not feel like one, and the king's little daughter, Deidameia, was one fine day obliged to confess blushingly to her mother, that she carried a child in her womb by her delicate fellow-pupil who was roaming about in girl's clothes. This child later became the famous hero Neoptolemus. In a celebrated picture by Polygnotus described by Pausanias, Achilles had been already represented dressed in feminine garb; a specially characteristic, strongly erotic picture from the hand of Giolfino hangs in the Museo Civico at Verona.

At the destruction of Troy Cassandra was obliged to consent to be torn away from the statue of the maiden Pallas, that her youthful bloom might be sacrificed to the might of the Locrian Ajax.

[1] It is well known that Odysseus, to avoid taking part in the Trojan war, feigned madness, thereby proving that he had yoked horse and ox together to the plough: Pausanias, i, 22, 6. On Achilles amongst the girls, cf. also Ovid, *Metam.*, xiii, 162 ff.; Statius, i, 206 ff. On works of art, O. Jahn: *Archäologische Beiträge*, p. 352; Overbeck, p. 287.

The so-called *Nostoi*, that is, the poems in which the return of the heroes from Troy is narrated, afforded many opportunities for the description of erotic adventures. Thus also the most beautiful and best known of these poems, the *Odyssey*, is rich in erotic situations. We need only mention the names of Calypso, Circe, Nausicaa, the Sirens, the Phæacians and others, to awaken in every reader the recollection of richly coloured and sensually painted pictures.

We have reached the end of our treatment of the religious and mythological views of the Greeks. Although this chapter has proved longer than was either expected or intended, I am fully conscious of the inadequacy of the representation, for the material is too vast and gigantic for the subject to be treated other than briefly in a single sketch. But even so the reader will have learnt, perhaps to his amazement, how the religion and mythology of the Greeks is saturated by erotic. I must point out again that what has been here discussed represents only a fragmentary selection; anyone who desires to be fully acquainted with erotic, which is at the bottom of the mythological conceptions of the Greeks, must refer to any of the elaborate handbooks on this subject.

CHAPTER VII

Erotic in Greek Literature

In a history of morals a summary sketch of literature and art is necessary, since the intellectual works set down in writing or shaped by plastic artists give a true reflected image of the times. Accordingly we shall be able to include in the circle of our treatment references to such works only as have a pronounced erotic character or of which erotic episodes form a substantial part. Also we shall pay no attention here to the extensive homosexual literature, since this will be treated in detail in a later chapter (pp. 411–98). Neither shall we have to speak here of tragic and comic poetry, since we have already examined the erotic character of these two kinds of poetry in the fourth chapter. Even with these limitations the quantity of material is still enormous.

The task is further rendered essentially difficult by the fact that up till now serviceable introductory works are almost entirely wanting, for the history of the erotic literature and art of the Greeks, which we so urgently need, still remains unwritten, and only here and there are modest intimations to be found. Thus the author had to examine the whole of Greek literature for the purpose stated without the assistance of any preliminary works worth mentioning. Anyone who has even a rudimentary idea of the extent of the Greek written works which remain to us, or whose content can be reconstructed by the exact method of philological research, will not demand what is impossible from a single individual, who in this case would need to attain absolute perfection. It is pre-eminently in the inexhaustible domain of classical archæology that the statement that our knowledge must always be incomplete holds good.

I. *The Classical Period*

1. EPIC POETRY

We begin our summary with mythical prehistoric times and start with the well-known remark of Cicero (*Brutus*, 18, 71), that there were already poets before Homer. This is undoubtedly correct, and indications that it is so are found in the Homeric poems themselves. But of all these poems nothing has been preserved; their creators were the pioneers who paved the way for Homer, modulated the language and created epic verse, the long line of the hexameter; their works fell into the shadows of oblivion when the sun of Homeric poesy rose in the literary sky. Nevertheless, much information has come down to us from this period, and the history of Greek literature informs us of an imposing number of poets who lived before Homer, although, to be sure, most of them are names merely—inventions of a later time to facilitate the connection of the oldest poetical creations with the more plastic conception of definite poets.

One of the earliest of these mythical poets was Pamphos, of whom Pausanias (ix, 27, 2) tells us that he wrote poems on Eros. This remark is valuable for us, since it shows that the Greeks already in the oldest times of their literary history assume the worship of Eros, and so we can with perfect right affirm that Eros stands at the beginning of Hellenic civilization, although certainly in the Homeric poems the god Eros does not happen to be mentioned by name. But in the *Theogony* of Hesiod (*Theogony*, 120) Eros is constantly mentioned among the oldest gods, that is, among those existing from the earliest times.

Essentially better known than the entirely mythical Pamphos is the half-fabulous Orpheus, who might be regarded as an emblem of the union of Dionysiac and Apolline religion. Although Aristotle (according to Cicero, *De Nat. Deor*., i, 38, 107) denied his existence, the poetical production of his time was so widely attributed to him personally that even to-day the historian of literature calls those times and that school "Orphic". Everyone knows how Orpheus descended into the lower world to gain back from its ruler, Hades, by the power of song, his wife Eurydice who had previously died from the bite of a snake. Hades was touched by the wonderful singing of Orpheus and allowed him to lead back his wife into life, but only on condition that he should not look round at her until he reached the light of day. This condition was too hard for mortal man and, compelled by longing, Orpheus looked back and his wife disappeared as a shade into the infernal regions, never more to be seen. Thus Orpheus, standing at the beginning of Greek literary history, is a shining example of the touching love of a husband; we shall meet him again (p. 462), though in somewhat other circumstances. (For Orpheus and Eurydice see Apollodorus, i, 14, and Conon, 45; cf. also Ath., xiii, 597 (*Hermesianax*); Virgil, *Geor*., iv, 454 ff.; Ovid, *Met*., x, 1 ff.)

The fact that the two great national epics of the Greeks, Homer's *Iliad* and *Odyssey*, are saturated with erotic and contain many pictures of highly sensual charm, glowing with colours and enriched by every device known to literary art, has been already frequently mentioned, so that their discussion is superfluous. The same holds good of the so-called *Homeric Hymns*, in the fifth of which the love of Aphrodite for Anchises is described with great charm, sensual passion, and not without a peculiar piquant flavour. I have elsewhere often had occasion to refer to the erotic contained in the *Homeric Hymns*. Nor need I go more closely into the poems of the so-called *Epic Cycle*, since the erotic contained in them is for the most part based on the glorification of youthful beauty and their male and female components have been previously examined. I need not even here discuss the poems of Hesiod, since the erotic elements therein, such as the myth of Pandora, the unamiable characteristics of women, their coquetry even at that time and their constant readiness to spring upon their victim, have been mentioned before.

Further, we possess a poem by Hesiod, entitled *The Shield of Heracles*. It describes the struggles of Heracles with the monster Cycnus, and derives its name from the description of the shield of Heracles that fills a great part of the poem. At the beginning, the poet relates how Zeus, in order to present the world with a saviour and healer, is inflamed with love for the beautiful Alcmene, the wife of the Theban King Amphitryon. " She far surpassed all earthly women in beauty of form and stature, and in intellect no woman born of mortals could vie with her. From her face and from her dark eyes breathed a charm like that of the gold-adorned Aphrodite. While Amphitryon, who, to atone for a deed of bloodguiltiness, did not touch his wife, is engaged in a campaign, Zeus approaches her. After he had enjoyed her love and departed, the husband returns, his heart filled with violent longing for his wife. As when a man with joy has escaped severe sickness or evil captivity, so joyfully and gladly did Amphitryon then return from the hard toil of war to his house. All the rest of the night he lay in the arms of his dear wife, rejoicing in the gifts of the gold-adorned Aphrodite." Alcmene becomes pregnant and bears twin boys, of which Heracles is the son of Zeus and Iphitus of Amphitryon.

Hesiod's *Melampodia*, 3, is interesting: " They say that Teiresias was once looking on two snakes in Arcadia while they were copulating. He wounded one of them, after which he became a woman, and from that time also had intercourse with men. But Apollo told him that when he again watched the snakes and wounded one of them, he would become a man again. This also happened. Now Zeus and Hera were once disputing which felt the greatest enjoyment in embracing, the man or the woman. Since Teiresias had experienced both, they asked his opinion, and received the answer: The man only enjoys one-tenth of the pleasure when sleeping with a woman, the woman only ten-tenths." (This is the explanation of the old Scholiasts on Lycophron, 683; according to others, the wife's share of enjoyment is nine-tenths, the husband's one-tenth (v. Kinkel).) "Hera was offended at this answer and made Teiresias blind, but Zeus by way of compensation bestowed upon him the gift of prophecy and long life."

2. LYRIC POETRY

We cannot glean much more from the lyric poetry of the Greeks than from their epic compositions just discussed. Certainly it is for the greatest part of an erotic nature, but—and this is one of the most essential differences between Greek and modern lyric poetry—the subject of its erotic is nearly always boys and youths; it is these who are sung of by Greek lyric poets. Hence we shall have to occupy ourselves later with Greek lyric poetry when we come to discuss pæderasty, and must confine ourselves here to some information about the love of the man for the woman.

The first Greek lyric poet who sings of the love between man and woman is Mimnermus of Colophon (late seventh cent. B.C.). Somewhat effeminate and sentimental, and always in love, he praises the joys of living and its sensual pleasures, and complains of the rapid fading away of youth and of happiness in love. His love and poetry had for its theme Nanno, a beautiful flute-player. The first really great lyricist of the Greeks is Archilochus of Paros (about 650 B.C.), a passionate, restless personality, for whom poetry means a confession of the overflow of his feelings. He was in love with Neobule, the daughter of the wealthy Lycambes: "A hot flame of love streams from his poems. Passion clasps his heart, tears from his breast the tender soul; it grows dark before his eyes, and he feels the torments of love to the depths of his heart. Yet Neobule listened to his stormy wooing. A lucky fate has preserved for us a picture of the fiercely loved girl: She wore a sprig of myrtle and smiled, fresh bloom of the rose mingled with her hair which fell in waves over her shoulders and down her back; hair and bosom sent forth perfume, so that even an old man could fall in love with her. But when her father, Lycambes, forbids the betrothal, the poet loses all moderation: he abuses not only the father for breaking his word, but dishonours his own love, by questioning the honour and chastity of his former betrothed. Later centuries have spoken with a shudder of the revenge of the poet Archilochus. He certainly knew himself best, when he compares himself to a hedgehog, which rolls itself together and turns its prickles against the enemy" (K. Heinemann, *Die Klassische Dichtung der Griechen* (1912); see also Bergk, *Poetæ Lyrici Græci*, I, p. 2 ff.).

Chronologically, Simonides of Amorgos (about 625 B.C.) should be the next to be mentioned, and his clever satirical poem on women already spoken of. Also Hipponax of Ephesus (about 540 B.C.) must be mentioned here, if only for the sake of the two very spiteful verses, preserved to us by Stobæus (*Florilegium*, 68, 8; cf. *Apostol.*, iv, 38*c*; Haupt in *Hermes*, iv, 159: "There are only two days on which a woman can refresh thee; on the day of marriage and when she is buried."

From Cercidas (Ath., xii, 554*d*) of Megalopolis,

who wrote lyrical satirical poems called *Meliambi*, in the time of king Philip, only the following verse interests us : " There once lived in Syracuse a pair of girls with fat buttocks "—a convincing proof of what the Greeks first and foremost thought of in their love for the female sex.

Alcæus of Mitylene, one of the greatest and most versatile of the Greek lyric poets, wrote a large number of love-songs, of which, however, only miserable fragments are preserved, like most of Greek lyric poetry. Sappho, " the sweetly smiling, with violet curly locks " was glorified by him in his poems, but he found no hearing from the beautiful poetess, whose heart would have nothing to do with a man's love.

Anacreon of Teos, who even in ripe old age would not give up wine or women, was a perfect harbinger of love and the more cheerful enjoyment of life. The remains of his poetry that have come down to us are quite scanty, for what was formerly admired as the poetry of Anacreon (the so-called *Anacreontea*) has proved to be a trifling imitation belonging to very different periods. What here meets us as love is certainly pretty, delicate, and agreeable to read, but it can make no claim to be considered genuine poetry.

But the purest gold of poetry meets us in the poems of Sappho, who undoubtedly must be reckoned among the greatest poetical geniuses of all time. In her verses speaks only the heart, loving and eager for love, and the figures and ideas which she evoked with the refined and never-failing feeling of genuine emotion remained for centuries the model, often imitated but rarely again attained, of the erotic poets. However, Sappho cannot here be discussed in detail, since it is homosexuality which fills up the life and poetry of the Lesbian prodigy ; hence we return to her later, and content here ourselves with pointing out that again the homosexual love of the Greeks does not indicate a decline but an advance of their civilization, in that it created for them intellectual values which last beyond all ages and ever provoke us anew to amazing astonishment.

Terpander had composed songs for girls' choruses, which were afterwards brought to the greatest degree of excellence by the greater Alcman or Alcmæon (about 650 B.C.). He deserves the credit of having promoted the musical development of the Spartan maidens. The relations between the poet and his singers, to whom he offers occasional homage in his poems, appear to have been personal and intimate, as might easily have been the case, considering the freer mode of life of Spartan maidens.

Equally as scanty as the fragments of the poems of Alcman are those of the Sicilian, Stesichorus, who flourished about 600 B.C. According to Plato (*Phædrus*, 243*a*; cf. Bergk, *PLG.*, III[4], p. 218) he had written an abusive poem on Helen's adultery, in consequence of which he was punished by the enraged heroine with the loss of his eyesight, which he did not recover until he wrote the famous "palinode", according to which it was not Helen herself, but an image created by Zeus that followed the seducer Paris to Troy and thereby became the cause of the Trojan war, so rich in sorrow; while the true Helen was carried away to Egypt. It is obvious that the story of the blinding of the poet and his healing by Helen cannot have been the true reason of the "palinode", which is indisputably attested. If, therefore, it cannot be believed that the poet thought himself obliged to explain an accidental and temporary affection of the eyes as an act of revenge on the part of the heroine, which is more than improbable, it must be assumed that the pressure of public opinion, for Helen was a cult-goddess in Dorian belief, compelled Stesichorus to recall his abuse of her, however strongly it might have been founded on tradition. If this explanation is correct—and every probability is in its favour—then we should have to see in the "palinode" of Stesichorus the first landmark on the way towards effeminacy, which certainly, advancing slowly but in a victoriously progressive manner through the centuries, finally led to the condition of modern feminism.

Stesichorus had also in a touching and affecting manner employed the motive of unhappy love, in the poem in which he told of the love of the beautiful Calyce, who committed suicide because she had been disdained by her lover, Euathlus. Athenæus (xiii, 601*a*) expressly attests that in the poems of Stesichorus the erotic impulse played a great part, and even among the fragments of his poems we find several erotic themes. Thus, he introduced into poetry the figure of the shepherd Daphnis that later became so popular; he was loved by a nymph but found a regrettable end owing to his infidelity. Stesichorus had also celebrated the cruel fate of Rhadina, who, although she was married to the ruler of Corinth, yet refused to leave her beloved Leontichus.

Erotic motives are also common in the poems of Simonides (556–468) and his nephew Bacchylides —and naturally so, since in both of them the myth, whose richness in erotic we earlier discussed in detail, plays a great part. But these motives are so interwoven with the poems, are so much an integral part of them, that an analysis of this erotic would mean an analysis of the individual poems. The same is also true of the poems of Pindar (about 518–442) that are preserved to us. He is the most powerful and the loftiest of all the Greek lyric poets, and we are so fortunate as to possess no fewer than forty-four of his *Epinikia* These are songs of very different compass, which were composed to celebrate victories at the four great national festivals; they were recited by a chorus, partly on the spot at the meal in honour of the victory, but mostly at home at the solemn entry into the victor's native town. The main substance of the song of victory is nearly always a myth told, by Pindar with masterly art, which has some special relation to the victor or his family. An imposing number of erotic motives could be elicited from these myths, if there were room in this book for a detailed analysis of them.

3. PROSE

Prose works of the classical period of literature also offer erotic rewards of various kinds to those who seek for them.

Pherecydes of Syros, whom the Greeks regarded as their oldest prose writer, had already written erotic stories, as is proved by the fragment only found a quarter of a century ago on an Egyptian papyrus, in which the "sacred wedding" of Zeus is pleasantly described (first ed. Grenfell-Hunt, *Greek Papyri*, series II, 1897 (No. 11)). In the historical work of Herodotus are also to be found some erotic tales, as that of the incest of Mycerinus and his daughter or the story of the wife of Intaphernes or the beautiful story of Hippocleides (already told by us, p. 164), who had "danced away his bride", and several others of which I have treated in a special essay.[1] The oldest example of a love-story in Greek, related in detail and with self-conscious art, is the touching history of Stryangæus, king of the Medes, and Zarinæa, queen of the Sacæ, written by the physician and historian Ctesias (Ctesias, 25–28; cf. Nic. Damasc. in *FHG.*, III, 364), who had lived seventeen years in Persia. Timæus (in Parthenius, 29, and frag. 23) told of the love-adventures of the beautiful Daphnis. He was also the first who mentioned the unhappy love of Dido for Æneas.

[1] "Sexuelles aus dem Geschichtswerke des Herodot." in *Jahrbuch für sexuelle Zwischenstufen*, Jahrgang, xxii (Leipzig, 1922), p. 65 ff. For Mycerinus see Herodot., ii, 131; for Intaphernes, iii, 118.

Phylarchus (in Parthenius, 15 and 31) introduced the subject of the beautiful but coy Daphne, who was loved by Apollo, but, praying to escape the violence of the god, was changed into a laurel. He had also told of Dimœtes, who found by the sea the washed-up corpse of a very beautiful woman and for a long time had sexual intercourse with her. When that was no longer possible, he buried the corpse and committed suicide.

Love stories are found in great numbers in the collections of local stories that sprang up almost everywhere, especially in the Ionic towns of Asia Minor. The local stories of the luxurious city of Miletus especially were so rich in erotic themes that Aristeides, the Greek Boccaccio, who lived about the beginning of the first century B.C., called his collection of erotic stories in at least six books, mostly of an indecent character, *Milesian Tales*. The great popularity enjoyed by these children of a lascivious muse is clear from the fact that they were translated into Latin by Cornelius Sisenna (fragments in Bücheler's *Petronius* (ed. 3, p. 237)), and also from a notice in Plutarch, according to which a copy of the work was found in the baggage of one of Crassus's officers in the Parthian war (53 B.C.) (Plutarch, *Crassus*, 32). These tales have not been preserved, but we can imagine them to be of a kind resembling those in the *Metamorphoses* of Apuleius. The story already told by us (p. 43) of the bride-bath in the Scamander may have been a *Milesian Tale*.

If we may consider the famous story of the Matron of Ephesus to be a *Milesian Tale*, then one of their ever recurring themes was to prove that no woman was so modest that she could not be sometimes madly inflamed with adulterous love for a paramour, as Eumolpus says in Petronius, who relates the story in the following form (Petronius, 111): "A certain lady at Ephesus was so famous for her chastity, that all the women from the neighbouring countries journeyed to see her because of the rarity of her disposition. When then the wedded husband of this lady died and was removed from the world, she was not contented with accompanying the corpse with dishevelled hair after the usual custom, and beating her bare breast before all the people, but she followed him even to his grave.

"The dead man was brought in the Greek fashion into a vault, where she began to keep watch over his dead body and to weep day and night. Her grief was so violent that she wanted to starve herself to death; neither kinsfolk nor friends could dissuade her.

"At last all the magistrates were sent to her, but were obliged to retire with a refusal. She had already passed five days without food, and everybody was touched by the virtue of the extraordinary woman, wept with her, and was deeply grieved on her account.

"This inconsolable lady was accompanied by a girl who was unusually attached to her, and wept, shedding tears with her as if the last man on earth had died; and if the lamp in the tomb seemed likely to go out, she refilled it with fresh oil. Nothing else was talked about in the city. Great and small, young and old with one accord confessed that the only true example of the purest chastity and love had appeared amongst them.

"Meanwhile, the commander of the province had crucified some rascals not far from the vault where the lady lamented her dead husband. The next night a soldier, who kept watch by the cross, so that no one might steal and bury any of the dead criminals, observed a bright light beneath the monuments and heard a mournful whimpering from that direction. After a mistake common to the whole human race his heart leaped up in his body in his anxiety to know what it was and what was going on there.

"Accordingly he crept up and entered the vault,

and when he beheld a charming woman, he stood still with astonishment, believing that it was a ghost and a delusion caused by evil spirits. But soon afterwards, when he was aware of the corpse beside her, and saw her tears, and her divine face scratched by her nails, he hit upon the truth and took her for a lady who was inconsolable for the loss of her husband. He pulled out a little food from his knapsack, offered it to her in a friendly manner with the addition of all the consolation he could think of, and entreated her with the greatest emotion not to persist in her useless grief or wear out her beautiful breast with unprofitable sighs. 'We must all die! That cannot be altered!' said he, 'we must at one time go into the same little house,' and did everything else to heal these sores in her heart. But her anguish increased still more at his words of consolation, she got angry, beat her bosom in a rage, tore her hair from her head and strewed it over her beloved husband.

"But the soldier was not a man to allow himself to be so easily discouraged; he continued his consolatory arguments and did all he could to persuade the lady to take some food. Her companion was at first overcome, the smell of the wine, like nectar, had excited her desires; she shyly reached out her hand to the friendly man, refreshed herself with food and drink, and began herself to attack her lady's obstinacy.

"'What good will it do you?' she said, 'if hunger now should consume you—if you bury yourself alive—if you drive your pure spirit away before destiny calls it from you? O dear lady, your departed husband knows nothing of your sorrow, your torments do not affect him! Can you restore him to life in spite of the unalterable will of destiny, should you not rather put aside your womanish prejudices and enjoy the joys of life so long as it is permitted you? Look, even this corpse should teach you how fugitive life is!'

"No one feels offended if urged to take food and live; and even this lady, hungry after fasting several days, at last allowed herself to be dissuaded from her obstinate resolve, and refreshed herself as greedily as the other with the food, the sight of which had previously overcome the girl.

"Well, you know what it is that a man wants, when he has eaten and drunk his fill! With similar flatteries to those with which the soldier had persuaded the lady no longer to want to die, he now attacked her modesty. The youth did not appear to her ugly and ill-bred, and the girl loyally supported him, for, indeed, the life that he had reawakened in her pleased her very well, and she cried to her virtuous lady: 'Will you ever obstinately withstand yourself? You love, and does your love flatter you? O do not pile sorrow on sorrow! He who *has* consoled you, madam, lies here!

"Why need I keep you longer? You know perhaps, how rapid is the passage from sadness to love? The lady no longer abstained from food and the conquering soldier soon persuaded her to give up the other kind of fasting also.

"So they not only passed this night together, enjoying in it all the delights of marriage, but also the next and the following day. Of course they shut the doors of the vault, so that any acquaintance or stranger who came to the monument might think that the most chaste woman on earth had given up the ghost on her husband's body; also, of course, the soldier was delighted, both with the lady's beauty and with his stolen pleasure, and he bought the best he could afford, and carried it at nightfall into the vault.

"When the relatives of the crucified men observed that there was no longer any guard present they got down into the vault at night and performed the last obsequies, while the soldier was sleeping on the bosom of his beloved and without being seen by him. At daybreak he noticed that one of the crucified thieves was missing. Terrified at the thought of being put to death, he told the lady he had consoled so well what had happened and declared that rather than undergo court-martial he would kill himself; one favour only he asked of her—to bury him on the spot, and let the same tomb embrace both her husband and her lover.

" The lady was as compassionate as she was chaste, and exclaimed : ' Ah ! the gods will not allow me to see at the same time the two mortals whom I loved most tenderly in one and the same grave. No! 'tis better that I should turn the dead to use than kill the living,' and having so said she ordered her husband's body to be taken from the coffin and hung upon the cross from which that of the thief had been stolen. The soldier availed himself of the artful woman's guile, and on the following day everyone was wondering what the dead man could have done that he should be crucified and could not understand it ! "

Among the writings of the Athenian Xenophon (about 430–354) is one devoted almost entirely to the erotic problem, the charmingly graceful *Symposium*. The meal was given by the wealthy Athenian Callias in honour of a beautiful favourite Autolycus, who had been victorious in the pancratium at the Panathenæa in 422. In contrast to the Platonic *Symposium*, jesters, female dancers and lute-players take part in it, and also a beautiful boy who treats the guests to his gymnastic and musical tricks. After all kinds of orations of a serious and cheerful character, Socrates delivers a speech on love, the pith of which is that one must allow oneself to be fascinated by the intellectual talents of a boy rather than by his bodily charms. The proceedings conclude with a mythological ballet, representing a love-scene between Dionysus and Ariadne, which makes such an impression upon the guests, that " the unmarried swear to take a wife as soon as possible, and the married to mount their horses and get home to their wives as soon as they can ".

The *Anabasis* also, in which Xenophon describes the ill-fated campaign of the younger Cyrus against his brother Artaxerxes and the painful and dangerous retreat of the Greek mercenary army, should be mentioned here, since at least occasionally erotic questions are touched upon: e.g., the love of a man still beardless for a bearded one, the rape of boys and girls, the touching story of Episthenes, the beautiful boy, and their courageous sacrifice, whereby the boy is saved from death (*Anabasis*, ii, 6, 28; iv, 1, 14; iv, 6, 3; vii, 4, 7–10). The *Œconomicus*, the treatise on the best way to manage a household, has been already mentioned (p. 38) and the charming description of the family life of the recently wedded Ischomachus quoted. In the *Hieron* also, a dialogue between Simonides and the Sicilian king Hieron, erotic questions are touched upon, to which we shall return later. Lastly, the *Cyropædeia* (the education of Cyrus), a pedagogic, political romance with a purpose, must be mentioned for the sake of the erotic stories that are introduced, the most enchanting of which is the story of Pantheia and her touching love and faithfulness.

That the works of Greek eloquence, consequently of the orators in the widest extent of the word, furnish contributions to the history of ancient erotic, might at first sight appear very surprising. And yet the fact is that not only are the orators fond of quoting examples and parallels from legend and history to emphasize their views and assertions, but also that many speeches treat legal cases of pronounced sexual character in a natural manner, the most important of which will be briefly discussed here. Thus, we have a speech of Antiphon, which an illegitimate son makes use of to accuse his stepmother of having administered a love-potion to her husband. It is interesting to see the way in which the orator Andocides succeeded in reversing the political verdict that had been given against him; he knew his fellow-citizens' unruly need for beauty, and accordingly, as Plutarch (*Moralia*, 835*b*, confirmed by the inscription *CIA*., 553, 21) relates, he equipped, from his ample means acquired abroad by lucky business transactions, a choir of boys in a most splendid manner, and so took all hearts by storm.

We must next mention the " erotic letter " of the orator Lysias, which Plato has inserted in his dialogue *Phædrus*, with the paradoxical subject that the reward of love should be given to one who does not love rather than to one who does. Other erotic letters of Lysias have also in part come down to us, and it seems as though he were the first to introduce this class of letter that later became so popular. The most famous of his speeches were those *Against Eratosthenes* and the speech in defence of a married man who, being outwitted most cunningly by the rascally Eratosthenes, had expiated the injury done to his honour as a husband by the murder of the adulterer.

That philosophy also grappled with the problem of love to a continuously greater extent and sought to probe the mystery of its nature, is both probable in itself and confirmed by philosophical written works. For love, as Plutarch once says, is " a riddle hard to understand and hard to solve " (in Stobæus, *Florilegium*, 64, 31; αἴνιγμα δυσεύρετον καὶ δύσλυτον), although no doubt philosophical speculation, corresponding to the Greek attitude, busied itself with the male Eros rather than with the female Aphrodite.

Of the writings of Plato, so far as they are occupied with erotic problems, the dialogues, *Charmides*, *Lysis*, *Symposion*, and *Phædrus* will be discussed later, as they are either entirely or at least in great part devoted to the homosexual question.

As time went on interest in the problem of

marriage increased; already the great Aristotle,[1] and then his pupil Theophrastus, had written books on marriage, and the latter especially had not said much that was favourable to marriage. His pupil and friend Demetrius of Phalerum, the well-known Peripatetic philosopher, who was also important as a statesman and was regent of Athens for ten years (317–307) had written an *Eroticus*, which has not come down to us. Nor has the work by Phanias of Lesbos on the tyrants, who were slain from motives of revenge, been preserved. The book abounded in erotic material of the character of a novel, as indeed many tyrants met their death owing to reasons of jealousy. Clearchus of Soli in Cyprus is also known to have written an *Eroticus* (more correctly *Erotica*). In this book, several fragments of which still exist, Clearchus had attempted to get to the bottom of the nature of love by mythological and historical examples. Therein was to be read the love of Pericles for Aspasia and the strong erotic longings of this most famous of all Greek statesmen; a doubtful love adventure of Epaminondas; the passionate affection of the Lydian king Gyges for his beloved wife, and the massive memorial which he caused to be erected to her after her death. Nor were singular anecdotes wanting: e.g., a goose had fallen deeply in love with a boy, and a peacock became so fond of a girl that it did not survive her death. But Clearchus had also spoken of the customs usual in wooing and their reasons; why lovers carry flowers and apples in their hands or crown the loved one's door with flowers. Anyone who likes may read these endless reflections in Athenæus, who quotes many passages from them (fragments in Müller, *FHG*. (Demetrius, ii, 362; *Phanias*, ii, 293; *Clearchus*, ii, 302); Ath., xv, 669 f.). Hieronymus of Rhodes, like many other writers

[1] The remains of Aristotle's Ἐρωτικός are collected by Val. Rose in *Aristotlelis quæ ferebantur librorum Fragmenta* (Leipzig, 1886), but they are only the well-known passages quoted by Ath., xv, 674*b*; xiii, 564*b*; Plutarch, *Pelop.*, 18; *Amatorius*, 17.

of this period, found pleasure in recounting all kinds of erotic anecdotes in his *Historical Memoirs*, of which several have been preserved by Athenæus relating to Socrates, Sophocles, and Euripides (Ath., xiii, 556*a*, 557*e*, 604*d*).

II. *The Hellenistic Period*

1. Poetry: (a) *Epic and Lyric Poems*

In the post-classical period of Greek literature, which is comprised under the name of the Hellenistic Age and is generally taken to begin with the death of Alexander the Great (323 B.C.), erotic plays a great, nay, almost a greater part than in the so-called classical period. It is a characteristic feature that the more foreign elements penetrate into the Greek spirit the more pæderasty retires into the background ; the female element begins to occupy more space when, especially in the large cities, the intercourse of young men with the hetairæ increased.

Many poems of this age have been lost and we are referred to their Roman imitations by Catullus, Tibullus, Propertius, and Ovid, from which we are enabled to draw an *a posteriori* conclusion as to the strongly marked sensuality of those poems. Thus Philetas of Cos, besides erotic elegies, had written an epic *Hermes*, the subject of which is the love-adventures of Odysseus with Polymela, the daughter of Æolus. His friend was Hermesianax of Colophon, who wrote three books of elegies, dedicated to his mistress Leontion, which contained stories of the almighty power of love. From this Athenæus (xiii, 597*b*) has preserved a long fragment of 98 lines, in which the poets, who up to his time had celebrated favourite women and girls in their poems, are enumerated with charming grace. In it he certainly permitted himself considerable freedom, as when he makes Anacreon the lover of Sappho, which indeed is excluded by chronological reasons. We are also fairly well informed by numerous quotations as to many other love stories treated of in his elegies. Thus he told how the wealthy but undistinguished Arceophon violently loved Arsinoë, the daughter of the king of Cyprus (Antonin. Liberalis, *Metamorph.*, 39). His wooing, however, was in vain and, in spite of his costly wedding presents, the father rejected him so he bribed the nurse to be his messenger of love. She was betrayed by the haughty Arsinoë to her parents, and they cruelly mutilated her and drove her from the house. Arceophon now killed himself from grief; and when the young man, beloved by all, was carried to his grave Arsinoë scornfully looked out of the window at the funeral procession, whereupon Aphrodite, who was angry at such hardheartedness, changed the haughty one into stone. This story gradually became a favourite theme of Hellenistic erotic and was afterwards told by different poets in ever new variations, so that it still lived in Cyprus in Plutarch's time (Plutarch, *Amatorius*; *Moralia*, 766*c*)

The most important poet of this period is Callimachus of Cyrene (about 310–240). Here we have no occasion to enter into detail about him, as he does not come into question as an erotic writer; at most a serenade to a girl he loved, named Conopion, might be mentioned and a few epigrams of erotic content, of which no fewer than twelve are devoted to the love of beautiful boys. In his *Hymn to Apollo* the poet has described the love of the god for the beautiful Cyrene with special satisfaction.

Apollonius Rhodius (about 295–215) is the author of the still extant epic *Argonautica*, which describes in four books the journey of the Argonauts to Colchis, their adventures there, and their return. This important and, save for running off the track in individual instances, very enjoyable work, of no fewer than 5,835 lines, contains not a few erotic episodes, executed with sensual fire and vigour. Love is the essential part of the whole epic; the representation reaches its culminating point in the third book, in which the poet, after invoking Erato, the muse of the poetry of love, describes the conquering of the king's daughter Medea by the darts of Eros that never miss their aim, with wonderful portrayal of her mental conflicts, consequently with strong accentuation of the psychological moment.

Of the numerous poems of Euphorion of Calchis (fragments collected by A. Meineke in *Anal. Alex.*, pp. 1–168) at least the epics were rich in erotic themes. He himself was not so particular in his love; in his youth he is said to have been the favourite of the poet Archebulus of Thera, for which he was ridiculed in a very biting epigram of Crates untranslatable because of the play on words.[1] Later, he lowered himself to become the lover of a voluptuous but rich old widow named Nicæa, whereby he obtained great riches and at the same time gave occasion to the proverb preserved in Plutarch's works (*Moralia*, 472*d*)—"to sleep with a rich old woman like Euphorion". Perhaps the anecdote, elsewhere only handed down in Suïdas, that the poet Hesiod was killed in mistake for the actual offender by the two brothers of a girl to whom violence had been offered (F. Nietsche in Rhein. Mus., xxviii, 1873), proceeds from him. Other poems of Euphorion, such as the *Thracians* and *Hyacinthus*, chiefly consisted of erotic stories. Thus in the *Thracians* among other things the love of Harpalyce for her father Clymenus was treated of; love between father and daughter also occurred in *Apollodorus*. Lastly, a number of erotic epigrams were written by Euphorion.

[1] Crates, in *Anth. Pal.*, xi, 218: *Χοίριλος 'Αντιμάχου πολὺ λείπεται. αλλ' ἐπὶ πᾶσιν Χοίριλον Εὐφορίων εἶχι διὰ στόματος, Καὶ, κατάγλωσσ' ἐπόει τὰ ποιήματα, καὶ τὰ Φιλητα 'Ατρεκέως ᾔδει· καὶ γὰρ 'Ομηρικὸς ἦν.*

(b) *The Poems of the Anthology*

The epigram, which in the classical period had been brought by Simonides in particular to a high state of perfection, had in course of time been removed more and more from its original use, that is to say, as an inscription, especially on a sepulchral monument. Gradually, and more particularly after the time of Alexander the Great, it was increasingly regarded as belonging to an independent class of poetry, the most popular form for poetical exchange of thoughts of the most varied kind. Seriousness and jest, joy and grief, friendship and love, the joys of the table and carousals, in short, whatever might show the mood of the moment, found eloquent expression in the epigram. Among the innumerable writers whose epigrams have been preserved, many a good-sounding name is found, and, although the wheat is not free from chaff, yet here also we are astonished at the infinite variety of forms in which Greek life meets us.

In the fourteenth century a monk named Planudes prepared another anthology in seven books, which certainly reproduces very many epigrams from the Palatine, but on the other hand not only frequently offers better readings, but also contains nearly 400 poems which are lacking in it. A supplement of erotic epigrams, omitted by Planudes, has been edited by L. Sternbach (Leipzig, 1890) under the title *Anthologiæ Planudeæ Appendix Berberino-Vaticana*.

The Palatine Anthology is divided into fifteen books, of which it is book V with which we are now chiefly concerned, since it contains only erotic epigrams. Sensuality certainly takes a back seat in the general collection, for fervid passion yields to the seriousness of death and makes room for recollection that survives the grave; but the sensual side of love stands out again in book XI, consisting of

442 epigrams which for the most part owe their origin to the cheerful, often jesting merry mood of one in his cups. Book XII contains pæderastic poems and will therefore be considered later.

In the following brief summary I shall abandon the arrangement in the Palatine MS. and place the epigrams that belong to each individual poet together, and, as far as possible, deal with them in chronological order.

Asclepiades of Samos, a contemporary of the previously mentioned Philetas, has left behind him some forty epigrams, most of which are of an erotic character. In one he admonishes the beloved maiden not to guard her virginity too prudishly, since she will find no lover in Hades—only here in this life can one be happy. We hear of three hetairæ, regular port-harlots, who strip their clients, seafaring men, down to their very shirts, and who in the poet's opinion are more dangerous than the sirens. In another poem we read: "Sweet in summer is a drink cooled with snow, sweet to sailors in need during a storm is a friendly star flashing in the sky, but sweeter it is to play the game of love under cover with one's girl."

Nicharchus makes fun of the fact that no one finds pleasure in embracing his own wife, but that only a strange bed enchants him.

Poseidippus of Alexandria in his epigrams has a leaning towards descriptions of merry carousals and adventures with hetairæ. The same is true of Hedylus (the Anth. Pal. poems mentioned above are: Asclepiades, v, 85, 161, 169; Nicharchus xi, 7; Hedylus, xi, 414; and Dioscorides, v, 52–6), from whom we have the pretty epigram: "From Bacchus, the limb-relaxing, from Aphrodite, the limb-relaxing, is born a daughter—Gout, the limb-relaxing."

Dioscorides, who will later meet us as a glowing enthusiast for the love of ephebi, has also left behind a number of strongly sensual epigrams on the love of a man for a woman:

They drive me mad, her rosy lips, The vermeil gate of song,
Wherefrom my soul its nectar sips, And her soft whispering tongue,
Her eyes a liquid radiance dart Beneath their lashes close,
Traps to ensnare my fluttering heart, And rob me of repose.
Her breasts, twin sisters firmly grown, A milky fountain pour,
Two hills that love their master own, More fair than any flower.

Anth. Pal., v, 56

A good-sounding name is Antipater of Sidon, or Tyre, whose epigrams are distinguished by a swing and flowery language; yet unfortunately only too few of his erotic poems, and those fairly unimportant, have come down to us.

Of far greater importance is Meleager of Gadara in Syria, who, as already mentioned, prepared the oldest collection of epigrams known to us. Of his own epigrams we possess still some 130, of which at least sixty are devoted to homosexual love. They are distinguished by liquid and graceful language, but also by sentimentalism: their theme is essentially love. Of the many young women to whom the gallant poet renders homage in ever new phrases it is especially Zenophila and Heliodora that fill his heart; in two elegant epigrams he gives us—like Leporello, in Mozart's *Don Juan*—an imposing list of his numerous sweethearts.

Among others he loved the white-cheeked Demo, but she appears to have preferred a Jew to him, or as the poet himself expresses it "the Jewish love".

Timarion, once so beautiful, is compared now that she has grown old, to an unrigged ship, and the biting comparison is carried through with obscenity into the most intimate details. The poet finds pretty words of love for the beautiful Phanion. Above all, he never tires of praising the charms of Zenophila and Heliodora. He praises their skill in music and clever conversation, their beauty outshines all the flowers in the meadow; he begs the flies to spare his sleeping love; but in vain, since even these unintelligent creatures rejoice in her voluptuous limbs. Another time he sends a fly as a messenger of love to her, or envies the goblet from which she sipped; he wishes he might be allowed to approach her as a dream-god, or he praises her charms—which she has received from Venus and the Graces themselves. His passion for Theodora went perhaps still deeper, and after her death he still retained loving memories of her, as is witnessed by the tender and heart-felt epitaph that he composed in her honour. The crown on her head, he says another time, fades, but she shines as the crown of crowns. He succeeds in one epigram with a pretty picture of how Heliodora plays with his heart, and in another with a touching prayer to Eros to still the fiery passion of his love.

The poet has yet other tones for his lyre. In an enchanting poem he sends a warrant of arrest after Eros as if he were a runaway slave; but Eros has not run away at all, he has but concealed himself in Zenophila's eyes. Or the poet complains of the irresistible power of this boy and the intolerable fire that he kindles, which appears the more wonderful, since his mother was Aphrodite, born from the cool waves. Therefore the useless, saucy fellow is to be sold; but as he looks at the poet so touchingly with tears in his eyes, he again takes pity on him; very well, then he may remain as Zenophila's playfellow (Meleager: Anth. Pal., v, 142, 213, 214, 176, 175, 177, 196, 197, 159 (cf. 171, 172), 203; xii, 53, 82, 83, 138, 139, 143, 150, 151, 170, 173, 194, 195; vii, 476).

The poet Archias, who is known to us through Cicero, complains that it is impossible to escape from love; but that that is quite natural, since Love has wings and so can always overtake a man.

"One should fly from Love, you tell me; but that is useless effort, for how can I escape on foot from one with wings who so closely pursues me?"—(Anth. Pal., v, 59.)

One of the most distinguished erotic poets of the Anthology is Philodemus of Gadara, a well-known Epicurean of Cicero's time, who describes him as a well-educated, amiable, and learned man. Of his extensive literary labours we are only interested here in the collection of epigrams edited by him and dedicated to Piso, in which he has set down in poetical fashion his own and Piso's ample experience in the department of love and drinking. If we may believe Cicero, he had in these " highly elegant verses described passions of every kind, every imaginable lewdness, revelry, drunken bouts, and finally his adulteries, so that one sees his life reflected in these things as in a mirror " (Cicero, *Piso*, 29, 70). Cicero adds that these verses enjoyed great popularity, and in Horace's notorious satire (*Satires*, i, 2, 120 ff.) on sexual excesses we find a quotation from Philodemus literally translated. This is the passage in which Horace states that one should not have intercourse with married women, since they always made excuses. At one time they said " Not now, later ", or again " Yes, if you pay more ", or " wait till my husband is away ". That might do for eunuchs, who had plenty of time to spare; he agreed with Philodemus, and prefers women who did not raise difficulties and were to be had cheaply.

In the interest of inquiry into the history of civilization it is to be regretted that these epigrams of Philodemus (Anth. Pal., v, 3, 12, 45, 114, 119, 122, 123, 305, 307, 309) have not come down to us complete. However, in the Anthologia Palatina at least twenty-four are preserved from the collection of Philippus, to which we cannot deny the credit of wit, grace, and elegance partly combined with great lasciviousness. He would have the lamp removed from the bedroom and the door shut; the bed alone should know what Venus offers in sweet secrecy. The hetaira Charito is already sixty years old, but the entanglement of her dark locks still charms, the marble-white globes of her breast are covered by no jealous bosom-band, innumerable delights still trickle from her as yet unwrinkled body—in short, he who longs for voluptuous love may still find here the very things for which he craves. The poem which describes the bargaining of a young man with one of those girls who are always ready to oblige for money is pretty, since it is dramatically enlivened. It is a play of question and answer, as the superscription in the MS. runs :

Good evening, miss. Good evening, sir, to you,
And what's your name ? What's yours, I'd like to know.
You're rather curious, miss. You're curious, too.
Are you engaged ? To anyone I please.
Then sup with me : how much ? No advance fees,
To-morrow you shall pay me at your ease.
Fair terms, my charmer ; now when will you come ?
Just when you please. At once ? Well, you are *some* ;
I'll tell you where I live, and you shall take me home.

Together with idle jests—e.g., that his name " Philodemus " accounts for his being obliged to love many girls called Demo—we find such an effective and lifelike picture as the words of the deceived lady-love : " At midnight I left my husband's bed and came secretly to thee, drenched with rain. That is why we sit doing nothing, nor do we sleep tired out, as lovers ought to sleep."

Another time in beautiful words he calls upon Selene, the moon-goddess, to shed her mild light upon him in the work of love ; she also has been once in love with Endymion, and hence knows what love is. A tender maiden, still almost a child, has a presentiment of the violent flame, which she will soon fan into a blaze ; already Eros is sharpening his unerring arrows on the whetstone.

His lady-love's petty jealousies and amorous whims give him occasion to complain : " You weep, utter miserable words, look round curiously, are jealous, often touch me, often kiss me. This is the behaviour of a lover ; but when I say ' I am going to bed ', and you dally, there is nothing of the lover at all about you."

The following epigram might well be entitled "Missed fire". "Wait, charming girl. What is your beautiful name? Where can I see you? I will give you whatever you want. You don't even say a word. Where do you live? I will send someone to fetch you. Are you engaged to anyone? Farewell, proud woman. You won't even say farewell? I shall approach you again and again, for I know how to soften even harder women than you. Now, farewell, madam."

As the poet gets older, his language becomes milder; gently complaining, he thinks of youth and its sweet games of love, whose place is now taken by wisdom and prudence; but in a spirit of resignation he consoles himself with the truth—everything in its time.

(c) *Farce, Cinædic Poetry, Mimus, Bucolic Poetry, Mimiambus*

Of the purely lyric productions of this period next to nothing has been preserved. Alexander Ætolus, so called from having been born in Ætolia, about the turning point of the third century B.C., in his elegy entitled *Apollo* had introduced the god of prophecy as foretelling stories of unhappy love. Parthenius has preserved a specimen of it—the story of the adulterous passion of the wife of Phobius for the beautiful Antheus, whom she in vain endeavours to seduce, and then out of revenge throws into the depth of a well.

In lower Italy, especially in voluptuous Tarentum (according to Plato, *Laws*, 637*b*, the whole city was drunk during the Dionysia), a special kind of farce had developed, the *hilaro-tragœdia* or the so-called *phlyax*, and coarse popular farces of this class had also spread throughout Greece. They had been introduced into literature by Rhinthon of Tarentum, to whom thirty-eight were ascribed, most of which appear to have been travesties of pieces by Euripides. Nothing of them has been preserved that is worth mentioning, but from vase paintings with phlyakian stage-scenes or from the Plautine tragi-comedy *Amphitruo* we can get an idea of the coarse, and in parts, highly obscene character of these popular entertainments. According to a note in Athenæus (Ath., xiv, 621 f.) *phlyakes* was also nothing but the lower Italian name for phallus-wearers. According to Aristoxenus (Ath., xiv, 620*d*, where there is more about these farces), the famous musician and biographer, there were two classes of these popular farces, the "hilarodia" or "Simodia," and the "magodia" or "Lysiodia" (the names are explained by the names of their poets—Simos and Lysis; "magodia" may perhaps indicate their magic effect), both accompanied by song and dance, yet with the difference that, in the first kind, the actor played male and female parts to the accompaniment of stringed instruments, while, in the second, kettledrums and cymbals supplied the accompaniment, the female parts being played in men's clothes, and indecent dances an important element (pp. 153–60).

According to Semos (Ath., xiv, 622*b*), the ithyphallic actors wore the *Tarentinidia* already mentioned, by which we are to understand a sort of "tights". These were also, according to Pollux (iv, 104), usually worn by the so-called *Gypones*, that is, dancers on stilts.

What is known as Cinædic poetry was not far behind the phlyakian in grotesque indecency. We shall return to the name and content of this poetical degeneracy in the chapter on homosexual literature, yet it must be mentioned here, since one of its most prominent exponents, Sotades of Maroneia in Crete (Ath., xiv, 621*a*: εἰς οὐχ ὁσίην τρυμαλιὴν τὸ κέντρον ὠθεῖς), used this form when he attempted to tell the entire truth about the great men and princes of his time, especially with reference to their sexual extravagances. Thus he had directed one of his poems against Belestiche, the mistress of King Ptolemy II (285–247 B.C.) to whom the king, according to Plutarch (*Amatorius*, 9; *Moralia*, 753*f*, and 11), had erected a temple as Aphrodite Belestiche. In an obscene verse he ridiculed the king's marriage with his sister Arsinoë, whence his name Philadelphus. The king was most deeply offended, and for a long time caused the poet to languish in prison, from which he finally managed to escape, but his escape was only temporary and he was again captured on the high seas by one of the admirals of the king, who ordered him to be thrown into the sea in a leaden chest.

Cleomachus, a boxer from Magnesia, if we may believe Strabo (xiv, 648*a*), fell in love both with a *cinædus* and with a girl who was kept by him, and was consequently induced to attempt a representation of these characters in dialogue form. The realistic trend of Hellenistic poetry and its preference for the genre pictures of every-day life favoured the development of the *mimus*, already spoken of (p. 154). Of the original mimes by a Sophron and others nothing worth mention has been preserved; of that which has come down to us the already highly conventionalized mimes of Theocritus take the first place. The place of bucolic, that is herdsmen's poesy, in the history of Greek literature and an appreciation of Theocritus do not belong to our task. We have only, as far as it is possible, to do with a brief record of the erotic in the thirty longer poems of Theocritus that we possess, to which may be added forty-four epigrams. For their extensive homosexual content we refer to a later chapter. Hardly one of the Theocritan poems is free from erotic; hence we can only mention what is most important, and must ask the reader to complete what is here said by reading the poems himself. In the first, in amœbæan (i.e. alternate) verse, the unhappy love of Daphnis, the chief hero of bucolic love poetry, his sufferings and premature death, are related by two shepherds. The second is the wonderful song of the lament of the abandoned girl and her attempt to win back her faithless lover by magic arts. In the depth of the night, by the light of the moon, she begins her sorcery, in which neither the magic iynx-wheel (p. 205) is wanting nor a waxen image of her loved one which she has made and melts in the fire, that the faithless one may melt away with heat like hers : " look, now the sea rests, the winds rest and are hushed ; yet my sorrow rests not, my sorrow deep within my bosom, but I am so utterly tortured with longing for him, who instead of a wife has made me a wretched harlot."

Her incantations grow stronger and stronger, and from them we can gain considerable insight into the love superstitions of that time. The mysterious herb *hippomanes* [1] is said to help, a flock of wool is pulled from the faithless one's garment and burnt in the fire, a lizard (for the erotic meaning of the lizard see p. 194) is ground to powder and mixed with a love-potion, which she intends to offer him at the first opportunity.

And now, alone and abandoned, in the depth of night, when everything sleeps and even the barking of the watchful dogs is mute, she recalls to mind the story of her unhappy love, how everything happened from the first glance she had of the wonderful youth in the company of his handsome friend, how then she returned home lovesick, and for ten days and nights lay prostrate in a burning fever. At last she can no longer restrain her yearning, and she sends her confidential friend to him : " And when thou'rt sure he's alone, give

[1] There were different ideas about hippomanes : (1) the herb mentioned here, which grew chiefly in Arcadia ; (2) a fleshy, tough excrescence on the forehead of a new-born foal, which the mother bites off immediately after its birth ; (3) a slime-like mass, which mares on heat drop from their private parts.

him a gentle nod o' the head and say 'Simætha would see him', and so bring him hither. Thus bidden, she went her ways and brought him that was so sleek and gay to my dwelling. And no sooner was I ware of the light fall o's foot across my threshold —*List, good moon, where I learnt my loving*—than I went cold as ice my body over, and the sweat dripped like dewdrops from my brow; aye, and for speaking I could not so much as the whimper of a child that calls on's mother in his sleep; for my fair flesh was gone all stiff and stark like a puppet's. *List, good Moon, where I learnt my loving.* When he beheld me, heartless man! he fixed his gaze on the ground, sat him upon the bed, and sitting thus spake: 'Why, Simætha, when thou bad'st me hither to this thy roof, marry, thou didst no further outrun my own coming than I once outran the pretty young Philinus.' *List, good Moon, where I learnt my loving.* 'For I had come of myself, by sweet Love I had, of myself the very first hour of the night, with comrades twain or more, some of Dionysus' own apples in my pocket, and about my brow the holy aspen sprig of Heracles with gay purple ribbons wound in and out.' *List, good Moon, where I learnt my loving.* 'And, had ye received me so, it had been joy; for I have a name as well for beauty of shape as speed of foot with all the bachelry o' the town, and I had been content so I had only kissed thy pretty lips. But and if ye had sent me packing with bolt and bar, then I warrant ye axes and torches had come against you.' *List, good Moon, where I learnt my loving.* 'But, seeing thou hadst sent for me, I vowed my thanks to the Cyprian first—but after the Cyprian 'tis thou, in calling me to this roof, sweet maid, didst snatch the brand from a burning that was all but done; for i' faith, Cupid's flare oft will outblaze the God o' Lipara himself'—*List, good Moon, where I learnt my loving* —'and with the dire frenzy of him bride is driven from groom ere his marriage-bed be cold, much more a maid from the bower of her virginity.' So he ended, and I, that was so easy to win, took him by the hand and made him to lie along the bed. Soon cheek upon cheek grew ripe, our faces waxed hotter, and lo! sweet whispers went and came. My prating shall not keep thee too long, good Moon; enough that all was done, enough that both desires were sped".

The third poem of Theocritus is a serenade offered by a young goatherd to his Amaryllis, who has become coy. The fourth, a conversation between two shepherds on all kinds of harmless subjects, finishes with coarse witticisms about a lustful old man.

Polpyphemus, known to every reader of the *Odyssey* as a repulsive cannibal, in a musical comedy by Philoxenus—which was popular in the time of Theocritus—becomes highly diverting as a languishing lover. He was enamoured of the beautiful nereid, Galatea, but met not with a favourable hearing, as is easy to understand.

Theocritus has twice occupied himself with the form of the love-sick giant. In the eleventh poem we read of his highly amusing love-complaints and the awkward and clumsy manner in which with all kinds of presents he hopes to make the shy nereid consent to his advances. He finally consoles himself with the thought that there are many other girls, yet much more beautiful, who will invite him "to sport with them during the night".

The Cyclops appears again in this mood in the sixth poem, in which the love-sick coxcomb is thoroughly made a fool of. It is a little drama between the shepherds Daphnis and Damœtas. At first Daphnis sings with him and shows her love plainly enough, but the Cyclops does not seem to notice it at all. Damœtas, in the part of the Cyclops, replies that he purposely pretends not to notice Galatea's wooing, in order to inflame the fire of her passion to the height of madness by his coldness.

The mixture of vanity, credulity, and rudeness in the love-sick fool is extremely comic.

The tenth poem is a dialogue between two reapers. The first confesses that the sorrow of love consumes his heart, and thereupon sings a song in praise of his girl. The second answers this sentimental song with a reaper's song of the good old sort, and laughs at the useless ideas about love which did not suit an industrious working-man.

In the fourteenth poem a young man complains to his friend how scornfully his lady-love treated him at a merry banquet; he has now found out that she is faithless and can think of no way to escape his affliction, except to wander into the wide world and go for a soldier. His friend appears and advises him to enter the army of King Ptolemy.

We have already spoken of the fifteenth poem (p. 119) and of the eighteenth (pp. 53 ff.).

The nineteenth,[1] the authorship of which certainly (and no doubt correctly) philological criticism denies to Theocritus, is an *Oaristys* (Lovers' Talk) between a cowherd named Daphnis, and a girl, who at first is coy, but afterwards shows herself quite ready to please, after Daphnis has solemnly promised to marry her.

It may be observed that the comparison of the breast with a pair of apples was a favourite one among the Greeks.[2] When the girl, half indignant and half pleased, complains that Daphnis has laid hands on her breasts, he says, "To test your heaving apples for the first time," after which the caresses became more and more intimate. The poem, which is not exactly one of the most valuable in Greek bucolic poetry, concludes as follows: "Thus they prattled in the joy of their fresh young limbs. The secret bridal over, she rose and went her ways for to feed her sheep, her look shamefast,

[1] The twenty-seventh, according to Liddell and Scott.

[2] The oldest passage in Greek literature comparing the female breasts with apples is the fragment of Crates in *CAF.*, I, 142.

but her heart glad within her; while as for him, he betook himself to his herds of bulls rejoicing in his wedlock."

Moschus of Syracuse lived in the second century B.C., and in addition to a longer poem *Europa* (165 lines) has left behind several poetic trifles. The subject of the *Europa* is the well-known story of the love of Zeus for Europa, the daughter of the Phœnician King, Agenor, and her abduction by Zeus, who approaches the maiden, while she is gathering flowers with her playmates in a meadow near the sea, in the form of a beautiful bull. It is so gentle and insinuating, that Europa caresses it, and finally seats herself on its back, whereupon the bull runs as fast as he can to the sea, and swims with his beautiful burden to Crete, where Zeus makes himself known in his true form and the solemn nuptials are consummated. The first little poem is very pretty: it is a kind of hue and cry, sent out after her runaway son, the roguish Eros, by Aphrodite, who promises a kiss as a reward to anyone who should bring him back to her.

The list of the Greek bucolic poets finishes with Bion of Phlossa near Smyrna, who lived about the end of the second century B.C. We have already mentioned his lament on the death of Adonis (p. 119); the *Epithalamium* of Achilles and Deidameia, which is certainly wrongly ascribed to him, has unfortunately reached us only as a fragment of 31½ lines. In this is told how the boy Achilles, that he may escape participation in the cruelties of war, is brought in girl's clothes by his anxious mother to King Lycomedes, of the island of Scyros, where for a time he was educated as a girl. Yet the natural instincts of the youth cannot be suppressed; he never leaves Deidameia, tenderly caresses her hand, and relieves her of many of her female tasks. " But his yearning and striving were ever set upon a common bed. So then he said to her: 'My love, the others, your sisters, all sleep together, but I sleep alone, and so also do you, O maiden. And yet we are both girls of the same age, we are both beautiful, and sleep alone in separate beds. The night is cruel, which with malicious spite separates you from me. For without you I cannot live.'" Here the fragment full of sensuality breaks off.

The fact that from other sources we know the further course of the story—that within a short time Achilles gains his object and Deidameia gives birth to Neoptolemus, and that soon afterwards he is tracked down by the cunning of Odysseus and enters the Trojan war as a brilliant hero—cannot console us for its loss.

The eighteen little poems and poetical fragments of Bion that are also preserved exhibit tender trifling and feeble sentimentality. Thus he tells of a dream, in which Aphrodite came to him, leading the boy Eros by the hand, and ordered him to instruct him in the art of bucolic poetry. This was done, and the teacher took the greatest of pains; but his pupil was obstinate and paid no heed to his lessons, preferring to sing love songs to him and to relate to the love adventures of gods and men. Or Bion addresses words of deep feeling to Hesperus, the evening star, the "golden light of the lovely foam-born goddess", and begs him to shed his gentle light, to shine upon him during the work of love at night. Or a boy, trying to catch birds, finds Eros sitting on a tree. He has never seen such a bird, and shows his find to an old husbandman, who is very fond of him. But the latter shakes his head cautiously and says: "Beware of this bird and keep your hands from him; it is a bad creature, and you will do well to keep far out of its way. You are happy, as long as you do not know it. As soon as you are grown up, it will come to you of itself and will get a firm footing in your heart."[1]

In 1891 the discovery of a papyrus in Egypt

restored to us a considerable number of poems by Herondas, of which only a very few were known until then from occasional quotations. Herondas probably came from the island of Cos, and lived in the middle of the third century B.C. His poems called *mimiamboi*, that is, *mimoi* in iambic "limping" trimeters, dive deeply into daily life, which they describe strikingly and with alarming truth. Seven scenes are preserved: the seductive behaviour of a procuress, the impudent manners of a brothel-house keeper, Attic oratory displayed before the court of justice in Cos, the schoolmaster who thoroughly flogs a good-for-nothing pupil at his mother's wish, the women admiring the temple of Æsculapius and offering sacrifice, a jealous woman who punishes and favours men as the fit seizes her, the two female friends who converse intimately about the source of supply of *olisboi* (artificial penises), and lastly, the visit of the women to the shop of the crafty shoemaker Cerdon. Of these scenes we have the procuress, already mentioned and in great part quoted (p. 64); the sixth, about the olisboi, will be discussed later.[1]

A few years after the resurrection of Herondas an erotic fragment, *The Maiden's Lament*, was found in a papyrus of the second century B.C.; this contains the passionate outburst of an abandoned hetaira who will not desert her faithless lover.

2. Prose

To give at least a brief account of the prose of this period, we must first mention the name of Phylarchus, already referred to (p. 248), the author of a large historical work in twenty-eight books,

[1] Mimiambi of Herondas, ed. Otto Crusius (Gottingen, 1893), *The Maiden's Complaint*, first published by Grenfell as *An Alexandrian Erotic Fragment* (Oxford, 1896); a similar piece in dialogue form, found on an ostrakon near Luxor (in ed. 4 of Crusius's *Herondas*); cf. *Eroticorum Græcorum Fragmenta Papyracea*, collected by Bruno Lavagnini (Leipzig, 1922).

which should be mentioned here, because it is full of erotic stories and sensual love-tales told in an undoubtedly amusing but yet unscientific manner. Thus in it were the stories of Apollo and Daphne, the love of Chilonis for her stepson Acrotatos, the infamous act of Phayllus, who out of love for the wife of Ariston became a robber of temples, and the ghastly story of the love for a corpse (p. 248). All that is known of it we learn in detail from Parthenius, while fragments of numerous other love-stories from Phylarchus are also to be found in Apollodorus and especially in Athenæus who is very keenly alive to such matters. Thus the inhabitants of Byzantium are said to have been such hard drinkers that they spent the night in taverns and hired out their own houses together with their wives to strangers. Or, on the Arabian gulf there was a spring, in which if anyone wetted his feet he found his member grow to an incredible size, so that it could only be brought back to its normal condition with the most violent pain and with great difficulty, or sometimes not at all. In India, too, there grew a white root of magical properties; anyone who bathed his feet in water in which it had been mixed became impotent and like a eunuch, and boys who had done this could never get an erection as long as they lived. He further spoke of Indian quack remedies, some of which, when laid under the feet during cohabitation, had an enormously stimulating effect, and others the opposite; and there is the story of the she-elephant, Nicæa, which had grown so fond of the thirty days' old baby of its female keeper that it was melancholy when it did not see the child, and indeed, took no nourishment; but when the little one slept the elephant waved over it bundles of straw with its trunk to keep the flies away, and if it cried it rocked the cradle with its trunk and put it to sleep.

Such stories appear to have specially pleased Phylarchus; yet he had also told of an eagle which struck up a touching friendship with a boy, that lasted beyond his death (Parthenius, ch. 15, 23, 25, 31 = Phylarchus, frag. 33, 48, 60, 81 (*FHG*.). For the numerous fragments of Phylarchus preserved in Ath., see *FHG*., I, 334*f*. The story of Byzantium is in Ath., x, 442*c*; the enlarged penis in Apoll. Dysc., *Hist. Comm*., 14; the white root, 18; the Indian remedy, Ath., i, 18*d*; the elephant, Ath., xiii, 606, and Ælian *De nat. anim*., xi, 14; the eagle, Tzetzes, *Chiliades*, iv, *hist*., 134, 288 ff., and Ælian, *De nat. anim*., vi, 29).

Even in the works on husbandry, which certainly are all lost in the original but from which a selection in twenty books, the so-called *Geoponica*, was made in the tenth century A.D., a wealth of erotic stories (Daphne, Cyparissus, Myrsine, Pitys, Dendrolibanos, Rhodon, Ion, Narcissus, Cittus) is to be found (for the passages from the *Geoponica*, see E. Rohde, *Der griechische Roman*, 2nd edn., p. 370).

III. *The Period of Transition*

1. POETRY

The period from about 150 B.C. to about A.D. 100 in the history of Greek literature is called the period of transition to classicism, and we naturally begin our summary of this short space of time, which is characterized by Oriental influence that more and more gains the upper hand, with its poets.

Parthenius of Nicæa, who lived chiefly in lower Italy and is known as Virgil's teacher, had written several poems of an erotic kind: elegies, an *Aphrodite*, *Metamorphoses*—in which erotic stories of change of form took up considerable space—and, for example, the unhappy love of the Megarian king's daughter, Scylla, for King Minos is related. He had also, as he himself boasts (*Erotica*, 11, 4), told the touching story of Byblis and Caunus in hexameter verse, six lines of which he quotes.

Byblis was inflamed with love for her brother Caunus, who, to escape her sinful passion, fled to the land of the Leleges, where he founded the town of Caunus. But the sister, overcome with grief, and more particularly blaming herself because her brother avoided his home, ended her life by her own hand; and from her tears arose a spring which was called Byblis. Further, Parthenius wrote in prose a still extant collection of *Stories of Unhappy Love*, as a kind of book of reference for his friend the Roman poet, Cornelius Gallus. In this book, already often cited by us, thirty-six examples of unhappy love-passion are collected from different sources, poets and historians (Scylla: Meineke, *Analecta Alex.*, p. 270 ff.).

Another reference-book—though indeed intended rather as a source of amusement—is the fifty mythological tales of Conon, which are preserved in a summary by Photius, patriarch of Constantinople (857–879). These also are rich in erotic themes, and are important, since they contain some stories which we do not otherwise know, or know at most only in another form.

Of the purely lyric poetry of this period little is preserved, and nothing at all suitable for our purpose. But we have again to speak of some writers of epigrams. Parmenion makes a harlot remark that Zeus won Danaë in the form of golden rain—"Zeus bought Danaë for gold, and I buy you for the same: I really can't give more than Zeus" (Anth. Pal., v, 34). Lollius Bassus (v, 125) tells the hetaira Corinna that he has no desire to flow with gold or to change himself into an ox or swan like Zeus; he offers her the usual two obols (about 3d.), but then he doesn't run away—that is, he is a regular customer.

Marcus Argentarius (Anth. Pal., v, 116, 118, 127, 128) tells how he loved the maiden dearly and at last takes her with him after he has tried many persuasive arts. Anxiously the lovers guard their sweet secret ; but suddenly her mother catches her, and says, " My daughter, Hermes is common." [1]

The dramatic production of the period is limited almost entirely to mime and pantomime ; at higher-class feasts, to be sure, one harked back to the great tragedies and comedies of the classical poets, but in general the people wanted the coarser fare that was more satisfying to their senses. We can get an idea of the mimo-dramas of the imperial period from the wall-paintings of the Villa Pamfili at Rome.

Such a mime, or at least its concluding part, is presented to us on an Oxyrhynchus papyrus (Oxyrhync. Papyri, III, No. 413, now printed in Crusius's *Herondas*, where the three other pieces named are to be found). It deals with the question of delivering the hetaira Charition from the power of the king of the Indians, who intends to sacrifice her to the moon-goddess. Her liberator is the girl's brother and she is assisted by a fool, who puts the enemies to flight by a fusillade of farts, and after the Indian king has been made senselessly drunk the rescue is successfully carried out. The piece is given to the accompaniment of kettle-drums and castanets.

We also know from papyrus finds the lament of a boy for his dead cock, the serenade of a young man before his lady-love's house, and the sentimental love-effusions of a nocturnal reveller.

In the *Pantomimus* (for the pantomimes see Lucian, *De Saltat.*, 34 ; Libanius, *Orat.*, 64F ; Choricius, *Apol. Mim.*) the content of thought almost entirely gives way to the titillation of the senses. We have already sufficiently discussed in detail this sensual type of ancient theatrical performances, so that only a few supplementary words need be added.

[1] A proverb used when one had made a lucky find, meaning " We go halves ". Another epigram runs : " Breast pressed to breast and nipple rubbing against nipple—pressing my lips firmly on the sweet lips of Antigone, I lay my body on hers ; of the rest I say nothing, only the lamp was witness " (Anth. Pal. v, 128).

Bathylus of Alexandria had developed the comic *Pantomimos* in Rome to the highest stage of refinement. Between the single scenes there were no doubt also choral songs, although they were certainly subordinate. These ballets or mimic dances, which were accompanied by instrumental music, cannot in any case be considered as literature. Although philosophers like Seneca and Marcus Aurelius declaimed against them (Seneca, *Quæst. Nat.*, vii, 32; M. Aurelius, *de se*, xi, 2), and emperors like Trajan and Justinian attempted to forbid them, the *Pantomimi* held their ground till the decay of the ancient world.

2. PROSE

Probably the beginnings of the Greek love-romance date from this period (E. Rohde, *Der griechische Roman*, 2nd edn., 1900).

The subject-matter of the so-called *Romance of Ninus* (edited by V. Wilcken in *Hermes*, xxviii (1893)), of which two fragments are contained in a papyrus of the Berlin collection, is the love of Ninus and Semiramis; and we may gain from these fragments an idea of the characteristic type of nearly all the Greek romances, and therefore need not enter more closely into the nature of the latter, the most meagre production of Hellenistic literature, especially as a detailed analysis is given in Erwin Rohde's excellent work. In the Ninus fragment the youth of the two lovers was first spoken of, then the wooing of the girl, the separation of the pair (here by war, elsewhere by pirates, etc.), and lastly, their happy reunion after dangers of all kinds. This, with more or less important variations, is the theme of all the Greek love-romances; and it would be drawing too much on the reader's patience were we to attempt to describe the unimportant variations of this motif in each one of the romances that have been preserved, which, with the exception of a few passages here and there, are very wearisome. But the Greek could attain no skill of any kind in the field of romance, for the essential secret of this form of literary art—the psychology of the love of man for woman—was, owing to his homosexual preoccupations, bound to remain hidden from him. So, in his romances it can only be a question of individual adventures and purely sensual longing, and never one of a properly psychological, deeply thought-out representation of the life of the soul.

A certain Protagorides of Cyzicus was the author of *Erotic Conversations* and *Funny Stories*, which are now no more than names. The same applies to the *Erotic Writings* of Asopodorous of Phlius, which Rohde takes to be a kind of " erotic poem in prose ".[1]

The *Bibliotheca* of Apollodorus, of the first century A.D., is a collection of stories from Greek mythology chiefly intended for school purposes. If we call to mind the details given in our sixth chapter, in which we discussed the number of Greek erotic stories, for the knowledge of which we are chiefly indebted to Apollodorus, from the modern point of view we are astonished at the simple naïveté of the Greeks towards sexual matters, even where the training and scientific education of the young was concerned.

In the time of Nero lived the learned Pamphila, the wife of a grammarian and herself a famous lover of learning, who collected together in thirty-three books the results of her reading in the history of literature. Of her little book on the *Enjoyments of Love* (*Περὶ ἀφροδισίων*, mentioned only by Suïdas: see *FHG.*, iii, 520) we know nothing but the name.

Physicians also gradually begin to show an interest

[1] On Protagorides cf. Susemihl, II, 396; on Asopodorus, Rohde, p. 265, note 1. Of the scientific prose of this period, there is little worth mentioning for our purpose.

in specifically sexual problems. Thus, in the time of the Emperor Trajan, Rufus of Ephesus (ed. by R. von Daremberg-Ruelle, Paris, 1879) wrote on satyriasis (swollen condition of the genitals) and spermatorrhœa, of which little treatise a few unimportant fragments are still preserved.

Plutarch of Chæronea (about A.D. 46–120) is so versatile a writer that it would be remarkable if he had not also shown the greatest interest in the erotic problem. In fact, in his numerous writings, a large number of passages with erotic details are to be found. We mention here only the monographs which touch upon erotic matters. Besides, many particulars from the rest of his writings are often mentioned and will be referred to later.

In his youthful and artistically not very valuable composition, *The Banquet of the Seven Wise Men*, erotic questions are frequently discussed. The important and beautiful treatise, *Erotikos*, which in a pleasant and suggestive manner deals with the subject so often discussed in ancient literature, whether the preference should be given to the love of boys or women, is entirely devoted to the erotic problem. In the delightful conversation, whose charm is enhanced by the insertion of several stories, the chief speaker is Autobulos, Plutarch's son, who, totally disagreeing with the opinion of Lucian in his *Erotes*, gives the preference to the love of women, and finally delivers a high encomium on marriage and on female virtue which is extolled by Plutarch on every possible occasion (Plutarch, *Erotikos*: trans. with introduction by Hans Licht, Dresden).

In the nine books of *Table Conversations*, erotic questions are here and there discussed.

We must also mention the *Marriage Precepts*, dealing with a newly-married couple, friends of Plutarch, which contain a number of partly quite humdrum, partly excellent instructions. Like Plato before him, Plutarch also is convinced of the moral equality of both sexes and endeavours to prove this by historical examples; with this purpose the *Virtues of Women* is composed. He had also written an essay (now lost) to show that women as well as men ought to be educated; and his writings *On Beauty*, *Love*, and *Friendship*, and *Against Wantonness* have likewise been lost. The five quite unimportant *Love-Stories*, handed down under his name, are not the work of Plutarch.

In regard to an appreciation of Plutarch, we have only to mention for our purpose that he values literary works of art according to their moral force. His highest ideal appears to be the purity of family life, which he warmly supported not only in his writings, but also in his own domestic life. Especially characteristic is his little essay *A Comparison of Aristophanes and Menander*, in which he quite plainly declares his opinion, that he unreservedly gives the preference to decent correctness over indecent literary genius. Plutarch from the moral point of view stands high, but his manner and method are essentially commonplace.

IV. *The Post-Classical Age*

1. SOPHISTIC: GEOGRAPHY: HISTORY: WRITINGS OF VARIOUS KINDS

For the sake of completeness, something must be said about the post-classical period of Greek literature, which is considered to begin about A.D. 100 and to end with the beginning of the sixth century A.D., although only what is most important can be noted.[1]

During this period, as before, erotic forms the chief subject of lyric poetry, to which the rhetorician Maximus of Tyre (*Dissertatio*, 29, p. 338) very rightly calls special attention, and confirms

[1] See W. Von Christ-Stahlin-Schmid, *Geschichte der Klassischen Literatur*, part 2, *Die nach Klassische Periode der griechischen Literatur* (second half from A.D. 100 to 530).

his statement by examples. Unfortunately the remains that have come down to us are for the most part very scanty, but in the numerous remains of the witty Syrian, Lucian of Samosata (about 120–180), erotic occupies so great a space that in 1921 the present writer published a special monograph on the subject, to which he begs to refer the student (Hans Licht, *Die Homo erotik in der griechischen Literatur ; Lukianos von Samosata*, Bonn, 1921).

An inexhaustible storehouse for the history of the erotic literature of the Greeks is the *Description of a Journey Through Greece* by Pausanias of Magnesia (second century A.D.), who travelled through the whole country, and recorded whatever he found or heard of that was remarkable in story, history, archæology, and art; this encyclopædic guide is of extraordinary importance to us, and it has with some justice been called " the oldest Baedeker ". It is impossible to give here all the love-stories it contains; many have already been given, and a few of the more important are mentioned below.[1]

Also Phlegon of Tralles (fragments of Phlegon in *FHG.*, III, 602), a freedman of the emperor Trajan, had handed down in his *Chronicle of History*, and especially in his *Wonderful Stories*, much erotic material, but the fragments that have survived are unfortunately quite unimportant in their subject-matter, with the exception of a long one, from which Goethe borrowed the subject matter of his ballad *Die Braut von Korinth.*

Neither can much be done with the fragments of Favorinus (in *FHG.*, III, 577 ff.), who is said to have been a hermaphrodite, and whom W. von Christ calls " the type of the learned gossip in rhetorico-philosophical garb, and therewith the founder of varied kinds of writing ". He had not only written on the love technique of Socrates, but also a

[1] i, 30, 1 (Meles and Timagoras); vii, 23, 1–3 (Selemnos and Argyra); viii, 47, 6 (Aristomelidas and the coy maiden); vii, 21, 1–5 (Koresos and Kallirrhoe); vii, 19, 1–5 (Melanippus and Comætho).

collection of anecdotes on the philosophers of the classical period and a large compilation entitled *Tales of Various Kinds* in twenty-four books.

Maximus of Tyre, of the time of the emperor Commodus (who reigned 180–192), has left forty-one essays on various subjects, of which especially one on the Socratic Eros (to be afterwards treated of) is specially important for us.

The following works by different writers who bore the name of Philostratus, not yet satisfactorily distinguished by philological science, should be mentioned here.[1] Firstly, *The Life of Apollonius of Tyana*, in eight books, which was written at the request of the Empress Julia Domna (died 217), probably to draw a parallel to Jesus Christ in the well-known miracle-worker, travelling apostle and swindler who lived in the first century, nevertheless contains a wealth of erotic details and is therefore an interesting proof of the impartial attitude of the times in regard to the sexual. To mention only a few examples: by the side of different homosexual passages we hear of the sensuality of Euxenus; the opinion of Pythagoras on sexual intercourse; the chastity of Apollonius, who as a boy and a young man had committed no sexual act and also later refused such; a piquant attempt of a eunuch upon a lady of the harem; a female panther caught on heat; the madness of the myth of Helen; the double sexuality of the æther; the numerous hermaphrodites in Ephesus; and many other things of a sexual character, which at the present day would hardly be found in a book dedicated to an empress.

Under the name of Philostratus sixty-four love-letters have also been preserved, amongst them one to the empress Julia Domna. The others are addressed partly to boys and partly to girls, the same theme

[1] In C. L. Kayser's edn. (Leipzig, Teubner, 1890): Euxenus, I, 6, 28; Pythagoras, 13, 6; chastity of Appolonius, 13, 8, and 13, 12; the eunuch, 38, 27 ff.; the female panther, 44, 14; the myth of Helen, 99, 14; double sexuality, 112, 8, and 125, 30.

sometimes having to do with a young man, sometimes with a young woman, although certainly we must say that by far the most charming are the letters to boys. Lastly, the *Pictures*, that is, descriptions of a gallery of sixty-five paintings in Naples, offer many kinds of opportunity for the voluptuous delineation of erotic scenes. We have also a description of seventeen more pictures by the grandfather of Philostratus.

Claudius Ælianus of Præneste near Rome, in his *On the Nature of Animals* in seventeen books, has put together a large selection of erotic stories from animal life. His *Varia Historia* in fourteen books is a copious collection of anecdotes with a wealth of erotic details. We have already given several quotations from both books. Twenty letters of his are also preserved; his indictment of the dead emperor Heliogabalus, the man-woman, is lost.

Perhaps no author in our description has been so often cited as Athenæus of Naucratis, who in the time of the emperor Marcus Aurelius wrote his gigantic compilation *The Banquet of the Learned* in fifteen books, an almost unfathomable source for archæology and more particularly for an account of the sexual life of antiquity.

The meal took place in the house of Larensius, a distinguished, highly educated Roman; and there were twenty-nine guests of all the faculties—philosophers, rhetoricians, poets, musicians, artists, jurists, physicians, and Athenæus himself, who in the work before us informs his friend Timotheus of everything that was said at the meal. The thirteenth book is devoted entirely to erotic fragments.

After invoking the Muse Erato, the subject is definitely stated to be " Conversations on love and the erotic poets ". The method of arrangement, which is interrupted here and there by occasional episodes, is easily recognized; at first marriage and married women are spoken of, the second part treats at considerable length of the character of the hetairæ in its many ramifications, while the third part is occupied with the love of boys.

The author has given an exhaustive analysis of this book in a separate essay (H. Licht: *Drei erotische Kapitel aus den Tischgesprächen des Athenaios*, 1909), so adds only a few details here. After drawing attention to the fact that an old man should not woo a young woman, there follows a long list of the miseries and sorrows which have been brought into the world through women. They have been the cause of many wars, from the Trojan to that which raged for ten years round the walls of the city of Cirrha for the sake of some girls who had been carried off. Whole families have been murdered for the sake of women and discord has entered many communities, which formerly were flourishing, through their jealousy and passion. The power of love is quite unconquerable, a truth which is supported by some beautiful quotations from Euripides and Pindar. But as Eros can disastrously kindle mighty passions, yet also the noblest and highest thing that mankind knows is the lofty ethical principle that brings human beings together to love. This is shown most beautifully and purely, according to the opinion of the Greeks, in the bond of love between two young men, after which naturally follow a few words on the subject, and the third part is entirely devoted to it.

Although the thirteenth book deals exclusively with the erotic problem, yet notices and episodes of erotic content also occur in other books in such masses that the compilation from the works of Athenæus of all the passages dealing with sex and of the other material important for the history of morals would fill a large volume.

Nor was there any lack of Dream-books in Greek literature, some of them very bulky. They must be mentioned here, since the dream reflects in a most subtle manner the workings of the mind, and is consequently very full of erotic. Hence naturally the ancient dream-books go also with great detail into erotic dreams, as is proved by the most important of the books of dreams preserved, that of Artemidorus of Ephesus. In it things, against which our feeling revolts (e.g. to dream that one is sleeping with his mother) are handled with the utmost naïveté and without any embarrassment.

2. THE LOVE-ROMANCE AND LOVE-LETTERS

Why the Greeks produced only indifferent love-romances, has already been briefly explained (p. 280). Following the purpose there expressed, we shall here briefly discuss the romances that have come down to us.

Chariton of Aphrodisias in Caria in the second century A.D. wrote the love-story of Chæreas and Kallirrhoe in eight books. The wedding of the pair is soon followed by ill-treatment of the wife by her jealous husband; apparently dead she is buried, but is carried away by robbers. In spite of the most enticing offers, she remains true to her husband, to whom she is again united after undergoing a great variety of adventures.

Xenophon of Ephesus in five books treated of the love of Abrocomes and Antheia. The hero of the story exhibits the type of the handsome, but prudish Hippolytus (p. 151). In this case also the marriage is soon followed by separation and all kinds of adventures gone through by the pair, who long for each other. Both victoriously withstand all attempts, find each other again, and celebrate a sweet night of love. The most interesting thing for the history of civilization is the strong prominence of the cult of Isis, with which the erotic happenings of the story are not unskilfully combined.

As for the *History of Apollonius, King of Tyre*, the so-called Trojan romance of Dictys and the numerous settings of the Romance of Alexander, we must refer to the handbooks of Greek literature.

The charming little story of Eros and Psyche also can only be mentioned here, as the probably very old material was certainly first represented in Greek prose, but only remains to us in the form given to it by Apuleius (*Metam.*, iv, 28–vi, 22)

The Syrian Iamblichus in his *Babylonian Stories* had told of the love of Rhodanes and Sinonis. Only an abstract of the work by Photius is preserved, which is not much to be regretted, as the author depends for his effects upon exciting situations and unreasonable exaggeration. The beautiful Sinonis awakens the desire of the king, who throws them into a prison from which they manage to escape; but they are pursued, and after a number of adventures Rhodanes is appointed the king's commander-in-chief, wins a victory for him, and finally is again united to Sinonis. The sensual-erotic element is very pronounced in this tale, at least so Photius affirms, without, however, giving any examples (Photius, *Bibliotheca*, cod. 94, 736; Bekker).

The longest of the Greek romances completely preserved to us, the love-story of Theagenes and Chariclea in ten books, is by Heliodorus of Emesa. It describes in a vivid and interesting manner, and at the same time decently, the fortunes of the Æthiopian king's daughter, who, exposed when a little child, after many perils is again solemnly recognized as such, and is wedded to Theagenes, whose acquaintance she made and whom she learned to love at the Pythian games.

The four books of the pastoral romance of Daphnis and Chloë, written by Longus of Lesbos, is of quite a different kind. In it there is nothing but "pagan" sentiment and sensual joyfulness. The little work describes in pleasant separate pictures the fortunes of two exposed children who are brought up by good-hearted shepherds; they are finally discovered to be the children of wealthy parents, but they cherish such attachment for the delightful village field of their happy childhood that they return thither to marry and to spend their lives far from the city. The fields of the country, which are described with great vividness, are enlivened by charming forms of pans, nymphs, and mischievous love-gods. Here also adventures and dangers threaten the pair of lovers; pirates carry off Daphnis, Chloë is dragged away, rich suitors woo her, the homosexual Gnathon tempts Daphnis, but all these adventures are only episodes, the author's main subject being his masterly and successful description of the relations of the two lovers which gradually developed from the first awakening of the erotic inclination into the greatest intimacy, as yet not understood, of the final sexual union. We here give some specimens from the romance. "Now they returned to their sheep and goats, inspected them, and when they saw that everything, the herdsmen, goats and sheep, was in order, they sat down on the trunk of an oak, and looked to see whether Daphnis had bruised himself in his fall or had drawn blood. He had suffered no injury at all, nor was there any bleeding, but his hair and the rest of his body was covered with earth and clay. Therefore Daphnis resolved to bathe, before Lamon and Myrtale noticed what had happened. So then he went with Chloë to the grotto of the nymphs, gave her his short coat and wallet to look after, drew near to the spring, and washed his hair and his whole body. His hair was black and thick, and his body sunburnt, so that one might think that it was browned by the shade of his hair. But to Chloë, who was looking on, Daphnis seemed to be very beautiful, and since then for the first time he appeared beautiful to her, she believed that the bath was responsible for his beauty. While she was rinsing his back, she felt beneath her fingers the soft, yielding flesh; then she secretly tested herself to see whether her own flesh was softer.

After this, Chloë's only wish was to see Daphnis in the bath again.

"When the next day they had entered the pasture, Daphnis sat down under the usual oak-tree, blew on his shepherd's flute, and at the same time inspected the goats, which lying on the ground appeared to listen to his songs; but Chloë sat down by his side, looked at the flocks of sheep, but still more at Daphnis. Again he appeared to her beautiful, when blowing his shepherd's pipe; and now she thought that the music was responsible for his beauty, so that she seized the flute after him, to see whether she could not also make herself beautiful. She persuaded him to take a bath again, looked at him in the bath, and the sight heated her blood; she praised his beauty when he returned and this praise was the beginning of love. Yet she did not know what was going on in her heart, since she was an inexperienced girl, who had grown up in the country, and had never yet heard the word 'love' uttered by any one. She no longer took pleasure in anything, she shed tears, and often called 'Daphnis'. She had no taste for food, she could not sleep at night, she did not care about her flocks; at one time she laughed, at another she shed tears; now she slept, now she sprang up; her face was pale, then again a flaming blush would cover it.

"If Daphnis was away from Chloë, he often chattered at random to himself: What in the world does Chloë's kiss do to me? Her lips are tenderer than roses, her mouth is sweeter than honeycomb, but her kiss is more bitter than the sting of the bee. I have often kissed little goats, puppies just born, and the calf that Dorcon gave us. But the kiss of Chloë is quite a different one; my breath throbs, my heart beats impetuously, my soul is sorrowful, and yet I want to kiss again. O fatal victory, O strange illness, to which I cannot yet give a name! Did Chloë, when she kissed me, take poison?

But then how could she remain alive? How beautifully the nightingales sing, but my pipe is mute! How merrily skip the goats, but I sit idle! How gloriously the flowers bloom, and yet I make no wreaths! Violets and hyacinths bloom, but Daphnis fades away! Thus the worthy Daphnis suffered and spoke, when for the first time he tasted the joys and began to know the meaning of love.

"When midday came, their eyes were dazzled by the things they saw. Chloë saw Daphnis undressed, was captivated by his beauty, and almost grieved that she could find nothing in him to blame. But Daphnis, when he saw her adorned in her doeskin and a wreath of pine, when she reached the cup to him, thought that he saw one of the nymphs from the grotto. He took the wreath from her head and put it on himself, after he had kissed it; but she put on his dress, which he had laid aside and which she had been stroking and kissing. Already they pelted each other with apples and decked their heads, while they arranged their hair tastefully. Chloë compared his hair, since it was dark, to the myrtle; but he rejoined that her face was like an apple, since it was white and suffused with a tender blush. He also taught her to play the pipe, and when she began blowing, he took the pipe away and himself made his lips run over the tubes, apparently to point out her mistakes, but as it were to taste Chloë's kiss upon the pipes. When Daphnis was once playing the pipe about midday and the flocks were resting in the shade, Chloë, unnoticed, had gone to sleep. When Daphnis observed this, he laid down his pipe, could not see enough of Chloë's whole form, just as if he was not ashamed, and said gently to himself: How softly her eyes slumber, how gently her mouth breathes! Neither apples nor pears are so beautiful. But I cannot venture to kiss them, for her kiss wounds my heart and makes it drunk like fresh honey; also I cannot help being afraid of waking her. O the chattering grasshoppers, they will not let her sleep with their loud chirping. And the goats also, eager for the fray, are butting one another; O cowardly wolves, more cowardly than foxes, that you have not stolen these goats. While he spoke thus to himself, a grasshopper, pursued by a swallow, fell into Chloë's bosom; the pursuing swallow could not reach it, and as it had come close to Chloë's cheeks it struck them with its wings. Chloë, unaware of what had happened, woke with a loud cry. As she now saw the swallow flying near her and Daphnis laughing at her fright, her alarm was allayed and she rubbed her eyes still heavy with sleep. Then the grasshopper chirped in her bosom, as if it were a suppliant giving thanks for its rescue. Chloë again cried out, but Daphnis laughed loudly. As the opportunity offered, he put his hand into her bosom and took out the fortunate grasshopper, which would not remain quiet in his hand. But Chloë was glad when she saw the little creature, kissed it, and put it back again into her bosom. After the burial of Dorcon, Chloë led Daphnis to the nymphs, bathed him, and now for the first time, before the eyes of Daphnis, bathed her white body, shining with beauty, which needed no bath to enhance it. Then they gathered flowers, such as were in season, crowned the images of the nymphs, and hung Dorcon's pipe on the rock as an offering. After that they went and looked after their goats and sheep. They were all lying there, without eating, without bleating, but longing for Daphnis and Chloë, who had disappeared. When they showed themselves, called to them as usual and blew the pipe, the sheep sprang up and grazed, and the goats skipped and jumped for joy, as though they were rejoicing at the return of their master. Daphnis, however, could not bring himself to rejoice, after he had seen Chloë undressed and her hitherto covered charms had been revealed to him. His heart was wounded as though he were consumed with gnawing poison; and now he began to pant for breath, as though pursued, or as though from panting he was utterly exhausted. The bath was more terrible to him than the sea, and he thought his soul was still among the robbers; he was still young, a child of the land and did not yet know the power of love."

Love-letters also (the earliest example of which may be the erotic letter of Lysias already mentioned (p. 254) and inserted in Plato's *Phædrus*, also belong to erotic literature. Hence we may also mention the note, which in the *Pseudolus* of Plautus (I, 1, 63) is written by the girl Phœnicium to her friend, since it probably derives from a Greek model. " Now as to our loves, manners, customs, jest, sport, talk, sweet kissing, close embracing of loving mates, soft little kisses with tender lips, gentle pressure of projecting breasts. From all these pleasures there comes a parting, a separation, a destruction, for me and in like manner for you, unless there is refuge for me in you and for you in me. I have taken care that you should know all that I knew; now I will test your love, and pretence of it. Good-bye! "

In the second century A.D. the rhetorician Lesbonax had published a collection of erotic letters, just as Zonæus had written erotic letters and Melesermus letters to hetairæ. Of the three last we know little more than the names,[1] but 118 letters of Alciphron, a younger contemporary of Lucian, have been preserved. Especially charming are the two letters, exchanged by Menander with his beloved Glycera; and there are also a number of letters to hetairæ, which originally filled the whole fourth book. These letters of Alciphron

[1] Some fifty immoral letters of Epicurus are mentioned, which have been proved to be forgeries by one Diotimos or Theotimos (see *Diog. Laërt.*, x, 3), who also ascribed some unpleasant letters from his own pen to the Stoic Chrysippus.

breathe glowing love for Athens and the fine Athenian culture, which are vividly portrayed; and in many of them sparkles a riotous, highly coloured sensuality of which the following specimen may be given:

MEGARA TO BACCHIS

"You are the only girl who has a lover, and you love him so well that you cannot leave him even for a minute. Dear Aphrodite, what bad taste! Glycera asked you to come to her sacrificial feast weeks ago—it was at the festival of Dionysus she gave us the invitation—and yet you were not there! It was because of *him*, I suppose, you could not bear to visit your old friends? You have become a virtuous woman and are devoted to your lover, but we are just wanton harlots. We were all there—Thessala, Moscharion, Thaïs, Anthrakion, Petalë, Thryallis, Myrrhina, Chrysion, Euxippe; also Philumene, although she is just married and has a jealous husband, came to us as soon as she had seen her dear to bed. You were the only one who was not there; but you of course had your Adonis to keep warm. I suppose you were afraid that some Persephone would get hold of him if you, his Aphrodite, left him by himself? Oh, what a party we had!—I mean to annoy you if I can—how perfectly charming it was! Songs, jokes, drinking till cockcrow, perfumes, garlands, and a delicious dessert! Our banqueting hall was under the shade of the laurel-trees, and the only thing we lacked was you—nothing else! We have often had a drinking party before, but seldom such a pleasant one as this. What amused us most, was a dispute between Thryallis and Myrrhina, as to which had the most beautiful and tenderest buttocks. First then Myrrhina loosed her girdle, and stood there in her silken undergarment, through which one could see her heaving posteriors, which shook like gelatine or congealed milk; then she looked back over her shoulders at the movements of her buttocks. At the same time she sighed gently, as if she were performing some sweet voluptuous action, so that I was struck with astonishment.

Thryallis was not backward, but surpassed her in wanton behaviour, saying, "I will not fight behind a curtain nor with prudish activity, but naked like the wrestlers."

3. PHILOSOPHY

Another world meets us, when we plunge into the *Enneades*, that is, the writings, each in nine books, of Plotinus of Lycopolis (third century A.D.). The indefatigable, half-blind, and physically shattered creator of Neo-Platonism often busies himself with the problem of love; but he regards sensuality as a sin, or at least a hindrance to spiritual knowledge, an act of self-destruction, as is shown by his famous allegory of the beautiful youth Narcissus, who falls in love with his reflection in the water and by its charms allows himself to be drawn into its fatal depths. Plotinus is absorbed in the thought that the wise man must allow himself to be so penetrated by the idea of the Pure and Beautiful, that, through familiarity with forms of the Beautiful in the sensible world and by freeing himself from the corporeal he may arrive at the highest happiness, which consists in the union with the idea of the purely spiritual. To him, therefore, the Beautiful, which he enthusiastically glorifies, is synonymous with the morally good, and on this basis the three splendid essays *On the Beautiful*, *On Eros*, and *On Spiritual Beauty* are constructed. The editor of his works, Porphyrius of Tyre, pushes the demands of Plotinus farther, when, for example, in his writings on *Abstinence*, he rejects the idea of flesh food, since it promotes sensuality. It should also be mentioned that he practised his teaching in his own life, by marrying Marcella, a widow with seven living children, as little blest as himself with the goods of this world, but on the other hand endowed with a rich philosophical spirit. No doubt as early as that there was gossip in the Christian camp, which represented this admirable deed as meaning that Porphyrius had married a faded old Jewess with many children from motives of avarice and had afterwards fallen away from Christianity.

It hardly needs to be mentioned that in the numerous lexicographical works preserved, and especially in the collections of proverbs, anthologies, and chrestomathies, erotic details are found without number ; but these works cannot be analysed here, as this is a case not of an independent class of literature, but only of excerpts from written works at hand.

V. *The Last Period*

It remains to give a brief summary of the last period of Greek literature, generally reckoned to be from about A.D. 300–530, and this is the time when Greco-Roman culture, a most precious bloom on the tree of humanity, gradually dies away. For its annihilation, the most lamentable catastrophe which until now had overtaken the human race, external agencies are to blame, such as the increasingly formidable attacks by barbarian peoples, amongst whom are to be named the Parthians and Blemmyes, and last, but not least, the Germanic hordes of Goths, and finally and perhaps most important of all, the evergrowing influence of Christianity. The so-called pagans, especially after the reign of the emperor Aurelian who, like so many men of culture, fell a victim to the daggers of conspirators, after a five years' reign in the year 275, had certainly attempted to combine the

Christian and pagan views of the world in the so-called cult of the sun—but in vain: " tolerant " Christianity did not take part in it, it was too full of unfortunate delusions to become the universal religion, and so the world went on its way, and earth was shovelled over the grave of beauty, the life of the senses that for so long had made joy a reality.

And not only that. The lofty names, which the old Greeks uttered with pride—freedom, independence, liberty of speech and others—faded before the autocracy of the Cæsars who ruled in the new capital of the world, Byzantium, or as it was now called, " the city of Constantine," and from these times of the Byzantine hierarchy of officials dates the servile tone, which even to-day is usual in the intercourse of " subject " and " superior ", and is hence rightly named Byzantinism.

1. POETRY

To begin here with poetry, at least the fragment of an epithalamium, preserved to us on a papyrus (see the catalogue of the Greek papyri in the J. Rylands Library, Manchester, 1911, No. 17), may be mentioned. That the visits of the Mimes and Pantomimes in the theatre little by little began to be felt defamatory, and were therefore at first forbidden to the students of the university of Rome and the governors, but gradually also to wider circles, will surprise nobody. But it was left for the emperors Anastasius and Justinian finally to forbid the Pantomimes. Certainly it had long become usual for the female parts to be taken by girls, and mostly by such as were of very doubtful character. The choral songs that connected the texts appear to have been quite incredibly indecent.

Quintus of Smyrna has left us an epic poem in fourteen books on " post-Homeric " events, which is nothing but a tedious infusion of old epic adventures. On the other hand, the forty-eight poems (*Dionysiaca*), in which Nonnus of Panopolis, in Egypt, sings of the fortunes of Dionysus in countless episodes of inordinate length, are full of glowing sensuality, of highly-coloured life, and of unadulterated paganism. This bulky work is an account of the journey of Dionysus to India, and the erotic details in this gigantic epic of travels are extremely numerous.

An amiable poet, probably belonging to the age of Justinian, is Musæus, who has left us the little epos (or rather *epyllion*) in 340 hexameters, on the love of Leander for Hero, an erotic motive which is known to everyone from Schiller's ballad. The little poem has been prettily called by H. Köchly, "the last rose from the fading garden of Greek poetry."

Musæus is possibly also the author of the beautiful poem, partly preserved in the Palatine anthology (ix, 362), on the love of the river-god Alpheus for Arethusa the nymph of the spring, whom he followed from Elis under the sea to Sicily and there had loving union with her.

From the second century A.D. we probably have the partly very discourteous verses from the *Mirror of Women* by Naumachius, preserved in Stobæus (Anth., xxii, 32; xxiii, 7).

In the second half of the sixth century A.D., the lawyer Agathias of Myrina published a collection of epigrams in seven books, of which the sixth contained love-poems, partly preserved in the Palatine anthology (*Agathias*, Anth. Pal., v, 269, 294): "I once was reclining at supper between two females; I desired one, but gratified the other; the one attracted me by her kisses; and, on the other hand, I, like a thief, kissed the other with grudging lip, beguiling the jealousy of the first one of whose reproach and love-breaking messages I was filled with dread. Then with a sigh I said:

'Perhaps it is a great sorrow for me to be loved and to love, since I am doubly punished.'"

"The jealous old woman lay by the side of the girl, across the bed leaning her back against the wall, like a projecting battlement, inaccessible; and, like a tower, a single blanket with ample folds covered the girl; also a grim maidservant having fastened the doors of the room, lay overcome with an unmixed draught of wine. Yet they did not alarm me; for, lifting up the hinge of the door with my hands without making any noise, I put out the burning firebrand by waving my cloak; and penetrating slantwise across the chamber, well eluded the sleeping guard, and dragging myself along on my stomach I crept gently beneath the girths of the bed and gradually raised myself, where the wall was passable; and pressing closer to the girl's bosom, I seized her breasts, and wantoned with her face by kisses, feeding my lips upon the softness of her mouth. My spoils were a beautiful mouth and I had a kiss as a pledge of the nightly contest. As yet I have not destroyed the fortress of her maidenhood, which is still kept intact by delay since I avoided a fight. Yet if the battle begins anew, I will verily destroy her walls of virginity, nor shall any battlements hold me back; and if I succeed, I will weave garlands for thee, O Cypris, bearing emblems of victory."

About the turn of the fourth and fifth century lived the epigrammatic writer Palladas of Alexandria, who remained a pagan. By profession he was a schoolmaster and so desperately poor that he was obliged to sell some of his editions of the classics; and he was, moreover, married to a devil of a woman.[1] Hence it is not surprising that no erotic epigrams are found in his collection, but several, in which he most bitterly expresses his loathing for

[1] His sale of editions of Pindar and Callimachus: Anth. Pal., ix, 171, 175; his "devil of a wife", ix, 165–8, 169; xi, 378, 381; reference to Christianity, ix, 528.

the female sex : " Every woman is gall and bitterness ; yet she has two delightful hours in her life —one in the nuptial chamber, the other in the grave."

From Paulus Silentiarius, a court-official of Justinian (reigned, 527–565), we have seventy-eight epigrams, chiefly erotic, which in sensuality could not be surpassed by any other epigrammatist (Anth. Pal., v, 252, 255, 258, 259 ; ix, 620) :

(*a*) " Full nakedness ! Cast off your linen white
and closely clinging, limb to limb unite ;
Off with these filmy veils : while they are on
Between us stand the walls of Babylon.
Join breast to breast, our lips together seal,
And ne'er shall blabbing tongues our joy reveal.

(*b*) I saw the lovers held in passion's chain, They
kissed and clipped, then clipped and kissed again,
If thus their endless thirst they might abate
And dull the torment of their parted state.
Fain were they in each other's heart to hide
And so at last a change of raiment tried.
He, as Achilles once on Scyros' shore A
maiden's smock upon his body wore ;
She, like Diana kilted to the knee, Strode
boldly forth in manly tunic free.
But soon their lips once more together pressed,
Unquenched the craving of their love confessed.
E'en as two stems unite to make one vine
And tendrils none can part together twine,
So close their bodies did they interlace With
limbs entangled in a soft embrace.
Thrice blessèd they on whom such fetters lie,
Who never know our parting's agony.

(*c*) The lines I see upon thy face Surpass the
bloom of youthful grace.

Thy quinces drooping in my hand Outshine
young breasts that upright stand.
Winter than summer seems more warm
And spring time yields to autumn's charm.

(*d*) How faint those limbs! how dull that eye!
Like one new-risen from her bed,
Your fragrant locks dishevelled lie, Your
cheek has lost its red.
A captive in the lists of love, Are these the
signs of your alarms?
Ah happy victor, who did prove His prowess
in your arms!
Or is it that in grief you pine With passion
still unsatisfied?
Dear sweetheart, then may it be mine To
clasp you to my side!"

Of a double bath, one for the male, another for the female visitors, he says: "Hope is near to love, but it is impossible to catch women; a little door keeps off the mighty Paphian goddess. But yet even this is sweet; for when people are stricken with love, hope is truly sweeter than the fulfilment."

From Macedonius (Anth. Pal., v, 243), also of the time of Justinian, we have:

" In my arms I held her tight, Saw her eyes with
laughter gleam,
Close together in the night; Though 'twas but
a dream.
All her body I caressed Nor did she reluctant
seem,
Each soft limb upon me pressed, Yielded—in my
dream.
But as every art I tried Plunging deep in Passion's
stream,
I by Cupid was denied, Lost my lovely dream.
Ah! he is a jealous boy, Lies in ambush, so I
deem:
Will not give us perfect joy Even in a dream."

About the same time that these wanton and frivolous poems came into being and enjoyed great popularity, the Neo-Platonist Proclus wrote his *Hymns to the Gods*, of which seven are preserved, amongst them two to Aphrodite. Here we find nothing sensual, everything is intellectual and moral; the theosophical poet has nothing to do with sensual enjoyment, but only with enlightenment and purification from the dross of the earthly, from the errors and sins of life. Even to Aphrodite he prays as if she were not the pagan goddess of love, but the Christian Madonna (Proclus, *Hymns*, 5, 14): "Lift up your souls from the dirt to purer beauty, that it may flee from the destructive charm of earthly desire."

2. PROSE

Of the prose authors of this period who are of importance and interest for our present purpose we must at least mention two brave men, namely, the sophists Libanius (314–393) and his contemporary Himerius, because of their energetic, though inevitably vain, struggle against the spread of Christianity. They had drunk their full of the beauty of antiquity, and from pious conviction ventured war upon the Nazarene enemy of life, a war which certainly, considering the state of things, was bound to remain without a prospect of success. Even the highly gifted, energetic nephew of Constantine I, Flavius Claudius Julianus, could not succeed, for in 351 he fell away from Christianity (for Julian's apostasy see his *Letters*, esp. 51, 52 and 25–27) and caused himself to be initiated into the mysteries of the cult of Mithras; but he proved himself no Heracles, he was unable to reduce the ever-growing heads of the hydra. The beginning of his reign (361), entered upon with so many beautiful hopes, was ended after two years by a melancholy stroke of fortune, since during his return from his victorious Persian war he succumbed to the mere accident of a wound. If Libanius is right, the fatal missile was thrown from his own ranks, by a Saracen incited by hatred of the Christians. The place where the last cultured man of antiquity received his death-wound on the 26th of June, 363, was the plain of Maranga in Phrygia on the bank of the Tigris. So far as I know, no one has set up a pious memorial of this world-catastrophe; but, on the contrary, the name of Julian was erased from several inscriptions in Asia Minor. History calls him the Apostate, the Forsaker, that is, of Christianity. With him died the last great hope of classical culture, and then began the downfall of the ancient civilization and the oncoming of succeeding centuries of wild madness. Since his accession to the throne he had in vain attempted to establish his religions, that is, the old pagan ideals, in writings as well as acts; he had in vain striven to convert the Christians of Alexandria to the worship of the sun; he in vain wrote the three books (unfortunately lost) of his polemic *Against the Christians*. In the course of time the great-hearted man and unfortunate emperor was stigmatized as "the accursed" (κατάρατος) by the triumphant Christians; later he was described as "the confederate of Satan"; and finally, in the literature of the nineteenth century, he became the tragic figure of Ibsen's powerful drama, *Emperor and Galilæan*.

A last attempt to save Hellenic sensual joyfulness from the gloomy resignation of Nazarenedom, was made in the fourth century by the love-romance. Achilles Tatius, a rhetorician in Alexandria, wrote in eight books the love-story of Cleitophon and Leucippe. The usual motives of the technique of the Greek romance (already mentioned, p. 279) are repeated here at wearisome length. Much of what happens is due to the working of significant dream-visions, two of which may be mentioned here on account of their curious nature. "When I was nineteen years old, and my father intended to make preparations for my wedding for the following year, I dreamed that I had grown together with my bride in the upper part of the body as far as the navel; but from there downwards we were two separate bodies. Then a woman appeared, of huge form and terrible, of wild countenance and bloodshot eyes; her cheeks were grim, and on her head she had snakes instead of hair. In her right hand she held a sickle, and a torch in her left. Drawing impetuously near to me, she lifted up the sickle, brought it down to the abdomen where I was grown together with the girl, and separated her from me." Another time the mother dreamed that "a robber with a naked sword had carried off her daughter, laid her on her back, cut up her body in the middle from the lower to the upper part, beginning with the sexual organs" (Achilles Tatius, i, 3; ii, 23). Further, the romance swarms with sophistical reflections and long-winded discussions on the nature of love, how it expresses and manifests itself in the most manifold varieties; we hear of the love of peacocks, plants and magnets; mythological motifs, such as the love of Alpheus and Creusa, are not wanting, any more than the favourite discussion, whether the love of women or of boys is to be preferred (ii, 35–38). A long chapter (i, 8) is occupied with the wickedness of women and the mischief that through them befalls humanity. A priest of Artemis delights in making a long speech, which consists of nothing but obscenities, although couched in expressions that sound harmless.

A number of letters are introduced, and descriptions of arts and technical trades, together with all kinds of trifles from legend, history, fables and natural history, and much more of the sort, are added as a piquant seasoning to this remarkable hotch-potch. We have a description of the hippopotamus, are told remarkable things about elephants, e.g. that it takes the female elephant ten years to work up the male seed internally and the same length of time to bring the embryo to maturity, and other singular things concerning the proboscidean, among which may be mentioned its "very sweet-scented breath", and the cause of this (Hippopotamus, iv, 2; Elephant, iv, 4 and 5).

Further, the love of Pan for Syrinx is prettily told: "Syrinx was a beautiful maiden who fled from Pan, who persecuted her with his love, into a dense forest. But Pan pursued her, and stretched out his hand to seize her. When he believed he had caught up with her and that he was holding her by the hair, he found that he had a reed in his hand, for, as the story goes, the maiden had sunk into the earth, and in her place a reed had grown. Pan then cut down the reed, being vexed that it had hidden his love from him; but, being still unable to find her, he bethought him that the maiden had changed herself into the reed, and he felt sorry for what he had done, since now he thought that he had slain his loved one. So he collected the pieces of reed that had been cut off as if they were parts of a body, held them in his hand and kissed them as if kissing the wounds of the beloved maiden. Therewith he sighed in the madness of his love and breathed his sighs into the pipes, at the same time kissing them. But his breath penetrated the narrow pipes and brought them to music, and so the shepherd's flute acquired its voice" (viii, 6).

The scene in which poor Leucippe is to die as a sacrifice at the altar is especially droll. Fortunately her friends had previously attached an intestine filled with animal's blood to her body, and it is this that is ripped up by the sacrificer with a dagger the blade of which slips back into its sheath.

To convict Melite of intrigue with Cleitophon during his absence, Thersander compels her to go down into the water of the Styx (viii, 11–14), which has the remarkable property of falling back before an irreproachable woman, while it rises up to the neck of those who have perjured themselves. Melite gets into the water, with a little tablet round her neck, on which the oath was written that she had never been intimate with Cleitophon, all the time that Thersander was away. She triumphantly endures the ordeal, for the truth was that she had never stepped aside with Cleitophon until after Thersander had returned.

We still possess two books of erotic letters by a certain Aristænetus, which frequently border upon the pornographic. Their theme is the ardent glorification of female beauty, together with a number of love-stories, partly from his own experience, partly from outside sources.

These are the last offshoots of Greek literature, so far as it comes into consideration for our task. What we have noticed in our literary-historical survey belongs to erotic literature in the widest sense of the word; pornography, as to which we shall have something to say later, has not so far been taken into account.

PART II

CHAPTER I

The Love of the Man for the Woman

In the present chapter we have only to do with normal sexual intercourse, that is, between a male and female partner, other kinds being treated of in later chapters. But as the mental components in the Greek sexual life have been already discussed in detail, here it only remains to describe the physical or purely sensual side. We remember that, in the opinion of antiquity and more particularly in that of the Greeks, love, that is, the physical part of love, is a disease, or a more or less violent form of madness. By the first expression they implied that love, and consequently the sensual erotic impulse, results from a disturbance of the healthy equilibrium of body and mind, so that under the compulsion of sexual desire the mind loses its mastery of the body; while the expression "madness" must be taken to mean that sexual desire in itself is only to be understood by the assumption of a transitory dullness of intellectual power of comprehension. It is quite interesting that modern sexual science, to explain sexual phenomena, presupposes the existence of a male and female substance, that is, chemical substances which are formed in the body and have a toxic effect, and consequently bring about a transitory depreciation of the intellectual faculties.

The great philosopher Hartmann (*Philosophie des Unbewussten*, Berlin, 1869, p. 583), like Schopenhauer before him (*Die Welt als Wille und Vorstellung*, 3rd edn., 1859, vol. ii, p. 586), adopts this view and draws the apparently logical conclusion when he says: "Love causes more pain than pleasure. Pleasure is only illusory. Reason would command us to avoid love, if it were not for the fatal sexual impulse—therefore it would be best to be castrated." I describe this conclusion as logical, since Hartmann did not know—or did not remember—that castration by no means does away with the sexual impulse. The Greeks knew that—as the story told by Philostratus (ed. Kayser (Leipzig, Teubner, vol. i, p. 38)), in which a eunuch makes an immoral attempt upon a lady of the harem, as well as many similar passages, amply proves. We shall have to speak later of the importance of castration in Greek civilization; here it is mentioned only to show that the Greeks knew that the knife brings no remedy against the disease of love. If Theocritus (*Idyll*, xi, 1 ff. and 21) begins his well-known poem, in which he sympathizes with the pains of love felt by his friend, the Milesian physician Nicias, with the words: "There is no other remedy against love, O Nicias, it seems to me, neither salve nor plaster, but only the Muses; and this is a gentle medicine and sweet to use upon men, but it is hard to find," he shows that the only remedy against love that there is was well known to the Greeks; it was, and is to-day, the conscious diversion of the mind by some intensive occupation, no matter what it be—hard work, as the simple fisherman, in another poem of Theocritus, advises, or, as Theocritus himself proposes in the poem just quoted, occupation with poetry, that is, with intellectual activity generally.[1]

Yet the Greeks, clever physicians of the soul that they were, knew not only the remedy for the disease of love, but also how this poison of the soul creeps into the organism and settles there.

[1] Children of nature, like Daphnis and Chloë in the pastoral romance of Longus (see p. 288) are certainly of a different opinion: "Against love there is no remedy, neither a potion, nor powder, nor song; nothing except kissing, fondling, and lying together naked are of assistance" (II, 7, 7).

The gate of entry for the *bacillus eroticus*, the carrier of the disease of love, was in their opinion the eye. "Irresistible," says Sophocles (*Antigone*, 795), "is the bewitching charm of the eyes of the bridal maiden, in which the goddess Aphrodite practises her irresistible sport." It is said in Euripides (*Hippolytus*, 525) that "Eros drips longing from the eyes, awaking sweet rapture in the soul of those whom he proposes to subdue", and Pindar (*Nemea*, viii, 1) begins "Queen of youthful prime, harbinger of the divine desires of Aphrodite, thou who sittest upon the eyes of maidens and boys. . . ."

Æschylus (*Agam.*, 714; *Supplices*, 973) speaks of the "gentle arrow of love, which beams from the eyes, the heart-gnawing crown of bodily charm" and of the "magic dart of the eye of a girl".

Lastly, Achilles Tatius (i, 4, 4) says: "Beauty inflicts a worse wound than a dart, and penetrates through the eyes into the soul, for the eye is a pathway for the wounds of love."

The cheeks of the maiden, blushing in gracious bashfulness, awaken love in man, as Sophocles (*Antigone*, 783), so beautifully says: "Eros keeps watch in the soft cheeks of the maiden," or Phrynichus (frag. 8 in Ath., xiii, 603*e*), "On her purple-red cheeks shines the fire of love." When then the maiden, as Simonides (frag. 72 in Ath., xiii, 604*b*) says, "Sends forth her voice from her rosy mouth," then the lover is conquered, and when then, in the words of Aristophanes (*Lysistrata*, 551), "But if charming Eros and Cyprian Venus breathe desire on our bosoms and thighs and produce a pleasant and morbid tension for men, I hope that we shall be called enders of strife," then there is no further resistance, then they prepare themselves for "the coaxing works of love".[1] Lips pressed

[1] "The coaxing works of love": Mimnermus, 1, 3; kissing and biting, Brandt on *Amores*; i, 7, 41; kissing with the tongue, B. on *Amores*, ii, 5, 24, and p. 214; kissing and biting on shoulders and breasts, B.

against lips, the two lovers long remain in tender embrace, the lips open and the tongues fondle each other,[1] while the hands of the youth clasp the breasts of the girl and wantonly touch the plump apples; kisses are followed by tender bites, especially on the shoulders and breasts, from which the youth has pulled down the clothes with feverish hand. Long before, he has loosed her maiden girdle; now he drags his beautiful prey on to the bed adorned with flowers and, after numerous mutual acts of tenderness and words of endearment, completes the sacrifice of love.

The individual phases of the game of love here mentioned, which could easily have been further amplified, are all taken from ancient writings, of which an account is given in the notes at the foot of this and the previous page. Of course the game of love is described only in a typical form; in reality among the ancient Greeks the phases of sensual love occurred—also as a matter of course—in succession, and were, besides, inexhaustible in their forms.

Among kisses the so-called handle-kiss (χύτρα: see Eunicus (*CAF.*, I, 781, from Pollux, x, 100), also Plutarch's *Moralia*, 38*c*) enjoyed special popularity. "Take me by the ears and give me the handle-kiss," occurs in a comedy of Eunicus. Both name and thing originally belong to the life of children; the child was taken by both ears and kissed, the child at the same time being obliged to catch at the ears of the kisser with his tiny hand.

An equally popular form of tenderness was the kiss on the shoulder or the breast, as is proved by a

on *Amores*, i, 7, 41; feeling the breasts, Nonnus, *Dionysiaca*, vii, 264, i, 348, xlii, 67, cf. 303 ff., 312; Theocritus, xxvii, 48; Aristoph., *Lysist.*, 83. Further, Brandt on *Amores*, i, 5, 20, and p. 203; also Aristænetus, i, 16; Aristoph., *Eccles.*, 903. On the comparison with apples, Anth. Pal., v, 59; 289. Undressing scenes: Aristoph., *Lysist.*, 615, 662, 686. Feeling of the sexual parts of woman by man, Ovid, *Ars*, ii, 707 ff.; and of man by woman, Aristoph., *Lysist.*, 363. The "loosing of the maiden's girdle", common in Homer, e.g. *Od.*, xi, 245.

[1] The Greek for "a billing kiss" of the kind is καταγλώττισμα (Arist., *Clouds*, 51).

host of passages in the poems of the Anthology and in elegies.

Ancient literature and art practised a true cult of the female bosom. Nothing puts the Greek enthusiasm for the beauty of the female bosom in a clearer light than the well-known story of Phryne and her defender Hypereides (Ath., xiii, 590*e*). Phryne is accused of a serious crime; the court of justice is assembled; the balance of opinion is that the beautiful sinner is to be condemned. Then Hypereides tears open her dress and lays bare the gleaming charm of her bosom, and the judges' sense of beauty causes them to shrink from condemning the bearer of such charms. A more enthusiastic glorification of the female bosom can, in fact, hardly be imagined. We may also recall what was said before about Menelaus (p. 25), who at the sight of Helen's bare breasts forgot her adultery and forgave her.

The man's delight in these charms is reflected also in the works of Greek literature and art. One would have to write a special book if all the passages were to be collected in which homage is paid to the beauty of the bosom, and where the delight of the man at the sight and the tender endearments of these charms finds expression.

At least a few of the passages may be mentioned. Nonnus calls the "little apples" of the female breast "the darts of love". In the same author we read how the lover "presses the heaving globe of the plump breast" or how Dionysus "brings his loving hand near to the breast of the girl standing before him, and how, apparently by accident, he touches the prominent roundness of the dress and, when he feels the heaving breasts, the hand of the god, mad for women, begins to quiver". In another passage in the same poem: "As a reward I hold two apples in my hand, which grew as twin-fruit from a single trunk." In Theocritus the girl asks: "What are you doing, you satyr, why do you grasp my breasts?" To which Daphnis answers: "to test your heaving apples for the first time." Aristophanes: "And what a beautiful round bosom you have!"[1]

For the scene of undressing and the shy resistance of the maiden let Ovid (*Amores*, i, 5, 13; cp. iii, 14, 21 and *Ars.*, i, 665) be quoted: "At last I tore off her tunic, which was so thin that it really meant very little, and yet she still strove to cover herself with it. Struggling as if indeed she did not wish for victory, she was easily self-betrayed and overcome. When she now stood naked before me, I could see no flaw in her whole person. What shoulders, what arms I saw and felt! The well-formed breasts, how fit to be caressed! How tense was her body beneath her swelling breasts, undisfigured by wrinkles, how beautifully formed and wanton her buttocks, how youthfully slender her thighs! Why need I go into details? Everything I saw was beyond reproach, and enchanted I pressed her naked form to my body. . . . May I often have such happy hours of love!"

Elsewhere Ovid says: "She will perhaps resist at first and say 'You naughty man' yet even while resisting she will show that she desires to be overcome."

Here also two epigrams (Anth. Pal., v, 131 and 54) in the Palatine Anthology (by Philodemus and Dioscorides) may be mentioned, which we have already referred to in another connection.

For erotic and especially quite intimate contact the left hand was employed by preference (Ovid, *Amores*, ii, 15, 11, cf. *Ars*, ii, 706, nec manus in lecto læva iacebit iners; Martial, xi, 58, 11). Thus Ovid says: "Then I wished you were with me, that I might feel your breasts and put my left hand beneath your clothes."

[1] The oldest passage known to me in Greek literature in which the female breasts are compared with apples, is frag. 40 of Crates (*CAF.*, I, 142), where they are also compared with the fruits of the arbutus (strawberry-tree).

CHAPTER II

Masturbation

The commonest and most important substitute for love is self-abuse or onanism,[1] an expression which, however false it is, must be kept, since the word "Ipsation", proposed by Hirschfeld, has not become naturalized.

As onanism played no small part in Greek life, it is impossible to avoid it entirely. It was not regarded amongst the Greeks as a vice, as it is by us; and, as was the case in regard to most sexual phenomena, they had not the moral scruples of the present day against masturbation. They certainly were aware that it could be indulged to excess and thus have an injurious effect, but they also know that this holds good of every pleasure. So they regarded onanism as a substitute, as a safety-valve created by nature, which prevented sexual ailments and thousands of sins against morality with their consequences—illegitimate motherhood, imprisonment, suicide.

On the terminology itself we must first observe that the Greek language has many noticeable expressions for it.[2] Thus we find *χειρουργεῖν*, *ἀναφλᾶν*, *ἀποτυλοῦν*, *δέφειν*, *δέφεσθαι*, *ἀποσκολύπτειν*. Aristophanes has the noun *ἀναφλύστηρ*, which gains force since there actually existed an Attic deme, Anaphlystos. The word "masturbation"

[1] The first scientific book on the subject was written by the Lausanne physician, S. A. Tissot, in 1760, entitled *De l'onanisme ou dissertation physique sur les maladies produites par la masturbation*. The term, as is well known, goes back to the first book of Moses (Gen. xxxviii, 9), where Onan, the son of Judah, practises something quite different from what is now understood by onanism—the so-called *coitus interruptus* or *reservatus*.

[2] The word employed in many medical works, *cheiromania* "passion with the hand" is not used classically since *cheiromantis* signified "one who divines by palmistry, a fortune-teller".

comes from the Latin *masturbare*, a contraction from *manus* and *turbare* or *stuprare*.[1]

Onanism was regarded in Greece as a substitute for natural sexual demoralization and practised by men who lacked the opportunity for sexual intercourse, as many authors attest.

In regard to the enormous spread of onanism, which is to-day as much a matter of course as it was in ancient Greece, it is easy to understand that plastic artists, especially in miniature, were fond of depicting such scenes on vases and terracottas. Thus, the Royal Museum at Brussels possesses a cup on which a youth with a garland on his head is represented as performing the act.

If the self-abuse of the female sex is not so often spoken of in Greek literature, the reason is only natural, since in the written authorities generally much less is said about women than men, and it would be a mistake to draw the *a posteriori* conclusion that Greek girls and women did not practise onanism as much as boys and young men. Many passages in ancient writers constantly speak to us of the mysterious conduct of the Greek girls. These passages prove, what we should with certainty assume without them, that the self-abuse of girls in ancient Greece also took place either with the hand or with the help of instruments adapted or constructed for the purpose.

These instruments, or "self-satisfiers", were called by the Greeks *baubon* or *olisbos*. They were chiefly

[1] For *Χειρουργεῖν*, see Diogenes Laërtius (with the addition of *αἰδοῖον*) in Lucian, *Peregrin.*, 17, and (without it), *Lexiph.*, 12; Aristoph., *Lysist.*, 1099, etc.; according to Pollux (II, 176), Aristoph. (*CAF.*, I, 401) used ἀναφλᾶν and ἀνακνᾶν for "to practise onanism". With this is connected the noun ἀναφλασμός, quoted by Suïdas from Eupolis (*CAF.*, I, 272), and singularly explained by him as τὰ ἀφροδίσια. *Ἀναφλύστιος* in Aristoph., *Frogs*, 427. The verb ἀποτυλοῦν literally means "to make hard by rubbing"; thus in frag. 204 of Pherecrates (*CAF.*, I, 203); cf. Pollux, ii, 176: *ἐκαλεῖτο δὲ καὶ τύλος τὸ αἰδοῖον, ὅθεν καὶ Φερεκράτης τὸ γυμνοῦν αὐτὸ τῇ χειρὶ ἀποτυλοῦν εἶπεν.* For δέφειν and δέφεσθαι cf. Eubulus, frag. 120, 5 in Ath., I, 25*c*; Artemidorus, i, 78; Aristoph., *Knights*, 24; *Peace*, 290; and often elsewhere. *Ἀποσκολύπτειν* in Soph., frag. 390 (*TGF.*, p. 223); *Ἀναφλύστιος*, Aristoph., *Frogs*, 427.

made in the wealthy and luxurious commercial city of Miletus, whence they were exported to all countries. We learn more details from the sixth mimiambus of Herondas, entitled *The two Friends, or Confidential Talk*, which describes how two friends, at first somewhat ashamed, afterwards converse without any embarrassment about these olisboi. Metro had heard that her friend Coritto already possesses one, or, as she calls it, a baubon. This has been lent by Coritto to an intimate friend, before she has made use of it herself; but this friend, Eubule by name, has indiscreetly passed it on to someone else, so that Metro herself has also seen it. She is terribly anxious to borrow the instrument and also to know the name of the maker who supplies such commodities. She is informed that his name is Cerdon, but is not satisfied, since she knows two master-workmen of this name, "to whom she would certainly not care to entrust such work"; and it is remarkable how well informed she is as to the cobblers of the little city, their expertness in their line of business, and as to the names of their customers. Coritto afterwards describes the master-worker more exactly and falls into raptures over the marvellous baubons made by him. Metro then goes off to get such a treasure for herself.

Such an olisbos was used by girls, sometimes alone in the discreet quietness of the bedroom, sometimes two used one together. A passage in Lucian's *Erotes*[1] points to the instrument being used in common.

The name baubon obviously reminds us of *baubo*, which later by reason of its nakedness became the symbol of shamelessness and is represented as riding upon a sow.

[1] *Amores*, 28 (translated and fully explained by the author, 1920). Charicles, virtuously indignant, exclaims: "Turning to account the invention of such shameless instruments, the monstrous imitation made for unfruitful love, lest a woman embrace another woman as a man would do; let that word which hitherto so rarely reaches the ear—I am ashamed to mention it—let tribadic obscenity celebrate its triumphs without shame."

CHAPTER III

Tribadism

The words of Charicles above quoted lead us naturally to the discussion of so-called Tribadism. By *tribads* we understand those women who commit sexual acts in common. For obvious reasons the author considers it unnecessary to describe the purely anatomical nature of the proceedings, and for this would refer the student to the medical handbooks. It is the literary aspect of the subject, that is, the expression that tribadism has found in literature, that interests us here.

The name "tribad",[1] in the Greek lexicographers, is the usual term, mostly taken over by the Romans, for a woman who is devoted to homosexuality; by the side of it occurs the expression *Hetairistria* and *Dihetairistria*,[2] both derived from *hetaira*.

As we know from Lucian,[3] according to the general view of antiquity female homosexual intercourse was especially common in the island of Lesbos, whence even to the present day " Lesbian love " or " Lesbianism " is spoken of. Lesbos was the birthplace not only of Sappho, the queen of the tribads, but also of that Megilla, the heroine of the famous tribadic conversations in Lucian's collection of the *Dialogues of Courtesans*. According to Plutarch[4] amours amongst women were also very frequent in Sparta. Yet these are, of course, only occasional mentions; as a matter of fact, female homosexual love in Greek antiquity was

[1] *τριβάς* in the old lexikons; *τριβακὴ ἀσέλγεια* (wantonness of the tribads) in Lucian, *Amores*, 28.

[2] *ἑταιρίστρια* in Plato, *Sympos.*, 191*e*; Lucian, *Dial. Meretr.*, 5, 2; *διεταιρίστρια* in Hesychius; *tribas* in Phædrus, iv, 14; Martial, vii, 67, 1; *frictrix*, Tertullian, *De Pallio*, 4; in late Latin we find *frictrix*, she who rubs (from *fricare*, to rub).

[3] Lucian, *Dial. Meretr.*, 5, 2.

[4] Plutarch, *Lycurgus*, 18.

obviously as little tied to time and place as in modern times.

By the side of literary testimony pictorial representations should also be briefly mentioned: A bowl of Pamphæus in the British Museum shows a naked hetaira who has two olisboi in her hand; apparently there is a similar representation on a bowl of Euphronius. The motif of the latter figure, a naked hetaira with a thigh-band on her right leg, is the leather olisbos, which she makes use of. The egg-shaped object, which the hetaira holds in her right hand, repeatedly occurs on vases of this period, e.g. in the hand of an ephebus in the interior of the bowl of Hiero in the Louvre. It is a flagon from which the hetaira drips oil upon the phallus. In the vase-collection of the Berlin Museum there is a vase with a very interesting representation, which appears to indicate that women were accustomed to wash themselves after using the olisbos. Furtwängler thus describes it: "A naked woman is in the act of binding her sandals on her left foot; she is bending forward, draws the red bands towards her with both hands, and, in order to be nearer her foot, has let herself down partly on her right knee, so that the space is admirably filled. A flat basin at her feet hints that she has just washed herself. On her right can be recognized the outline of a large phallus in the open space turned towards her."

Several terra-cottas in Naples with such subjects are described by Gerhard and Panofka: in No. 20 a naked woman sits, embracing a phallus, which lies like a bladder over her in front; No. 16 is a bald-headed old woman, her left arm supported on a pillow, and she looks at a phallus lying in front of her.

In addition, mention should be made of the red-figured vase painting of an Attic *hydria* (water-vessel) of the fifth century B.C. in the Berlin Antiquarium. It represents a naked girl with full breasts and still fuller buttocks, who is carrying a gigantic phallus in the form of a fish under her left arm.

A famous tribad was Philænis of Leucadia, certainly, according to Lucian, the first who wrote an illustrated work on tribadic postures, though in an epitaph upon her by Æschrion of Samos it was denied that she wrote this obscene book. Whether the Philænis often mentioned by Martial is identical with her, cannot be decided with certainty; more probably the name is invented by Martial, in order to have a collective address for the extravagances described by him.

The most famous and the most important woman, for the purposes of our present inquiry, was Sappho, or as she calls herself in the Æolic dialect "Psappha", the celebrated poetess, "the tenth Muse" (Anth. Pal., ix, 506; vii, 14; ix, 66, 521; vii, 407), as the inspired Greeks call her or, as Strabo says (Strabo, xiii, 617*c*), "the marvel among women". She was the daughter of Scamandronymus, born about 612 B.C. at Eresus in the island of Lesbos, or according to others, in Mitylene. She had three brothers, one of whom, Charaxus, lived for a considerable time in Naucratis (Egypt) with the coquettish hetaira Doricha, called Rhodope (rosy-cheeked); his indiscretion is blamed by his sister in a poetical fragment (frag. 138). The second brother, Eurygius, is only known by name; the third, Larichus, owing to his remarkable beauty, was appointed cupbearer in the prytaneum (town-hall) of Mitylene. Her marriage with Cercylas of Andros, only mentioned by Suïdas, is improbable and certainly to be referred back to comedy, in which the private life of Sappho was criticized at an early date, and she herself, contrary to the truth, was ridiculed as longing after men (frag. 75).[1] Also, the statement that she had a daughter, named Claïs, is nothing more than a deduction from some

[1] Andros = the city of men; Cercylas, derived from *kerkos* = penis.

passages in her poems, in which she says of a girl Claïs, that " I have a daughter fair, and none so loved as she : Not all the Lybian land, Nor Lesbos' lovely strand, Can weigh her worth to me."

Since in all the fragments love for man is only mentioned once and then decidedly rejected, Claïs is more likely to have been one of Sappho's girl friends than her daughter. Her amour with the handsome Phaon is certainly to be banished to the realm of fable ; and similarly, the famous leap to death into the sea, alleged to have been taken because Phaon tired of her, is to be attributed to a misunderstanding of the metaphor current among the Greeks —" to spring from the rock of Leucadia into the sea ", that is, to purify the soul of passions.

Sappho's life and poetry are filled with the love of her own sex ; she is in antiquity—perhaps in all time—the best-known priestess of this type of love, which from early times, as we have seen, had been styled " Lesbian ". Sappho gathered a circle of young girls around her, of whom Anagora, Euneica, Gongyla, Telesippa, Megara, and Claïs are named in the fragments, and we hear too of Andromeda, Gorgo, Eranna, Mnasidica, and Nossis. Her union with these friends was chiefly combined with poetical and musical interests ; in her " house of the Muses " (frag. 136) the girls were instructed in all the musical arts, playing, singing, and dancing. She loves her girls so intensely, and expresses this love in the scanty fragments of her poems with such passion, that to attempt again what Welcker and others have already attempted—to whitewash Sappho of the reproach of love for those of her own sex—with whatever good intention would be an endeavour lacking any prospect of success. In accordance with the Greek outlook, and its comparative indifference to such things, Sappho's tendency was not regarded as a vice ; she did not, of course, escape occasional ridicule—but she was ridiculed not on account of her impulsive nature, but because of the frankness with which she laid bare her inmost soul, and because of the emancipation which she sought from the limitations in domestic life which at that time were still demanded from the Greek women.

Horace hits the mark, when he calls Sappho "the male" (*mascula*) (*Ep.*, i, 19, 28—*temperat Archilochi Musam pede mascula Sappho*). The male part of her character explains her love and is the key to the understanding of her poetry. She is shaken by the almighty power of love "like oak-trees by a storm". Her poetry is saturated with the nameless happiness as well as the abysmal pain of love. The god in her breast gives convulsive expression to the torments of jealousy as well as to the pain of the ingratitude that she has suffered. The dearest of her loved ones was Atthis; and from the lamentably mutilated remains of the poems the heartfelt romance of the two girls, distinguished by mental and physical beauty, can even yet be recognized, at least in individual phases.

For the start of Sappho's love we should perhaps put the words with which she herself confesses the passion that flames up with mighty power:

> "Love's palsy yet again my limbs doth wring,
> That bitter-sweet, resistless creeping thing."[1]

Once again she becomes aware of the power of the god, which she is unable to resist, and gives expression to it in a new image:

> "Love again hath fluttered my heart, as a squall
> That down from the hills on the oaks doth fall."

Certainly, she still seeks to force back passion, and from her breast the touching complaint breaks forth with a struggle that betrays how her soul is torn in two directions: "I know not what I am to do, my soul is divided." Yet the struggle with love is in vain, she confesses it to herself: "As a child to its mother, so I fly to thee." And when

[1] This and the following quotations from Sappho are from *Sappho, her Poems and Fragments*, by C. R. Haines, M.A., Broadway Translations, Geo. Routledge & Sons, Ltd., 1926.

she sees that it is a useless undertaking to renounce the wish of her soul, then she turns with a childishly pious prayer to the great goddess, who understands her sorrow, and from her poetical mouth springs forth the immortal song to the "craft-weaving" Aphrodite. It was allowed her to tell her sufferings, and so the ode is an expression of a heart, pious, but thrilling with hot passion. She calls on the goddess to help her in the present need of her soul; may she as once before float down from heaven and alleviate her sorrow. With genuine poetic fancy she recalls the image of the goddess, how she formerly appeared to her in person, asked with charming sympathy what was the cause of her sorrow and promised her the fulfilment of her heart's desires. To this recollection is added the prayer and the hope that this time also the immortal will be favourable to her and render her support:

Immortal Cypris of the marbled throne, Daughter of Zeus, for all wiles are thine own,
Crush not my soul, O lady queen, with care and teen;
But hither come, if thou in days gone by Didst ever leave thy father's home on high,
Deigning from far my prayers to hear with listening ear,
And camest in thy golden car, that straight Thy dainty sparrows down from heaven's gate,
With quick winds winnowing the air o'er dark Earth bare,
And lo! were here; and thou, O lady blest, Thy lovely face in smiles immortal drest,
Didst ask what ails assailed me? Why this wistful cry?
For what new boon with frenzied soul I prayed Above all else; and "Who", saidst thou, "the maid
Whose love you fain would win? Who so works Sappho woe?
If now she spurns, she soon shall seek your side, If gifts she scorns, to give shall be her pride,
If she kiss not, she soon shall kiss, coy though she is."
Come, Queen, now also, and thy suppliant save From carking cares,
All that my heart would crave
Bring thou to pass, and be my friend still to the end.

The kindly goddess was unable to resist such a prayer; at least she filled the heart of her protégée with courage and joyful confidence in love, so that she brought herself to open her soul to the loved one in the second of the songs completely preserved for us, quoted by Longinus as an example of the

Sublime, which is attained by the bringing into prominence and gathering up of the chief moments :

> " Like to the gods I deem him blest, Who, face to face with thee, thy guest,
> Sits welcome with ears rapt to hear thy voice so sweet, so near,
> Thy lovely laugh : that sight doth make The heart within my bosom shake !
> When I but glance at thee, no word from my dumb lips is heard,
> My tongue is tied, a subtle flame Leaps in a moment o'er my frame,
> I see not with mine eyes, my ear can only murmurs hear,
> Sweat dews my brow, quick tremors pass Through every limb, more wan than grass
> I blanch, and frenzied, nigh to death, *I gasp away my breath*."

" One must not be astonished," we read further in Longinus, " how she groups together soul, body, ear, tongue, eyes, colour, of whatever different kind they may be, and, uniting the opposites, at the same time grows cold and hot, loses her senses, and finds them again ; she shivers and is near to death, so that it is not merely a single passion that shows itself in her, but a conflict of passions."

We certainly agree with this judgment, and add that we should not care to regard the poem as a song of farewell (as some do), but as the song of wooing of a hot and open soul, who, perhaps after a long struggle, at last finds courage to afford the loved being a glance into her inmost feelings, into her wishes not yet fulfilled. It is not in contradiction with this that she regards a man as happy to whom it is permitted to enjoy the sight of a beloved female friend ; the expression is very indefinitely worded and there is little doubt that what she really means is that every one who sits facing his loved one and at the same time thinks chiefly of himself, is happy ; in which case it may still be possible that she is intentionally obscure, for her soul, hurrying forward with lively fancy, has already been attacked by the gloomy foreboding that she would some day belong to a man, and consequently the sting of jealousy has made its way into the soul of the poetess, even before she herself has enjoyed the happiness of love. On the other hand, our conception of the poem as a song of wooing is confirmed by the fact that Catullus has translated it almost word for word, in order to confess his yearning for his loved one and to woo her love. Now, Catullus's Clodia—Catullus, however, named her Lesbia after her favourite poetess—was too well acquainted with Sappho's character for us to believe the sensitive Roman capable of the *gaucherie* of wooing the love of his Sappho with " a song of farewell " by the genuine Sappho.

So then in the two pearls of Sapphic poetry her love for Atthis has found a pure and affecting expression, which did not close the heart of the divinely inspired songstress to such wooing of love. The two girls found themselves united by a long-standing bond of friendship, from which certainly much that was magnificent originated, many a tender and intimate song of friendship, love, and innocently joyful pleasure in life, and many a lofty majestic hymn, when the god took possession of the poetess and unsealed her lips. All this has been lost to us through the unkindness of fate, and it is only occasionally that we find a few words of the Lesbian maid that witness to her friendship for Atthis; certainly, the confession that one day she makes to her in an hour of joy was made in a time of unclouded happiness—" I loved you, Atthis, with all my heart, before you as yet suspected it."

Considering the passionate warmth which Sappho felt for this girl we cannot be surprised that our poetess was not exempt from the pangs of jealousy; she gives expression to her pain with words that suggest reproach, though, as they are still informed by love, they are not meant too angrily:

> "Atthis, all thought of me thou now dost hate,
> And hoverest ever at Andromeda's gate."

Was the jealousy well-founded, or was it merely

a temporary separation from Sappho that elicited the touching complaint, so full of feeling?

> "The Moon and Pleiades have set, Midnight is nigh,
> The time is passing, passing, yet alone I lie."

Another time the anxious fear breaks forth with a struggle from her lips: "Certainly thou lovest another of the human kind more than me." But her love for Atthis is the more intimate since she had already found pleasure in her at a time when she was merely a little girl from whom the hour of betrothal was still far distant.

That Atthis later separated from Sappho, we learn from the fragment of a poem, which in 1896 was acquired, together with numerous other pieces of papyrus, by the Egyptian department of the State museums in Berlin. The poem, unfortunately mutilated, is addressed to a common friend, perhaps Andromeda, who, like Sappho, feels it especially painful that the beloved Atthis is now lingering in distant Lydia—"Among the women of Lydia she shines, as the moon surpasses the stars in brightness when it rises over the sea." And the poem concludes with a heartfelt description of a moonlight night on flowery fields, while in the calyx of the flowers the dew sparkles, and there is a scent of roses and sweet clover. "And often," Sappho continues, "longing will fill thy heart, when thou thinkest of the sweet voice of Atthis."

If therefore what is known to us of Sappho's bosom friend from a few fragments of her poetry is quite scanty, yet we can give even less information about her other friends and pupils. We hear the oath of eternal loyalty in the beautiful words: "Fair comrades mine, to you My thoughts are ever true."

In a comparatively longer fragment, but which unfortunately has not come down to us without several lacunæ, one of her pupils, who feels as if she is going to die, takes an affectionate farewell of Sappho, who tells her in answer that she should be of good courage, but must never forget her She should think of the goddess whom she is now leaving, and remember all that is beautiful, all that they had both enjoyed in her service. And she reminds her of the wreaths of violets and roses, which with Sappho she laid down to adorn the temple, and of the service in which they were both devoted to the goddess. (Sappho, frag. 35, 31, 36; Longinus, *De Sublim.*, 10. The famous poem is imitated by Catullus, li.)

In the friendship of Sappho with her pupils the ancients saw a counterpart of the intimate relations of Socrates with his pupils, a certainly significant and very useful parallel for judging of the relationship, which the philosopher Maximus of Tyre (*Dissert.*, 24, 9), who lived in the time of the Roman emperor Commodus, describes in detail in the following manner: " What then is the passion of the Lesbian songstress but the love-technique of Socrates? For both of them seem to me to have the same idea of love, the former the love of girls, the latter of youths. What then an Alcibiades, Charmides and Phædrus were to Socrates, a Gyrinna, Atthis, and Anactoria are to Sappho; what rivals such as Prodicus, Gorgias, Thrasymachus, and Protagoras were to Socrates, so are Gorgo and Andromeda to Sappho. Now she scolds and refutes them, and at the same time employs the same irony as Socrates. 'Hail to thee, my Ion,' says Socrates. 'Hail to thee and blessing, little daughter of Polyanax,' says Sappho. Socrates declares that he has loved Alcibiades for a very long time, but has been unwilling to approach him as long as he did not think him capable of understanding what he said—'You seemed to me to be still a little child without grace,' says Sappho. Everyone makes fun of the attitude and seat of a sophist: 'What an uncultured woman in boorish attire,' she says. Eros, says Diotima to Socrates, is not the son, but the companion and servant of

Aphrodite, and also in an ode of Sappho she says to her, 'Thou and Eros thy servant.' Diotima says that Eros prospers to overflowing and dies in want; this Sappho has comprehended in the words—'bitter-sweet and bringing pain.' Socrates calls Eros a sophist, Sappho a rhetorician. The former is senseless before love of Phædrus; love convulses the heart of the latter, as a storm on the mountains assails the oaks. Socrates reproaches Xanthippe for lamenting his approaching death; Sappho says to her Claïs—'Never, where lovers of the Muses dwell, Should dirges sound; for us that were not well.'"

This parallel of Sappho with Socrates is thoroughly justified. In both the extraordinary susceptibility to personal beauty is the foundation of the friendly intercourse with youth, and of the presumption of the erotic character of such friendship. Socrates will be spoken of later; but in regard to Sappho, as already said, judging from the remains of her poetry and the almost unanimous testimony of antiquity there can no longer be any doubt of the erotic character both of her odes and of her intercourse with her friends. Even Ovid, who, be it observed, could read the poems of Sappho in their complete form, says that there can be nothing more sensual than her poetry, and therefore recommends the reading of it to the girls of his time as of most pressing importance. In another passage he expressly says that all Sappho's poetry was a unique course of instruction in female homosexuality. Lastly, Apuleius remarks that "Sappho has written passionate and sensual verses, certainly wanton, but yet also so graceful that the wantonness of her language captures the reader's favour by the sweet harmony of words". All these are authors who still had her complete works before them and whose judgment must therefore be decisive, especially as it agrees with our own conclusions from the remains of Sapphic poetry that have come down to us. But it is just these fragments that make it clear that Sappho's poetry not merely breathed the sensual glow of passion, but also was illuminated by feeling derived from the very depth of her soul.

Gradually no doubt, and chiefly through Attic comedy, but later more by unsound erudition, the element of soul was more and more denied, and Sappho came to be regarded as partly a woman mad for men, and partly as an unblushing tribad. We know of six comedies called *Sappho*, and of two called *Phaon*. Of these only scanty fragments are preserved, but it is firmly established that in them the glowing sensuality of the poetess was revealed, but brutally exaggerated and even made ridiculous. From the island of Lesbos, the home of the poetess, the phrase "Lesbian love" gradually came into fashion, and "to play the Lesbian" already occurs frequently in Aristophanes in the sense of practising immorality in the Lesbian manner. Certainly the Lesbians generally were regarded as immoral, so that "a Lesbian woman" is but another name for a whore (*laikastria*). Further, Didymus, the savant who lived in the time of Ciccro, examined the question whether Sappho was a common harlot; and the immoral character of her relationship with her friends was emphasized by the humanists Domitius Calderinus and Johannes Britannicus, and by the commentators of Horace—Lambinus, Torrentius, and Cruquius. If we conscientiously examine everything, especially the fragments of her poetry that have been preserved and the information given by antiquity, we shall be forced to the conclusion that Sappho was an inspired artist, a poetical phenomenon of the very first rank, but that she was at the same time a tribad of unbounded sensuality, however illuminated by the gold of her poetry.[1]

[1] Opinions of ancient writers on Sappho: Ovid, *Ars Amatoria*, iii, 331, *Nota sit et Sappho, quid enim lascivius illa?* *Tristia*, ii, 365, *Lesbia quid docuit Sappho, nisi amare puellas*; cf. also Martial, vii, 69; x, 35, 15, *and* Apuleius, *Apologia*, 413. λεσβιάζειν, Aristoph.,

Towards the end of the fourth century B.C. lived Nossis, a poetess from the lower Italian city of Locris, who ventured proudly to put herself on a level with Sappho. "Stranger," she says (*Anth. Pal.*, vii, 718), "if thou sailest to Mitylene, the city of lovely dances which kindled (?) Sappho, the flower of the Graces, say that the Locrian land bore one dear to the Muses and equal to her, and that her name was Nossis. Go!" She showed enthusiastic admiration for her friends in pretty epigrams, some of which are preserved; and in one (*Anth. Pal.*, v, 170) she confesses that there is "nothing sweeter than love", and that, unless Venus be gracious, one can never know how precious are its flowers.

Birds, 1308, *λεσβίζειν*, *Wasps*, 1346; Hesychius s.v. *Λαικάστρια*; Didymus, *An Sappho publica fuerit*, see Seneca, *Epist.*, 88, 37 (M. Schmidt, *Didymi Chalcenteri Fragmenta*, 1854). On all questions concerning Sappho, cf. P. Brandt, *Sappho. Ein Lebensbild aus den Frühlingstagen altgriechischer Dichtung* (Leipzig, 1905).

CHAPTER IV

PROSTITUTION

1. GENERAL REMARKS

If in the course of this presentation of Greek manners and culture it has repeatedly been necessary to remark that it was a question of working upon entirely new ground, or that, in the case of a particular chapter, preliminary works of reference were non-existent, no such complaint can be made as we pass on to describe the nature of Greek prostitution. Rather the contrary would be the truth, and an author might almost apologize for the abundance of works treating of his subject, the number of which in this case can scarcely be estimated. Hence we have but to work up the material supplied by easily accessible handbooks so far as is necessary to complete the general picture, and then to occupy ourselves rather with details taken from more remote and therefore less-known sources.

In Greek antiquity these things were considered without prejudice. Not only were women who could be bought for money called *hetairæ*, which may be translated " life-partners " or " friends ", but these priestesses of Venus were spoken and written about openly and without embarrassment, and the immense part which they played in private life is reflected also in Greek literature. There was a vast number of writings on the hetairæ, either generally, or on those of particular cities, such as Corinth and Athens especially. Even the great grammarian and philologist Aristophanes of Byzantium (Ath., xiii, 567*a*; A. Nauck, *Arist. Byz. Grammatici Alexandrini fragmenta*, 1848) did not disdain to publish investigations of the life-history of Athenian prostitutes. According to the list given in Athenæus, among others his pupil Callistratus (Ath., xiii, 591*d*), the famous student of Homer, and the philologists Apollodorus, Ammonius, Antiphanes, and Gorgias may be mentioned (Apollodorus, see Susemihl, II, 41, 54; Ammonius, ib. II, 155, 43; Gorgias, Ath., xiii, 567*a*, 583*a*, 596*f*.).

Of all these writings little more than the title is known. But the witty *Dialogues of Courtesans* by Lucian have come down to us, and various others are translated below or at least summarized according to their subject.

Alciphron's still extant *Letters of Courtesans* have been already mentioned and represented by specimens. The *Chreiæ* of Machon, a collection of anecdotes, will be spoken of in the course of this chapter.[1]

Terminology. The Greeks, if they wished to avoid the ugly name "whores" (πόρναι), delicately called girls who sold themselves for money by the name of ἑταῖραι, properly "comrades", "companions". There were also many more or less coarse designations, several dozen of which are enumerated by lexicographers like Pollux and Hesychius. Among the expressions collected by the latter are: ἀπόφαρσις, the chopper-up; γεφυρίς, the "bridge-woman", one who gads about the bridges; δαμιουργός, parish worker; δημίη, public woman; δρομάς, "runner"; ἐπιπαστάς, "bedroom-article; κασαλβάς (Aristoph., *Eccles.*, 1106), and κασάλβη, according to the scholiast on the *Knights*, 355, compounded of καλεῖν and σοβεῖν, since whores "entice" men and then "drive them away"—a very doubtful explanation; also the word κασαλβάζειν (*Knights*, 355) to "abuse like a prostitute"; see Hermippus in the scholiast on

[1] Of modern descriptions of the nature of prostitution among the Greeks may be mentioned: F. Jacobs, *Vermischte Schriften*, iv, p. 311; Becker-Göll, *Charicles*, ii, p. 85 (Berlin, 1877); Limburg-Brouwer, *Histoire de la civilisation morale et religieuse des Grecs*, ii, p. 174 (Groningen, 1883); Pauly-Wissowa-Kroll, *Realenzyklopädie der klassischen Altertumswissenschaft*, viii, col. 1331 (Stuttgart, 1913).

the *Wasps*, 1164. Similar expressions for "whore" are κασαύρα, κασαυράς, κασαυρίς, κασωρίς (Lycophron, 1385), κασωρῖτις, (Antiphanes in Eustathius, 741, 38), and κάσσα (Lycophron, 131). To these names may be compared the terms for a brothel, κασάλβιον, κασαύρεῖον (*Knights*, 1285), and κασώριον.

Of further expressions for whores Hesychius enumerates (Pollux, vii, 203; Hesychius, περὶ ἑταίρων καὶ πόρνων; cf. also Eustathius on Homer, *Il.* xxiii, 755) κατάκλειστος "the shut in" (Corinthian), of girls kept in a brothel; λυπτά (the gloss, probably wrongly handed down, would properly mean "she-wolf", indicating their greed and covetousness); λωγάς, perhaps the same as λαικάς (Aristænetus, 2, 16); also λαικάστρια (Aristoph., *Acharnians*, 529) and λαικάζειν, to play the whore (Aristoph., *Thesm.*, 57, *Knights*, 167) and λαικᾶν in the same sense (Hesychius), and λωγάνιος, properly "dice", since whores are taken in men's hands and then thrown away; μαχλάς (Anth. Pal., v, 301, 2) and μαχλίς, also μαχλοσύνη (Homer, *Iliad*, xxiv, 30), μαχλότης (Schol. Lycophron, 771; *Etym. Mag.*, 524, 24) and μαχλοῦν, to play the whore, μαχλεύειν, to practise prostitution (Manetho, iv, 315), μαχλικός, wanton (Manetho, iv, 184), all from μαχλός, unchaste, lascivious, applied to women, while λαγνός was used of men in the same sense (Lobeck on Phrynichus, 184). With this word, which is certainly connected with λαγώς, hare, known for its lustfulness, belongs λαγνεία = emission of seed (Aristotle, *Hist. anim.*, vi, 21), but generally "lust" (Tim. Locr., 103*a*; Xenophon, *Memorabilia*, i, 6, 8; also λαγνεύειν and λάγνευμα in Hippocrates, generally meaning "to be lustful" (Lucian, *Rhet. præc.*, 23).

Other expressions in Hesychius: πῶλος, "foal"; Eubulus (*CAF.*, II, 193) had called the hetairæ the "foals of Aphrodite". Σαλαβακχώ is a whore in Aristoph., *Knights*, 765, *Thesmoph.*, 805, and was used generally by the inhabitants of

Attica as their name. Σινδίς, properly a woman from the land of the Sindi at the foot of the Caucasus, therefore a whore; σποδησιλαύρα (Eustathius, 1921, 58), properly the street dust-sweeper; στατή (certainly wrongly handed down) explained by Hesychius with κάρδοπος = kneading-trough; στεγῖτις properly room-furniture; χαμαιτύπη (Timocles in Athenæus, xiii, 570 f. and elsewhere) properly "lying on the ground"; also χαμαιτυπεῖον, brothel (Lucian, *Nigrinus*, 22 and elsewhere); χαμαίτυπος (Polybius, viii, 11, 11) whoremonger and whore; χαμαιτυπία (Alciphron, 3, 64) whoremongering; χαμαιτυπικός, like a whore; χαμαιτυπίς, a whore, also χαμεταιρίς and χαμευνάς (Lycophron, 319).

For brothelhouse-keepers, procurers, bullies, etc., the Greek language has many names, partly extremely drastic, for which the philologically trained reader may consult the index in Vol. IV of Moriz Schmidt's large edition of Hesychius (Jena, 1857) and also the article in Pauly-Wissowa-Kroll's *Realenzyklopädie* mentioned at p. 330 (*n*).

2. BROTHELS

The whores who were quartered in brothels (πορνεῖα) occupied the lowest rank in the social position of *filles de joie*; they were not distinguished as hetairæ, but were called simply "whores". In Athens the foundation of brothels was referred to the wise Solon.

In brothels whores stood very lightly clad or even quite naked for show, that every visitor might make his choice according to his personal taste. The statement by itself is quite credible, but there is abundant evidence to prove it. Thus Athenæus (xiii, 568*e*; Eubulus, frag. 84, *CAF.*, II, 193) says: "Do you not know how, in Eubulus's comedy *Pannychis*, it is said of the music-loving, money-enticing bird-catchers, the dressed up foals of Venus, that they stand there in order on parade, in transparent dresses of fine-spun fabrics, like the nymphs on the sacred waters of Eridanus? Amongst them you can buy pleasure for a trifle to your heart's desire and without any risk."

In the comedy *Nannion* (frag. 67, *CAF*., II, 187) it is said: "Who watches stealthily for a forbidden bed, is he not of all men the most unhappy? While he can see the girls standing naked there in the bright sunlight," etc.

Further, Athenæus says "But also Xenarchus (frag. 4, *CAF*., II, 468) in his comedy the *Pentathlon* blames people who live like you and are keen after expensive hetairæ and free women, in the following words, 'the young people in our city do what is terrible, terrible, and a thing that can no longer be endured.' Where one sees only comely girls in the brothels—one can look at them and see how, with bared breasts in thin dresses of gauze drawn up in a row they exhibit themselves in the sun; any man may pick out the one that pleases him—thin, fat, roundish, lanky, crooked, young, old, moderate-sized, mature—you need not set up a ladder to enter secretly, you need not creep in through the dormer-window, nor cleverly smuggle yourself in in heaps of straw; they themselves drag you almost with violence into the house, calling you, if you are already an old man, 'daddy,' otherwise 'little brother' and 'little youngster'. And you can have any one of them for a small sum without any risk, by day or towards evening."

It appears that admission to the brothel cost but a trifle—according to the passage already quoted from the comic writer Philemon one obol (about 1½d.). This agrees with a passage from Diogenes Laërtius (vi, 4) where we read: "When Antisthenes once saw an adulterer running away, he said: "You ass, you could have had that without any risk for an obol!" Of course the price of admission was regulated by place and time and must have differed according to the quality of the houses, yet we may be allowed to assume that in no case can it have been very high, since brothels represented the lowest, and hence the cheapest, form of prostitution. It must be added that, of course, in any case besides the entrance-money a " present " had to be given to the girls, the amount of which was determined by the demands made upon them. If the author rightly understands a note in Suïdas, this present varied between obols, drachmæ, and in better houses even staters.[1]

Out of the revenue obtained from the honorarium of the girls the brothel-keeper (πορνοβοσκος) (cf. Demosth., 59, 30; Æschin., 1, 188; 3, 214) had to pay a yearly tax to the State, the so-called prostitute-tax (τέλος πορνικόν) (Æschin., 1, 119), which a special official, the *pornotelōnēs* (πορνοτελώνης) (Philonides in Pollux, ix, 29; *CAF*., I, 255, and Böckh, *Public Economy of Athens*), or several, was appointed to collect. Similarly, the honorarium (μίσθωμα) which the visitor had to pay the girls (Ath., xiii, 581*a*, xii, 526*b*), was fixed by special officials, the *agoranomi* (ἀγοράνομοι). The brothels, as well as the whole system of prostitution generally, stood under the supervision of the city officials, the *astynomoi* (ἀστύνομοι), whose duty it was to maintain public decency, and also to decide disputes.

In the cities by the sea most brothels were probably to be found in the harbour quarters, as Pollux expressly states was the case at Athens (Pollux, ix, 5, 34). But in the ward named Ceramicus, according to Hesychius (s.v. Κεραμεικός), there were also numerous brothels of all grades.

The Ceramicus, the " potters' quarter ", extended from the market in a north-westerly direction as far as the so-called Dipylon, the double gate, and then, beyond this gate, under the name of the

[1] A drachma = about 9d., a stater about £1.

Outer Ceramicus by the side of the Sacred Way leading to Eleusis. It is interesting to note that the sanctity of this religious festal street does not seem to have been affected by the numerous brothels existing in it. Through this district a long, broad street, called Dromos (Corso), led from the interior of the city, on both sides adorned with colonnades, in which there were numerous shops.

Greek writers have not told us much about the arrangement of the brothels, their equipment, or their internal management, but we may assume that they did not differ much from Roman and Italian brothels, as to which we are well informed. Indeed, it is even to-day possible to visit a Greco-Roman " house of joy ". Every one who knows Pompeii will understand what I mean : in the Fourth Region ins. 12, no. 18, at the corner of the *Vicolo del Balcone Pensile* is the house *Il Lupanare*, in which Pompeii's young men sowed their wild oats, of which even to-day numerous obscene wall-paintings and inscriptions remind us. It is interesting also to notice that a separate entrance led from the street direct into the second story by a gallery (*pergula*).

Horace and the author of the *Priapea* (Horace, *Sat*., i, 2, 30; *Priapeia*, 14, 9) call the Roman brothels (*fornices* or *lupanaria*) evil-smelling, which would indicate dirt and uncleanliness, so that according to Seneca (*Controv*., i, 2 : *redoles adhuc fuliginem fornicis*) visitors took the smell away with them, which Juvenal (vi, 131) in his biting satire remarks with grim satisfaction about the empress Messalina who prostituted herself in the brothel. In each brothel there were of course a number of rooms or chambers, called *cellæ* (Juvenal, vi, 122, 127; Petronius, 8; Martial, xi, 45); above each was written the name of the girl (Martial, xi, 45; Seneca, *Controv*., i, 2) who inhabited it, with perhaps also a mention of the lowest price she would take. Authors also mention the different coverlets (Petronius, 20; Martial, xiv, 148, 152) (*lodices*, *lodiculæ*), which were spread over the bed or on the floor, and as a matter of course the lamp (*lucerna*) (Martial, xiv, 39–42; Horace, *Sat.*, ii, 7, 48; Juvenal, vi, 121; Tertull., *Ad uxorem*, ii, 6).

The price had to be paid to the girls in advance, as a passage of Juvenal seems to show (vi, 125: *excepit blanda intrantes atque aera poposcit*). Whores were also called *nonariæ* by Persius (Persius, i, 133, and Scholiast: *nonaria dicta meretrix quia apud veteres a nona hora prostabant, ne mane omissa exercitatione illo irent adulescentes*), for the houses were not allowed to open until the ninth hour, that is, towards four o'clock in the afternoon, "so as not to keep young men away from their exercises." To entice passers-by the girls stood or sat before the *lupanaria*, whence they were also called *prostibula* (for *prostabulum* see Nonius Marcellus, v, 8; for *proseda* see Plautus, *Pœnulus*, i, 2, 54) or *prosedæ*, the former of these words being derived from *prostare*, whence "prostitution". If a girl had a visitor in her cell, she shut the door, having first hung upon it a ticket bearing the word *occupata*, "engaged" (Plautus, *Asinaria*, iv, 1, 15). At a certain hour, probably towards morning, the brothels were shut, as we may conjecture from a passage in Juvenal (vi, 127). We should have imagined that the walls were adorned with obscene pictures and paintings even had the finds from the Pompeian "house of joy" not expressly confirmed this.

The opinion of the ancients in regard to the sexual prevented them from seeing anything offensive in visiting the brothels, as is undoubtedly clear from several passages of ancient writers. So Horace (*Sat.*, i, 2, 31) says in the well-known satire, in which he is speaking about sexual life: "When a very famous man had once visited a brothel, he said: praised be to eternity the sensible opinion of the old Cato. As soon as desire brings the blood in the veins of young men to boiling heat, it is right and just that they should go this way and not seduce respectable married women."[1]

We return to Greece after this digression upon the character of Roman prostitution. The numerous prostitutes who roam about, and girls who regard prostitution as a sort of secondary trade, occupy an intermediate place between the whores of the brothel and the hetairæ. We need not say any more about street prostitution, since it was carried on in forms not essentially different from those of modern times. In accordance with the nature of the case, the manner in which the whore dealt with the customer or vice versa was infinitely various. Some interesting specimens are preserved in the Palatine Anthology; one of which I have already given.

Here is a second example (Anth. Pal., v, 101):

He. Good day, my dear.
She. Good day.
He. Who is she that walks in front of you?
She. What is that to you?
He. I have a reason for asking.
She. My mistress.
He. May I hope?
She. What do you want?
He. A night.
She. What have you for her?
He. Gold.
She. Then take heart.
He. So much (*showing the amount*).
She. You can't.

We have an epigram of Asclepiades (v, 185), the subject of which is that he sends his friend to

[1] On this the Horatian scholiast observes: Once, just as Cato was pausing by a brothel, a young man, very embarrassed at the sight of him, came out and did his best to sneak secretly round the corner. But Cato called to him and said, that there was nothing to blame in what he was doing. When then he afterwards saw the young man frequently coming out of the same brothel, he stopped him and said: "I praised you then, since I assumed that you came here now and again, not that you lived here." (Cf. also Horace, *Satires*, ii, 7, 47.)

the market to make some purchases for a jovial meal with a little whore—three large and ten small fish and twenty-four prawns; and he must not forget to buy six wreaths of roses (characteristic of the Greeks).

An epigram of Poseidippus (v, 183) describes a drinking-bout of four young men with four whores. One large jar of Chian wine is not sufficient, so that the boy attendant is sent to the wine-merchant Aristios, to tell him that at first he sent one only half full—"it is two gallons short certainly". It has already been mentioned that such scenes frequently recur, especially in vase paintings.

The ritual adopted by these wandering priestesses of Venus when they wanted to catch a man was much the same as it is to-day, and nothing really original can be said about it. The shoe of such a street-walker has been accidently preserved. On the sole of this shoe, of which there is a copy in Daremberg-Saglio's monumental work, the word *ΑΚΟΛΟΥΘΙ* (that is, 'follow me') is nailed, so that, while the girl is walking along, the word is impressed on the soft ground of the street, and the passer-by can have no doubt as to her trade.

Asclepiades (v, 158) mentions that he once amused himself with a girl named Hermione, who wore a girdle embroidered with flowers, on which were to be read the words: "Love me always, but be not jealous if others also have me." Certainly this can hardly be a wandering prostitute of the lower class, but an hetaira.

The wandering prostitutes naturally roamed about wherever a lively street traffic invited; hence they were to be found in specially large numbers in the harbours and in the streets leading to them. They took their customers into their own or hired rooms, or gave themselves to them in dark nooks and corners (Catullus, lviii), or even between the high sepulchral monuments that bordered certain streets (Martial, i, 34, 8), and also in the public baths

(Martial, iii, 93, 14). There were also houses of accommodation and inns (see the lexicons under *ματρυλλεῖον, ματρύλλιον, μαστρύπιον*; on the taverns, Ath., xiii, 567*a*; Philostratus, *Ep.*, 23), called in Greek *ματρυλλεῖα*; but the taverns and inns also, especially in the harbour district, afforded shelters at any time for such purposes.

That the light-hearted companies of flute and cithara-players, acrobats, etc., were to be had for love and money, needs no special remark.

3. The Hetairæ

The hetairae stand on a much higher level and occupy a far more important position in Greek private life. They are distinguished from the girls of the brothel especially by the social respect they enjoyed and by their education. "Many of them," says Helbig,[1] "are distinguished by refined education and a wit quick at repartee; they know how to fascinate the most distinguished personalities of their time—generals, statesmen, men of letters, and artists, and how to keep their affection; they illustrate in the manner indicated a mixed existence of fine intellectual and sensual pleasures, to which the majority of the Greeks at that time paid homage. In the life of almost every more important personality, prominent in the history of Hellenism, the influence of well-known hetairæ can be proved. Most of their contemporaries found nothing offensive in it. In the time of Polybius (xiv, 11) the most beautiful houses in Alexandria were indicated by the names of famous flute-players and hetairæ. Portrait statues of such women were set up in the temples and other public buildings by the side of those of meritorious generals and statesmen. Indeed, the degraded sense of honour of the Greek free states condescended to honour

[1] *Untersuchungen über die kampanische Wandmalerei*, p. 195 (Leipzig, 1873).

those hetairæ who were intimate with influential personalities, with garlands and sometimes even with altars and temples" (Ath., vi, 253*a*).

Yet another honour paid to the hetairæ, the most characteristic that can be imagined, is known to us. It is in the nature of things that their occupation flourished chiefly in the large towns and centres of foreign intercourse, and most especially in the powerful maritime and commercial city of Corinth, on the isthmus and between two seas. Of the wantonness and licentiousness of life in this metropolis of ancient trade, so wealthy and so favoured by nature, it would be difficult to give an account that should err by exaggeration. The inscription, found on a brothel in Pompeii, HIC HABITAT FELICITAS, "Here dwells Happiness" (the inscription was not found in an actual brothel but in a pastry-cook's, where also whores were frequently kept for the customers), might with equal justification have been written in gigantic letters across the harbour of Corinth.[1] What human fancy elsewhere was content merely to imagine in the way of licentiousness, found in Corinth its home and visible exemplification, and many a man who could not find his way out again from the whirlpool of the naturally very expensive pleasures of a great city, thereby lost reputation, health, and fortune, so that a verse became proverbial: "The journey to Corinth does not profit every man."[2] The priestesses of venal love crowded about the city in incalculable numbers. In the district of the two harbours were swarms of brothels of every degree, and prostitutes without number lounged about the streets. To a certain extent the focus of unmarried love and the high school of the hetairæ

[1] On life in Corinth, cf. *Dion Chrysost.*, 37, 34, who calls it the most wanton (*ἐπαφροδιτοτάτην*) of all early and present cities. The note on the thousand temple girls is from Strabo, viii, 378: cf. Horace, *Ep.*, i, 17, 36: *non cuivis homini contingit adire Corinthum.*

[2] That is, few persons have money enough for the expensive vices of Corinth: from Strabo, viii, 378.

was formed by the notorious temple of Venus, in which no fewer than a thousand hetairæ or *hieroduli* (temple-servants), as they were euphemistically called, practised their profession and were always ready to greet their friends.

On the uneven ground of the citadel, the stronghold Acrocorinthus, known to everyone from Schiller's poem *The Cranes of Ibycus*, on a terrace walled round by mighty blocks of stone, rose the temple of Aphrodite (cf. Pausan., ii, 5), visible from afar to seafarers approaching either the east or from the west. To-day a Turkish mosque stands on the spot where once a thousand temple-girls welcomed the stranger.

Now it was in 464 B.C. that the Hellenic people in Olympia once again celebrated the great games, and that the noble and wealthy Xenophon of Corinth, the son of Thessalos, gained the victory in the Stadium and also in the Pentathlum. To celebrate the victory, Pindar, the most powerful of all Greek poets, wrote a splendid song of victory, still preserved, which was perhaps recited in the presence of the poet himself, either when the victor was solemnly met by his fellow-citizens or at the procession to the temple of Zeus for the dedication of garlands (Pindar, *Olympia*, xiii).

Before Xenophon had entered the hard struggle, he made a vow (Ath., xiii, 573 ff.) that in the event of victory falling to him he would dedicate a hundred girls to the service of the temple. Besides his Olympian *Ode* Pindar wrote a hymn (W. von Christ, frag. 122) that was sung in the temple and danced to by these hetairæ, who had received an honour such as was never either before or after bestowed upon their class and which was conceivable only in Greece. Unfortunately only the beginning of this ode is preserved: "O girls much sought after in wealthy Corinth, loyal attendants of Peitho (Persuasion), you who piously send up the golden tears of fresh incense, and in spirit often guide your flight to Aphrodite, the heavenly mother of Love, who from above grants you sweet forgiveness. O girls, begging that you may cull the fruit of tender youth in the joys of love . . . Cyprian Queen! Xenophon has brought hither to this grove a herded troop of a hundred girls, in glad fulfilment of his vow."

Where a conception of the problem of prostitution existed so free from prejudice, it is easy to understand that literature also—and certainly not, as amongst ourselves, predominantly medical and forensic, but belletristic literature likewise—went painstakingly into the question of the priestesses of Aphrodite. There existed among the Greeks an extensive literature of the hetairæ, some works of which, like the famous *Dialogues of Courtesans* by Lucian, are preserved completely, others in more or less bulky fragments. Lucian sketches for us a picture extremely rich in colouring of the varied life of the hetairæ in its manifold gradations.

Under the title *Chreiæ* (that is, all kinds of things worth knowing) Machon of Sicyon (flourished between 300–260 B.C.), most of whose life was spent in Alexandria and whose date is approximately settled by the fact that he was the tutor of the grammarian Aristophanes of Byzantium, has cleverly and wittily related for our benefit all kinds of anecdotes from the *chronique scandaleuse* of the court of the Diadochi in iambic trimeters. That the hetairæ played an important part in this book, the loss of which is much to be deplored, is probable in itself and is confirmed by the detailed excerpts made from it by Athenæus. Besides Machon, Athenæus had at his disposal many other books on the life of the hetairæ, out of which (especially in the thirteenth book of his *Deipnosophistæ*, or "Banquet of the Learned") he gives us a wealth of detail, from which we now offer a concise selection.

Hetairæ

The Most Famous Hetairæ, Their Life, Anecdotes, and Witty Sayings

We begin with some who at the same time were appearing on the stage as heroines of comedy. Of course this must not be taken to mean that they actually appeared as performers, for at that time female parts were still filled by men, but we mean those hetairæ whom the comic poets introduced as sustainers of the action of a comedy.

Klepsydra (*CAF.*, II, 182) was the heroine of a comedy by Eubulus, hardly any fragments of which are preserved. Her proper name was Metiche, and Klepsydra was the name bestowed upon her by her friends; the name signifies a water-clock, and she was so called because she manifested her favours exactly " according to the clock ", that is, until it was emptied.

Pherecrates had written a comedy called *Corianno* (*CAF.*, I, 162), after an hetaira of the same name, the scanty fragments of which show no more than that the liking of the priestesses of Aphrodite for wine was ridiculed. The old theme of comedy was also turned to account: father and son fell in love with the same girl and strove together for her favour, in the course of which struggle excited explanations are given by the son and his parent, of which the fragments give us a small specimen.

Eunicus wrote a comedy, *Anteia* (*CAF.*, I, 781), yet we can say nothing more explicit of the hetaira of this name nor of the comedy itself than that from it only a single verse is preserved—" Take me by the ears and give me the handle-kiss " (see p. 310).

Of the hetairae and comedies named after them—the *Thalatta* (*CAF.*, I, 767) of Diocles, the *Opora* of Alexis (*CAF.*, II, 358), and the *Phanion* of Menander (*CAF.*, III, 142), nothing further is known.

The same Menander had brought yet another hetaira into a comedy on the stage, no less a person than Thaïs (*CAF.*, III, 61), in whose person the first splendid star in the heaven of Greek prostitutes rises. Thaïs of Athens could boast of having been the mistress of Alexander the Great, and is one of the many hetairæ who misused the power of their beauty in political affairs. Not far from the ruins of Nineveh Alexander had defeated the far superior host of the Persians in the battle of Gaugamela (331 B.C.). While King Darius saved himself by flight, Alexander marched into Babylon, captured the city of Susa, and then entered the old Persian capital, Persepolis. There he celebrated a drunken feast of victory in which a crowd of hetairæ took part, amongst them Thaïs, the most beautiful of all. When the intoxication of wine and passion had brought men's blood to fever heat, Thaïs cried out to the king that the moment had now come for him to crown all his previous deeds of glory with immortality. Alexander should let the Persian royal palace be consumed by fire and so exact vengeance for the sins committed by the Persians when they burnt the temple and the sanctuaries of the Acropolis at Athens in the time of Xerxes. The proposal was noisily approved by the drunken youths who were celebrating the feast of victory with the king, and the monstrous idea urged him on. At once torches, to the accompaniment of song, flute-playing, and the sound of pipes, are brought up to the palace, with Thaïs like a raging Bacchant at the head of the procession. There stands the proud magnificence of the capital of the dynasty of the Achæmenides. Alexander hurls the first burning torch, Thaïs the second, then they rush on from all sides, and soon the wonderful building has become a mere sea of flames (Diod. Sic., xvii, 72 ; Plut., *Alex.*, 38).

After Alexander's death his mistress and hetaira Thaïs rose to the dignity of queen by her marriage with Ptolemy I, King of Egypt. That she was made the heroine of a comedy by Menander has already been mentioned ; but unfortunately the fragments are so scanty that we can only conjecture its contents. A very well-known line from this play is preserved—the words often quoted in ancient times and by the Apostle Paul in the first epistle to the Corinthians, "evil communications corrupt good manners" (φθείρουσιν ἤθη χρήσθ' ὁμιλίαι κακαί). According to others, the line is from Euripides, and it would certainly be possible that Thaïs quoted it in the comedy of Menander. On another occasion she shows that she was well acquainted with Euripides, where she wittily and humorously answers a somewhat coarse question with a verse from the Medea (Ath., xiii, 585*e*). When on the way to a lover who smelt of perspiration she was asked where she was going, she said: "To live with Ægeus, the son of Pandion." The point of the witty answer is twofold, and indeed remarkable. In Euripides the banished Medea says that she will flee to King Ægeus in Athens in order to live with him, that is, under his protection. But Thaïs uses the word in its erotic sense. The second point is that she derives the name Ægeus from *aig-* the stem of the word which in Greek means "goat" (ἄϊξ, αἰγός), and the goat has a very unpleasant smell.

This *bon mot* of Thaïs leads on naturally to further sayings of hetairæ, which afford the reader an insight into the conversation of the Greek *jeunesse dorée*, often strongly seasoned with shameless *doubles entendres*. That the hetairæ were certainly well up in classical literature—placed by Ovid, the past-master in the art of love, before the fashionable ladies of his time as an unavoidable condition of their social education—is shown not least of all by their partiality for the employment of quotations from the poets (cf. Ovid, *Ars*, iii, 311).

Lamia of Athens (Ath., xiii, 577*c*) was one of the most famous hetairæ in the time of Demetrius Poliorcetes. By profession a flute-player, she had acquired such considerable prosperity by her art and popularity, that she rebuilt their ruined picture-gallery for the Sicyonians.[1] Such splendid foundations were by no means rare among Greek hetairæ: thus, according to Polemon, Cottina (Ath., xiii, 574*c*) had dedicated the bronze statue of a cow at Sparta and numerous similar examples are to be found in old writers.

On one occasion, Demetrius had to send ambassadors to Lysimachus. When they were talking with Lysimachus, after political matters had been settled, they noticed large scars on his arms and legs. Lysimachus told them that they were due to the bite of a lion with which he had once had to fight. The ambassadors answered laughing, that their king Demetrius also showed on the back of his neck traces of the bites of a dangerous beast, the lamia (Plutarch, *Demetr.*, 27).

An admirer of Gnathæna (Ath., xiii, 579*e*–580 f., 583 ff.) sent her a small bottle of wine, remarking that it was sixteen years old. "For its years it is very small," she replied jestingly.

In Athenæus we have a number of sayings of Gnathæna, some of them more witty and piquant than can be reproduced in a translation without circumstantial explanations or paraphrases, for they depend chiefly upon puns and the point would inevitably be lost. Gnathæna's profession was carried on by her grandchild Gnathænion (little cheeks). It happened that a distinguished stranger, almost ninety years old, who was staying in Athens for the festival of Kronos, caught sight of Gnathæna with her granddaughter in the street, and, since she pleased him, asked her what was her charge for a night. Gnathæna, judging the stranger's money by his excellent clothes, asked for 1,000 drachmæ (about £40). The old man thought that beat everything and offered half. "Very well, old man," said Gnathæna, "give me what you

[1] Inhabitants of Sicyon, in Peloponnesus, about 10 miles west of Corinth.

like; I know well enough that you will give my granddaughter twice as much" (Ath., xiii, 581).

The queens of Love, Laïs and Phryne. There were two hetairæ named Laïs, and both were celebrated in various anecdotes and epigrams, without, however, being clearly discriminated. The elder Laïs was a native of Corinth, lived in the time of the Peloponnesian war, and was famous for her beauty as well as for her greed. No less a man than the philosopher Aristippus was reckoned among her adorers [1]; and in the words of Propertius (ii, 6, 1) the whole of Greece had at some time languished before her doors. The younger was born at Hyccara in Sicily, and was the daughter of Timandra, the friend of Alcibiades. Among her lovers the painter Apelles (Ath., xiii, 588*c*) and the orator Hypereides are mentioned. Later, she followed a certain Hippolochus or Hippostratus to Thessaly (Pausan., ii, 2, 4; Plutarch, *Amor.*, 21, 768*a*) where she was said to have been killed by some women who were jealous of her beauty (Ath., xiii, 589*b*; App. Anth. Pal., 342).

In what follows we select some anecdotes from the abundant store attached to the name of Laïs, without making the hopeless attempt to distinguish between the two bearers of the name.

When Laïs was not yet an hetaira, but still a maiden, she was going to Peirene, the famous spring near Corinth, to draw water. Carrying her jug on her head or her shoulders, after she had filled it she set out for her home, and as she walked Apelles caught sight of her charming form, and his artist's eye could not gaze enough upon the wonderful beauty of the girl. Soon afterwards he introduced her to the circle of his boon-companions; but they became noisy and asked him sarcastically what a maiden had to do with a men's drinking-bout, he ought rather to have brought an hetaira with

[1] See Wieland's romance *Aristipp*, in which Laïs plays a considerable part.

him; but Apelles replied: "Don't be surprised, my friends; I will make an hetaira of her soon enough."

The beautiful bosom of Laïs was especially famous, and painters crowded in from far and near to perpetuate this divine breast in a picture.

Aristippus, who, as a philosopher, was frequently reproached for his intercourse with Laïs, on one such occasion made the famous reply: "Laïs is mine, I am not hers."

Further, it is related, that Aristippus lived with Laïs on the island of Ægina for two months every year during the festival of Poseidon. When his steward reproached him for spending so much money on Laïs, while Diogenes the Cynic enjoyed her favours for nothing, he replied: "I am generous to Laïs in order that I may enjoy her; not in order to prevent another from enjoying her as well." (Ath., xii, 544*d*, 555*bd*; xiii, 588*c*, 599*b*).

Diogenes himself had no such superior ideas. He once said to Aristippus in his affectedly coarse language: "How can you be so intimate with a whore? Either become a cynic or give up the intimacy." Aristippus replied: "Do you think it absurd if one puts up at a house in which others before him have lived?" "By no means," said Diogenes. "Or," Aristippus went on to ask, "if one goes on board a ship, in which many others before him have travelled?" "Certainly not." "Then you can have no objection, if one lives with a woman, whom many others have already possessed" (Ath., xiii, 588*e*).

Phryne, properly Mnesarete, came from the little Bœotian town of Thespiæ; she was the most beautiful, the most famous, but also the most dangerous of all the hetairæ in Athens, so that the comic poet Anaxilas (Ath., xiii, 558*c* (*CAF*., II, 270)) compares her with Charybdis,[1] who swallows up the shipowner and his entire vessel.

[1] Charybdis also was a hetaira-name: cf. Aristoph., *Knights*, 248.

She owes her immortality not only to her wonderful beauty, but also to a scandalous story, the truth or otherwise of which need not here be questioned. Phryne was accused before the court. The famous orator Hypereides, who had undertaken to defend her, saw that his case was almost lost. Then a sudden inspiration flashed into his mind, and he tore off the clothes from his beautiful client's bosom and disclosed the shining glory of her breast. " But the judges were seized with holy awe of the divinity, so that they did not venture to kill the prophetess and priestess of Aphrodite " (Ath., xiii, 590*d*; cf. Hypereides, frag. 174 and 181).

Athenæus then proceeds : " But Phryne was in fact more beautiful in the parts which one is not accustomed to show, and it was not easy to see her naked, for she usually wore a tight-fitting *chitōn* and did not use the public baths. But when the whole Greek people was assembled at the Eleusinia and the festival of Poseidon, she took off her clothes for all to see, loosed her hair, and went into the sea naked, and this it was that suggested to Apelles his Aphrodite rising from the sea. Praxiteles also, the famous plastic artist, was one of her admirers and took her as a model for his Aphrodite of Cnidus " (Ath., xiii, 590 *f*).

Phryne once asked Praxiteles which of his works he considered the most beautiful. But as he refused to say, she invented a trick. Once, when she was staying with him, a servant rushed in with every sign of affright and said that the studio was in flames, that much, but not everything, was already destroyed. Praxiteles sprang up in alarm and cried out : " All is lost, if the fire has destroyed my Satyr and my Eros." Phryne, with a smile, quieted him and told him he could stay where he was, for she had only invented the story of the fire, to learn which of his works he himself prized the most. (Pausan., i, 20, 1). This story is greatly to the credit of Phryne's astuteness, and we can readily believe that Praxiteles in his joy allowed her to select one of his statues for a present. Phryne chose the Eros, but did not keep it for herself; she dedicated it to the temple of Eros in her native place Thespiæ, the result of which was that the little place became for a century a much visited Mecca for pilgrims. How astonishing at the present day does that time appear to us, when artists favoured by the gods made presents of their works of art—works whose magnificence still fills us with delight, to their hetairæ, and that they dedicated such treasures to the divinity! The greatness of the act remains, even though we calmly admit, as we very well may, that personal vanity might have had much to do with the matter. That it was not entirely free from such a motive is proved by the fact that she had offered to rebuild the ruined walls of the city of Thebes, if the Thebans agreed to put on them this inscription: *Destroyed by Alexander, rebuilt by Phryne the hetaira*, a story which makes it clear that the handiwork of Phryne had a "foundation of gold", as is expressly stressed by ancient writers (Ath., xiii, 591*d*).

The inhabitants of Thespiæ, besides, showed themselves grateful for the magnificent gift of the Eros statue and commissioned Praxiteles to execute a statue of Phryne decorated with gold. It was set up on a column of Pentelic marble at Delphi between the statues of King Archidamus and Philippus, and no one took offence at it except the Cynic Crates, who declared that the image of Phryne was a memorial of the shame of Greece (Ath., xiii, 591*b*).

On another occasion, as Valerius Maximus (iv, 3, ext. 3) relates, some insolent young men of Athens made a wager that the philosopher Xenocrates, who was celebrated for his strict morality, would yet succumb to the charms of Phryne. At a luxurious banquet she was cleverly placed near the virtuous man; Xenocrates had already drunk heartily of the wine, and the beautiful hetaira did not fail to provoke him by exposing her charms, by stimulating words and contact. But all was in vain, for the seductive arts of the prostitute proved powerless against the inflexible will of the philosopher: indeed, she was even obliged to put up with jesting remarks to the effect that, in spite of her beauty and refinement, she had been beaten by an old man, and, moreover, by one who was half drunk. But Phryne did not lose her head, and when the party of carousers demanded from her the price of the lost wager, she refused, on the ground that the wager had meant a man of flesh and blood, not an insensible statue.

From what we have previously said it will be seen that the Greek, especially the Attic hetairæ, did not lack sprightliness and wit, and that many social talents, which most of them had made their own, dignified their calling, so that we can understand, not only that the chief men of the nation did not choose to abandon their intercourse with hetairæ, but that no one reproached them with it; indeed the love for Aspasia (Plutarch, *Pericles*, 24) of Pericles, who was a husband and father as well as a powerful statesman, has become almost world-famous, and yet Aspasia was nothing but an hetaira, although perhaps the one who stood, socially and intellectually, on a higher level than any of those known to us in Greek antiquity.

Born in Miletus, she came early to Athens, where, by her beauty, cleverness, and social talents, she soon succeeded in assembling in her house the most important men of her time. Even Socrates was not ashamed to associate with her and it is remarkable that Plato attributes the funeral oration in the *Menexenus* to Aspasia, and puts it into the mouth of Socrates. Pericles divorced his wife to marry her, and from that time her political influence increased so much that Plutarch even makes her instigate the war between Athens and Samos for the sake of her native town Miletus. In any case the preference for Aspasia shown by Pericles afforded a welcome excuse for his opponents to attack him; people would not hear of a woman having anything to say in political life, especially one who was not an Athenian but was brought from abroad, and even from Ionia (Ath., v, 220*b*), which was notorious for the immorality of its women. The marriage of Pericles to Aspasia was according to Athenian ideas a *mésalliance:* the beautiful Milesian was not considered a legitimate wife, but a concubine, a subsidiary wife. Hence she was very severely criticized by the comic poets, and when people called Pericles " the great Olympian ", the nickname "Hera" was ready to hand for Aspasia; but the comic poets ridiculed her power over the great statesman by putting her on the stage now as the domineering Omphale and now as the nagging Deianeira, thereby suggesting that as Heracles grew feeble under their sway so does Pericles under the arbitrary will of the foreign adventuress. At the present day gossip of all kinds equally irresponsible has settled upon her name; it was insisted that she procured free women for her husband; indeed, according to a statement in Athenæus (xiii, 569 f.) she was said to have maintained a regular brothel. Even Aristophanes endeavours to connect the outbreak of the great war with Aspasia's supposed " house of joy ", when in *The Acharnians* (524 ff.) he makes Dicæopolis say: " But some young tipsy cottabus-players [1] went to Megara and stole the fair Simætha. Then the Megarians, excited by their griefs, stole, in return, two of Aspasia's harlots. From these three strumpets on the Hellenic race burst the

[1] The game of cottabus, of which there were various kinds, was a favourite at drinking-bouts. The essential point was that the player was obliged to squirt some wine from the mouth or drinking-cup into little scales or metal basins which oscillated above small bronze figures, so that the basin sunk upon one figure and then, by the counter-thrust, upon the other figure, and so on alternately. Or the wine was spirted into little floating basins, which were thereby caused to sink. For a description of the game see Ath., xv, 666, Pollux, vi, 109, Scholiast on Aristoph., *Peace*, 343, 1208, 1210, and Scholiast on Lucian, *Lexiphanes*, 3.

first beginnings of the war. For then, in wrath, the Olympian Pericles thundered and lightened, and utterly confounded Hellas, enacting laws which ran like drinking-songs, decreeing that the Megarians should not remain in our territory or our markets, nor on the sea nor on the mainland." When she was accused of *asebeia* (impiety) and procuring, Pericles defended her and secured her acquittal. After the death of Pericles she married Lysicles, a man of low origin, who thereby obtained great influence.

Cyrus the younger named his mistress Milto, who came from Phocæa, Aspasia, after the great prototype. She accompanied him on his campaign against his brother Artaxerxes, and when Cyrus fell at Cunaxa (401 B.C.) became the prize of the Persian king, Artaxerxes Mnemon, whom also she ensnared by her amiability. Later, she became the cause of dispute between him and his son Darius. The father gave in, but on condition that she became a priestess of Anaitis.[1] This made the son rebel against his father, but he had to pay for his rebellion with his life.

To complete what has been said about the life of the Greek hetairæ I give a few further trifling particulars—such as are to be found scattered throughout Greek literature—and first from the Palatine Anthology. Mæcius (Anth. Pal., v, 130) visits the hetaira Philænis, who refuses to admit her lover's infidelity although her flowing tears give the lie to the words. It was just as common, if not more common for the hetaira to be unfaithful to her lover or to displace him. Asclepiades complains that the hetaira Niko, who had solemnly sworn to visit him at nightfall, does not keep her word. The perjured woman! The time of the last night-watch is already drawing to an end. Put out the

[1] An originally Babylonian divinity, whose cult took different forms in different countries. In Armenia it was combined with temple-prostitution (Strabo, xi, 532); in Cappadocia and Pontus the goddess was worshipped in the holy cities by numerous male and female hieroduli (Strabo, xii, 559; xv, 733).

lights, boys! she will never come (Anth. Pal., v, 150, 164). If we may be permitted to combine these epigrams of Asclepiades with another by the same poet, this hetaira Niko at that time had a daughter, named Pythias, who followed the same calling as her mother; the trade would then, so to say, have remained in the family, and we should have a parallel to Gnathæna and Gnathænion. The poet, however, had also had a bad experience of Pythias; she once made an appointment with him but allowed him, when he came, to find her door shut; and while he calls upon the goddess of night to witness the wrong he has suffered he prays that the faithless Pythias may soon have to suffer a similar insult before a lover's shut door.

Together with the infidelity and inconstancy of the hetairæ their lovers find special cause of complaint in their covetous avarice, the expression of which is everywhere to be found in Greek poetry. In an epigram of Hedylus (or Asclepiades) the three hetairæ Euphro, Thaïs, and Boidion are said to have turned three merchant seamen out of doors after having robbed them of everything but their shirts, so that they were now even poorer than when they had suffered shipwreck. "Therefore," the epigram concludes, "avoid these corsairs of Aphrodite and their ships, for they are more dangerous than the sirens" (Anth. Pal. v, 161).

This complaint is very old and a constantly recurring motif of erotic literature ever since the time when love began to be purchasable with gold. To quote at least one other example, there are the words of Chremylus in the *Plutus* (149 ff.) of Aristophanes: "And they say of the hetairæ of Corinth that if a poor man longs for their love they pay no attention to him, but that if he is rich they at once turn their buttocks towards him."

An example of the eternal susceptibility of the hetairæ to gold, very drastic in its effective brevity, is to be found in Alciphron's letter of Philumena the courtesan, to her friend Criton (Alciphron, i, 40): "Why do you trouble yourself," she writes, "with long letters? I want fifty gold pieces, but no letters. If therefore you love me, pay up; but if you love your money more, then you needn't bother me any more. Good-bye!"

It is greatly to be wished that the Anthology gave some information as to the prices asked by the hetairæ. The Athenian hetaira Europa was on the average satisfied with a drachma, if one may draw general conclusions from an epigram of Antipater (Anth. Pal., v, 109). But, on the other hand, she is always ready to oblige in every respect, and makes things as pleasant as possible for her visitors; there is no lack of soft coverlets on the bed—indeed, if the night should be cold, she does not spare the expensive coal. Bassus (Anth. Pal., v, 125) goes deeper into the scale of prices, and decides with grim humour that he is not Zeus, to be able to let money flow into the open lap of the loved one, nor has he any intention of impressing her with the arts of the god who changed himself into a bull to carry off Europa, or into a swan to make Leda happy—he simply pays the hetaira Corinna "the usual" two obols and there is an end of it! That would certainly be an extraordinarily low price, and we shall be obliged to be very careful about drawing such general *a posteriori* conclusions. Neither do the ever repeated complaints about the greediness of the hetairæ agree with this; nor the unamiable descriptions by which they are frequently commemorated. Thus Meleager once calls a hetaira (v, 184, 6) "you evil beast of my bed" (κακὸν κοίτης θηρίον) and Macedonius Hypatos (v, 244, 8) names the hetairæ "the hirelings of Aphrodite, who brings happiness in the bed".

If their daily, or more correctly, nightly, incomes may not have been on the average very high, they certainly would not have been able to defray the expense of such costly votive presents as have been spoken of, unless at least sometimes they had been considerable, on which point a reference may be made from the Palatine Anthology. Simonides (v, 159; Polemon in Ath., xiii, 574*c*), if the epigram be really by him, mentions two hetairæ, who dedicated girdles and embroidery to Aphrodite; the poet is talking to a tradesman and whimsically remarks that his purse knows where these costly gifts come from.

We hear especially of dedicatory gifts of the hetairæ to Priapus, and quite naturally, since he was the god of sensual love. According to the epigram of an unknown poet (Anth. Pal., v, 200, 201) the beautiful Alexo in memory of the sacred night-festival dedicated garlands of crocus, myrrh, and ivy, plaited round with bands of wool, to the "sweet Priapus who caresses like a woman". Another also unnamed poet says that the hetaira Leontis, after she had enjoyed herself with the "golden" Sthenius till the rising of the morning star, dedicated the lyre on which she had played to Aphrodite and the Muses. Or was this Sthenius a poet in whose poetry she found pleasure? Perhaps both interpretations are right; certainly the wording leaves the question open.

The epigrams of Asclepiades and others (v, 202, 203, 205, etc), in which the peculiar votive presents of hetairæ are spoken of, are also to be noted.

From another poet, also unfortunately not known (v, 205), comes the beautiful epigram on the hetaira Niko. She has presented as a sweet gift to Aphrodite an iynx (see p. 205), that wheel, "which is able to entice a man over the distant sea and a boy from his modest bedroom, which is artistically set with gold, carved from radiant amethyst and bound round with a soft flock of lamb's wool."

Cosmetics, in the widest extent of the word, of course play an extraordinarily important part in the life of hetairæ, and from a vast number of ancient authorities, which treat of such things, I give a few specially characteristic samples. In the first place, an epigram of Paulus Silentiarius (Anth. Pal., v, 228) informs us that young men, when they visited their hetairæ, attached special value to carefully chosen dress. The hair was nicely curled, the nails neatly cut and polished, and a particularly tasteful, purple-coloured dress was put on. Lucian (xi, 408) ridicules an already oldish hetaira, who wants to disguise her wrinkled face with all possible arts of the toilet, means for colouring the hair, white-lead and rouge: "Don't trouble yourself," he adds grimly, "paint will never make a Helen out of a Hecuba." From Lucilius (xi, 68) we have the biting epigram: "Many people declare, Nicylla, that you dye your hair—but you bought it jet black in the market." A fragment of Aristophanes (frag. 320, in Pollux, vii, 95; *CAF.*, I, 474) contains a complete list of things used by women as aids to beauty and as cosmetics, and amongst others are mentioned: clippers, mirrors, scissors, grease-paint, soda, false hair, purple trimmings, bands, ribbons, red paint (i.e. alkanet), white-lead, myrrh, pumice stone, bosom-bands (bust-holders), bands for the posteriors,[1] veils, seaweed paint, chains for the neck, eye-paint,[2] soft woollen garments,[3] gold ornament for the hair, hair net, girdle, mantilla, morning dress,[4] dress purple-hemmed on both sides and with a purple border, dress with a train,[5] shifts, combs, ear-rings, necklaces adorned with precious

[1] *Ὀπισθοσφενδόνη*. Perhaps used to tie up too fully developed buttocks and reduce their volume; or it was directly put round the buttocks, and served to raise them and make them more prominent. The word *σφενδόνη* in Pollux, v, 96, is a head-band used by women, or a bandage used by physicians like Galen and Hippocrates in the case of a menstruating woman.

[2] The so-called *ὑπόγραμμο* or *στίμμι*, antimony ore, burnt and pulverized. It was used for painting under the eyes, and also for darkening the brows and eyelashes (Pollux, v, 101; *Etym. Magnum*, 782, 9).

[3] *τρυφοκαλάσιρις*

[4] *τρύφημα*, so I translate this word, not otherwise known to me as a female article of dress.

[5] *ξυστίς* a long robe of state.

stones, ear-pendants, ear-pendants in the form of bunches of grapes, bracelets, arm buckles, hair buckles, foot buckles, ankle buckles, ornamental chains, finger rings, beauty plasters, hair supports, self-satisfiers,[1] precious stones, necklaces, twisted ear-pendants, and numerous other things with names of which we do not even know the meaning.

The writer of comedies, Alexis (see p. 148) in a humorous fragment describes how skilful the hetairæ are at enhancing already existing charms and faking up such as are non-existent.

The profession of the hetairæ required not only the careful use of cosmetics, but also great cleverness in behaviour, knowledge of male weaknesses and no small acuteness in changing these weaknesses into as much ready money as possible. One may say that in course of time regular catechisms for hetairæ came into being, which at first were propagated by oral tradition, but in time were actually set down in writing. No such manuals for hetairæ have survived, but ancient writings contain enough passages to enable us to have a sufficient idea of the plan of these books. A poem of Propertius (iv, 5) is well known, in which a procuress delivers a regular lecture on the means by which a girl can extort as much money as possible out of her lover. Above all, says the procuress, you must know nothing about loyalty; you must understand the art of lying and dissimulation, and you must not pay any heed to the laws of modesty. You must act as if you still had other lovers: that keeps a man in suspense and goads on his jealousy. If the lover then sometimes becomes furious, so that he pulls your hair, that doesn't matter; on the contrary, a fresh opportunity is offered for squeezing money out of him, for which superstition supplies many pretexts. Tell him that it is the day of Isis or else some religious festal day, on which one abstains

[1] The ὀλισβός.

from sexual connection. Arouse his jealousy anew over and over again by writing letters in his presence, or take care always to show him traces of bites on your neck and breast, which will cause him to believe that they have been made by another lover. Let not Medea's importunate love be your model, but the hetaira Thaïs and the methods by which in Menander's comedies she succeeds in plundering her lovers. Let your porter have strict instructions; if there should be a knock at your door at night he should open it only to rich people; if a poor man knocks it must remain shut. Also, do not reject people of the lower classes, such as soldiers or sailors; even though the hand is rough, remember that it brings money to you. And as to slaves, if only they come with money in their pockets, you ought not to scorn them for having been put up for sale in the Forum. What do you get from a poet, who praises you heavens-high with his verses, but cannot make you any presents? As long as your blood is lively and your face free from wrinkles, make use of the opportunity and of that youth of yours, which vanishes so quickly.

We read of a similar procuress's catechism in the *Amores* of Ovid (i, 8). After the Introduction, which makes us acquainted with the name, the secret arts and charms and the disgraceful calling of the old procuress, the poet, who by chance had overheard the lesson, makes the old woman give a προαγωγεία (lecture on the trade of procuring) worked out to the smallest detail. A young man is in love with you, she says to the girl, and as a matter of course on account of your beauty. If you were only as rich as you are beautiful, it would certainly not be my loss! Yet the time is favourable, and he is rich and handsome as well. You are blushing? Red suits your white complexion, but the blush of shame does not befit you; leave that to the respectably modest females of old times. Now there is another thing to remember: modesty is a privilege of old maids. Yet even Penelope, the model of chastity, prized the true power of a man. Think of old age that comes creeping on, and make use of your beauty as long as you have it: the more lovers the better. Your present one is only a poor needy poet, genius is a trifle, the chief thing is to make a man pay as much as possible. Under such conditions you might even make a slave happy. Neither can you impress me with your fine gentleman's famous family, nor with his beauty, which he may use in your interest. All you have to do is gradually to drain him; attract him with love, but make him pay; continually feed him with hopes of getting what he wants, then give in again—but only if he pays. You must pretend to be ill, but don't exaggerate, lest nothing comes of the skirmishing. Don't spare tears or oaths. The chief thing is: always get something given to you, also to your sister, mother or nurse. Never tire of inventing reasons for that. Don't forget to make your lover jealous—for that will strengthen love. What he doesn't give you, borrow from him; get it out of him by honied words—you needn't give it back. You will be eternally grateful for my teaching. Here the poet's indignation breaks out: "If I could only get at your withered body, you disgraceful procuress!" and curses upon the old woman conclude the effort of Ovid to put into Latin verse motives borrowed from comedy and elegy.

The last sentence contains my justification for appealing to Latin sources in a representation of Greek manners. What the two Roman poets (Propertius and Ovid) here give us, is the common property of the Greeks, a reflection of Greek life, as characterized by comedy and taken over from the love-elegies of the Alexandrines, which finally passed into the armoury of Roman poetry. I have already had the opportunity of analysing (at least in outline) a Greek hetaira-catechism, that of

Herondas (pp. 64–7); and have also mentioned (p. 63) Lucian's *Dialogues of Courtesans* which contain an abundant wealth of material for the present subject. Thus, in the sixth dialogue, we read the following instructions given by a mother to her daughter:

" *Crobyle*: So then, my Dorinna, you have learnt that it was not such a terrible thing as you thought to become a woman instead of a virgin, since you were with a handsome young man and received a mina as your first present, out of which I am going to buy you a necklace presently.

" *Corinna*: Yes, mummy. And see that it has some stones as bright as fire, like Philænis's.

" *Crobyle*: Of course. And now listen to some other things which you must do, and learn how to behave towards men, for we have no other means of livelihood. But you don't know how poorly we have lived during the two years since your blessed father died. While he was alive, we had plenty of everything; for he had a smith's business and was well known in the Piræus; you can hear everyone vowing that there will never be such another smith as Philinus. But after his death, I first had to sell his firetongs, his anvil, and hammer for two minæ, on which we lived; after that, sometimes by weaving, sometimes by spinning, or twisting the warp, I just managed to get food; and I brought you up, my daughter, waiting patiently and hoping.

" *Corinna*: Are you talking about the mina?

" *Crobyle*: No, but I reckoned that when you had reached your age you would support me; and that you would easily deck yourself out, and be rich, and have purple robes and servants to wait upon you.

" *Corinna*: What are you talking about, mother, what do you mean?

" *Crobyle*: If you go with young men, drink with them, and sleep with them for money.

" *Corinna*: Like Lyra, the daughter of Daphnis?

" *Crobyle*: Yes.

"*Corinna*: But she's a whore.

"*Crobyle*: That's nothing terrible; for you will be as rich as she is and will have many lovers. What are you crying for? Don't you see how many whores there are, and how much they are sought after, and what money they get? I knew Daphnis, when she was in rags, before she reached maturity. And you see how she has got on—gold, embroidered dresses, four maids.

"*Corinna*: How did Lyra get such things?

"*Crobyle*: In the first place, she dressed herself decently, was well-behaved and pleasant to all—not that she burst out laughing as easily as you are in the habit of doing, but smiling sweetly and in an attractive manner. In the next place, she associated with men wisely, neither tricking anyone who came to see her or who sent for her, nor yet on the other hand fastening herself upon them. And whenever she goes to supper, after anyone has given her a little present, she never gets drunk—for it is ridiculous, and men hate women like that—nor does she gorge herself greedily, but only touches her food with the tips of her fingers, and takes her mouthfuls silently, not stuffing them into her jaws; she drinks quietly, not greedily, but in sips.

"*Corinna*: But supposing she should be very thirsty, mother?

"*Crobyle*: Then she must be most careful. And she never talks more than is necessary, nor does she make jokes about any of the guests, but gazes only at the man who has hired her, for which everybody likes her. And when it is time to go to bed, she will not do anything wanton or indecent, but her sole endeavour is to get him into her power and to make him her lover. For this again everybody praises her. If you learn this, we also shall be happy, and with your superior attractions . . . I say no more, if only you live!

"*Corinna*: Tell me, mother, are all those who hire us like Eucritus, with whom I slept yesterday?

"*Crobyle*: Not all; some are better and already grown to manhood; others are not naturally good-looking.

"*Corinna*: Shall I have to sleep with them as well?

"*Crobyle*: Certainly, my girl; for they give larger presents; handsome men only want to pay with their person. Do you always think about more money, if you want all the women in a short time to be pointing you out [1] and saying, Do you see Corinna, Crobyle's daughter, how rich she is and how she has made her mother thrice happy? What do you say? Will you do the same? I know you will, and you will easily eclipse them all. Now go and have a bath, in case the young man Eucritus should come to-day: he certainly promised he would."

In the first dialogue the hetairæ Glycera and Thaïs are discussing a distinguished officer, who, after having loved the beautiful Abrotonon and then Glycera, has now inconceivably fallen in love with an ugly girl. With comfortable satisfaction they enumerate the ugly points of the girl: her scanty hair, her bluish lips, her thin neck with very prominent veins, her long nose. But they are fair enough to appreciate her tall slim form and her seductive laugh. They can only explain the officer's error of taste by the fact that he has been bewitched by the girl's mother, an infamous witch and poisoner, who is able to draw down the moon and flies about by night out of doors.

4. SUPERSTITION IN MATTERS OF SEX

Superstition plays a most important part in sexual matters and therewith also in the practice of the hetairæ, to which I have already had occasion to refer when discussing the second idyll of Theocritus p. 40). That no enlightened ideas could prevail—rather that superstitious ideas were ineradicable,

[1] It was not considered derogatory to a person, but rather a compliment, thus to be pointed at; cf. *Persius*, i, 28, digito monstrari et dicier "Hic est!"

is clear amongst other things from the express warning against "Thessalian arts" which Ovid feels bound to give in his *Art of Love* (*Ars.*, ii, 99). He says: "All this hocus-pocus, such as the famous hippomanes (p. 268), magic herbs, formulæ of exorcism, and love potions have no effect, as the example of Medea and Circe shows; both were famous enchantresses, and yet their black art did not avail to prevent the unfaithfulness of their husbands, Jason and Odysseus." But such enlightened voices remained isolated, the masses firmly believed in them, as is the case even to-day, and the tribe of hetairæ, to whom love was and was bound to be a material content of life, will never be able to free itself entirely from superstition.

Without claiming that the account is even approximately complete, a few supplementary remarks are here added on the superstition of the Greeks, so far as it has reference to sexual life. According to Pliny the sap of the plant κραταιόγονον (flea-wort) was most effective in securing the birth of boys, and in order to obtain sons, the parents were obliged to drink the sap three times fasting for forty days. Glaucias (in Pliny, xx, 263) ascribes the same effect to the thistle. I have already mentioned that agnus (Pliny, xxiv, 59; Dioscorides, *Mat. Med.*, i, 134), owing to its causing weakness of the sexual impulse, was strewn over the bed by women during the Thesmophoria (p. 111). According to Xenocrates (in Pliny, xx, 227), the sap of mallows, as well as three of its roots bound together, excited the passion of women. If mallow-seed in a little bag was fastened on the left arm, it was a protection against pollution. According to Dioscorides (Dioscorides, *m.m.*, iii, 131; Pliny, xxvi, 95; xxvii, 65) men must eat the larger root of the "boy-cabbage", if they wished to beget boys, and women the smaller, if they wanted girls. If they drank it fresh in goat's milk, the sexual impulse was excited; if they ate it dry, it would diminish. If the plant *pesoluta* (Pliny, xxi, 184) was laid under them, it made them impotent. Satyrium (Diosc., *M.M.*, iii, 134; Pliny, xxvi, 98 and 96) also had a stimulating effect, if carried in the hand; its root was believed to have the same qualities as the "boy-cabbage". The root of the cyclamen (sowbread) (Theophrastus, *Hist. Plant*, ix, 9, 3; Diosc., *M.M.*, ii, 193; Pliny, xxv, 114) as an amulet accelerated childbirth; if a pregnant woman trod upon it, it caused abortion. The root was also used for love-potions. Anyone who drinks of "sea-roses" (water-lilies) has to pay for it by being impotent for twelve days (Pliny, xxv, 75). If one put *habrotonum* (southernwood) under the bed, a strengthening of the sexual impulse was to be expected (Pliny, xxi, 162); it was also infallible in counteracting charms intended to prevent conception. One who wore asparagus root (Diosc., 151) as an amulet became barren.

The ashes of the plant *brya* (Pliny, xxiv, 72) mixed with the urine of an ox made one impotent; according to the magicians it might also be mixed with a eunuch's urine. The plant *telephilon* (poppy) according to Theocritus (iii, 28) was used for love-oracles; one of its leaves was laid in the palm or on the bare arm and struck smartly with the hand; if a loud crack resulted that was a good omen.

To protect oneself against the "evil wolf" (hæmorrhage between the muscles of the buttocks), one must put absinthium (vermuth) on the posteriors (Scholiast on Aristoph., *Knights*, 1578; Cato, *De Agricultura*, 159; Pliny, xxvi, 91). The pith of a branch of the pomegranate-tree, about which Theophrastus tells some incredible stories, raised the sexual potency (Pliny, xxvi, 99), another means of increasing which was to wear the right testicle of an ass in a bracelet (Pliny, xxviii, 261).

If a pregnant woman ate the testicles, womb, or rennet of a hare (Pliny, xxviii, 248), she bore boys. Eating the fœtus of a hare was said to remove barrenness permanently. If hens crowed in a farm-yard, this was a sure sign that the owner was henpecked (Schwarz, *Menschen und Tiere im Altertum*, " Man and Beast in Ancient Times," 1888). Since the cock had helped Leto in her difficult birthpangs, a cock (Ælian, *Hist. An.*, iv, 29) was brought to pregnant women to ease childbirth; and another way to ease the birthpangs of a pregnant woman was to touch her hips with the placental skin of a dog, which had not come into contact with the earth. If a woman ate a cock's testicle immediately after conception, she could be sure of having a boy (Pliny, xxx, 123); and if one made water where a dog had already done so, " the vigour of the loins dried up," and one became impotent (Pliny, xxix, 102; xxx, 143).

There was a remarkable superstition about the hyena (Pliny, viii, 105) that it changed its sex every year, an idea combated by Aristotle (*De Generatione Animalium*, iii, 66). A female crab pounded in a mortar and ground with fine salt and water after the full moon was said to heal carbuncles and cancerous ulcers of the womb (Pliny, xxxii, 134).

If it was desired to make men impotent, they were daubed with mouse-dung (Pliny, xxviii, 262). If a woman carried a *mullus* (an edible sea-fish) her menstrual blood lost its poisonous effect (xxviii, 82). It was believed that the raven had had intercourse with a woman with its beak; hence, if one was brought into the house of a pregnant woman, the result was difficult labour; also, if a pregnant woman ate a raven's egg she had an abortion through the mouth (Pliny, x, 32; Aristotle, *De gen. an.*, iii, 66; Pliny, xxx, 130). If a woman at the time of conception eats veal roasted with the plant *aristolochia* (Pliny, xxviii, 254) she will bear a boy. It was believed that cow's milk (Pliny, xxviii, 253) promoted conception.

To the superstitious the private parts, also, were of great importance; this is a subject upon which Reiss (*Realenzyklopdiäe*, i, 85 ff.) has collected a mass of information, among which we find the following:—

The exposure by a woman of her organ of generation—with which action the gesture of the "fico" is associated—broke magic spells, and consequently its image or symbol was carried as an amulet. The exposure of the organ was especially efficacious against hail, bad weather, and storms at sea; the effect was heightened if the woman were menstruating at the time; and, indeed, when this "charm" was invoked for agricultural purposes—particularly the destruction of vermin—the best results could hardly be expected unless menstruation was in progress, for then the malignant powers attributed to women in this condition would come into play with their fullest effect.

Pliny, among others, has described in very lively fashion the baneful influences brought to bear on all around her by a menstruous woman. If she touched rue it withered; cucumbers and pumpkins dried up or, at the least, turned sour as a result of her mere glance; young vines were ruined by her touch, linen in the wash-tub became black, razors blunt, brass rusty, the very mares miscarry, and the mirror into which a menstruous female looks becomes tarnished—though, to be sure, if she afterwards gazes steadily on its back it recovers its brightness.

Especially potent is the power of a woman menstruating for the first time, or for the first time after the surrender of her virginity; and the menstrual discharge itself, even without actual contact with the object to be attacked, was effective. For instance, that of a maiden was buried with laurel in a field to ward off hail; a rag soaked in it will cause any nut-tree beneath which it is buried to wither away; while if it is spread on door-posts all evil spells are excluded from the house within.

The urine, also, of a menstruous woman was to be feared, but all urine was powerful in that it could counteract every magical charm—and Hierocles is said in the *Geoponica* to have preferred the urine of a man [1] to that of even a menstruating woman in the case of certain horses' complaints. The slave of a friend of Porphyry, for instance, understood the language of birds, but his mother one night made water in his ear when he was asleep and so deprived him of this gift. Pliny tells us further that the power of urine as a counter-charm was increased if the person urinating spat into it immediately upon its being voided, and that it had certain healing properties which were strengthened if one used one's own in one's own case. A drop placed on the crown of the head instantaneously cured the bite of the centipede; for snake-bites one should drink either one's own urine or that of a boy not yet arrived at puberty; nuts were placed in it five days before planting; menstrual stains could be removed only with the urine of the woman who had produced them; while that of a eunuch was especially efficacious in promoting female fertility.

The fæces were not so powerful as urine though, according to Æschines, they were used as a remedy for various ailments when baked, and the excrement of a new-born child introduced into the uterus was a specific against barrenness.

Healing qualities were also attributed to the milk of women, especially of mothers, and a dog that had once tasted the milk of a woman who had recently had a son would never go mad. The milk of the mother of a girl was an aid to beauty only, but a person treated with a salve composed of the milk of mother and daughter enjoyed life-long immunity against affections of the eyes.[2]

[1] The *sordes virilitatis* were used too, according to Pliny (*Nat. Hist.*, xxviii, 52), as a remedy against scorpion bites, the consequences of which could, it is also said, be transferred by a man to a woman through copulation.

[2] The source of these and many similar curious superstitions will be found in Pliny's *Nat. Hist.*, vii, 64 f.; xvii, 266; xxviii, 38, 44, 52, 65, 67, 73, 77, 79, 81, 82, 84, 85, ; xxix, 65; Columella's *De re rustica*, x, 358 ff.; xi., 3, 38, 50, 64; Cassianus Bassus's *Geoponica*, i, 15; x, 2, 3, 64, 67; xii, 2, 5, 8, 20, 25; xvi, 2, 10; Porphyry's *De abstinentia*, iii, 3; and Dioscorides' *Materia medica*, ii, 99.

It is not without interest that many of these folk-medicines were in favour in remote parts of Europe until comparatively recent times.

We have already had occasion to refer—especially in connection with our notices of the phallus-cult—to the great importance attached by the Greeks to the male organs of generation; the subject is also touched upon in subsequent chapters, so that here only a few remarks need be made. The word βασκαίνειν is reproduced in the Latin verb *fascinare*; both words signify "to enchant", but also "to break a spell". The spell most dreaded in antiquity was the evil eye,[1] to which everyone is always exposed, often without any evil or injurious intent by another. Indeed, we may say that everyone who exhibited any peculiarity in the appearance or position of his eyes—especially such as might suggest evil intention—was believed to be capable of exerting this baneful influence; and even to-day the dread of "the evil eye" is very real in the South.

The means of protection against it are extremely numerous, and what is common to all of them is their alleged power of averting the dreaded glance by means of sudden fright or discomposure. This confusion was considered to be most effectually attained by causing the evil eye to fall upon pictures or models of the sexual organs. Of course, the idea was not that "the eye at once turned away for shame", but that the "hostile" eye was so enchanted and fascinated by the sight of the obscene, that it sees only the obscene and for the time being is harmless to everything else. This explains why sexual organs—by preference male—were painted or imitated in plastic art wherever it was thought that the evil eye was especially to be feared. Thus the phallus—often of colossal size—is to be

[1] *Fascinum*: e.g. Horace, *Epod.*, 8, 18, *minusve languet fascinum,* on which Porphyrio says: *fascinum pro virile parte posuit, quoniam præfascinandis rebus hæc membri difformitas apponi solet.*

seen almost everywhere ; on houses and gates, in public places, on implements in daily use, such as vessels and lamps, on dress and ornaments, on rings, buckles, etc. ; it was also carried by itself on a handle ; it was believed that its effect was sometimes heightened if it was made in the form of an animal, with claws and wings, or if little bells were attached to it, since the clang of the metal was considered an effective protection against witchcraft and ghostly beings of every kind. Thus is to be explained the vogue of the phallic amulet, which to the modern spectator would appear as the height of shamelessness, if he were ignorant of the inner reasons for it. I have already pointed out that, even at the present day, one can easily see and buy phallic amulets in the south.

In antiquity the amulet in the form of the female sexual organ is far less common, but this can readily be explained. The Greeks ascribed greater power to the man, and therefore his genitals would have the greater effect in averting the evil eye.

Instead of representing the actual female organ on amulets it was suggested by symbolism, and usually in the guise of the *fico* (fig, Greek σῦκον), which often recurs in the specimens extant.

These amulets were made of very different sizes and of every kind of material ; they were carried singly or in batches strung together, for it was even then believed that " many a mickle makes a muckle ". They could be carried openly or secretly, and so convinced were people of their power that their mere possession was considered sufficiently effective.

Of course superstition also played a great part in the sexual life proper. The so-called " knot-tying " (any charm intended to prevent conception) was well known to the wise women of antiquity and to their female clientele ; one could bewitch a hated rival by enchantment, so that her hair fell out or she lost other personal charms (Ovid, *Amor.*, i, 14, 39), and envious and jealous girls could rob a man of his best powers, temporarily or permanently. Different methods were employed —sometimes incantation; sometimes a narcotic such as a weak infusion of hemlock (Ovid, *Amor.*, iii, 7, 27), to mix which in the victim's drink opportunity had to be found; and sometimes the puppet method was used, for which it was only necessary to form a wax model (ib., 29 f.; *Heroïdes*, 6, 21) of him who was to be bewitched and to stick a needle into the position of the liver, whereupon the man himself became impotent, for the liver (Theocritus, 30, 10; Horace, *Odes*, i, 13, 4; 25, 13) was regarded by the ancients as the seat of sensual desire.

Secret powers, amongst them that of making people impotent, were also ascribed to wollen thread (cf. e.g. Anth. Pal., v, 205; Horace, *Sat.*, i, 8, 30), and this, according to Clement of Alexandria (*Stromata*, vii, 4, 843), was especially feared.

How widespread this superstition was is clear from the fact that the rules and precepts with which it was believed that love could be awakened, unfruitfulness changed into fruitfulness, in short, all a lover's wishes be fulfilled, were brought into a system and written down, so that gradually a whole literature of such books sprang up, by the help of which lovers, in every imaginable difficulty, would take refuge in the ever-open arms of superstition. The longer specimen which follows, from this literature, may just now be of special interest, since it cannot escape an attentive observer that so-called "occult science" has lately been gaining a good deal of ground. Spiritism and Theosophy are the magic words which offer salvation to a certain part of alarmed humanity. Sittings innumerable of occult unions in great and moderate-sized cities reveal their secrets to believers who shiver in mystic enchantment; the wise women, who with the assistance of the arch-backed tom-cat, know how to foretell the future from the patterns of coffee-grounds and the fall of cards, have no need to complain that business is bad. In just the same way in ancient Greece, it was believed that by correctly making use of the powers of nature, and also by such compulsion as could be exercised directly on the gods, one could be assured of all kinds of beautiful things, e.g. health and wealth, and above all of love, or could bewitch an enemy with sickness and death. The earlier the time, the simpler are the usual formulæ of enchantment, which gradually, especially in the Hellenistic period, became so complicated under the influence of Oriental secret science, that they were set down in writing. The single precepts were collected together in large books of incantations, of which several (about twelve) have been preserved, dating from the later period of Greek antiquity. The most important and most interesting of these books (Richard Wünsch, *Aus einem griechischen Zauber-papyrus*, Bonn, 1911), now in the National Library of Paris, was written down in the fourth century A.D. —at a time, that is to say, when the old superstitions had not yet completely given place to the new.

From this MS., so valuable for the history of civilization, there follow a few samples, and what is necessary by way of explanation for the non-philologist has been added in brackets. By way of introduction it may be observed that our specimen is a love-charm; it contains a prescription for ensnaring the love of a girl, and, with the aidance of the goddess Hecate, influencing her in the way the enchanter desires. In Greco-Oriental magic Hecate is identical with the moon-goddess Selene, while the latter again becomes one with Artemis and Persephone, the goddess of the underworld, so that Hecate, corresponding to her triple functions, is represented in three forms; and she thereby also becomes the goddess of the Three Ways, which, according to superstitious fancy, were peopled from time immemorial by ghostly forms. The idea at the bottom of this love-charm is that the goddess is to bring the girl, who is desired by the one who works it, to him " by torture "; but in order that the goddess may do this, she is first addressed in a " slander ", of which the girl has been guilty towards her. It is easy to smile at such naïveté; but we must not forget what many men to-day expect from the gods—to say nothing of the customs of such tribes which, even to-day, imagine that they honour their god all the more the more they spit on his image.

A complete Greek magic charm consists of the following parts. First, the powerful effect of the recipe is praised; then the essential parts of the necessary offering or victim, and how the particular sacrifice in the charm is to be treated are described; then follows the formula of the *logos*, of the prayer in accordance with which incense must again be thrown upon the sacrificial fire; then measures of precaution are given, to prevent the charm from injuring the charmer himself—for the spirits are at such times very sensitive. Next follow directions for preparing an amulet, and a second prayer—for the purpose of making still more sure of obtaining the desired effect—and one or more hymns in verse, in which the power of the goddess is praised, with, as a counterpart, a poem setting forth the evil deeds of the girl so that the goddess may pursue her and, as was said above, drive her by " torture " to the suppliant. The laudatory hymn is written in the metre of heroic poetry, the epic hexameter, and the abusive poems in iambics, which had been specially used for abuse since the time when the washerwoman who thereby became famous recalled the poet Archilochus from the classic spheres of poetry to prosaic reality: " Get away, fellow, you are upsetting my wash-tub " (Dracon. Straton., 162, Herm., ἄπελθ', ἄνθρωπε, τὴν σκαφὴν ἀνατρέπεις).

And now let the old book of charms speak for itself.

(*Laudatory.*) " Preparation of the smoke sacrifice that conjures up the moon-goddess. It brings hither without resistance and on the same day the soul (of the one to be charmed); it drives (the enemy) to the sick-bed and surely kills; it sends blissful dreams and has shown itself effective in most enchantments. Pancrates, the priest of Heliopolis, brought this offering before the emperor Hadrian and therewith proved to him the power of his divine magic; the spell followed in an hour, sickness in two, death in six hours; it plunged the emperor himself into dreams, while he saw clearly and announced the enchantment that lay upon everything around him. Astounded at the prophet's art, he ordered a double honorarium to be given to him.

(*Prescription.*) " Take a shrewmouse and 'idolize' it in spring-water (that is, kill it, but this word must not be used because it was ill-omened); do the same with two moon-headed beetles, but in running water; then take a crawfish, fat from a speckled virgin goat, dung from the dog-headed ape, two ibis eggs, two drachmæ each of gum, myrtle-resin, and crocus; four drachmæ each of Italic Alpine herb and incense and an onion without any sucker. Place all these things in a mortar, pound them carefully, and keep the mixture in case of necessity in a leaden receptacle. When you want to use it, take some and go up to the loft with a coal-pan, and when the moon rises, offer the mixture with the following prayer, and Selene will immediately appear.

(*Prayer.*) " Let the gloomy veil of the clouds disperse above me and let the goddess Actiophis rise brilliantly before me and listen to my holy prayer, for I have to disclose the insult of the shameful and impious N.N. (here the enchanter inserts the name of the girl concerned). She has betrayed the holy mysteries to men. N.N. has also said: 'I saw the great goddess leave the vault of heaven and roam over the earth with naked feet, a sword in her hand, and silent.' N.N. also said: 'I saw how she drank blood.' N.N. said that; I did not. Actiophis Ereschigal Nebutosualethi Phorphorbasa Tragiammon (magic names of the goddess, influenced by Oriental magic)! betake thyself to N.N., deprive her of sleep, throw the firebrand into her soul, and punish her with the unrest of madness, pursue her and bring her from every place and every house to me!

"After these words make the offering and utter loud cries (to keep the attention of the goddess), and come down backwards, and at once the soul of the one called upon will appear. But then open the door, else it will die (since it is pursued by the wrathful goddess, and while waiting would be overtaken).

"If now you wish to make anyone ill, use the same prayer and add: 'Make N.N., the daughter of N.N., sick.' If she is to die, then say: 'Take the breath, mistress, from the nose of N.N.' If you wish to send a dream, pray thus: 'Come to her in the form of the goddess, whom N.N. serves.' If you yourself desire a dream, then say: 'Come to me, mistress, and give me during sleep advice on such and such a thing,' and she will come to you and tell you all without deception. But do not employ the charm too rashly, but only when you have a serious reason for it.

(*The amulet.*) "There are also measures of precaution to be taken that you may not have an accident. If anyone should practise such enchantment incautiously, the goddess is accustomed to make him leap about in the air, and to dash him from on high down upon the earth. Therefore I thought it useful also to describe the amulet. But keep it a secret! Take a leaf of best papyrus and carry it on your right arm during the offering. On the leaf should be the words: 'Mulathi Chernuth Amaro Mullandron! Protect me from that evil spirit, be it male or female!' Yet keep it secret, my son!"

In the original text there follow the hymns mentioned, the laudatory in hexameters, the abusive in iambics. The laudatory is very like the Orphic, the words sound solemn and mysterious, and awaken in certain minds a feeling of reverential awe, such as does, for instance, the twilight in the marble dome of Milan. But the iambics, which, as already said, contain the outrage, with which the person to be enchanted is said to have insulted the goddess, give us a deep insight into the might of superstition, by whose gloom the uneducated were surrounded even in the fourth century A.D. The details cannot be made intelligible without lengthy explanations; but this much may be said, that the eating and drinking of human flesh and blood at that time appeared to believing minds compatible with the character of a divinity. Thus the book of spells, of which we have only given a small section, represents a noticeable document of ancient times, and who can tell how many made use of this and similar conjuring formulæ to obtain the object of their wishes—or not to obtain?

To-day, to be sure, no one casts spells according to this prescription; yet it is not the fact, but only the form that has changed, and Schiller's words remain eternally true: "Against stupidity the gods themselves fight in vain."

5. Lucian's Dialogues of Courtesans

After this excursus on love-charms we return to Lucian's *Dialogues of Courtesans*. In the second the hetaira Myrtion complains to her lover Pamphilus that he is now leaving her to marry the daughter of a shipbroker. Thus all his oaths of love were idle, he has now forgotten his Myrtion and further, at a time when she is eight months gone with child—"the worst thing that can happen to an hetaira."

She will not expose the child, especially if it should be a boy; but she will call it Pamphilus and bring it up as a painful consolation. Besides, he has picked out an ugly girl for his wife, with sky-blue squinting eyes.

Pamphilus replies that she is certainly foolish to serve up such nursery-tales, or she must have a bad head, although yesterday she did not have too much to drink. Finally, it turns out that everything rests on a misunderstanding: Doris, Myrtion's too eager maid, had seen garlands on Pamphilus's house and heard the sound of festal enjoyment proceeding from it; she had hurried post-haste and told her mistress that the ship-broker's daughter had made her entrance as a young wife. Only in her haste she had confused Pamphilus's house with that of his neighbour. Now, of course, great joy is the result, and how the two lovers celebrated the happy solution of the misunderstanding is delicately left by Lucian to the reader's imagination.

Jealousy is the foundation of the third dialogue, here fully translated :—

"*Mother* : Were you mad, Philinna, or what was the matter with you yesterday at the banquet? For Diphilus came to me in the morning all in tears and told me how badly you had treated him. He declared that you were drunk, got up in the middle of the meal and danced, although he tried to prevent you; next, you kissed his companion Lamprias; and when he was angry with you, you left him and went to Lamprias and embraced him. While this was going on, Diphilus was choked with rage. And you didn't even sleep with him, I believe, but left him in tears and lay by yourself in the next bed, singing and annoying him.

"*Philinna* : He didn't tell you what he did himself, mother; otherwise you would not support anyone who behaves so insultingly as he. He didn't tell you that he left me first and talked with Thaïs,

Lamprias's friend, before he had arrived. When he saw that I was annoyed and made a signal to show what he was doing, he took hold of the top of Thaïs's ear, and bending back her neck kissed her so vigorously that he almost tore her lips. Then I began to cry, but he laughed and said something in a whisper to Thaïs, evidently meant for me. And Thaïs smiled, looking at me. When they perceived that Lamprias was approaching and they had had enough kissing, I nevertheless reclined by his side, and I did not believe that Diphilus could afterwards reproach me. After the meal Thaïs got up and danced with bare feet, as if she was the only girl whose ankles were beautiful; and after she had finished Lamprias was silent and said nothing, but Diphilus praised to excess her graces and the way she danced, saying how well her foot kept time with the lyre, how beautiful her ankle was, and hundreds of other things, as if he were praising Sosandra of Calamis, not Thaïs; and you know what she is like, from her bathing with us. And how Thaïs immediately began to scoff at me and say, 'Let anyone who is not ashamed of having thin legs get up and dance!' What could I say, mother? I certainly got up and danced—and what would you say I should have done—put up with it and confirm the joke and leave Thaïs mistress of the feast?

"*Mother*: You let jealousy get the better of you, my dear; you ought not to have taken any notice. But tell me what happened after that.

"*Philinna*: The rest approved of what I did; only Diphilus had thrown himself on his back on the couch and kept looking up at the ceiling until I was tired out.

"*Mother*: But was it true that you kissed Lamprias and went over and embraced him? Why don't you answer? Such actions are unpardonable.

"*Philinna*: I wanted to annoy him in return.

"*Mother*: And then you didn't sleep with him, but even sang while he was in tears? Don't you understand, my daughter, that we are poor ; do you forget how much he has given us ? What a winter we should have had to get through, unless Aphrodite had sent him to us ?

" *Philinna* : What then ? Am I to suffer his insults because of that ?

" *Mother* : Be angry, but don't return insult for insult. Don't you know that lovers, when insulted, soon turn round and blame themselves ? But you have always been too severe with men ; mind you don't break the cord by pulling it too tight, as the proverb says."

The fourth dialogue starts with the supposition that Melitta's lover has been unfaithful to her. She complains of the wrong to her friend Bacchis and tells her that the young man keeps away from her without any reason. He has found written on a wall in the Ceramicus, " Melitta loves Hermotimus," and a little below, " The ship's captain Hermotimus loves Melitta." But that is all silly nonsense ; she doesn't even know a ship's captain named Hermotimus. Now would her friend be good enough to see if she could not hunt out one of those old women who are said to be able by their adjurations and spells to recall an unfaithful lover to his duty and to patch the pieces of broken love together. Luckily Bacchis knows such a witch, " a tolerably vigorous, rough woman, a Syrian," who had once helped herself in a similar love trouble, and is not even expensive ; she only asks a loaf of bread and a drachma in ready money. " Besides," says Bacchis, " you must have on the table a portion of salt, seven obols, some sulphur, and a torch ; also a jug of wine which she will drink up alone. Then something belonging to your dearest must be there, some article of clothing, or boots, or a tuft of his hair, or something else of that kind." " Yes, I have some of his boots." " These Bacchis hangs on a nail and fumigates with sulphur, while she sprinkles salt on the fire. She also utters my own name and his. Then she brings out from her bosom a little wheel, which she turns round, and also pronounces a spell in a barbarous language, terrible to hear, with ever increasing rapidity. Thus she acted in my case, and after a short time my faithless lover returned to me. One cannot really ask more. Then she taught me a charm for producing hatred against Phœbis, who had seduced my dearest; I was obliged to pay attention to her footstep, and as soon as she left a trace, then I had to put my right foot on the mark of her left foot and conversely, at the same time saying: 'I have trodden upon you, and am over you.' And I did so on that occasion. No sooner had Melitta heard this, than she earnestly begged her friend to fetch the wise woman; at the same time she ordered her maid to procure everything necessary for the charm."

The fifth dialogue is devoted to Lesbian love, and does not concern us in the present connection; while the sixth has already been given on pp. 361 ff.

In the seventh, between a mother and her daughter Musarion, the entirely low views, certainly also the worldly-wise experiences, of the maternal procuress who thinks of nothing but money are represented, while the inexperienced little daughter still believes in ideal love and is enthusiastic about marriage with her most handsome lover, although he is assuredly as poor as a beggar. The naïveté of the girl is described as delightfully as the action of the mother, whose only object is what is material, so that it is to be regretted that necessary considerations of space forbid the reproduction of this splendid cabinet picture.

The eighth dialogue takes place between the hetaira Ampelis, who has been in the profession for twenty years, and Chrysis who has practised for eighteen. After a few short remarks about the usefulness of jealousy in the affairs of love, and of how it is often invaluable as a means of working a lover up to concert pitch, Ampelis relates how once she treated a certain gallant of hers. He never gave her more than five drachmæ (about five shillings) a night, but she brought him to such a state by arousing his jealousy that, rather than be supplanted by another, he parted with a whole talent (about £250) for sole possession of her for eight months!

The ninth is not of sufficient importance to be translated or even summarized.

The tenth shows that pupils also sometimes visited hetairæ; I shall return to it later, since for other reasons it is very important for the history of Greek morals.

In the eleventh dialogue we see a young man named Charmides with the hetaira Tryphæna on a bed. But instead of doing homage to the joys of love, the young man sobs like a little child. After long persuasion, Tryphæna succeeds in getting the reason from him: namely, that he is madly in love with the hetaira Philemation, but has been unable to obtain his desire for, as his papa keeps him very short, he cannot pay the fairly high figure she puts on herself. So she has dismissed him and opened her door to Moschion, of course chiefly to vex him; while he himself, also wanting to grieve her, has come to Tryphæna. But Tryphæna knows how to cure his trouble. She points out to him without any pretence, that the adored Philemation by every kind of false and deceiving art of the toilet is enabled to wear a youthful appearance, but that she is really forty-five years old. It would truly bring no happiness worth having to see this "funeral urn" quite naked and to possess her. Charmides is at once converted by these revelations; he removes the sheet that separates them, which he had piled up between Tryphæna and himself in the bed, to avoid being touched by her and sinks into her arms full of emotion and longing for love, with the words "the devil take Philemation!"

After what has been said about the Greek hetairæ, we need only briefly point out that intercourse with them by no means necessarily implies an enjoyment that happens but once, which of course was by no means rare, but that often we have to do with affectionate relationships which last for longer or shorter periods, and in which faithfulness and unfaithfulness, quarrels and jealousy play great part.

The twelfth dialogue likewise discloses a picture of jealousy. The hetaira Ioëssa reproaches her lover Lysias at length, for purposely offending her and intentionally showing in her presence a preference for other hetairæ. "Lastly," she says, "you bite a piece off an apple, and aiming it cleverly, spit it into Pyrallis's bosom, without even attempting to conceal it from me. But Pyrallis kissed the piece of apple and stuck it between her breasts under the bosom-band. All this and yet much more you do to me, although I have never asked you for money, and have never kept the door shut against you, with the words 'I have someone with me already', and have refused many suitors, amongst them some wealthy ones, for your sake. But remember, there is a goddess to punish and revenge. You will perhaps be sorry, if you hear one day that I am lying there dead, having hanged myself or jumped into a well, that the sight of me may no longer annoy you. Then you may triumph in the idea that you have accomplished a great and glorious deed. Why do you look at me so gloomily and gnash your teeth? Here, let my friend Pythias judge between us."

Pythias of course takes her friend's part. "He is a stone, not a man," is her opinion; "certainly you have spoilt him inexcusably."

At last Lysias also has his say. He turns the tables and declares that Ioëssa has no ground for complaint at all, since he recently caught her in someone else's arms. He climbed through the window on his friend's back, crept up to her bed, and noticed that she was not lying there alone, that she had a bedfellow, and, as he made certain by touching him gently, one who was " a beardless, tenderly girlish youngster, who had not a hair on his body and was highly scented ".

The little drama of jealousy finds an end that satisfies everyone, when it is established that the supposed young man was no other than her friend Pythias, who, not to desert her friend in her sorrow, had spent the night with her. Yet Lysias is not entirely satisfied. " Then she had no hair and now, after less than a week, she has a thick head of hair," he expresses his opinion doubtfully. " Yes, that is easy to explain," is the laughing answer. " She was obliged to have her hair cut off for some ailment, and since then she has worn a wig. Prove it to him, take off your wig, and show him who the youngster really was of whom he was so jealous as of a supposed lover." This is done and after a festive drink reconciliation is decided upon, in which Pythias also, the guilty-innocent object of jealousy, is to take part. She willingly consents, on condition that Lysias does not let out the secret of her wig to anyone.

In the thirteenth dialogue the Miles Gloriosus, the vain officer, supposedly covered with glory, boastful but with nothing in him, plays the swaggerer. With blustering speeches and endless bombast, with contradictory and silly idle talk he boasts of his heroic deeds, in which he is vivaciously seconded by his equally silly and empty-headed friend Xenidas. " Yes, that is all true," says the latter, " and you yourself know how earnestly I begged you not to expose your valuable life too much to danger. For I should not have been able to live any longer, if you had fallen ! " His friend's praise encourages General Rodomontade. But now comes the sudden effect of the psychologically fine satire. Far from being enchanted by his heroic deeds, as he had naturally hoped, the somewhat more humanely disposed and not uneducated hetaira declares that she will have nothing to do with such a murderer on a large scale, dripping with blood, and gives him his dismissal on the spot. Let Lucian himself tell us the result of the dialogue :

" *Leontichus* : But I took courage and flung myself into the line of battle, as well armed as the Paphlagonian, for I also wore armour of pure gold, so that a great shout arose from our side, as also from our enemies. Speak, Xenidas, with whom did all compare me ?

" *Xenidas* : With whom else, deuce take me, but with Achilles, the son of Thetis and Peleus.

" *Leontichus* : When it now came to a duel, the enemy wounded me slightly, merely scratching me above the knee, but I pierced his shield through and through with my lance, so that it penetrated his breast. He fell ; then I ran up to him and without any trouble cut off his head with my sabre, took of his armour, which I kept as a trophy ; then I spitted his head on my lance, and so returned, loaded with trophies of victory and dripping with blood, back to my ranks.

" *Hymnis* : Get away, Leontichus, if you can tell such cruel deeds of yourself. Who would so much as look at you, if you take such delight in murdering, or drink with you, to say nothing of sleep with you ? Anyhow, I'm off.

" *Leontichus* : I'll pay you twice as much.

" *Hymnis* : Quite impossible ; I couldn't go with such a murderer.

" *Leontichus* : Don't be afraid, Hymnis. I did such things in Paphlagonia, but now I am a man of peace.

" *Hymnis* : No, you are an abominable fellow, and the blood of the Paphlagonian, whom you spitted on your lance, cleaves to your hands. And should I exchange tenderness with such a man and enjoy love? Far be it from me! I would rather embrace the headsman.

"*Leontichus*: If you could only have seen me in my uniform and my feats of arms, you could not have helped falling in love with me.

"*Hymnis*: I felt ill merely at hearing of them, I shuddered; I thought I saw the phantoms and corpses of those whom you have slain; especially the unfortunate Paphlagonian officer, whose head you split open. What do you think would have happened to me if I had been obliged to see your feats of arms with you and the dead men lying there in their blood? I should have died on the spot with terror—I who cannot even bear to see a young cock killed."

After these and a few more words ("Good-bye, you hero of an officer, and go on murdering as much as you like"), Hymnis positively turns her back upon the boaster dripping with blood and flees to her dear mother. The braggart, whose eagerness is now inflamed, tries to re-establish intercourse by the help of Xenidas. The latter knows that most of his heroic deeds are a simple fraud, and it is only after the confession has been very reluctantly wrung from the boaster that he has shamelessly exaggerated, which Xenidas is to tell Hymnis, that hope springs up again that he may soon hold Hymnis in his arms.

The fourteenth dialogue is of such importance for the knowledge of the *milieus* here to be described that it is presented in a complete translation:

"*Dorion*: Now you shut your door upon me, since I have become a beggar; but when I could give you large presents, then I was your lover, husband, master—in a word, everything. But since it can no longer be concealed that I am ruined and you have found the Bithynian wholesale merchant as a lover, then I am for you worth nothing and may stand weeping before your closed door, while he is loved by you, and may stay with you the whole night, and you even declare that you are with child by him.

"*Myrtale*: That pains me enough, my dear Dorion, especially when you say how much you have given me, and that you have ruined yourself for me. Come, tell me all from the beginning—what sort of presents have you give me?

"*Dorion*: Agreed! Let us reckon. First, Sicyonian shoes—two drachmæ. Put down two drachmæ.

"*Myrtale*: But for that you had two nights with me.

"*Dorion*: Then, when I came back from Syria, I brought an alabaster scent bottle for you, which again—by the living gods—had cost two drachmæ.

"*Myrtale*: But I gave you, before you put out to sea, the most beautiful shirt that came down to the knees, which you were to wear while rowing. That second mate had left it lying about, after he had spent a night with me.

"*Dorion*: That's true enough, but soon after in Samos, Epiurus took it away from me, because he recognized it as his, and that led to a severe quarrel between us. Then I brought you onions from Cyprus, five herrings, and four perch. And—look you—eight ship's biscuits in little wicker-baskets, sandals with gold threads, you ungrateful woman! Oh! And a large cheese!

"*Myrtale*: That may perhaps have made five drachmæ.

"*Dorion*: Yes, Myrtale, and quite enough for a poor sailor to spare from his little bit of pay! Now I have the whole right bench under my command, and you don't want to hear any more about me! Besides, I have recently laid a silver drachma at the feet of Aphrodite during her festival, begging her to procure me your favour; I have also put by two drachmæ for shoes for your mother, and I have often pressed two, or four obols in your maid's hand. That is altogether quite a fortune for a sailor.

"*Myrtale*: The onions and the herrings?

"*Dorion*: Yes, for I could not give more. Should I give myself up to the rower's bench, if I were a rich man? But your Bithynian has never once even brought a head of garlic for your mother. I should certainly like to know what presents you have had from him!

"*Myrtale*: Well then! In the first place this expensive chemise, which he bought for me. Then he bought me this thick string of pearls.

"*Dorion*: He bought you that? Why, you had it long before you knew him!

"*Myrtale*: No, the one you mean was much thinner and besides had some small emeralds. Further, he gave me these ear-rings and the beautiful carpet and recently two minæ (about £8) and paid the rent for me—not like you, a pair of cheap shoes and cheese and other trifles!

"*Dorion*: Of course, you say nothing about what a miserable object your new bedfellow is! He is over fifty, quite bald in the front of his head, and his face is as red as a crab's! Have you ever looked at his teeth? In fact, he possesses—the gods punish me!—many charms, especially when he opens his mouth to sing and tries to act the regular dandy, when all he is is the real ass who wants to play the lute, as the proverb goes. But I wish you luck with such a lover, since you deserve him, and may you have a child like its father. I shall find another girl very soon, Delphis perhaps, or Cymbalion, or my neighbour the flute-player, or certainly someone. Everyone cannot give whores carpets and necklaces or two minæ as payment.

"*Myrtale*: Yes, she is worth envying who gets you for a lover! I congratulate you on your Cyprian onions and your greasy cheese!"

The fifteenth and last dialogue shows us the brutal results of jealousy, which leads to wild scenes of flogging, which are sure not to end without bloody noses and severe injuries. In this dialogue also the hero is a swaggering soldier.

6. TEMPLE PROSTITUTION

If Lucian's *Dialogues of Courtesans* afford us a deep insight into the life and manners of the *demi-monde* of Greece, many additional and interesting details may still be gathered from other written sources. Thus we read in Athenæus (xiii, 573*c*): "From ancient times there has existed a custom in Corinth, as the historian Chamæleon also attests in his book on Pindar, that the city when it offers prayers to Aphrodite in a great procession, draws as large a number of hetairæ as possible into it, and these pray to the goddess and later are also present at the sacrifice and sacrificial feast. This is in commemoration of the time when the Persian led his enormous masses to the temple of Aphrodite and the hetairæ also proceeded thither and prayed for the deliverance of the fatherland, and this is also confirmed by the historians, Theopompus and Timæus. When afterwards the Corinthians set up to the goddess a dedicatory tablet, still in existence, with the names of the hetairæ upon it who had taken part in the procession, Simonides composed the following epigram: 'These girls united in a devout prayer to the heavenly Cyprian goddess for the Greeks and their brave champions; therefore the divine Aphrodite did not think of handing over the acropolis of the Greeks to the Persian bowmen.' And private persons vow to Aphrodite their willingness to admit the hetairæ to her temple, after hearing their prayer."

Thus Athenæus, who, in proof of his assertion, cites as an example the gift of the Corinthian Xenophon, who, as already stated (p. 341), after his victory at the Olympian games conducted a hundred girls to the temple of Aphrodite.

It is here obviously a question of religious or temple prostitution (see pp. 124, 195, 205). As there was a temple of Aphrodite Porne at Abydos (Ath., xiii, 572*e*), so also there was one in Cyprus (Herodotus, i,

199), Corinth (Ath., xiii, 573*c*; Strabo, viii, 378), and other places, and, according to the historian Demochares (Ath., vi, 253*a*), the nephew of Demosthenes, the Athenians had even dedicated their own temples of Aphrodite to famous hetairæ, Lamia and Leaena. At Abydos the temple of Aphrodite had been dedicated to the goddess because one of the hetairæ, when the citadel was occupied by foreign forces, made the guards drunk with love and wine and had handed over the keys of the citadel to the authorities, so that they could attack the sleeping guards and the city could be freed.

Of the temple of Aphrodite Porne at Corinth Strabo says: "The temple of Aphrodite was so wealthy, that it was able to keep more than a thousand hetairæ who were dedicated to the goddess by men and women. For the sake of these girls strangers crowded hither, so that the city became rich thereby. Ship's captains only too easily spent their money there, and thus arose the proverb: 'The journey to Corinth does not suit every man'."

One hetaira is said to have answered another who had reproached her for not being industrious and not wanting to know anything about work at the loom, "and yet in a short time I have lifted no less than three weaver's beams." [1]

Religious prostitution already existed in the Babylonian cult of Mylitta and in the similar service of Aphrodite of Byblos, a city in Phœnicia, the modern Jebeil. Herodotus (i, 195) mentions the following as being, in his opinion, the most intelligent of the Babylonian customs, and remarks that he has heard that it was also practised among the Eneti, in Illyria. Once a year, he says, in every village the numerous marriageable young women were assembled together at an appointed place, round which the men soon collected. A herald then offered each one for sale, and first of all the most

[1] There is a play on the word *ἱστούς*, which means (1) ship's masts, i.e. in this case, seamen, and (2) weaver's beams.

beautiful among them. After her sale had brought in a large sum of money, he offered the next most beautiful. But the girls were only put up for sale as lawful wives (that is, not as slaves). The rich men, and youths among the Babylonians ripe for marriage, outbid one another, to buy the most beautiful girls; but the people of the poorer clases—who set no great store on beauty—could marry the uglier girls and get money with them, for when the herald had disposed of all the more attractive he would offer the most ill-favoured, or, perhaps, one who was deformed, and she fell to him who was willing to accept the smallest dowry with her; the necessary funds were supplied by the sale of the beautiful girls, so it was they who, in fact, furnished the dowries for their less favoured sisters. But nobody could hand over his daughter to whomsoever he would; and, further, no buyer might take away his purchase until he had given good security that he would indeed make her his wife. Also, if it turned out later that the couple were not suited to each other the law annulled the marriage and ordained that the dowry should be returned.

Herodotus adds that these customs no longer existed in his time, but there was another which allowed an impoverished man to sell his daughter for money. He had already said the same of the Lydians (i, 93): "In the land of the Lydians all the daughters go whoring so as to procure a dowry, and they do this until they are regularly married."

If the complete passage from Herodotus shows further how the Babylonians brought their daughters to men, and not only those that were beautiful and had fine figures but also the ugly ones, this is religious prostitution in the truest sense of the word. He says: "The most disgraceful law among the Babylonians is the following. Once in her lifetime every native woman must sit down in the precincts of the temple of Aphrodite, and have intercourse with a stranger. Many women, proud of their great wealth and desirous of keeping themselves apart from the vulgar, travel in a closed and covered carriage followed by a number of maidservants, into the temple. But the majority seat themselves in the sacred plot with garlands of cords [1] round their heads, and there is a great multitude of them coming and going. Before and behind, right and left of each, a straight road is left, so that strangers can enter conveniently from all sides, to find their choice. When a woman has once become seated she does not return home until one of the strangers has thrown a gold piece into her lap and has had intercourse with her outside the temple; but as he throws her the money he must at the same time say 'I demand you in the name of Mylitta' ('Mylitta' is the Syrian name of Aphrodite). The amount paid is at the discretion of the purchaser, who need not fear to be rejected since the woman's refusal would be a sin as the money belongs to the goddess; she is obliged to follow the first man who selects her, and it never happens that anyone is rejected. When the woman has given herself to the stranger and has thereby fulfilled her sacred duty to Aphrodite and made herself holy in her sight she returns home, and henceforth no offer, however great, will buy her. Beautiful and well-formed women are, of course, quickly selected, but the ugly must often wait a long time before they can fulfil the law—many of them three or four years. There is also a similar law in the island of Cyprus" (i, 199; see also Strabo, xvi, 745).

Thus Herodotus, whose statements are confirmed by the so-called "Epistle of Jeremy" in the Book of Baruch (vi, 43), where it is said: "The (Chaldean) women also with cords about them, sitting in the ways, burning bran for perfume: but if any of them drawn by some that passeth by, lie

[1] As a symbol of being bound, and of the service which they owe to the goddess.

with him she reproacheth her fellow that she was not thought as worthy as herself, nor her cord broken."

In Cyprus there were also especially the holy cities of Aphrodite-Astarte at Paphos and Amathos, in which religious prostitution was usual, as to which Lactantius (i, 17) in his honest piety falls into a rage. This religious custom had also penetrated to Armenia and the service of Anaïtis, as to which we read the following in Strabo (xii, 532): "What the Medes and Persians regard as sacred, is also honoured amongst the Armenians; but amongst them the cult of Anaïtis flourishes most. For her young male and female slaves prostitute themselves. That is not astonishing, but even the most distinguished persons in the land sell their maiden daughters, and the law orders that they must not wed until they have served the goddess a long time, without anyone disdaining them as wives. Besides, they behave so amiably to their lovers, that they even keep guest-friendship with them and often give them larger presents than they themselves receive since they come from well-to-do families."

We conclude the list of ancient testimony as to religious prostitution with a note of Lucian (*Dea Syria*, 6): "In Byblos I also saw the great temple of Aphrodite and became acquainted with the orgies that are common there. The inhabitants believe that the death of Adonis when he was killed by a boar took place in their country, and in memory thereof they beat their breasts every year and lament, and great mourning prevails throughout the country. When they have finished with beating and lamentation, they perform the obsequies of Adonis and on the following day they pretend that he has awakened to life, place him in heaven and shave their heads, like the Egyptians on the death of Apis. But all the women, who refuse to let their hair be cut off, suffer the following punishment: On a fixed day they are obliged to prostitute themselves, and to this market only strangers have admission, the proceeds being given to the temple of Aphrodite."

To understand temple prostitution, one must remember that according to ancient ideas Aphrodite not only bestows the enjoyment of love, but that this enjoyment is also her divine command, so that it appears quite consistent if it is furthered by her cult. If girls earned their dowry by prostitution, marriage was thereby promoted and consequently a work of piety performed ; and if the girls who gave themselves for money put their profits into the temple treasury, that was also a work of piety, since it was regarded as a thank-offering to the goddess, who was the source of all female beauty, maturity, and fruitfulness, and thus the goddess was honoured in her sanctuary. We know of many peoples and many times, when more value was put upon the girl who gave herself to her husband before marriage than upon the one who brought her virginity with her into the married state. The arrangement is to be found amongst other peoples that *hieroduli*, that is, girls given to prostitution, were to a certain extent appointed to the temple of the love-goddess, not only for the purpose of offering themselves to visitors to the temple but also to give, by means of their dancing and musical talents, greater brilliancy to the festivals held in honour of the divinity. As late as Roman times there existed in the temple of Venus Erycina on mount Eryx in Sicily the service of the *hieroduli* of which Strabo (63 B.C.–A.D. 23) certainly speaks with the almost regretful addition that " the colony no longer counts as many male inhabitants as before, and the number of the sacred bodies (meaning the hieroduli) was considerably reduced " (vi, 272). After Sicily became a Roman province, the Romans, clever politicians as they were, took the temple and the hieroduli under their special protection, gave large sums of money to the temple treasury (at the expense, it is true, of seventeen Sicilian towns), and put two hundred soldiers in the sacred district as a standing protection to the hierodouli and for other purposes. So we are told by Diodorus Siculus (iv, 83), who also gives a concise account of the glorious history of the temple of Eryx.

Anyone who in spite of all these facts does not regard Greco-Oriental temple-prostitution with sympathy, should remind himself that also among the ancient Indians, who must be reckoned next to the Greeks, or perhaps even their equal, as the most cultivated people in the world, quite similar institutions have arisen, and some reference may here be made to these people for purposes of comparison. No one has given a more judicious description of prostitution in ancient India than Karl Gjellerup, the Dane, from whose novel, *Der Pilger Kamanita* (Frankfurt a. M., 1907—p. 84) I take the following in a slightly abbreviated form: " My native place Ujjeni is famous throughout India for its gaiety and noisy joy in life no less than for its brilliant palaces and magnificent temples. Its broad streets resound by day with the neighing of horses and the trumpeting of elephants and by night with the lute-playing of those in love and the song of merry carousers.

" But in particular the hetairæ of Ujjeni enjoy an extraordinary reputation. From the famous hetairæ, who live in palaces, found temples for the gods and public gardens for the people, and in whose reception-halls one finds poets and artists, actors, distinguished foreigners, and indeed, often princes, down to common harlots, all exhibit healthy, strong-limbed beauty, and indescribable grace. At the great festivities, shows and pageants, they form the chief ornament of the streets, which are beautifully decorated with flowers and with fluttering pennons. In cochineal-red dresses, with fragrant garlands in their hands, redolent of perfumes and sparking with diamonds, you see them then, O brother, sitting on the splendid seats allotted them, or passing along the streets with amorous looks, exciting gestures, and laughing words of banter, everywhere fanning to a bright flame the sensual glow of those who desire enjoyment.

"Honoured by the king, adored by the people, sung of by the poets, they are called the varied crown of flowers of Ujjeni with its towering rocks, and make us the envy of the less favoured neighbouring towns. Frequently the most prominent of our beauties visit there: indeed it even happens that such a one has to be called back by order of the king."

7. FURTHER REMARKS ABOUT THE HETAIRÆ

In ancient Greece it might have been the same. That the life of the hetairæ was not devoted only to procuring the indispensable means of sustenance for themselves and to satisfying the sensual desires of others, but that also the slavery and commonness attaching to this as to other trades was dignified by a beauty of its own, is shown amongst other things by the festivals of Aphrodite, which were celebrated in honour of the goddess by the hetairæ in numerous places in Greece. Athenæus (xiii, 574*b*) has given some details on this point, which it would be superfluous to quote after all that has been said; but the same lesson is abundantly taught by the large number of really charming love-stories told of the Greek hetairæ. One of these at least must be related here, from the tenth book of the *Stories of Alexander* by Chares of Mitylene (Ath., xiii, 575*b*): "Once Odatis saw Zariadres in a dream, and fell in love with him, as he did with her. So they yearned without ceasing for each other, since both had had the same dream. Odatis was the most beautiful woman in Asia and Zariadres also was very handsome. So Zariadres sent a messenger to her father Homartes and demanded her hand in marriage. But the father did not consent, since in default of male descendants he intended to betroth his daughter to one of his kinsfolk. Not long afterwards Homartes invited the royal princes, together with his friends and relatives, to his daughter's wedding feast, without saying to whom he intended to betroth her. When drunkenness had reached its height, he called his daughter Odatis into the hall and told her, so that all the guests could hear, 'We desire now, my daughter Odatis, to wed thee. Look now round the hall and upon all the guests, and after that take a golden cup, fill it with wine and give it to whom thou wilt, and his wife shalt thou be.' But when Odatis had examined all, she went weeping into the space before the room, in which stood the mixing jar, since she did not see Zariadres amongst the guests; for she had conveyed a message to him that her marriage was about to take place. He was at that time engaged in a campaign on the Don, but had secretly crossed the river, accompanied only by his charioteer, and had travelled in his chariot about 800 stadia (*c.* 100 miles). When he drew near to the place where the feast was being celebrated, he left conveyance and driver behind and proceeded on foot in Scythian dress. Entering the hall and seeing Odatis standing by the mixing jar, weeping and only filling the cup slowly, he went up to her and said, 'Here am I, Odatis, as you have longed for me; I am Zariadres.' When then she looked at the stranger and perceived that he was handsome and like the man whom she had seen in her dreams, she was full of joy and gave him the cup, but he took her to his chariot and bore her off. And the slaves, who knew about this love passion, said nothing; and when her father ordered them to speak, they declared that they did not know where Odatis was." This story is often told with pride by the non-Greek inhabitants of Asia Minor, and is represented by painters in temples and kings' palaces, even in private houses, and many distinguished citizens call their daughter Odatis.

If this story also does not deal with the hetairæ

themselves, it might yet be given here, as it belongs to the "erotic stories", as they were told by the hetairæ in sociable meetings with their lovers, in order to incite them to be more stedfast in their faithfulness or, according to circumstances, to be more generous in giving. I conclude the chapter on the hetairæ, about whom everything of importance has now been said, by adding a few little-known remarks thrown together almost at random from old authorities.

Idomeneus (Ath., xiii, 576*c*; xii, 533*d*—*FHG*., II, 491), a pupil of Epicurus, had given in his work *On the Demagogues*, a *chronique scandaleuse*, certainly not of unquestionable authority, of the great politicians of Athens. In this, e.g., he related that Themistocles, at a time when drunkenness was still rare, once, in broad daylight drove through the market-place thronged with people in a carriage to which were harnessed like horses four of the best-known hetairæ of the day. Unfortunately, we are not informed what costume these "foals of Aphrodite" (p. 129) wore. According to another reading the hetairæ did not draw the carriage, but sat in it as his companions. In this connection it may be remembered that Themistocles himself was the son of a hetaira, Abrotonon, a Thracian woman, upon whom, as Amphicrates (Ath., xiii, 576*c*—*FHG*., IV, 300) in his book *On Famous Men* related, an epigram had been written, to the effect that Abrotonon was only a Thracian hetaira and yet had borne the great Themistocles.

Antiphanes (Ath., xviii, 587*b*) had said in his book on hetairæ, that the hetaira Nannion was called "mask", because she had a finely-cut face, and wore gold ornaments and expensive clothes, but when naked she was deadly ugly. She was the daughter of Corōnē, the daughter of Nannion, so that she was given the name of 'Tethe' (grandmother) in consequence of the trade having been carried on in the family through three generations.

Xenophon, in his *Memorabilia* (iii, 11, 1, quoted in Ath., xiii, 588*d*)), says of Socrates that: "When anyone affirmed that the Athenian hetaira Theodota was beautiful beyond description, and that the painters preferred her as a model, the master said, 'Let us go and see this woman, for one must not judge beauty from simple hearsay.' So they repaired to Theodota and found her standing as model for a painter. Xenophon then tells us that they found all their expectations surpassed, and that Socrates conversed with the beautiful hetaira and the others who were present on the best way of gaining true friends. Beauty alone, he said, does not secure this: goodwill and a correct moderation in the bestowal of favours are also necessary."

If here it is only a question of the visit of the great wise man and the most important educator of youth to a public courtesan without necessarily ending in a more intimate connection, which, according to the erotic attitude of Socrates (to be spoken of in detail later) is more than improbable, one need only transfer the scene described to modern times and conditions, to estimate the enormous contrast. At that time such a thing caused no offence to anyone: it was publicly spoken of, and even as squeamish a writer as Xenophon has no scruple about mentioning with perfect frankness these things in his *Memorabilia*, which originated in an enthusiastic affection for Socrates. Other intellectual princes of Greece at that time went much further than Socrates.

In Athenæus (xiii, 589*c*) we read: "Aristotle had a son Nicomachus by the hetaira Herpyllis and loved her till his death, since, as Hermippus (*FHG*., III, 46) says, the needs of the philosopher had found with her the necessary attention, and did not the handsome Plato love Archeanassa, an hetaira from Colophon, as he himself testified in the epigram that he wrote upon her?

Athenæus after repeating this epigram, speaks of

the love of Pericles, already mentioned, for the hetaira Aspasia, with whom Socrates also had friendly intercourse. He then goes on to say: "Pericles in general was inclined to sensual pleasures." He also was on intimate terms with his son's wife, as is attested by his contemporary Stesimbrotus (*FHG.*, II, 56). Antisthenes adds that Pericles went in and out of Aspasia's house twice a day. When she was later accused of impiety, she was defended by Pericles when he sought to induce the judges to have compassion on her by shedding more tears and lamenting more than when his own life was at stake. And when Cimon had unlawful connection with his sister Elpinike and was obliged to go into exile, Pericles, as a reward for permitting him to return, received permission to take her as his mistress.

It is naturally impossible at the present day to establish which of these stories, which readily multiplied about many other men, are true; nevertheless, this much is certainly clear—and this is the reason why I have spoken of such things here—that at that time no one found fault with illegitimate sexual intercourse, but looked upon it as a matter of course and spoke with the utmost frankness about it. The attitude of antiquity in this respect can hardly be better rendered than in the words ascribed, rightly or wrongly, to no less a person than Demosthenes (*In Neæram*, 122): "Man has the hetairæ for erotic enjoyments, concubines for daily use, and wives of equal rank to bring up children and to be faithful housewives."

Demosthenes himself, besides, is also said to have been very dissolute, if we may believe Athenæus (xiii, 592*e*) when he writes: "It is said that the orator Demosthenes also had children by an hetaira. He himself brought the children during a lawsuit into the court to arouse sympathy with them, but not the mother, although that would have been allowed according to the custom of the times."

Of the further love-affairs of the great orator we shall speak later, since they are of a pæderastic character.

Athenæus (xiii, 594*b*) tells the following story of the famous hetaira, Plangon : " As she was extremely beautiful, a youth from Colophon fell in love with her, although he already loved Bacchis of Samos. The young man spoke to Plangon of the beauty of Bacchis, and since she wanted to get rid of him, she demanded the famous necklace of Bacchis as a present. Bacchis yielded to his impetuous haste and handed over to him the necklace, which he delivered to Plangon. The latter, touched by the generosity of Bacchis, sent the necklace back to her, and allowed the young man to enjoy her favour again. From that time the two hetairae were inseparable friends and between them made the young man happy with their love. The Ionians were proud of such magnanimity and ever afterwards called Plangon ' Pasiphile ' (friend to all), as is attested by Archilochus (frag. 19, quoted by Ath., as above) in an epigram, in which Pasiphile is compared to a fig-tree, which feeds many crows.

From the Palatine Anthology also (of the contents of which we have spoken on p. 250 in detail) some few further particulars of the life of the Greek hetairæ may be added. According to an epigram of Rufinus (Anth. Pal., v, 44, compared with 161) two specially dangerous hetairæ, named Lembion and Cercyrion made the harbour of Samos unsafe; the poet impressively cautions young men against these " female pirates " in the same words used by another poet in an epigram already communicated.

Paulus Silentiarius (v, 281) relates with amusing seriousness how once, after a copious drinking-bout, he repaired to the house of the hetaira Hermonassa, and began to ornament her door with flowers. But she was unkind and poured water on his head from the upper window. With comic pathos he complains that she had completely ruined his tastefully arranged head of hair. The disdainful young woman certainly failed in her object, for as it was the jug which she was in the habit of touching with her sweet lips the water had received the ardour of love, and hence only inflamed the lover the more.

Unceremoniousness went so far that even on gravestones people were not afraid of speaking of the harlot's profession, and out of several epigrams referring to this, one by Agathias (Scholiast on Anth. Plan. 80) may serve as an example. It says: "I was a harlot in the city of Byzantium and granted to all the love that I sold. I am Kallirrhoë, experienced in all the arts of voluptuousness; lashed by the stings of love, Thomas has placed this epitaph on my grave, and thereby showed what passion dwelt in his soul; his heart melted and became as softened wax."

Even though it is not impossible, and even though—as is the case—it is highly probable that this sixth century A.D. "epitaph" by the epigrammatist, Agathias, is fictitious, there still remains to us plenty of incontrovertible evidence of the manner in which dead hetairæ were regarded in Greek antiquity. Athenæus says (xiii, 594*e*): The Macedonian Harpalus, Alexander the Great's governor of Babylon, after he had carried off much gold, fled to Athens and there fell in love with the hetaira Pythionike, who gradually relieved him of a fortune. After her death he had a very splendid memorial erected to her; according to the testimony of Poseidonius (*FHG.*, III, 259), her body was attended to the grave by choral songs sung by the most prominent artists and with musical accompaniment on every possible instrument.

Dicæarchus (*FHG.*, II, 266), in his book on the *Descent to the Cave of Trophonius*,[1] says: "The traveller who comes from Eleusis to Athens by the

[1] At Lebadæa in Bœotia Trophonius had a famous underground dream-oracle (see *Pausanias*, ix, 39).

so-called Sacred Way, has lived to see a real wonder. When he has arrived at the place where for the first time a view of the temple of Athene and the city opens to his view, he sees erected in the street a more imposing funeral monument than any other in the neighbourhood. He will at first conjecture that it is the tomb of Miltiades or Cimon or of some other great man of Athens, and he will believe that it has been erected by the State at the public expense. If he then hears that it is the grave of the hetaira, Pythionike, what will he expect next?"

This is, moreover, substantiated by Theopompus in his letter to Alexander (*FHG.*, I, 325), in which he severely criticizes the licentiousness of the governor, Harpalus: "Consider and hear exactly what the Babylonians report about the splendour he displayed in the burial of the hetaira, Pythionike. She was originally a maid of the flute-player Bacchis, herself a maid of the Thracian Sinope, who had transferred harlotry from Ægina to Athens, so that she must be called not only a triple maid, but also a triple harlot. He has now erected two memorials to her costing more than 200 talents (about £50,000). What all of us now are especially astonished at is this: to those who fell in Cilicia for thy kingdom and for the freedom of Greece neither this excellent governor nor anyone else has erected memorials: but for the harlot, Pythionike, we shall now see with astonishment one in Athens, besides that in Babylon, which has long been finished. The friend of this harlot, of whom we all know that she gave herself to anyone who desired her for paltry sums of money, who boasted also of being thy friend, ventured to dedicate a sanctuary and temple district to her and to disgrace a temple and altar by naming them after her Pythionike-Aphrodite, thereby proving himself to be not only a scorner of divine punishment, but also one who attempts to tread thy reputation under foot."

Athenæus (xiii, 595*d*) says further: " After the death of Pythionike Harpalus sent for Glycera, who was also a hetaira, as Theopompus attests," and he says also that " Harpalus did not wish to be distinguished with a garland, unless the harlot were crowned at the same time. He erected a bronze statue of Glycera in the Syrian city of Rhossus just at the place where he now intends to set up a statue of thee and of himself. He further gives her permission to live in the royal castle at Tarsus, and has in view that royal honours shall be bestowed upon her by the people, that she shall be called queen and all the reverence paid her which is due to thy mother and thy wife." With this the author of the satyric drama *Agen* *TGF*., 810) agrees; *Agen* was performed at the time of the Dionysia on the Hydaspes, when Harpalus was already driven out and had fled overseas. The poet here mentions Pythionike as a very beautiful woman already dead, but thinks that Glycera is living with Harpalus and that through her the Athenians received magnificent presents.

Athenæus then quotes some lines from this satyric drama, in which the " famous temple of harlots ", already briefly referred to, is named. According to this passage some magicians offered to bring Pythionike back again from the underworld to Harpalus.

Athenæus still further tells us (xiii, 596*b*): " There were also famous hetairæ distinguished for their beauty at Naucratis in Egypt." Thus Doricha, who is abused by the beautiful Sappho (frag. 138—Bergk; cf. also the wonderful ode in Diehl, *Supplementum Lyricum*, Bonn, 1917, p. 29) in her verses because, being her brother's mistress, she had estranged him from his sister when he had come to Naucratis in the course of his business journeys. In Herodotus (ii, 135) Doricha is called "Rhodopis"; and the historian does not seem to have known that this name belonged to that other famous hetaira who had at Delphi, according to Cratinus (*CAF.*, I, 110) set up the so-called "obelisks" which were, in reality, iron roasting spits. This is made clear by Herodotus, who, among other notices of Doricha Rhodopis, says: "Rhodopis, originally a Thracian slave, after various adventures came to Naucratis, where she gave herself up to her master," until she was bought off for a large sum by Charaxus of Mitylene, the brother of the poetess Sappho. She afterwards remained in Egypt, and as she was a well-known harlot, she earned a great deal of money, at least for a hetaira, but not enough to enable her to erect a pyramid. Now Rhodopis "wanted to leave a memorial of herself in Greece, such as no one else would easily accomplish for himself, and the like of which was not to be found in any temple. So she planned to set up something in Delphi in memory of herself, and therefore caused to be made, out of the tenth part of her earnings, a number of iron spits,[1] each of them so large that one could roast a whole ox upon it, and set them up at Delphi, where they are still preserved at the present day, behind the altar erected by the inhabitants of Chios".

Athenæus quotes an epigram of Poseidippus on Doricha, which finds its point in the idea that one would remember her in Naucratis, as long as a ship on the Nile puts out to sea.

Athenæus further says (xiii, 596*d*): "Archedike, a beautiful hetaira, also came from Naucratis." The hetaira from Eresus, who had the same name as the poetess Sappho and who fell in love with the beautiful Phaon, as Nymphis says in his *Voyage Round Asia* (*FHG.*, III, 16), was also famous.

Nicareta of Megara was an hetaira of excellent family, much sought after for the sake of her learning, for she had been a pupil of the philosopher Stilpon. The hetaira Bilistiche of Argos, who carried back her family to the Atridæ, was also famous,

[1] A spit was in Greek *ὀβελός* and *ὀβελίσκος*; hence the confusion with the "obelisks".

as was also the hetaira Leæna, who was beloved by the tyrannicide Harmodius, and who, when later she was treated injuriously by the adherents of the tyrant Hippias, died under torture without betraying any of the State secrets.

The hetaira Lerne, also called Parorama, was the mistress of the orator Stratocles. She was also, since she went to any man who desired her for two drachmæ (1*s*. 6*d*.), sometimes known as Didrachmos.

A certain Heracleides wrote a letter to King Ptolemy IV, Philopator (still preserved : in *Sudhoff*, *Ärztliches aus griechischen Papyrusurkunden*, p. 108, *Bull. Hellen.*, xxvii, 1903), in which he complains of the conduct of the hetaira Psenobastis. When he went by her house, she lay in the window and invited him to come in, and when she was unsuccessful she came out of the house and seized him by the arm. When he rejected her importunity, she tore his cloak off him and spat in his face. When some passers-by tried to take the old man's part, she went back into the house and then poured urine over him from the window.

We know from Plautus (*Menæchmi*, 388) that in Epidaurus the hetairæ sent their servants or maids to the harbour to invite arriving travellers to come into their house, and we may fairly assume that this was the usual thing in harbour towns.

That the hetairæ were everywhere accessible to presents is in the natural order of things, and has been already demonstrated by several passages from authorities. It is also confirmed by vase paintings. Thus, we see on a red-figured box a young man offering a necklace to an hetaira sitting before him in an arm-chair, and we have no doubt that she will accept and put it into her jewel-box that is open beside her. " When love has seized anyone," says Plautus (*Trinummus*, 242), " then all one's property is gone to the deuce ! ' Give me something, my lump of sugar,' whispers the little harlot, ' if you really love me ! ' And the lover says,

'Of course, my darling, and if you want still more, you shall have it!'" In Alciphron (i, 36) the hetaira Petale writes to her lover: "I wish that a courtesan could keep house with tears. I should be well off then; for I have plenty of them from you. But, as things stand, it is money that I need, and clothes and furniture and servants. On that the whole business of my life depends. Unfortunately I did not inherit an estate at Myrrhinus, nor do I possess any shares in silver mines. I have only the money I earn and such miserable tear-stained presents as my silly lovers make me."

That even in the more primitive brothels a bath was not wanting may, considering the fondness of Greeks for them, be assumed without more ado, but is also expressly confirmed by Plautus (*Pœnulus*, 702). It might appear less intelligible to us that, according to the same passage of Plautus, it was customary to make the body supple with olive-oil before connection. It seems as if this was done for hygienic reasons rather than to heighten the enjoyment, for the famous physician Galen has devoted no less than two chapters of his treatise on the *Preservation of Health* (Galen, *De sanitate tuenda*, iii, 11) to the method of anointing the body with oil before sexual intercourse.

To the arts of the toilet, already described in some detail, it may be added that in Plautus (*Mostellaria*, 273), the old maid of the hetaira Philemation expresses the certainly heretical but very sensible idea that "a woman only smells as she should, when she does not smell at all. For those vamped-up, toothless old women who besmear themselves with ointments and hide their bodily defects with dye, when once perspiration has united with the cosmetics such a smell arises from the hags as when a cook mixes together a number of soups".

The author of the *Gods of Love* (falsely ascribed to Lucian) (*Amores*, 39), ridicules still more the female arts of the toilet: "If anyone could see women getting up from bed in the morning, he would think them more disgusting than those animals (apes) whose names must not be mentioned in the early morning. That is no doubt the reason why they carefully shut themselves inside the house and let no man see them; old women and a crowd of maids, as ugly as their mistresses, stand round them on all sides and treat their unhappy faces with all kinds of cosmetics, for a woman does not plunge into a stream of pure water to dissipate the heavy sleep that covers her eyelids and then at once set about some serious occupation; she tries to disguise the unpleasant colour of her face with innumerable paints and powders; and, as if they were part of a public procession, the lady's-maids are lined up with various appliances, to say nothing of silver dishes, pitchers, and mirrors. Piles and rows of boxes, such as one sees in a chemist's shop—vessels full of lies and fraud—in which are stored means of whitening the teeth or artificially blackening the eyebrows, fill the room. But it is the dressing of the hair that takes up most of the time, for some treat it with lotions and such-like that make it shine like the midday sun; and as one colours wool, so do they dye it reddish-yellow, accounting its natural colour ugly; while, if they happen to be satisfied with black hair, they spend their husbands' money on anointing it with all the perfumes of Araby. Then there are iron instruments, heated in a gentle flame, which serve to crimp the hair and twist it into long ringlets. What pains are taken to make it lie back over the eyebrows! Hardly any space is left for the forehead, and the locks behind float proudly over the back and shoulders. After this, bright-coloured sandals are so tightly fastened on that they cut into the flesh, and then—merely as a matter of form, that they may not seem to be naked—a garment of the finest texture, through which everything beneath is more easy to recognize than the face, with the exception of the breasts, which fall down shapelessly and which they always keep prisoners. What need is there to narrate the more expensive of these evils? Erythræan stones suspended from the ears, several ounces in weight; or those snakes round the wrists and arms (would that they were really snakes instead of gold!); and a diadem surrounds the head, starred with Indian gems; expensive necklaces encircle and hang down their necks, and the wretched gold is even about their feet, squeezing whatever part round their ankles is bare—it were better that the ankles should be confined with iron! And when the whole body has thus been magically made up with the deceptive beauty of spurious charms, they redden their shameless cheeks with dyes smeared on, so that the 'flower of purple' may provide a striking contrast upon their excessively whitened and grease-painted skin."

For harlots and hetairæ to wear a special, showy costume (Pauly, *Realenzyklopädie*, viii, col. 1353) may have been the custom in individual places and times, but it can hardly have been the general rule, as a large number of vase paintings show, and perhaps all that can be safely said is that the costume of the hetairæ would change with the fashions.

Nicknames were customarily bestowed upon well-known hetairæ, such as the following:—

"Anticyra" (hellebore) (Ath., xiii, 586 f.) was considered a remedy against mental disturbances by the ancients, and so the hetaira Hoia was named Anticyra, with reference to her habit of going with highly excited or mad fellows or, as was subsequently said, because her protector, the physician Nicostratus, left her nothing but a bundle of hellebore after his death.

Laïs was surnamed "Axine" (axe) (Ælian, *Var. hist.*, xii, 5; xiv, 35) because of the sharpness—or the bluntness?—of her demands.

"Aphyē" (anchovy) (Ath., xiii, 586*ab*) was the

name of several hetairæ, because of the colour of their skin, their slender forms, and large eyes.

"Kynamyia" (dog's snout) (Ath., iv, 157*a*) was the name given to the hetaira Nikion, from the expression of her face.

"Lychnos" (lamp) (Ath., xiii, 583*e*) was the nickname of the hetaira Synoris, perhaps on account of her eternal thirst, which sucked up all sorts of wine as a lamp-wick sucks up the oil.

"Pagis" (running knot) (Lucian, *Dial. Meretr.*, xi, 2) was the name given to the hetaira Philemation, who ensnared men with her charms.

"Proscenion" (stage-curtain) (Ath., xiii, 587*b*) was the nickname of the hetaira Nannion, because she possessed a pretty face and expensive toilette, but an ugly body.

"Ptochhelene" (begging Helen) (Ath., xiii, 585*b*) was the name given to Kallistion because of her poor dress. Athenæus records that she was once hired by a good-for-nothing fellow, and that as he lay naked by her side, she saw the marks of some recent thrashing and asked him what they were. He replied that when a boy he had spilt some hot broth over his body; whereon she laughingly rejoined "that it must have been 'veal-broth'".[1]

"Hys" (swine) (Ath., xiii, 583*a*) was another name of Kallistion, which does not necessarily imply greedy or bestial habits, but may refer simply to her lack of cleanliness.

"Phthelropyle" (Ath., xiii, 586*a*) was the nickname of Phanostratē, who once was seen standing at her door and picking lice off herself.

There were many pet names, given to the hetairæ by their lovers, of which the following may serve as characteristic examples :—

Little sister, nightingale, goldfinch, little vine, abyss, honeycomb, little cow, little swallow, womb, gazelle, hind, ivory, sweetie, naked frog, sink (in

[1] Whips for flogging slaves were made of calves' skin.

Greek ἱππάφεσις, properly the place in the race-course from which the horses were let go), fig, darling, snail, gnat, crow, luteplayer, huntress, bitch, hare, leveret, little glowworm, lioness, little one, little dish, wolf, lyre (lute), kneading trough, little mother, boy's lover, bee, little calf, fly, little doll, skiff, clover, early fruit, wrestler and wrestling place, much little love, vigil, little miss, little torch, little kiss, little licker, toad, cuttlefish, sparrow, snubnose, wick, tiger.

CHAPTER V

Male Homosexuality

1. General and Introductory

Henry Beyle (Stendhal) writes in his book *De l'Amour*: "There is nothing more comical than our usual views of the ancients and ancient art. As we read only superficial translations, we do not recognize that they devoted a special cult to the Naked, which repels us moderns. In France only the feminine is called 'beautiful' by the masses. Gallantry did not exist among the ancient Greeks, but on the other hand, only a love which appears perverted to us to-day. . . . They cultivated, we may say, a feeling rejected by the modern world."

From this feeling the fact is no doubt to be explained that the generally known and in other respects excellent handbooks pass over this subject in almost complete silence. To give an example: In Holm-Deecke-Soltau's book of almost 600 pages (*Kulturgeschichte des Klassischen Altertums*, Leipzig, 1897), homosexuality is not mentioned at all; in L. Schmidt's profound work in two volumes (*Die Ethik der alten Griechen*, Berlin, 1882) the subject is limited to something less than three pages; in the four gigantic volumes of Burckhardt's *Griechische Kulturgeschichte* one finds next to nothing, and indeed in the new and revised edition of Pauly's well-known *Realenzyklopädie der klassischen Altertumswissenschaft* (increased to ten volumes each of at least 1,300 pages) the catch-word *Päderastie* contains four pages by the distinguished Breslau university professor W. Kroll, in which certainly much that is correct is stated, yet so incompletely, that though it might perhaps suffice as a summary, it is unworthy of monumental work which professes to treat exhaustively the whole culture of classical antiquity. The article "Hetairen" in the same encyclopædia fills twenty pages.

The result of this treatment, which is to be found throughout present-day literature, is to give the reader, who is himself unable to consult the authorities, the idea that in the case of Greek homosexuality it was a merely subsidiary phenomenon, something which happened in isolated instances, rarely, and only here and there.

Without anticipating the argument, listen first to the great philosopher Plato, who wrote: "Since then Eros is acknowledged to be the oldest god, we owe to him the greatest blessings. For I cannot say what greater benefit can fall to the lot of a young man than a virtuous lover and to the lover than a beloved youth. For what those who intend to live a noble life ought to regard as their whole life, this neither kinship nor wealth nor honours nor anything else can afford us so well as love. And what is this? I mean modesty in regard to shameful things, in good things ambition; for without these it is impossible for any city or private individual to perform great and noble deeds. Therefore I assert that a man who loves, if he is found doing or suffering anything disgraceful at anyone's hands, without defending himself through cowardice, would not be so pained if he were seen by his father or his companions or anyone as he would were it by his favourite. Similarly, we see that a young man who is loved is specially ashamed when his lover sees him committing an offence. If then there were any means whereby a state or army could be formed of lovers and favourites, they would administer affairs better than all others, provided they abstain from all disgraceful deeds and compete with one another in honest rivalry. And such men together with others like them, though few in number, so to speak would conquer the world.

For the man who loves would be ashamed to abandon his post or throw aside his arms in the presence of his favourite more than in the presence of anyone, and would often prefer to die in his place. For no one is so base as to leave his beloved in the lurch and not to help him when in danger, for Eros himself inspires him with valour, so that he behaves like a man of the greatest courage. For, as Homer says, this courage is breathed into the souls of some of the heroes by the god, but this love of itself inspires it in those who love " (*Symposium*, 178*c*).

In order to be able to face the problem, the solution of which at the same time indicates the key to the understanding of the whole of Greek culture, it is necessary first of all to become acquainted with the facts that are accredited and undisputed.

2. TERMINOLOGY

The word most frequently used, " pæderasty " (*παιδεραστία*), comes from *παῖς* (boy) and *ἐρᾶν* (to love), and consequently denotes the spiritual and sensual affection for a boy, though it should be noted, as will later be more fully shown, that the word " boy " is not to be understood offhand in the modern colloquial sense. In the Greek language the word " pæderasty " had not this ugly sound it has for us to-day, since it was regarded simply as an expression for one variety of love, and had no sort of defamatory meaning attached to it.

The word *παιδέρως* is only once found in the sense of " pæderast ", but the verb *παιδεραστεῖν* frequently. Lucian once has the expression *τὰ παιδεραστικά* for " pæderasty ". Frenzied, uncontrolled passion for boys was called *παιδομανία*, and a man filled with such passion *παιδομανής*, both words being derived from *μανία* (passion, frenzy). The word *παιδοπίπης* (one who stares at or spies after boys) had a harmlessly jesting additional note which again represents a different shade of meaning, i.e. one who gapes after, or ogles boys with fair hair.

The words παιδοτρίβης and παιδοτριβεῖν, harmless in themselves and originally meaning a teacher of boys in the art of wrestling, are also used obscenely, and the secondary sense is easy to understand, since the words are connected with the verb τρίβειν.

Later authors, especially the Fathers of the Church, prefer to use, in an obscene sense, the words παιδοφθορία, παιδοφθόρος, παιδοφθορεῖν (seduction of boys, seducer of boys, to seduce boys).

In addition to the above the expressions παίδων ἔρως and παιδικὸς ἔρως (love of boys, boyish love) were in common use.

The word *ephebophilia* is not ancient, but a new formation; it means the love for an ephebos (ἔφηβος), by which was understood a young man who had passed the age of puberty; certainly, however, the adjective φιλέφηβος (fond of young men) existed. So far as I know, the noun παιδοφιλία (love of boys) does not occur in any Greek author; but the verb παιδοφιλεῖν (to love boys) and παιδοφίλης (lover of boys) are fairly frequent.

A boy's lover had different names in the several Greek dialects; as, for example, on the island of Crete, where the love of boys flourished from the earliest times, he was called ἐραστής, and after the alliance was completed, φιλήτωρ, a word difficult to translate—perhaps " wooer and friend "; the boy who was the object of affection was called ἐρώμενος (loved), as long as he was still courted, but if he became the friend of a great personage he was called κλεινός (the famous, the celebrated). The word φιλοβούπαις stands by itself, and is used of one who is fond of over-matured boys. The word βούπαις denoted what we call " a big young man ".[1] The word φιλομεῖραξ also rarely

[1] According to Hesychius, the syllable βου means " big ", but also " much "; it may be connected with βοῦς (ox, bull). Also, according to the same, among the Spartans βοῦα denoted a definite division of bigger boys (ἀγέλη παίδων), and the word βούπαις might very well be derived from this.

occurs; it is derived from μεῖραξ, by which a boy in his best prime was meant, and consequently signifies one who especially loves beautiful boys. In Athens it was the title of honour given to Sophocles.

The expression which meets us most frequently in the Greek writings to denote the beloved boy or young man is τὰ παιδικά (boyish things, things connected with boys), and the explanation is that a man loved in the object of his love just "what was boyish", that is, the qualities of mind and body that distinguish the boy; that he held him dear, since he beheld in him the embodiments of boyhood. I do not know a translation that completely reproduces the idea of this word and am unable to coin one.

In the Doric dialect the usual word for the lover was εἴσπνηλος or εἰσπνήλας, literally "the inspirer", which contains the hint that the lover, who indeed, as we shall see later, was also responsible for the boy in every sort of connection, inspired the young receptive soul with all that was good and noble. Therefore the Dorians used the word εἰσπνεῖν in the sense of "to love", if it was a question of a boy. That this "blowing in" is to be understood in the above-mentioned ethical sense is expressly stated by Ælian. Even more definitely and indisputably Xenophon expresses himself: "By the very fact that we breathe our love into beautiful boys, we keep them away from avarice, increase their enjoyment in work, trouble, and dangers, and strengthen their modesty and self-control."

With this the Dorian name for the loved boy—ἀΐτας, the "listening, the intellectually receptive"—agrees.

By the side of these highly serious terms there grew up in course of time a number of others, which owed their origin to joking or derisive caprice. These will be discussed later; but it may be mentioned in passing that, by a secondary meaning easy to understand, the lover was sometimes called the "wolf", while the loved boy would be the "lamb" or "kid". The wolf was to the ancient Greeks the symbol of greediness and audacious fierceness. Thus we read in an epigram of Straton: "Going out in revel after supper, I, the wolf, found a lamb standing at the door, the son of my neighbour Aristodicus, and throwing my arms round him I kissed him to my heart's content, promising on my oath many gifts."

Plato has an epigram: "As wolves love lambs, so do lovers love their loves."

Occasionally the lover was also called a "raven", while "Sathon" and "Posthon"[1] were tolerably frequent names for the boy favourite. Both these words were also serious family names, the Greeks being in all sexual matters astonishingly naïve.

3. Boyhood and the Greek Ideal of Beauty

When discussing the Greek love of boys, one thing especially must not be forgotten: that it is never a question of boys (as we mostly use the word), that is, of children of tender age, but always of boys who are sexually matured, that is, who have reached the age of puberty. This age alone is meant by the word παῖς in by far the greater number of passages of the Greek authors, so far as we are here concerned with them; indeed, in not a few an age which we should never consider a boy's age but rather that of a youth, corresponding sometimes to what we should call "a young man", is indicated. We must also bear in mind that in Greece, as in all countries of the so-called Sotadic zone,[2] puberty sets in earlier than in the north, so that we can well keep to the word "boy", if we do not forget that all

[1] Both σάθων and πόσθων are nurses' baby talk or pet names, formed from σάθη and πόσθη, both of which = *membrum virile*).

[2] Countries in which the south European climate calls forth an early awakening and evident intensification of the sexual impulse—Spain, Southern France, Italy, Greece, Asia Minor, and Northern Africa.

these boys have reached the age of puberty. Sexual intercourse with boys in our sense of the word, that is, sexually immature youths, was of course punished, and sometimes very severely, in ancient Greece; of this we treat in a later chapter.

On the different ages of boys and youths who were loved by the Greeks, a treatise might be written, with a motto from Goethe, who, in regard to this problem, so unintelligible to most of the men of the present day, showed himself to be the universal intellect that knew and understood all; for in the *Achilleïs* we read: "Now to the son of Cronos came Ganymede, with the seriousness of the first look of youth in his childlike eye, and the god rejoiced."

We should also recall a passage in Homer's *Odyssey* (x, 277), where we hear how Odysseus, in order to explore the island of Circe, went into the interior of the country. On the way he is met by Hermes (of course unknown to him) "in the form of a youth with the first down of his beard upon his chin, in whom the charm of youth is fairest".

The Greek poet Aristophanes (*Clouds*, 978) also praises his Greek boys in the same manner, except that the down he speaks of is not the down of their cheeks and lips.

The beginning of the *Protagoras* of Plato refers to the passage from Homer quoted above: "Whence come you, Socrates? And yet I need hardly ask the question, for I know that you have been in chase of the fair Alcibiades. I saw him the day before yesterday, and he had got a beard like a man—and he is a man, as I may tell you in your ear. But I thought that he was still very charming.

"*Socrates*: What of his beard? Are you not of Homer's opinion, who says that 'Youth is most charming, when first the beard appears?' And that is now the charm of Alcibiades."

On the different degrees of age Straton (Anth. Pal., xii, 4) says: "The youthful bloom of the twelve-year-old boy gives me joy, but much more desirable is the boy of thirteen. He whose years are fourteen, is a still sweeter flower of the Loves, and even more charming is he who is beginning his fifteenth year. The sixteenth year is that of the gods, and to desire the seventeenth does not fall to my lot, but only to Zeus. But if one longs for one still older, he no longer plays, but already demands the Homeric 'but to him replied'."[1]

To facilitate the understanding of the Hellenic love of boys, it will be as well to say something about the Greek ideal of beauty. The most fundamental difference between ancient and modern culture is that the ancient is throughout male and that the woman only comes into the scheme of the Greek man as mother of his children and as manager of household matters. Antiquity treated the man, and the man only, as the focus of all intellectual life. This explains why the bringing up and development of girls was neglected in a way we can hardly understand; but the boys, on the other hand, were supposed to continue their education much later than is usual with us. The most peculiar custom, according to our ideas, was that every man attracted to him some boy or youth and, in the intimacy of daily life, acted as his counsellor, guardian, and friend, and prompted him in all manly virtues. It was especially in the Doric states that this custom prevailed, and it was recognized so much as a matter of course by the State that it was considered a violation of duty by the man, if he did not draw one younger to him, and a disgrace to the boy if he was not honoured by the friendship of a man. The senior was responsible for the manner of life of his young comrade, and shared with him blame and praise. When a boy on one occasion uttered a cry of pain at gymnastic exercises, his older friend, as Plutarch relates (*Lycurgus*, 18), was punished for it.

[1] That is, he demands the return of love, which the poet expresses by Homer's oft-repeated τὸν δ' ἀπαμειβόμενος.

If this originally Doric custom was not also spread throughout Greece, yet the daily intercourse of the male youth with men, the close community of life from early morning till late evening, was a matter of course in all Greece. Thereby in the man was developed that understanding of the soul of the boy and the young man, and an almost unexampled zeal to scatter the seed of everything good and noble in the young, receptive hearts and to bring them as near as possible to the ideal of an excellent citizen. For the ideal of male perfection the Greek has coined the formula καλὸς κἀγαθός, good and beautiful, or " beautiful in body and soul ". Thus, then, a value was placed upon the bodily development of boys, the importance of which it would be difficult to overestimate. We may affirm without exaggeration that Greek boys spent three-quarters of the day in the palæstræ and gymnasia, which, in contrast to the German—though not to the English—sense of the word, served essentially for bodily development. In all these bodily exercises boys and youths were naked, to which the derivation of the word (from γυμνός, naked) points.

4. Boyish Beauty in Greek Literature

From the immense number of passages available, some few may be selected as especially characteristic. As early as the *Iliad* youthful beauty is glorified, when the poet speaks of Nireus, who outshone all the other Greek youths in beauty. Indeed, the beauty of Nireus afterwards became proverbial and is mentioned constantly (*Il.*, ii, 671).

The æsthetic pleasure of the Greek eye in beautiful youth is prominent in the *Iliad* in another exquisite passage, where Hector's father, the aged King Priam, standing in great distress before Achilles and begging for the dead body of his beloved son, can yet find it in his heart to glance with admiration upon the beauty of the youth who had slain his

Hector (*Il.*, xxiv, 629). On this passage Gerlach (*Philologus*, xxx, 57) finely observes: "We must accordingly form a higher idea of the beauty of Achilles than of the charms of Helen; for Priam, on whom the most unspeakable sorrow has been inflicted by the former, admires it and is able to be surprised at it, at the very moment when he is begging for the dead body of his son."

In a fragment of his poetry the wise Solon (frag. 44) compares the beauty of boys with the flowers of spring. We may quote the verses from the poems of Theognis (1365 and 1319): "O most beautiful and charming of boys, stand before me and listen to a few words from me"; and "O boy, since the goddess Cypris has given you charming grace and your beauty of form is the admiration of all, listen to these words and place my gratitude in your heart, knowing how hard it is for men to bear love."

Ibycus (frag. 5), known to everyone from Schiller's ballad, does homage to the beauty of his favourite with the words: "Euryalus, offshoot of charming Graces, object of the fair-haired maidens' care, Cypris and mild-eyed Persuasion have reared you in the midst of rosy flowers."

Pindar (*Nemea*, viii, 1) sings the praise of boyish beauty with the words: "Queen of youthful prime, harbinger of the divine desires of Aphrodite, thou that, resting on the eyes of maidens and of boys, bearest one in the hands of gentle destiny, but handlest another far otherwise—'tis sweet for one who hath not swerved from due measure in aught that he doeth, to be able to win the nobler prize of love."

Licymnius (frag. 3 in Ath., xiii, 564*c*), the lyric poet born in the island of Chios, had related in one of his poems the love of Hypnos, the god of sleep, for Endymion: "He was so fond of looking at the eyes of Endymion, that he did not allow him to shut them when he put him to sleep, but made him keep them open, that he might enjoy the charm of looking at them."

Straton (Anth. Pal., *a*, xii, 195, *b*, 181) is above all a eulogist of the beauty of boys: (*a*) "The meads that love the Zephyr are not abloom with so many flowers, the crowded splendour of the spring-tide, as are the high-born boys thou shalt see, Dionysius, all moulded by Cypris and the Graces. And chief among them, look, flowers Milesius, like a rose shining with its sweet-scented petals. But perchance he knows not, that as a lovely flower is killed by the heat, so is beauty by a hair." (*b*) "It is a lying fable, Theocles, that the Graces are good and that there are three of them in Orchomenus; for five times ten dance round thy face, all archers, ravishers of other men's souls."

The verses of Meleager (Anth. Pal., xii, 256) describe the beauties of various boys: "Love hath wrought for thee, Cypris, gathering with his own hands the boy-flowers, a wreath of every blossom to cozen the heart. Into it he wove Diodorus the sweet lily, and Asclepiades the scented white violet. Yea, and thereupon he planted Heracleitus when, like a rose, he grew from the thorns, and Dion, when he bloomed like the blossom of the vine. He tied on Theron, too, the golden-tressed saffron, and put in Uliades, a sprig of thyme, and soft-haired Myiscus the evergreen olive shoot, and despoiled for it the lovely boughs of Aretas. Most blessed of islands art thou, holy Tyre, which hast the perfumed grove where the boy-blossoms of Cypris grow."

Nor is the great poet Callimachus (Anth. Pal., xii, 73) ashamed to sing the praises of the beauty of boys: "It is but the half of my soul that still breathes, and for the other half I know not if it be Love or Death that hath seized on it, only it is gone. Is it off again to one of the lads? And yet I told them often. 'Receive not, ye young men, the runaway.' Seek for it at . . .; for I know that it is somewhere there that the gallows-bird, the love-lorn, is loitering."

It is a matter of course for Greek thought and feeling, that even the lofty pathos of serious tragedy is not ashamed to pay homage to boyish beauty on every possible occasion (see p. 134).

Sophocles (frag. 757: ὅτῳ δ' ἔρωτος δῆγμα παιδικοῦ προσῆν; cf. also Pindar, frag. 123: "wound from the bite of youthful beauty"), in one of the fragments that we still possess, praises the beauty of the youthful Pelops with words given elsewhere (frag. 433). Even Euripides (frag. 652: ὦ παῖδες, οἷον φίλτρον ἀνθρώποις φρενός), the great negationist, gives expression to his enthusiasm in the words: "O what a magic comfort are boys to men!"

Comedy also often finds occasion to speak of the beauty of boys. Thus in 421 B.C. Eupolis had brought on the stage his comedy *Autolycus*. The hero of the piece, Autolycus, was a youth of such beauty, that Xenophon (*Sympos.*, i, 9) says of him admiringly: "As when a light flashes up in the night and draws the eyes of all upon it, so the shining beauty of the youthful Autolycus guided all eyes towards it."

The following verses are preserved from an unknown comedy of Damoxenos (Ath., i, 15*b* (*CAF.*, III, 353)), in which the beauty of a boy from the island of Cos is described: "A youth about seventeen years old was throwing a ball. He came from Cos, the island that produces seeming gods, and whenever he looked at those who were seated, or took or gave the ball, we all raised a shout, for symmetry and character and order were seen in everything he did. It was the perfection of beauty; I had never seen or heard of such grace before. I should have fared worse, if I had remained longer; and now I do not think that I am well."

An unknown poet (*CAF.*, III, 451, in Plutarch, *Moralia*, 769*b*) of Greek comedy has left us the lines: "And beholding his comeliness, I made a slip. . . . A beardless, tender, and beautiful youth . . . would that I could die embracing him and gain an epitaph."

Anyone who, after reading the above passages, should be of the opinion that for such glorification of the beauty of boys we are indebted only to the poetically idealized caprice of the poet, would be greatly mistaken. Greek prose also is full of inspired praises of beauty, indeed of enthusiastic hymns on the beauty of boys. A whole volume could be put together, from the letters of Philostratus alone, of which the following are instances :—

(1) *To a Boy.*—These roses desire with longing to come to you and their leaves as wings carry them to you. Receive them kindly as a memorial of Adonis, or as the purple blood of Aphrodite, or as the choicest fruits of the earth. The crown of olives adorns the athlete, the towering tiara a great king, the helmet a warrior; but the rose is the ornament of a beautiful boy, since it resembles him in fragrance and in colour. It is not you who will adorn yourself with roses, but the roses themselves with you.

(2) *To the Same.*—I have sent you a crown of roses, not (or at least not exclusively) to give you pleasure, but out of affection for the roses themselves, that they may not fade.

(3) *To the Same.*—The Spartans clad themselves in purple-coloured garments, either to frighten their enemies by the obtrusive hue, or in order that they might not see when they were wounded, owing to the resemblance of the colour to blood. So must you beautiful boys arm yourselves only with roses, and let that be the equipment that your lovers will present to you. Now the hyacinth suits a fair-haired boy well, the narcissus a dark-haired one, but the rose suits all, since once it was itself a boy. It infatuated Anchises, deprived Ares of his weapons, enticed Adonis; it is the hair of spring, the brightness of the earth, the torch of love.

(4) *To the Same.*—You reproach me for not having sent you any roses. I omitted to do so, not from forgetfulness, not from want of affection, but I said to myself, you are fair and beautiful, and on your cheeks your own roses bloom, so that you need no others besides. Even Homer does not set a garland on the head of the fair-haired Meleager—that would have been adding fire to fire—nor on that of Achilles, nor of Menelaus, nor of any other who is famous in his poems for the beauty of his hair. Also this flower is of a sorry kind, for its appointed time is only brief, and it soon fades away, and, as we are told, the first beginning of its existence is melancholy. For the thorn of a rose pricked Aphrodite as she passed by, as the people of Cyprus and Phœnicia tell. Yet why should we not crown ourselves with the flower, which spares not even Aphrodite ?

(5) *To the Same.*—How did it happen that the roses, which, before they came to you, were beautiful and smelt delightfully—else I would never have sent them to you—withered and died away so quickly when they reached you ? I cannot tell you the real reason, for they would disclose nothing to me ; but probably they did not want to be overcome in comparison with you and were afraid to enter into competition with you, so that they died at once, when they came in contact with the more charming fragrance of your skin. Thus the light of the lamp is darkened, conquered by a blazing flame, and the stars became extinct, since they cannot endure the sight of the sun.

(6) *To the Same.*—The nests afford shelter for the birds, the rocks for the fishes, and the eyes for beauty. Birds and fishes roam around, change places, wander hither and thither wherever chance leads them ; but if beauty is once fixed firmly in the eyes, then it never again abandons this shelter. So you dwell in me, and I carry you in the nets of the eyes everywhere. If I go oversea, you rise up from

it, like Aphrodite in the story ; if I cross the meadow, you shine from the flowers to meet me. What grows there that is like you ? The flowers also are beautiful and charming, yet they bloom only for a day. If I look up to heaven, I think the sun has set, and that you are shining in its place. But when the dusk of night surrounds us, I see only two stars, Hesperus [1] and you.

The vast number of passages from prose literature, in which the beauty of boys is praised, makes it impossible to enumerate them all, yet at least a small selection may be given from Lucian.

In the first *Dialogue of the Dead* (Diogenes and Polydeuces) " fair hair, black flashing eyes, ruddy complexion, tight sinews and broad shoulders " are named as marks of manly beauty.

Lucian's *Charidemus* is entirely devoted to the nature of beauty : " The occasion for our conversation, which you would like to know, was the beautiful Cleonymus himself, who sat between me and his uncle. Most of the guests who, as has been mentioned, were ignorant persons, could not keep their eyes from him, they saw nothing but him, and forgetting nearly everything else, vied with one another in praising this youth's beauty. We learned people could not help fully appreciating their good taste, but we were obliged to consider it unpardonable negligence to let ourselves be overcome by laymen in what we regarded as our own speciality ; so we naturally hit upon the idea of making little impromptu speeches, which we were to deliver one after the other. For, for the sake of decency and to avoid increasing his self-conceit, it did not appear suitable for us to enter into a special praise of the young man."

Then Philo began his panegyric on beauty : " All men desire to have beauty, although only few have

[1] Hesperus is the Greek name for the planet Venus, which the ancients considered the most beautiful star : cf. Sappho frag. 133 : *ἀστἑρων πάντων ὀ κάλιστος* ; *Catullus*, lxii, 26, Hespere quis caelo lucet jucundior ignis ?

been thought worthy of it. The few who have obtained this boon are always supposed to have been the happiest of men, being honoured as they deserved by gods and men alike. And here is a proof of this. Among all the mortals who have ever been thought worthy of associating with the gods there is not a single one who has not had to thank his beauty for being thus preferred. It was simply thanks to his beauty that Pelops shared the ambrosia of the gods at their table, and Ganymede, the son of Dardanus, had such power over the chief of the gods, that Zeus would not allow any of the other gods to accompany him when he flew down to the heights of Ida to fetch this his favourite to heaven, where he now remains with him for all time. When Zeus approaches beautiful youths he becomes so gentle and mild and just to all, that he always seems to put off the character of Zeus, and for fear of not being pleasant enough to his favourites in his own form, he assumes the form of someone else, always one so beautiful that he can be certain of attracting all who look at him. Such is the honour and respect paid to beauty ! "

Zeus, however, is not the only one among the gods over whom beauty exercises such power, and anyone who looks into the history of the gods will find that in this matter they all have the same taste —Poseidon, for example, fell a victim to the beautiful Pelops, Apollo to Hyacinthus, Hermes to Cadmus. If then beauty is something so noble and divine and in the eyes of the gods themselves is so highly valued, should it not be our duty to imitate the gods in this and to contribute to its glorification by doing all we can to assist, both in words and actions ?

Lastly, Philon expresses the pleasure which one has in the national games where he can feast his eyes upon the courage and steadfastness of the competitors, their beautiful bodily forms, the vigorous structure of their limbs, their inconceivable cleverness and skill, their invincible strength, boldness, condition, patience, and perseverance, and their inextinguishable desire to be victorious.

Further, we read in Lucian's *Scytha* (xi) of a youth who " will capture your heart at the first glance by his manly comeliness and noble stature, but as soon as he begins to speak he will lead you away fettered by the ears. As often as he speaks in public our feelings are such as the Athenians experienced towards Alcibiades. The whole city listens to him with such eager attention, that it seems desirous of swallowing with mouth and eyes everything he says. The only difference is that the Athenians soon repented of their enthusiastic love for Alcibiades, whereas here, on the contrary, the whole State not only loves the athlete, but finds him, in spite of his youth, worthy of respect."

5. BOYISH BEAUTY IN GREEK ART

To how great an extent the boyish ideal appeared to the Greeks the embodiment of all earthly beauty may be further appreciated from the fact that in plastic art specifically female beauty is represented as approximating to the type of the boy or youth ; and the truth of this assertion can be proved by rapidly turning over the pages of any illustrated history of Greek art. Indeed, even the prototypes of female charm and female seductiveness—the Sirens—were often enough represented as boyish. In Greek art, and especially in vase-paintings, boys and youths are portrayed far more frequently and with much greater attention to detail than are girls, as must strike everyone who even casually examines one of the great works on vases ; a favourite subject above all is the youthful Eros, together with Hyacinthus, Hylas, and other boy-favourites, of whom Greek mythology tells us.

Further, it must be remembered that in mythological handbooks whole chapters were filled with a list of beautiful boys, as in Hyginus's book of myths for schools (*Fabularum Liber*, 271); and here also may be mentioned the *Erotes* of Phanocles, to be afterwards discussed—a poetical list of many beautiful boys and their lovers.

A further proof that the Hellenes saw the ideal of beauty in the boy and the youth, is the very remarkable fact that the inscription καλός (beautiful boy) occurs on an enormous number of vases, while the inscription καλή (beautiful girl) is comparatively rare. In regard to these so-called inscriptions on favourites the following account may be given.

It was (and is, in certain sections of the community) a common custom everywhere to write down, carve, or scrawl hurriedly the names of specially beloved friends, wherever opportunity offers or the material to hand permits. It was the same in ancient Greece, and we have a very large number of passages from which it is clear that it was customary to write the name of a favourite boy or girl on the walls, the doors, or wherever there was room—especially in the Ceramicus at Athens (of which we spoke when discussing Lucian's *Dialogues of Courtesans*) or to cut them on the bark of trees.[1] Indeed, the great artist Pheidias was not ashamed to do homage to his favourite by inscribing "beautiful Pantarkes" (*Pausanias*, v, 11, 3; vi, 10, 6; 15, 2; Clem. Alex., *Protrepticon*, 35*c*) on the finger of his mighty statue of Zeus at Olympia. A brick has been preserved on which a workman named Aristomedes has scratched the words: "Hippeus is beautiful! Ἱππεὺς καλὸς Ἀριστομήδει δοκεῖ, *CIGr.*, 541), so it seems to Aristomedes." Indeed, sentimental lovers write the name of the dead loved one (female) with the addition of the

[1] Names of favourites on walls outside and inside houses, Aristoph., *Acharn.*, 142; Plutarch, *Gryllus*, 7; Lucian, *Amores*, 16; Anth. Pal., xii, 130, 49; on doors, Aristoph., *Wasps*, 97; Plautus, *Mercator*, ii, 3, 74; in the Ceramicus, Lucian, *Dial. Meretr.*, 4, 10; Strabo, xiv, 674; on bark of trees, Scholiast on Aristoph., *Acharn.*, 144; Callimachus, frag. 101; Aristænetus, *Ep.*, 1, 10.

" beautiful " with their own blood (Iamblichus in Photius, *Bibliotheca*, 94—p. 77, Becker) on the grave.

The names of favourite boys were also written on graves, as is shown by an epigram of Aratus (Anth. Pal., xii, 129) : " Philocles the Argive is beautiful; this the pillars of Corinth and the tombstones of Megara announce. It is written that he is fair as far as the baths of Amphiaraus.[1] But what need is there of the testimony of the stones? Everyone who knows him will admit it."

It was only a step to the inscribing of these love-tokens also on vases. The word " beautiful " is sometimes found alone, more frequently in the form " The boy is beautiful ", or combined with a name as an inscription on Greek vessels; also on columns, shields, basins, footstools, pillars, altars, chests, bags, discus rims, and a large number of other objects. Indeed, many vases exhibit regular dialogues—such as one at Munich where between the ornamentation stands the inscription written in wavy letters :—

A. Beautiful is Dorotheus, O Nicolas, beautiful!

B. To me also he appears to be beautiful, indeed; but so also the other boy, Memnon, is beautiful.

A. To me also he is beautiful and dear.

It may also be mentioned that the epithet καλός for the favourite is found even on vases where scenes from the school-room are represented: e.g. on a red-figured bowl of Duris which has often been copied and is now kept in the Antiquarium of the old Berlin Museum.

Although for these inscriptions on favourites a comprehensive literature already exists, the nature and purpose of them have not even yet been adequately explained; but the results of the investigations hitherto carried out can be fairly summarized in the following propositions :—

[1] A spring near Oropus (Harma) in Bœotia; cf. Pausanias, i, 34, 4; ii, 37, 5.

(1) Essentially the names of favourites were only usual on vase paintings in Attica and only during a period of about 70 years of the fifth century B.C.

(2) The inscription καλός (beautiful) has different meanings. Sometimes the artist wanted to praise himself; at other times the inscription had to do with individuals of the figures represented by him, whereby he meant to express the naïve joy which he felt because this or that form had been especially successful.

(3) But more frequently the vase painter wanted to offer homage to the boy who was his favourite.

(4) Many also, who ordered vases from the artist, caused the addition "the beautiful Hippias" or whatever the name happened to be, to be put upon the vessels, in order to delight the boy to whom they intended to present the vase, by praising his bodily charms, especially as at that time every boy was proud of his beauty, and did not think it a disgrace but a high distinction when he found anyone to admire his mental and bodily excellencies.

(5) Lastly, the vase painters also wrote on their vessels the names of those boys and youths, about whose beauty and daring tricks the whole city was enthusiastic. It may be assumed that many a manufacturer could dispose of his wares more readily, if they were ornamented with the name of a boy who at the time was idolized by everybody.[1]

6. Analysis of the Greek Ideal of Boys

After having thus considered the Greek ideal of beauty in its main features and made the attempt to render the understanding of it easier to the modern point of view, we have to go more closely

[1] On the numerous places where different variations of καλός may be found cf. Charicles, i, 314; on the Munich vase, O. Jahn, *Beschreibung der Vasensammlung König Ludwigs in der Pinakothek zu München* (1854, p. 101), when different possibilities are given, such as the Greek words καλός, Νικόλα, Δωρόθεος καλός· κἀμοὶ δοκεῖ ναί. χἄτερος παῖς καλός, Μέμνων· κἀμοὶ καλὸς φίλος grouped together; K. Wernicke, *Die griechischen Vasen mit Lieblingsnamen* (Berlin, 1890, with older literature given).

into the details of the Hellenic ideal of boys. Of all the bodily charms of a boy there is none by which the Greek was more enchanted than by the eyes, which accordingly enjoy their greatest triumphs in poetry. Sophocles has perhaps found the most beautiful words, when in the fragment (certainly difficult to translate) he says of the eyes of the youthful Pelops: "His eyes are the infatuating magic charm of love [1] (frag. 433 (Nauck [2]) in Ath., xiii, 564*b*); they are flames, with the fire of which he warms himself and scorches me." And in the drama the *Lovers of Achilles* (frag. 161 (Nauck [2])), Sophocles had spoken of the "longing inflamed by the flash of the eyes", of the eyes "which hurl the darts of love". Hesychius (iii, 203: ὀμματειος πόθος διὰ τὸ ἐν τῷ ὁρὰν ἁλισκεσθαι ἔρωτι· ἐκ γὰρ τοῦ ἐσορᾶν γίνεται ἀνθρώποις ἐρᾶν. Καὶ ἐν Ἀχιλλέως ἐρασταῖς ὀμμάτων ἀπὸ λόγχας ἵησιν.), who quotes these words, reminds us that the eyes of the one to be loved are the entrance-gates of love, for, according to a Greek proverb, "love arises in men by beholding."

We have already (p. 420) mentioned how Licymnius spoke of the beautiful eyes of his favourite. Sappho begs (frag. 29 (Bergk [4]) in Ath., xiii, 564*d*): "Stand in front, my friend, and shed thy grace over the eyes."

From Anacreon we have the verses (frag. 4 (Bergk [4])): "O boy, with a maiden's look, I seek thee, but thou dost not hear, not knowing that thou ridest thy chariot over my heart."

The mighty-voiced Pindar (frag. 123 (Bergk [4])) begins a skolion not preserved with the words: "Right it were, fond heart, to cull the flower of love in due season, in life's prime; but whoever, when once he hath seen the rays flashing from the

[1] In the original ἴυγγα θηρατηριαν ἔρωτος, "the magic wheel of love that seizes the victim." The words are those of Hippodameia. For the Iynx, cf. p. 205.

eyes of Theoxenus, does not swell with desire, his black heart with its frozen flame is forged of adamant or iron."

The great philosopher Aristotle (frag. 81R, Ath., xiii, 564*b*), the mightiest and most universal thinker of antiquity confesses: "Lovers look at none of the bodily charms of their favourites more than at their eyes, wherein dwells the secret of boyish virtues."

Of course, the lyric poets are not behindhand in eulogizing boys' eyes. Thus Ibycus celebrates them in a poem (frag. 2 and 3) beginning: "Eros again, gazing languishingly at me from beneath his dark eyelids with the greatest possible charm, flings me into the inextricable nets of Cypris."

At another time he compares the eyes of a boy with the stars, which sparkle in the sky when dark with night.

With especial frequency the praise of boy's eyes is sung by the poets of the Palatine Anthology. Thus Straton (Anth. Pal., 196) says of a boy: "Thy eyes are sparks, Lycinus, divinely fair; or rather, master mine, they are rays that shoot forth flame. Even for a little season I cannot look at thee face to face, so bright is the lightning from both.

And in another passage (ibid., 5): "Nor do I dismiss brown eyes; but above all I love sparkling black eyes."

These few questions in which beautiful eyes are praised give an idea of the homage paid by the Greeks to the bodily charms of their boys; and although it is a fact that other parts of a boy's body were lauded quite as much as the eyes, there is no need to weary the modern reader by considering each bodily charm and systematically supplying appropriate quotations from the Greek writers concerning each, and it will suffice to mention briefly the other physical attractions that evoked special attention.

At the sight of a boy on whose cheeks the charming

blush of bashful confusion had flamed up Sophocles quoted the verse of the tragic poet Phrynichus (frag. 13; *TGF.*, p. 723, in Ath., xiii, 604*a*): " There shines on his ruddy cheeks the fire of love " ; and Sophocles (*Antigone*, 783) himself had said that " tender cheeks are where Eros keeps vigil ".

To the Greeks one of the chief beauties of boys was the hair. Horace (*Odes*, i, 32, 19) certifies of the great poet Alcæus : " He sang of Bacchus and the Muses and Venus and the boy who always clung to her side, and of Lycus, distinguished by his black eyes and black hair."

If we may believe Cicero (*Nat. Deor.*, i, 28, 79) Alcæus for a while took special pleasure in a mole on the finger of this boy, Lycus (see p. 469).

The comic writer Pherecrates (frag. 189; *CAF.*, I, 201) had praised a boy who was adorned with fair curly hair with the words : " O thou, who shinest in curly golden hair."

When Anacreōn stayed at the court of Polycrates, ruler of Samos, he had fallen in love with the beautiful Smerdis (Ælian, *Var. hist.*, ix, 4) amongst other royal pages, and was never tired of gazing at the lad's splendid curly hair or of celebrating the dark abundance of these locks in his poems. In boyish vanity Smerdis was highly pleased at the praise so bountifully lavished upon him. But Polycrates, in tyrannical caprice and a fit of jealousy had his hair cut off, to annoy the boy and the poet. The latter, however, showed no annoyance, but behaved as if the boy of his own free will had deprived himself of the ornament of his hair, and reproached him for his folly in a new poem, which thereby became an act of homage. From it only the words are preserved : that " he cut off the irreproachable bloom of his soft hair, whereas before he was wont to throw it back so saucily ". Of the boyish ideal of Anacreon (frag. 48, 49) we can even to-day form a living idea.

Another favourite of his was Bathyllus (cf.

Maximus of Tyre, xxxvii, 439; Horace, *Epod.*, 14, 9), who enchanted the poet not only by his beauty, but also by the skill with which he played the flute and cithara. Polycrates had had a statue of the youth set up in the temple of Hera at Samos, described by Apuleius (Apuleius, *Florilegium*, ii, 15), who had seen it.[1]

According to the ancient conception, love is nothing but the longing for the beautiful, and so, after all we have described, it is by no means surprising if the sensual love of the Greeks was also directed towards their boys and that they sought and found in intercourse with them community of soul. There was added to the ideal of beauty the richer and more highly developed intellectual talents of the boys, which made rational conversation possible, where with girls a man could only have jested. Thus the Greeks took refuge in their trusted sexual companions not only in a social sense but also intellectually. The old Greek love of boys (παιδοφιλία) appears to us modern men as an insoluble riddle, but it can be proved, from the history of the Greek love of boys and its expression in literature, that it was just the most important and influential supporters of Greek culture who held the most decidedly homosexual opinions.

Theodor Däubler, in his book on Sparta (Leipzig, 1923) has expressed this as follows: "Anyone who is unable to regard the love of the Hellene for boys, or Sappho's inclination for her own sex, as something elevated and sacred, denies it in the face of Greece. We are more indebted to their heroic lovers than to mankind's most glorious art for Europe's freedom and the complete destruction of the Persian despotism in face of the diversity of the natural impulses in man. . . . Any attack on the love of boys in Sparta's prime would have acted with

[1] Considering the Greek idea, this is a highly remarkable fact. People were not afraid to set up statues of boy favourites in the temple of Hera, the protecting goddess of women and marriage.

destructive effect, would have been considered unwholesome, and as a betrayal of the people." (Cf. Lucka, *Die drei Stufen der Erotik*, p. 30; M. Hirschfeld, *Die Homosexualität des Mannes und der Weibes*, 1914).

7. FURTHER PHASES OF THE GREEK LOVE OF BOYS

If the qualities sketched in the preceding pages are existent, then the boy is worthy to become an object of consideration.

In the twelfth book of the Palatine Anthology, a hymn of the love of boys is preserved to us. In the literary and historical survey we must return to this, but we may content ourselves at present with describing individual phases of pædophilia from poetical passages contained in this collection, and with occasional quotations from the poems themselves.

If Straton (Anth. Pal., xii, 198) once confesses that "everything boyish" enchants him, he thereby reveals not only his own soul but that of most of the Greeks and has therewith spoken from the heart to many Hellenes.

Another time (Anth. Pal., xii, 192) he confesses: "I am not charmed by long hair or by needless ringlets taught rather in the school of Art than of Nature, but by the dusty grime of a boy fresh from the playground, and by the colour given to his limbs by the gloss of oil. My love is sweet when unadorned, but an artificial beauty has in it the work of a female Cypris."

Wherever drinking-bouts are represented in ancient literature and art, we also find boys who present wine to the guests, joke with them, or even offer their luxuriant hair as a towel, as Petronius informs us (27, 31, 41) to mention only one example. He relates how "boys from Alexandria pour water cooled with snow over the hands of the guests, while others wash their feet and pare their nails with the utmost care". In another passage of the same author it is said: "After we had thus conversed, a very beautiful boy came, crowned with vine-leaves and ivy, carrying round a little basket of bunches of grapes, and singing at the same time with a voice as clear as a bell. And we kissed the beautiful boy, as he flitted about, to our heart's content."

How intimately the boyish ideal was connected by the Greeks with their drinking-bouts is quite clear from the story told by Philostratus (i, 105, 13 (Kayser)), that in the palace of a mighty Indian king there were four costly tripods which were carried by bronze automatons in the form of boys "who were as beautiful as the Greeks imagine their Ganymede or Pelops to be". Often enough boys may also have taken part in the carousal, as appears from a fragment of the comic writer Philyllios (Ath., xi, 485*b* (*CAF*., I, 783)).

8. MALE PROSTITUTION

Love has at all times and among all peoples been purchasable for money, and always will be, however much it may be regretted for very various reasons. Male prostitution also is as old as love itself. We have already said often enough that among the temple prostitutes beautiful boys as well as women were to be found. How widespread male prostitution was at Athens in Solon's time is clear from the fact that this great statesman, poet, and philosopher, not only forbade pæderasty to slaves by legislation, since this freest manifestation of man's self-determination was only permitted to free men, but laid under a penalty those who made a trade of their beauty. "It is to be feared," says the orator Æschines (*Tim*., 13, 138, 137), to whom we are largely indebted for our knowledge of these laws of Solon—of which, certainly, some details as transmitted are vague—"that anyone who sells his own body for money will also lightly sacrifice the common interests of the State."

However much the Greeks at all times approved of the relation between man and youth that rested upon mutual liking, they in the same manner rejected it if the boy sold himself for money. This is not only clearly attested by Æschines in his famous speech against Timarchus, but it is clear from many passages in other authors. Professional male love was called ἑταίρησις or ἑταιρεία, and to sell oneself for money ἑταιρεῖν.[1]

It remains to quote the numerous passages from Greek authors, which prove that boys and youths were to be had everywhere for money or presents or for both. By way of proof, we may be reminded of the lines of Aristophanes (*Plutus*, 153): "And they say that the boys do this very thing, not for their lovers', but for money's sake. Not the better sort, but the sodomites; for the better sort do not ask for money."

Hence we must not pass by in silence the complaints of the poets upon the greediness of boys, especially as they know how to conceal this avarice by all the arts of coquetry. Thus Straton (Anth. Pal., xii, 212) complains: "Woe is me! Why in tears again and so woe-begone, my lad? Tell me plainly; I want to know; what is the matter? You hold out the hollow of your hand to me. I am done for! You are begging perhaps for payment; and where did you learn that? You no longer love slices of seed-cake and sweet sesame and nuts to play at shots with, but already your mind is set on

[1] It is noteworthy that precisely those words were chosen which originally denoted something quite noble—first, male fellowship; later, political clubs; lastly male prostitution (cf. the similar development of the English *hussy*. ἑταιρησις, e.g. Æschines, *Tim.*, 13; ἑταιρεία, Andoc., i, 100; Diod. Sic., ii, 18; for ἑταιρεῖν see the Lexika, also ἑταιρεύεσθαι) chiefly of the man, so Polyb., vii, 11, 10; Diod. Sic., xii, 21, but also of women, Plut., *Antonin.*, 18, also ἑταιρίζειν in this sense, e.g. Schol. Aristoph., *Thesmoph.*, 254, Pollux, vi, 168; Plutarch, *De adul. et am. discr.*, 30, φιλία ἑταιροῦσα is opposed to φιλία ἀληθινὴ καὶ σώφρων.

gain. May he who taught you perish! What a boy of mine he has spoilt!"

With slight changes this unpleasant subject recurs very frequently in the motifs inspired by the Muse of boys, but we may be satisfied with this single representative specimen.

Especially prominent or handsome men could hardly resist all the boys who offered themselves. Thus Carystius (Ath., xii, 542*f*—*FHG*., IV, 358), in his *Recollections*, relates: "All the boys of Athens were so jealous of Diognis, the special favourite of Demetrius, whose acquaintance they were anxious to make, that the most beautiful boys in the city, when he went for a walk in the afternoon, all came where he was in order to be seen by him."

Boys were not merely to be bought for money: they could even be hired by contract for a longer or a shorter time. Besides other evidence, we have a particularly interesting testimony in the speech written by Lysias in 393 B.C. for an Athenian who loved a boy from Platææ, named Theodotus, and was accused by a certain Simon, who was also in love with the boy, of intentional violation of his body, which at that time was an offence punishable by banishment and confiscation of property. In this memorable legal document it is related, with the greatest detail and frankness, and quite as a matter of course, that a man hired a youth by contract for the purpose of using him in this way. By the terms of settlement, Theodotus is said to have received 300 drachmæ (about £12).

Yet more. We have several written authorities, from which it appears to be tolerably certain that in Greece, at least in Athens and other harbour towns, there were brothels or houses of accommodation, in which boys and youths were to be had alone or with girls for money. Thus Æschines says: "Look also at those who are acknowledged as carrying on the trade, if they sit in the 'public' houses. They also draw a kind of curtain to hide their shame and shut the doors" (*Tim.*, 30).

Often enough the inmates of such houses may have been young people who had been taken as prisoners of war and afterwards sold. The best-known example of this is Phædo of Elis (Diog. Laërtes, ii, 105), with whom Socrates on the day of his death held the famous dialogue on the immortality of the soul. Pheado belonged to a distinguished family and, at the time of the war between Elis and Sparta, and while still very young, had fallen into the hands of the enemy who sold him to Athens, where he was purchased by the possessor of a "public" house. There Socrates made his acquaintance, and induced one of his well-to-do adherents to buy him off. It is surely a remarkable fact, that the much-admired dialogue *Phædo*, perhaps the most touching that Plato ever wrote, is named after a young man, and is carried on for the most part with one who, although under compulsion, only a short time before was at the disposal in a brothel of anyone who cared to pay for him.

But free youths also voluntarily roamed about in such houses, to earn money by the sale of their bodies. Æschines thus reproaches Timarchus (*Tim.*, 40): "As soon as he had left his boyish years behind him, he stayed in the Piræus in the bathing-place [1] of Euthydicus, on pretence of learning this trade, but in fact with the purpose of selling himself, as the event has shown."

From what Æschines says further it is clear that boy-prostitutes were not only visited by their lovers in the "public" houses (brothels with male inmates are also mentioned by Timæus in Polyb.,

[1] In the original ἰατρεῖον, the consulting room of a physician—who was at once physician, surgeon, bath-proprietor, and chemist. There he had his assistants, but also young people were trained for the medical profession. Idlers of all kinds were also to be found there, to talk or make interesting acquaintances, cf. Ælian, *Var. hist.*, iii, 7; Plautus, *Amphitruo*, iv, 1, 3.

xii, 13—*FHG.*, I, 227—τῶν ἐπὶ τέγους ἀπὸ τοῦ σώματος εἰργασμένων), but also went to them to their own homes, to be at the disposal of the master of the house alone or, at festivitics, of the guests. "There is, O Athenæus," says Æschines, "a certain Misgolas, otherwise a man of honour and beyond reproach, who is excessively devoted to the love of the boys and cannot live unless he always has some singers and players on the cithara about him. As soon as he observed why Timarchus stayed in the bathing-place, he took him away from there after paying something on account and kept him with him, since he grew up wanton, young, voluptuous, and thoroughly adapted for the things which he had resolved to do himself, and Timarchus had decided to tolerate. Timarchus had no scruples about doing this, but submitted to him, although he would have had no lack of anything provided his claims had been moderate." One of the Athenian boys' brothels appears to have been on the rocky cone of mount Lycabettus that rises some 900 feet above the city of Athens, as may be concluded from a passage in the comic poet Theopompus (in Schol. Pind., *Pyth.*, 2, 75—*CAF.*, I, 740), where mount Lycabettus personified says: "On my rocky height boys willingly give themselves up to those of the same age and to others."

9. The Ethics of Greek Love of Boys

In spite of these facts, it would be entirely wrong to assume that sensuality denoted the only (or at least the most important) element of the Hellenic love of boys. Quite the contrary is the case: everything that made Greece great, everything that created for the Greeks a civilization which will be admired as long as the world exists, has its root in the unexampled ethical valuation of the masculine character in public and private life. Allusion has already been made to Plato's high opinion of the love of boys (see Lagerborg, *Die platonische Liebe*, Leipzig, 1926), and it is now time to describe in greater detail the ethical tendencies of Greek pædophilia.

Eros is the principle not only of the sensual, but also of the ideal side of Greek pædophilia. A beautiful vase painting in the Berlin Antiquarium represents this ideal side symbolically and has hence been called " the ecstasy of Love ". We see a winged Eros flying away towards the heights of heaven with enraptured look and carrying up with him a boy, who appears to be struggling, but at the same time lovingly regards Eros. Hartwig says rightly (*Meisterschalen*, p. 659): " Perhaps what is here intended is that generic Eros, who brings to boys sometimes a flower, a lyre, or a hoop, who addresses them with lively gesture or impetuously hurls himself down upon them : an ideal representation of the wooing of men in love, which the pictures on the cups of this period so often realistically present."

Pædophilia was to the Greeks at first the most important way of bringing up the male youth. As the good mother and housewife was to them the ideal of the girl, so καλοκἀγαθία, the symmetrically harmonic development of body and soul, was that of the boy. For the Greeks the most excellent way of approaching this ideal was the love of boys ; and while, especially among the Dorians, the State expected that every man should choose a youth as his favourite, and, further, while a boy was blamed if he failed to find an older friend and lover—a lapse that appeared to be intelligible only if he had some moral taint—both man and boy exerted themselves as far as possible to develop manly virtues. As the older was responsible for the behaviour of the younger, the love of boys was not persecuted, but fostered, to become the power that maintained the State and upheld the foundation of Greek ethics. These ethical tendencies we find proved in numerous passages of Greek literature, best of all in the words of Plato already quoted (p. 412).

That Plato, however, does not indulge in optimistic dreams is shown by historical facts. This was why at Chalcis (Plut., *Amat.*, 761) in the island of Eubœa songs were sung in praise of good fellowship ; this was why the Spartans before the battle sacrificed to Eros (Ath., xiii, 561*e*) ; this was why the Theban army, named the sacred band (ἱερὸς λόχος), was the pride of the nation and the object of the admiration of Alexander the Great ; and this was why, before they went into battle, friends at the tomb of Iolaus in Thebes took the last oaths of fidelity.

When the Chalcidians were at war with the Eretrians, Cleomachus came to their assistance at the head of an imposing squadron of cavalry ; but he loved a youth. The battle was furious, for the enemy's cavalry was well equipped. Cleomachus asked his favourite, whether he would like to see the battle with him. He said yes, kissed his friend, and set his helmet on his head. Then high spirit filled the elder man's heart and in contempt of death he sprang into the enemy's ranks. He gained the victory but only at the price of his own heroic death. The Chalcidians buried him with all honours and erected on his grave a column, an eternal remembrance for coming generations.

According to Athenæus, the reason why before the battle the Spartans offered sacrifice to Eros was that " they were convinced that in the comradeship of a pair of friends fighting side by side lay safety and victory ".

The " sacred band " of the Thebans also has given for all time the best evidence of the lofty ethics of the Greek love of boys. This band of men of noble blood, 300 in number, who had exchanged the oath of love and friendship, was formed, it is said, by Gorgidas. A witticism used to be quoted which Pammenes (Plutarch, *Pelop.*, 18 ; also Philip's exclamation), the friend of Epameinondas, had coined. He blamed Homer, since in the *Iliad* (ii, 363) Nestor once makes the people draw themselves up for battle " arranged according to clans and tribes ", and thinks that he ought to have formed the order of battle of pairs and friends, since it would then have been indissoluble and unbreakable. The sacred band proved itself brilliantly in the battle of Mantinea, in which Epaminondas fell with Cephisodorus, and the traditions of the gallant band maintained themselves unconquered until the defeat of Chæronea, in which the flower of Greek freedom was broken. When the victor, King Philip of Macedon, surveyed the field of battle after the engagement and saw that all the bodies of the 300 had fatal wounds in their breasts, he could not suppress his tears, and said : " Woe to them who think evil of such men."

It is easy to quote parallels to the Theban sacred band. The words with which Plato attests the greater excellence in war and the lofty joy of sacrifice of these hosts have already been quoted, although Socrates indeed in Xenophon's *Symposion* (8, 32) does not declare his agreement with them unreservedly. But let one read the story in Xenophon's *Anabasis* (VII, iv, 7) of the emulation of Episthenes and a boy, how each is ready to suffer death for the other. It was that same Episthenes of Olynthus, who later " formed a whole company of beautiful youths and proved himself a hero amongst them ". In the *Cyropædia* (vii, 1, 30) it is said once that " it has been shown many times on other occasions that there can be no stronger order of battle than one composed of comrades who are close friends ", which is confirmed in the battle between Cyrus and Crœsus, no less than in the battle of Cunaxa (Anab., i, 8, 25 ; i, 9, 31), in which together with the younger Cyrus his " friends and messmates " also suffer the death of heroes. All this is confirmed by Ælian (*Var. hist.*, iii, 9), who explains the joy of sacrifice by saying that one who loves is animated by two gods, Ares and Eros, while the warrior who does not love is only inspired by Ares. Even in the *Eroticus* of Plutarch, which does not approve of the love of boys, the power of love in war is shown by many examples. Wolfflin (*Philologus*, xxxiv, 413) has drawn attention to the company of friends in the army of Scipio and Cæsar speaks of a league of youth in the land of the Sontiates, a Gallic tribe (*Bell. Gall.*, iii, 22).

After these parallels, which could easily be increased, one will no longer find what is reported of the Theban " sacred band " to be exaggerated. Certainly the life of this phenomenon, like that of the whole of Hellenism itself, was only of short duration. We hear of it first at the battle of Leuctra (371 B.C.) and after the unhappy battle of Chæronea (338 B.C.) its end had come ; thus it existed only 33 years.

The story told by Plutarch (*Lycurgus*, 18) also deserves mention. When a youth uttered a painful scream in battle, his lover was afterwards punished by the State.

Consequently, one who loves will, with the assistance of Eros who inspires him " go through fire, water, and raging storm " (Plut., *Amat.*, 760*d*) for the loved one (as a line from the unknown tragedian runs), and the courage of the lover even defies the divine wrath. When the sons of Niobe (Soph., frag. 410—*TGF.*, 229) were shot by Apollo for their mother's sin, the friend endeavours to protect the tender body of the youngest daughter, and when this is in vain, he carefully wraps the body in the sheltering garment. Even of the ideal of Greek heroic might, of Heracles, it is related that his mighty deeds became easier, when he carried them out before the eyes of his beloved Iolaus, a gymnasium and shrine in honour of whom existed until comparatively late times before the gate of the Prœtidæ in Thebes (Pausan. IX, xxiii, 1 ; cf. also

Plut., *Pelop.*, 8). In memory of the love between Heracles and Iolaus there was celebrated in Thebes the Iolæia (Pind., *Olymp.*, vii, 84, and Schol.) consisting of gymnastic and equestrian games, in which arms and brazen vessels were given as prizes to the victor.

In Pausanias we read that an Athenian named Timagoras loved a certain Meles (i, 30, 1) or Meletus, but had been scornfully treated by the boy. Once, when he found himself on a steep mountain slope with Timagoras, Meles requested him to hurl himself down, and he did so, since he valued his life less highly than the absolute fulfilment of any wish expressed by his favourite. In despair at the death of his friend Meles then threw himself also down from the rock.

If we are to draw conclusions from what has been said as to the ethics of Greek love of boys, the following emerges as an undeniable fact: The Greek love of boys is a peculiarity of character, based upon an æsthetic and religious foundation. Its object is, with the assistance of the State, to arrive at the power to maintain the same and at the fountain-head of civic and personal virtue. It is not hostile to marriage, but supplements it as an important factor in education. We can also speak of a decided bi-sexuality among the Greeks.

That passion yields to the seriousness of death and makes room for the clarified happiness that revels rather in recollection—that friendship lasts beyond the grave, is shown to us by many epitaphs which, in tenderness of language, dignity of subject, and beauty of form belong to the noblest remains of Greek poetry.

The seventh book of the Palatine Anthology, with its 748 epitaphs, some of them quite excellent, show with what choice taste and tactful feeling the Greeks adorned the grave of their dead heroes and erected tokens of honour of them. I have already collected those devoted to the love of boys in an earlier work, so that it may be sufficient to give only the most beautiful of them here. This epigram was written by the poet Crinagoras (Anth. Pal., vii, 628) to his boy, whom he named Eros; the boy died early on an island and was buried there, and so the poet wishes that this and the neighbouring islands may henceforth be called the Islands of Love. "Other islands ere this have rejected their inglorious names and named themselves after men. Be called Erotides (Love islands), ye Oxeiai (sharp islands); it is no shame for you to change; for Eros himself gave both his name and his beauty to the boy whom Dies laid here beneath a heap of clods. O earth, crowded with tombs, do thou lie light on the boy and do thou lie hushed for his sake."

10. NEGATIVE AND AFFIRMATIVE OPINIONS

In Greek antiquity there were also of course not wanting opinions which, either generally or under definite assumptions, repudiated the idea of the love of boys. Thus the epigram of Meleager (Anth. Pal., v, 208), which contains the thought that "one who gives this love cannot at the same time also receive it", is negative. Certainly, Meleager did not always hold the same opinion, since we possess numerous epigrams of his, in which love of youths is extolled.

In the romance of Xenophon of Ephesus (ii, 1) the pair of lovers, Habrocomes and Antheia, fall into the hands of pirates, the leader of whom conceives a violent passion for Habrocomes. But the latter says "Oh, the unhappy gift of beauty! So long kept I myself chaste, only now to yield in shameful lust to the love of a pirate! What then is left to me to live for, if from a man I must become a harlot? But I will not submit to his desires, I would rather be dead and save my chastity!"

The seduction of boys was in any case unreservedly repudiated. Thus it is said in a comedy of Anaxandrides (frag. 33, 12, in Ath., vi, 227*b*—*CAF*., II, 147) "and a little boy in the bloom of youth, by what kind of charms or by what seductive words could anyone succeed in catching him, if one did not also make use of the art of the fisherman ? " In a comedy of Baton (frag. 5 in Ath., iii, 103*c* and vii, 279*a*—*CAF*., III, 238) an indignant father complains of a philosopher who has corrupted his son by his false doctrines.

Further, it was quite generally made the subject of reproach if a boy gave himself up for money or any other kind of payment. I have already proved this by a quotation from the *Plutus* of Aristophanes (153 ff.), and poets are never weary of recalling the good old times when a boy, as a reward for favours granted, was satisfied with a little bird, a tomtit, a missel-thrush, a robin, a quail, or even a ball to play with and such-like trifles.

Here it may be mentioned that women, as was to be expected, on the whole objected to everything that had to do with this love of boys, and thus, in a comedy by an unknown author, a woman says : " I do not care for a man who himself wants one " (frag. in Lucian, *pseud*., 28—*CAF*., III, 497).

That hetairæ also were jealous of the homosexual intrigues of their customers was a matter of course, but is also confirmed by the conversation of the two hetairæ Drosis (the dewy) and Chelidonion (the little swallow) in Lucian (*Dial. meretr*., 10). Drosis has received a letter from the pupil Cleinias in which he writes that he cannot visit her any more, since the teacher Aristænetus watches every step. She complains of her trouble to her friend Chelidonion :—

" *Drosis* : Meanwhile, I am dying for love. Now Dromon [1] tells me that Aristænetus is a pæderast and only uses his knowledge as an excuse to attract the most beautiful young men ; he talks much and often secretly with Cleinias and makes him great promises, as if he would make him equal to

[1] Servant of Cleinias, who had brought the letter.

the gods. He also reads to him certain erotic dialogues of the old philosophers with their pupils, and, in a word, he is always about with him, but Dromon has threatened to tell the young man's father.

" *Chelidonion*: You ought to have greased his palm properly!

" *Drosis*: I have done that, but he is mine without that, for he is violently in love with that maid of mine, Nebris.[1]

" *Chelid.*: If that is so, be of good courage: everything will turn out as you wish. I think I will also write on a wall of the Ceramicus,[2] where his father is in the habit of walking, in large letters: 'Aristænetus is corrupting Cleinias,' so that I may support Dromon's accusation."

(Perhaps the writer might attain her object, to separate the lover from his rival; but it would at the same time terribly compromise the loved one. In ancient Greece there was no idea of this kind. It is, of course, not so much the reproach of pæderasty as such, with which she hopes to injure Aristænetus, as the fact that he misuses his influence as teacher. While the father hopes that the son is being brought up by his teacher to become a famous man, he is only regarded by him as a favourite.)

" *Drosis*: But how will you write that without anyone seeing you?

" *Chelid.*: By night, Drosis, with a lump of coal.

" *Drosis*: Good luck to you! If you help me to fight, I still hope to get the better of that windbag Aristænetus."

[1] The name means "Fawn", from her particoloured dress.

[2] It was a special meeting-place for lovers of boys. Boys were also found in large numbers in barbers' shops (κουρεῖα, Demosth. in Aristog., 52, 786; Theophr., *Charact.*, 8, 5; Aristoph., *Plutus*, 338); in perfumers' shops (μυροπωλεῖα, Aristoph., *Knights*, 1375); in the physicians' rooms (ἰατρεῖ α, see p. 439, *n.*); the baths (Theophr., *Charact.*, 8, 4), and many other places, especially the lonely and dark Pnyx (Æschin., *Tim*, 34, 81), a hill west of the Areopagus, surrounded by ruined buildings, where male prostitution took place.

II. HISTORY OF GREEK LOVE OF BOYS

Naturally, it cannot belong to our task in the present book to examine more closely the different theories, especially of medical men, as to how the problem generally is to be explained. It would also be superfluous, since not only have these different attempts at explanation been clearly and conveniently collected in Hirschfeld's standard work, but also that Greek love of boys at least, of which alone we are speaking here, in general needs no explanation at all as a phenomenon difficult to understand. Some space may be given, however, to a description of its historical development.

Goethe's assertion that " the love of boys is as old as humanity " is confirmed by modern science. The oldest literary testimony hitherto known dates back more than 4,500 years, and is to be found in an Egyptian papyrus which proves not only that pæderasty was at that time widespread in Egypt, but also that it was presumed to exist amongst the gods as a matter of course.

The first beginnings of the Greek love of boys are lost in prehistoric times, even in the darkness of Greek mythology, which is completely saturated with stories of pædophilia. The Greeks themselves transfer the beginnings to the oldest times of their legendary history. The assertion, often naïvely made, that in the Homeric poems there is as yet no trace of the love of boys to be met with, and that it was a phenomenon which first appeared during the so-called decadence is, in my opinion, false, for I have already shown in an earlier work (in *Anthropophyteia*, ix, pp. 291 ff.) that the bond of friendship between Achilles and Patroclus (the most important passages are *Il.*, xxiii, 84; ix, 186, 663; xviii, 22 ff., 65, 315, 334; xix, 209, 315), however ideal it was, yet contains a high percentage of homoerotic sentiment and action; that the Homeric epos also abounds in undoubted traces of ephebophilia, and that no one in the ancient times of Greece ever supposed otherwise.

The *Iliad*, the greatest old epos of the Greeks that has come down to us, represents a hymn to friendship. From the third book onwards the love of the two youths, Achilles and Patroclus, runs through the whole poem until the conclusion, and is represented in such detail that one can no longer speak of mere friendship. This shows itself still more when Achilles learns that Patroclus has fallen in battle. Terrible is the sorrow of the unhappy youth, who stands, a prey to gloomy forebodings, on the seashore, tormented by uncertainty; words die on his lips, while his soul is torn by sorrow; he strews dust upon the crown of his head; then, quite overcome, he throws himself upon the ground, pulling out his hair. After the first rage of his sorrow has gradually calmed down, when the elementary burst of passion is followed by a slow bleeding to death of the soul, then his only thought is to take vengeance on him who has robbed him of what he loved best. He desires neither food nor drink, and his soul thirsts only for revenge.

He vows to his dead friend that he will not celebrate his obsequies "until he has brought him the weapons of Hector, the murderer. He will also slay twelve noble youths before the funeral pyre, Troy's noble sons, in anger at thy murder". But before he can carry out his revenge, he relieves his heart by a touching lament for the dead. Among other things he says: "O never could anything more bitter come upon me, no, not even if I should hear of my father's death."

All this is language of love, not of friendship, and so the ancients have nearly always regarded the bond. To give only one piece of evidence, one of the poems of the Anthology (Anth. Pal., vii, 143; cf. Pindar, *Olymp.*, x, 19; Xen., *Sympos.*, 8, 31; Lucian, *Toxaris*, 10; Ovid, *Tristia*, i, 9, 29) says: "Two men most distinguished by friendship and in arms, farewell, son of Æacus, and thou, son of Menœtius."

It is clear from the Odyssey (xxiv, 78; cf. iii, 109; xi, 467; xxiv, 15) that, after the death of Patroclus, Antilochus took his place with Achilles, meaning, of course, that Homer is unable to imagine the chief hero of his poem without a favourite. From this passage we further learn that Achilles, Patroclus, and Antilochus were buried in a common grave, as the three were often named together in life.

The bond of friendship between Achilles and Patroclus was referred to by the great tragic writer Æschylus as based on sensuality, and this author was still near enough to the age of the Homeric epos to understand its underlying spirit perfectly. A drama of Æschylus that is not preserved was called the *Myrmidons* (frag. in *TGF.*, 42 ff.; cf. Ath., xiii, 601*a*, 602*e*) and its subject was as follows: Achilles, grievously offended by Agamemnon, in his animosity abstains from fighting, and consoles himself in his tent with the joys of love. The Chorus consisted of the Myrmidons, the vassals of Achilles, who finally persuade him to let them take part in the battle under the leadership of Patroclus. The piece ends with the death of the latter and the wild sorrow of Achilles.

This is confirmed by Lucian (*Amores*, 54; cf. Plut., *Amat.*, 5, *De adul. et amico*, 19; Xen., *Sympos.*, 8, 31; Æschines, i, 142; Martial, xi, 44, 9), who says: "Patroclus also, the favourite of Achilles, did not merely sit opposite to him listening to his lyre, but the driving-power of this friendship also was lust."

It may be mentioned that Phædrus (Plato, *Sympos.*, 179*e* ff.), in his speech on Eros, reverses the situation, making Patroclus the lover, and Achilles, as the younger and handsomer, the loved one.

But still further proofs could be brought to show that it is false to assert that the Homeric epos knows nothing of homosexuality. Homer already speaks not only of the rape of the Phrygian royal boy Ganymede (*Il.*, xx, 231), and expressly declares that he was carried off because of his beautiful figure, but also of an extensive trade in boys, who were chiefly bought by Phœnician shipmasters, or more frequently carried off, to fill the harems of wealthy pashas (*Od.*, xiv, 297, xv, 449; cf. Movers, *Phönizien*, ii, 3, 80). When Agamemnon and Achilles are finally reconciled, Agamemnon offers the latter a number of gifts of honour, amongst them several noble youths (*Il.*, xix, 193). If the war-chariot of Achilles is called "sacred" (*Il.*, xvii, 464), Nägelsbach has already recognized that the "sacred fellowship of the warrior and his charioteer is thereby meant to be indicated" (*Homerische Theologie*, p. 50).

Thus, homosexuality meets us from the oldest times when we have any certain information concerning the Greeks. How the exercise of its sensual functions was handed down to posterity by formal documents is sufficiently shown in the rock inscriptions of the island of Thera—the modern Santorin—in the Cyclades. So it remains to the end of the ancient world, and in this historical summary only individual phases of development need be mentioned.

An important turning-point is indicated by the name of Solon (Æschines, *Tim.*, 138; *Charicles*, ii, 262 ff.), who, himself a homosexual, issues important laws for the regulation of pæderasty, providing in the first place, especially, that a slave might not have connection with a free-born boy. This shows two things: first, that pædophilia was recognized in Athens by the legislator, and secondly that the legislator did not consider the feeling of superiority of the free born to be diminished by intimate relations with slaves. Further, laws were issued (Æschines, *Tim.*, 13–15) which were intended to protect free-born youths from abuse during their minority. Another law deprived those of their civic rights who incited free boys to offer their charms for sale professionally; for prostitution has nothing to do with pædophilia, of which we are speaking here, and in which we must rather think always only of a voluntary relationship that is based upon mutual affection.

Further, these laws of Solon only affected Athenian full citizens, while the great mass of *Xenoi*, that is, non-Athenian immigrants, had complete freedom in this matter. Thereby the efficiency of these laws early became questionable; even the severity [1] of the punishments cannot have acted too much as a deterrent, since the *πρόφασις φιλίας* always was a way out, that is, the protestation that it was done "out of affection"; and of course youths certainly often chose the momentary advantage, without troubling about the loss of civic privileges that eventually threatened them in the distant future. But that these laws were not meant to strike at pæderastia itself, indeed not even at its organization and use as a profession, is shown by the fact that the State itself levied a tax on those who put boys and youths at the disposal of lovers, as well as on the public women's houses (Æschines, *Tim.*, 119).

Diogenes Laërtius (Xen., *Mem.*, ii, 6, 28) says that Socrates, when a boy, had been the favourite of his teacher Archelaus, which is confirmed by

[1] Strikingly severe, for instance, is the punishment of death for an unauthorized person who sneaks into a boy's school (Æschines, *Timarchus*, 12). The law further says: "And the owners of gymnasia shall not allow anyone beyond the age of boys to sneak in with them at the feasts of Hermes; otherwise he is to be punished according to the law concerning the violation of the body." That this law which impresses us as quite barbarous can only have existed on paper, is sufficiently proved by the well-known custom of the Greeks, according to which they spent a great part of the day in the gymnasia and palæstræ in gossiping. The law also concerned entering the gymnasia at definite times, e.g. the dissolute festivals of Hermes. To explain the prohibition mentioned by Æschines the Scholiast observes that: "In the inner part of the house at schools and palæstræ there were columns and chapels, with altars to the Muses, Hermes, and Heracles. There was also drinking water there, but many boys under pretence of drinking, came in and practised immorality."

Porphyrius, (ib., 201) who says that Socrates when a youth of seventeen years was not averse from the love of Archelaus, for at that time he was much given to sensuality, which was later supplanted by zealous intellectual work.

Further, Xenophon makes Socrates say: " And perhaps I may be able to help you in the search for good and noble boys, since I am given to love; for whenever I terribly love men I strive with my whole heart that, while loving them, I may in my turn be loved; and desiring them, may in my turn be desired; and that, when desiring to be with them, my society may be sought in return."

In the *Symposion* of Plato (177*d*, 198*d*) Socrates says: " I profess to understand nothing but love-affairs " and " I affirm that I am capable in matters of love ", with which several passages in Xenophon's *Symposion* (i, 9; iii, 27) agree: e.g. " I can mention no time, when I was not madly in love with some-one ", or when Socrates describes the impression which the young Autolycus makes upon him: " As a fire flaming up in the night draws all men's eyes to him, so the beauty of Autolycus at first captivates all men's looks, none who looked upon him remaining unmoved in heart."

The effect produced when Critobulus sat next him is thus described (Xen., *Mem.*, i, 3, 12): " That was a bad thing. I have been obliged to rub my shoulder for five days, as if an animal had stung me, and into my very marrow I thought I could trace the pain such as an animal inflicts."

Are these the words of a man who has renounced the sensuality of love? It is also clear from the Platonic *Alcibiades*, i, and *Symposion* that the beauty of Alcibiades made a violent and lasting impression on Socrates.

Certainly there are several passages in which Socrates not only did not do homage to sensual love of youth, but even tried to dissuade his friends from it. One such passage is contained in a conversation held by Socrates with Xenophon, in which a warning is given even against kissing a youth: "Do not beautiful boys with their kisses inspire you with something fearful, even though you cannot see it? Do you not know that that animal called Beautiful and Blooming, is much more dangerous than poisonous spiders? These can only hurt by contact, but the other animal, without any contact, pours in its poison that clouds the understanding, even from a great distance, if one only looks at it. Therefore, my dear Xenophon, I advise you, when you see a beautiful boy, to take flight as rapidly as possible." Further expressions of the same kind may be found in Kiefer.

On the other hand, it must not be concealed that Greek antiquity itself did not believe so readily in the pædophilia of Socrates as being only of an intellectual kind; and that is the decisive point so far as we are concerned, for men living in—or so near to—the relevant time were in a very advantageous position for passing an essentially better judgment than is possible for us with our still very fragmentary knowledge. In the *Clouds*, certainly, the humorous comedy of Aristophanes, in which Socrates is made fun of in every conceivable way, there is no single word from which one might conclude that the master was addicted to coarsely sensual pædophilia.

To sum up: Socrates, as a Hellene, certainly always had an open eye for boyish and youthful beauty; intimate companionship with the ephebi was also indispensable for him; but he himself as far as possible abstained from giving any practical bodily proof of his affection. He was even capable of renouncing the sensual, since his incomparable art of regulating the souls of youths and of leading them towards the greatest possible perfection, offered sufficient compensation. This power of abstinence he also sought to place before others as an ideal; that he would have required it from all was nowhere suggested nor would it have been held to be consonant with the wisdom of " the wisest of all the Greeks ".

12. LOCAL DETAILS

To begin with the Cretans, since these, according to Timæus (Ath., xiii, 602*f*) were the first Greeks who were fond of boys, we must first remember that, according to the incontestable testimony of Aristotle (*De Republica*, ii, 10, 1272), the love of boys in Crete was not only tolerated but was also regulated by the State in order to prevent over-population. The extent to which the love of boys was a national practice there, is clear from the fact that the Cretans ascribed the rape of Ganymede—which, according to an elsewhere unanimous tradition, was carried out by Zeus—to their ancient King Minos, as could be read in the *Cretan History* of Achemenes (Ath., xiii, 601*e*). Whether it was Zeus or Minos who carried off Ganymede, certainly in Crete as in many other Greek states the rape of boys had long been an established custom.[1] The Cretan rape is attested by many writers: it is described most fully by Ephorus of Cyme (Strabo, x, 483*f*; also Plutarch, *De lib. educ*, 11 *F*; Plato, *Laws*, viii, 836), who composed a grandly planned *History of the Greeks* from the earliest times to the year 340 B.C.

" Three or four days beforehand, the *erastes* (lover) announces to his friends that he intends to carry out the rape. To conceal the boy anywhere or to forbid him to go to the street agreed upon, would indicate the greatest disgrace, since it would only mean that the boy does not deserve such a lover. If they have met, and the lover in rank and the like is equal to the boy or is even superior to

[1] The rape is the most primitive form of all marriage connections, and thus ætiologically for the love of youths the rape of Ganymede by Zeus or Minos was invented.

him, for the sake of the traditional custom they pretend to pursue the lover, but in reality gladly let him go on his way. But if the lover is not his equal, then they snatch the boy from him with violence. But they only pursue him until the lover has brought the boy into his house. But the one who is distinguished for beauty is considered less worth desiring than one renowned for bravery and modesty. After that the boy is presented by his friend with a present, who takes him where he pleases. But the witnesses of the rape accompany them ; then a solemn meal takes place, after which they return to the city. After two months the boy is dismissed with rich presents. His legally established presents are a military equipment, an ox and a goblet, besides a number of valuable gifts, so that his friends contribute towards the expenses. He offers the ox to Zeus and gives his friends a meal from it. But if a beautiful boy of good family finds no lover, this is considered a disgrace, since the reason for it must be in his character. The boys who are given preference by the rape are specially honoured. Thus they receive the best place in the dances and racing competitions, are allowed to wear the dress with which the lover has presented him, and that distinguishes them from the others, and not only this, but even when they are grown up they wear a special garment, by which everyone, who has become *κλεινός* can be immediately recognized ; the loved one is called *κλεινός* (the famous, the celebrated), the lover *φιλήτωρ*."

The rape of boys also existed in very ancient times in Corinth, as to which Plutarch (*Amat. narr.*, 2, 772*f*) has left us an instructive story : "The son of Melissus was Actæon, the most beautiful and the most modest of those of his own age, so that very many desired him, but chiefly Archias, whose family went back to the Heracleidæ and who was prominent among the Corinthians for his wealth and power. Since the boy refused to be persuaded, he resolved to rape him with violence. He consequently rode at the head of a number of friends and slaves before the house of Melissus and attempted to carry off the boy. But the father and his friends offered a bitter resistance, the neighbours also assisted, and during the struggle between the two parties the lad was dragged hither and thither, was fatally injured, and died. But the father lifted up the boy's dead body, carried it into the market-place, and showed it to the Corinthians, while he demanded from them that they should punish those who had been guilty of his death. They sympathized with him, but otherwise did nothing. The unhappy father afterwards repaired to the Isthmus and threw himself down from a rock, after he had summoned the gods to take vengeance. Soon afterwards a bad harvest and famine visited the state. The oracle declared that it was the wrath of Poseidon, who would not be appeased, until the death of Actæon was expiated. When Archias, who was one of those sent to consult the oracle, heard of this, he did not return to Corinth, but sailed to Sicily and founded the city of Syracuse. There, after he had had two daughters, Ortygia and Syracusa, he was murdered by his favourite Telephus."

Such is the story. Its meaning is clear. The rape of boys must remain a seeming one. To employ violence, if the father is not agreed, becomes a crime, the sin of which the gods themselves avenge, and (herein lies the tragic irony) by the hand of the boy; this follows the *Dikē* of Hybris and agrees with the "Laws of Gortyn", which avenge the offering of violence to a boy by severe punishment.

In Thebes the rape of boys was referred to the ancient King Laïus who, according to the Theban version, had inaugurated pæderasty by carrying off Chrysippus the son of Pelops and making him his favourite (Ath., xiii, 602; Ælian, *Hist. an.*, vi, 15; *Var. hist.*, xiii, 5; Apollodorus, iii, 44).

As in Thebes (Xen., *Symp.*, viii, 32*f*; Plato, *Symp.*, 182*b*), so also in Elis the love of boys had a sensual element, although the religious feeling was not wanting. Plutarch also attests the combination of sensuality and a sacrificing heroic spirit in Chalcis (Plut., *Amat.*, 17; there also the song) on the island of Eubœa and its colonies. A song that became popular there has been preserved and also a similar one of Seleucus (Ath., xv, 697*d*) by whom the love of boys is called more valuable than marriage on account of the knightly fellowship of which it is the cause. The song of the people of Chalcis, the author of which is unknown, is as follows: "O ye boys of brave fathers, shining in the grace of your charms, never grudge the companionship of your beauty to honourable men, for in the cities of Chalcis, in union with manly virtue still ever blooms your gracious, heart-infatuating sweet youth."

According to Aristotle (Plutarch, *Amat.*, 761), this song went back to the bond of love between the heroic Cleomachus and his young friend, already spoken of p. 442); or it may, perhaps, have arisen out of the belief that Cleomachus's victory was due to his enthusiasm having been encouraged and sustained by the presence of his friend as a witness of his bravery. What taste the Chalcidians had for beautiful boys is also proved by the notice of Hesychius, that χαλκιδίζειν is synonymous with παιδεραστεῖν. This is confirmed by Athenæus, who adds that the Chalcidians, like others, made claim to the honour that Ganymede was carried off from a myrtle grove near their city, and they proudly showed this place, which they called *Harpagion* (the place of the rape) to strangers.

According to Xenophon (*Rep. Lac.*, 2, 13) the love between a man and a youth was considered entirely as a conjugal union.

Throughout Greece there were festivals which served for the glorification of boyish and youthful beauty, or at which it at least appeared conscious of its aim. Thus at Megara the spring-festival *Diocleia* (Theocr., xii, 30) was celebrated, at which contests of boys and youths in kissing took place; at Thespiæ (Plut., *Amat.*, 1; Pausan., ix, 31, 3; Ath., xiii, 601*a*) the festival of Eros, at which prize songs on the love of boys were sung; at Sparta the festival of the naked boys, the *Gymnopædia*, also the *Hyacinthia*; and the island of Delos (Lucian, *De Saltat.*, 16) is said to have specially rejoiced in the round dances of boys (see pp. 109, 115, etc., and 164).

When Plutarch (*Prov. Al.*, i, 44), speaking of the boys of the Peloponnesian city of Argos, says that " those who have kept their youthful bloom pure and uncorrupted, as an honourable distinction lead the procession at a festival with a shield, according to old custom ", he does not mean that these boys have not been the favourites of men of standing, but only that, so long as they were still boys, they had abstained from female intimacy.

The question of the love of boys in Sparta (Xen., *Rep. Lac.*, 2, 13; *Sympos.*, 8, 35; Plut., *Lyc.*, 17*f*; *Ages.*, 20; *Cleom.*, 3; *Institut. Lac.*, 7; Ælian, *Var. hist.*, iii, 10) is very difficult to decide, since on this point the reports of ancient times are actually contradictory. Xenophon and Plutarch assert that the Spartan love of boys certainly depended upon the sensual pleasure in corporeal beauty, but did not arouse sensual desires also. To have designs upon a boy sensually was put on the same level as a father seeking his son or a brother his brother, and whoever did so was throughout his life " without honour ", that is, he was deprived of his rights as a citizen.

Maximus of Tyre (*Diss.*, xxvi, 8), a rhetorician who lived in the time of the Antonines and Commodus and so wrote very late, says that in Sparta the man only loved a boy as a beautiful statue, many men one boy and one boy many men.

This is not only improbable according to the Greek idea of the nature of the love of boys that has been sufficiently described, and above all from physiological reasons, but has also been abundantly proved incredible by the following considerations. Xenophon (*Rep. Lac.*, 2, 14) himself is obliged to admit that it never occurred to any Greek to believe in this ideal side of the Spartan love of boys and no more; the Attic comic poets also have in constant outbursts thrown light upon just that sensual character of the Spartan love of boys, which is still further strengthened by the terms collected by Hesychius and Suïdas (s.v. *κυσολάκων*, *λακωνίζειν*, *Λακώνικον τρόπον*), with which the language of daily life indicated the Spartan peculiarity. But that which turns the scale is that the man who was best acquainted with such matters, namely Plato (*Laws*, i, 636; viii, 836; cf. also Cicero, *Rep.*, iv, 4), decidedly rejects the idea that the Dorian love of boys dispensed with sensuality.

I. *Epic Poetry*

1. The Mythical Pre-Historic Period

Pamphos (Pausan., ix, 27, 2) had already written hymns to Eros, so that it may be justly affirmed that Eros stands at the beginning of Hellenic culture.

Part of the story of Orpheus, whose existence is denied by Aristotle (Cic., *De nat. deor.*, i, 38, 107), and who is taken by Erwin Rohde [1] to be a symbol of the union of the religions of Apollo and Dionysus,

[1] *Psyche* (3rd edn.), ii, 52. On Orpheus see Apollod., i, 14; Conon, 45; Hermesianax in Book III of the *Λεόντιον* (*Ath.*, xiii, 597); Virgil, *Georg.* iv, 454; and Ovid, *Metam.*, i, 10; for the head of Orpheus see Phanocles (acc. to Stobæus, *Flor.*, 64, 14); similarly Lucian, *Adv. indoct*, 11; Ovid, *Metam.*, xi, 50 ff.

has been already told (see p. 240), but after the final disappearance of Eurydice, his wife, into Hades, there comes a singular sequel. Orpheus, in his loneliness, returns to his Thracian mountain home, where the famous singer is surrounded by enthusiastic crowds of women and girls because of his touching love for his wife. But he " rejects all female love ", whether it be that he has had unfortunate experience of it before, or whether he was unwilling to be unfaithful to his wife. But he certainly taught the Thracians to turn their affection to the love of tender boys, and, " so long as youth laughs, to enjoy the brief spring of life and its flowers." So says Ovid. An extremely important passage, since it shows that the solitary husband compensates himself with the love of boys, and, what is even more important, that according to the ancient idea of homosexual intercourse this was not regarded as an offence against wedded faithfulness, " since he was unwilling to be unfaithful to his wife." And henceforth he is so devoted to this Greek form of love, that not only does marriage become for him merely an episode but the songs now sung by him contain nothing but the glorification of the love of boys.[1] Thus the paradox becomes a fact ; Orpheus, who even at the present day is most widely known as a model of conjugal fidelity, is for antiquity the man who introduced the love of boys in his home in Thrace and was so devoted to it that girls and women, who felt themselves spurned, finally attacked him, cruelly mutilated and killed him. Further, the legend informs us that his head was thrown into the sea and finally cast up on the shore of the island of Lesbos. Of Lesbos ? That is, of course, not accidental, for there later Sappho arose, who was for Greeks the greatest advocate of homosexual love.

[1] The songs which Ovid (Met., x) makes Orpheus sing are : " The love of Apollo to Cyparissus " (86–142) ; " The rape of Ganymede " by Zeus (155–61) ; " The Love of Apollo for Hyacinthus " (162–219).

2. THE EPIC CYCLE

In the *Œdipodeia* it was told how Laïus, the father of Œdipus, fell desperately in love with the beautiful Chrysippus, the son of Pelops, and finally carried him off by violence. Pelops uttered a fearful curse against the robber (p. 134).

The *Little Iliad* (*Ilias Parva* (see Kinkel, *Epicorum Græcorum Fragmenta*, Leipzig, 1877, p. 41, frag. 6)) of Lesches treated as an episode the rape of Ganymede (*Il.*, xx, 231 ; v, 266), the young son of the Trojan King Laomedon, upon whom Zeus bestowed as a recompense a vine fashioned of gold by the art of Hephæstus, while in Homer Ganymede is a son of King Tros, who receives a pair of thoroughbred horses as a recompense.

The rape of Ganymede is described in the fifth of the so-called Homeric Hymns (v, 202 ff.) in still greater detail.

3. HESIOD

In his *Shield of Heracles* (57) the poet Hesiod had told of the struggle with Cycnus which Heracles had to endure. He summons his favourite and brother-in-arms Iolaus, who was "by far the dearest of all men to him". The length of the conversations between them prevents their being given here ; their tender language and their whole tone prove that already Hesiod, as all later writers, considered Iolaus to be, not only the companion-in-arms, but also the favourite of the hero.

From a fragment we learn that Hesiod himself loved a youth named Batrachus (Suïdas, in Kinkel —see above—p. 78), on whose early death he had written an elegy.

4. PHANOCLES

At a time which cannot be accurately defined, Phanocles [1] had composed a garland of elegies

[1] Philetæ Coi Hermesianactis Colophonii atque Phanoclis reliquiæ disposuit, emendavit, illustravit Nic. Bachius (Halle, 1829) ; cf. Preller, *Phanokles und die Mythologie der Knabenliebe* (Rhein. Mus., N.F. iv, 1846, pp. 399–405), and the article *Phanokles* in Ersch-Gruber.

entitled Ἔρωτες ἢ καλοί (" Love stories, or Beautiful Boys "). These elegies represented what may be called a history of the love of boys in poetic form with abundant examples from stories of the gods and heroes. Among the fragments a longer one of 28 lines (longer frag. in Stobæus, *Flor.*, 64, 14) in which the love of Orpheus for the boy Calaïs and the fearful murder of the singer by the Thracian women is described, is prominent. It is interesting to find that the Christian Fathers of the Church—such as Clement of Alexandria, Lactantius, and Orosius—used the poems of Phanocles to prove the immorality of paganism, while Friedrich Schlegel (Werke, iv, 52) translated fragments from him.

5. DIOTIMUS AND APOLLONIUS

Diotimus (Ath., xiii, 603*d*; Schol., *Iliad*, xv, 639; Clem. Rom., *Homil.*, v, 15; Suïdas, s.v. Εὐρύβατος) of Adramyttium in Mysia in the third century B.C. wrote an epos—the *Struggles of Heracles*, in which he endeavoured to prove the rather silly idea that the mighty deeds of Heracles are to be ascribed to his love for Eurystheus.

Apollonius of Rhodes (Apol. Rhod., I, 1207; III, 114 ff.), the most important of the Alexandrine epic writers, lived in the third century B.C. Only the most famous of his poems is preserved, namely, *Argonautica*, that is, the adventure of the Argonauts, in four books. The poem, abounding in charming details, contains the story of the love of Heracles for Hylas, his carrying off by the nymphs of the spring, and the boundless sorrow of the hero at the loss of the boy.

I here quote the episode of Eros and Ganymede: " They were playing for golden dice, as like minded boys are wont to do. And already greedy Eros was holding the palm of his left hand quite full of them under his breast, standing upright and on the bloom of his cheeks a sweet blush was glowing. But the other sat crouching hard by, silent and downcast, and he had two dice left which he threw one after the other, and was angered by the loud laughter of Eros. And lo, losing them straightway with the former, he went off empty-handed."

6. NONNUS

Nonnus, a Greek of Panopolis in the Egyptian Thebaid, who lived in the fourth or fifth century A.D., is the author of a bulky poem in no fewer than 48 cantos called *Dionysiaca*, that is, the life and deeds of Dionysus. The vast epos describes in bewildering superabundance the victorious expedition of Dionysus to India, interwoven with so many episodes and separate myths, that the whole represents a work that is certainly extremely valuable and interesting, but by no means a unity. The singular thing is that the author was a Christian, but he has created an enthusiastic hymn of Bacchantic, and consequently heathen ecstasy, such as might stand alone in the whole of literature. Hence, there occur in the work so large a number of homosexual episodes that what is most important can only be mentioned here, not given in detail.

The beauty of the youthful Hermes (iii, 412 ff.) is eloquently described, while the beauty of Cadmus (iv, 105) takes as many as fifty-six lines. The Erotes are represented dancing at the wedding of Cadmus and Harmonia (v, 96); with obvious satisfaction the poet tells of the games that Dionysus shared and enjoyed with boys (ix, 160 ff.), and describes in detail how he bathes in company with the wanton and lascivious satyrs (x, 139).

The idyll with the boy Ampelos occupies considerable space (x, 175 to xii), and his beauty is painted in glowing colours; Dionysus sees the boy and the description of the love with which he is inflamed for him runs, with various episodes, through two cantos. Like a second Eros, only without wings and quiver, Ampelos appeared to the god as he formerly revealed himself in a forest of Phrygia, and he is excessively happy because of the love which Dionysus shows towards him. There ensues a love idyll, which is painted by the poet in detail and with great beauty. Dionysus has only the one fear, that Zeus may see the boy and carry him off, since he is even more beautiful than Ganymede. Zeus, however, does not begrudge him his happiness, and that in spite of the Greek idea that everything that is beautiful in the world is destined to find a speedy end. In youthful desire for adventure, Ampelos betakes himself to the hunt, laughing at Dionysus with boyish insolence as the god warns him against the wild animals of the wood. Terrified by an evil omen, Dionysus goes after the boy, finds him safe and clasps him in his arms enchanted. But destiny does not slumber; an evil spirit prompts Ampelos to ride against an apparently harmless bull, but the bull suddenly turns on him and throws him off his horse, so that he is fatally hurt and dies.

Dionysus is inconsolable, covers the body of the boy, still beautiful in death, with flowers, and strikes up a touching lament. Afterwards he prays to his father Zeus to recall the loved one to life only for a short hour that he may hear once more from his lips words of love; indeed, he curses his immortality, since he cannot now be together with the boy for the whole length of eternity in Hades.

Eros himself takes compassion upon the despair of the mourner's boundless grief; he appears to him in the form of a satyr, speaks to him affectionately and advises him to end his sorrow by taking a fresh love, "for," he says, "the only remedy for an old love is a new one; look about therefore for a more excellent boy—even as did Zephyrus who, after the death of Hyacinthus, became enamoured of Cyparissus"; and, further to console the bereaved diety and to encourage him to take a fresh love, Eros then gives him a detailed account of the story of Calamus and his favourite Carpus.

"Calamus (Kalamos), a son of the river-god Mæander, was united in tenderest love with Carpus (Karpos), the son of Zephyrus and one of the Horæ, a youth of surpassing beauty. When both were bathing in the Mæander and swimming for a wager, Carpus was drowned. In his grief Calamus is changed into a reed, and when it rustled in the wind the ancients heard in the sound a song of lamentation; but Carpus becomes the produce of the fields, which returns every year."

A gap in the text does not allow us to know what effect this had on Dionysus. Probably very little, for now with glowing sensuality a wanton round dance of the Horæ is described, which can be introduced here only with intent to bring the god, who is consumed by longing, to other thoughts. With this "orgy of the legs, which in the furious whirlwind of the dance are seen through their transparent robes", the eleventh book of the story of Dionysus closes.

In the twelfth it is related how the gods, out of compassion for the sorrow of Dionysus, change the boy Ampelos into a vine. The god, enchanted, accepts the glorious plant, which is henceforth sacred to him, and so invents the precious gift of wine, which he praises in an enthusiastic address. Then the first gathering and pressing of the newly created wine takes place, after which a Bacchic orgy concludes the feast that has developed into a riotous merry-making after a time of deepest sadness.

Between Rome and Florence a beautiful marble group of Dionysus and Ampelos was found (cf. Himerius, *Orat.*, 9, 560; Pliny, xviii, 31, 74) which is to-day one of the most valued treasures of the British Museum. The boy[1] is represented just in the act of being changed, offering a bunch of grapes to Dionysus who is tenderly embracing him.[2]

All our extracts from Nonnus, the last epic offshoot of Hellenic beauty and sensual enjoyment, have been taken from the first twelve books, a quarter of the vast poem; the remaining thirty-six cantos contain numerous other homosexual episodes and many descriptions of boyish beauty.

II. *Lyric Poetry*

As lyric poetry is the most direct expression of personal states of mind and feelings, it is only to be expected that in that of the Greeks homosexual love should occupy a large space; and it is, indeed, quite correct to say that lyric poetry generally had its origin in homosexual love. But unfortunately only a lamentably small fragment of Greek lyric has come down to us.

1. THEOGNIS

Under the name of Theognis, who lived, chiefly in Megara, in the middle of the sixth century B.C., a collection of maxims and rules of life in 1,388 lines has come down to us. The last 158 lines are entirely devoted to the love of youths, especially to the poet's favourite Cyrnus. The latter, the son of Polypais, was a noble and beautiful youth, to whom the poet was attached by paternal, but also by sensual love. He desires to teach him worldly wisdom and to bring him up as a true aristocrat. The collection is therefore rich in intrinsic ethical value, which caused it to be used in ancient times as

[1] According to Ovid (*Fasti*, III, 407), the boy met with an accident while trying to break off a tendril from a vine which was creeping up an elm-tree, whereupon he was placed among the stars by Dionysus as *Vindemitor* (vine-dresser, vintager).

[2] It should be mentioned that the Brit. Mus. authorities disagree with Herr Licht's interpretation of this group (No. 1636): the figure that Dionysus is embracing, they say, is female and represents not Ampelos but the personification of the vine.—*Ed.*

a school-book, and at the same time contains a number of love-terms of strong, sometimes ardent sensuality.

The poet hesitates between love and indifference, he cannot do without Cyrnus, and yet it is hard to love the modest boy. Indeed, he even threatens to put an end to his life, so that the boy may realize what he has lost. Another time he complained of offended love; that he was sympathetic to Cyrnus, but not Cyrnus to him. The loved one will be famous through him; at all festivals he will be sung of, and even after death he will never be forgotten.

2. PLATO

Under the name of Plato (*PLG.*, frag. 1, 7, 14, 15; cf. Apuleius, *De magia*, 10), the great philosopher and pupil of Socrates, several homosexual epigrams have come down to us. A tender epigram is: "When I kissed you, Agathon, I felt your soul on my lips: as if it would penetrate into my heart with quivering longing." Another epigram is an epitaph on the favourite Dion, "who filled the heart with the madness of love." Two epigrams owe their origin to the beautiful Aster (star). The poet envies the sky, which looks down on his Aster with many eyes, when he, himself a star, looks up at the stars.

3. ARCHILOCHUS AND ALCÆUS

Even among the fragments of Archilochus of Paros, who is known for his passionate love for Neobulē, the beautiful little daughter of Lycambes, there is one (frag. 85) containing the admission that "yearning for the boy relaxes his limbs and overpowers him".

Of Alcæus of Mitylene, who was both a poet and hero, mention has already been made (p. 433). The Lycus there referred to (if Bergk's reading be correct) occurs in a fragment (58) in which the poet, in an attack of ill-humour, says that he will no longer celebrate him in his songs. In another of the few existing fragments (46) he begs someone "to send for the charming Menon, else he would have no enjoyments at the feast ".

4. IBYCUS

Only a few of those who enjoy Schiller's beautiful ballad of the *Cranes of Ibycus*, are aware that the hero of the poem, whose death at the hands of a wicked murderer is certain to awaken general sympathy, was called in ancient times "the most frenzied lover of boys" (Suïdas, sub *Ibycus*: ἐρωτομανέστατος περὶ τὰ μειράκια). That he did homage to boys all his life, is attested by Cicero (*Tusc.*, iv, 33, 71); even in old age this passion blazed in him to such an extent that Plato expressly drew attention to it (*Parmen.*, 137*a*); an anonymous epigrammatist in the Palatine Anthology refers to him (vii, 714) as a "lover of boys", and in the same collection he is mentioned in a short list of lyric writers (ix, 184) as one who, during his life, did "cull the sweet bloom of Persuasion and of the love of lads". All this is confirmed by his poetry, of which only a few fragments are preserved. Besides those mentioned above (p. 420) the following (frag. 1) may be quoted: "In spring the quinces, watered by the river streams, bloom in the unspoiled garden of the maidens; and the first shoots of the vine, guarded beneath shady leaves, grow and blossom; but for me love—that, like the Thracian north wind, blasting beneath the lightning and rushing, dark and fearless, from Cypris with scorching madness—is never at rest, and holds possession of my mind throughout my life."

5. ANACREON AND THE ANACREONTEA

Anacreon of Teos, the always cheerful and amiable poet, was born about 560 B.C.; according to Lucian he lived to the ripe old age of eighty-five, and even in his latter years happiness for him seems to have consisted largely in love and wine. Of his works the Alexandrians still possessed various poems in five books altogether, most of which have been lost by the unkindness of time. All his poetry is dedicated to love, says Cicero (*Tusc.*, iv, 33, 71; cf. Ovid, *Tristia*, ii, 363). Although he did not disdain female love—and for the sake of example he once complains half jestingly (frag. 14) that a pretty Lesbian girl refuses to play with him, yet during his life it was the ephebus who had just reached his prime to whom his heart and song were devoted, and an imposing list of names is known to us, the bearers of which had inflamed his heart. After a stay at Abdera in Thrace we find him together with Ibycus at the court of Polycrates, the well-known and refined lover of art and magnificence, and ruler of Samos, who had surrounded himself with a court-household of carefully selected pages (Ælian, *Var. Hist.*, ix, 14). Maximus of Tyre says: "Anacreon loves all who are beautiful and extols them all; his songs are full of praise of the curly hair of Smerdis, the eyes of Cleobulus, the youthful bloom of Bathyllus" (xxiv, 9, 247—frag. 44). Again he says that everything that is good is beautiful to love. "I should like to sport with you, O boy, for thou hast the love-charm of the Graces" (ibid., 120), and "For the sake of my verses boys would love me; for I sing graceful songs, and I know how to say graceful things" (ibid., 45).

Several epigrams (esp. Anth. Pal., vii, 25, 27, 29, and 31; see also ibid., 23, 23*b*, 24, 26, 28, 30, 32, 33; and vi, 346) also attest the poet's love for his Smerdis; in the first mentioned, for instance, Simonides in an epitaph says: "Alone in Acheron he grieves not that he has left the sun and dwelleth there in the House of Lethe, but that he has left Megistheus, graceful above all the youth, and his passion for Thracian Smerdis." Of Anacreon's extant fragments at least four are addressed to Smerdis. Thus we read of a stormy wooing, in which he confesses to him that Eros had dashed him down again as powerfully as the smith wields his hammer.

His love for Cleobulus was inflamed in the poet by avenging Nemesis herself, as Maximus of Tyre insists in an anecdote (frag. 3). This love filled the poet with fervent ardour; he entreats Dionysus (frag. 2) to incline the heart of the boy towards him and confesses that he loves Cleobulus, raves after him, looks out only for him.

There is a fragment, in which it is said that no one, if Bathyllus plays the flute, may dance to it, since he cannot turn his gaze away from the charming form of the player (frag. 30). Another fragment is addressed to Megistes (frag. 41; and see Bergk, *Der Ausgabe des Anakreon*, p. 151, Leipzig, 1834), who takes part in the feast, crowned with a wreath of *agnus castus*, or "tree of chastity", a plant concerning which the ancients gave profound and curious accounts (see esp. Pliny, *Nat. hist.*, xxiv, 38).

Other fragments treat of his love for Leukaspis and Simalos (frags. 18, 22), while others again have come down to us without the name of the favourite. The boy at the mixing-jug is to bring wine and garlands, "that I may not succumb in a boxing-match with Eros." Of a song to Eros, "to whom gods like men are subject," five lines are preserved. The poet also has to complain of rejected love, and at another time he threatens that he will fly up to Olympus, and complain to the Loves, that "my boy will not pass the time of youth with me". He complains that Eros, when, already grown so grey, at last he saw him, waving his gold-glittering wings, flew heedless by. He comically threatens Eros, that he will no longer sing a beautiful hymn in his praise, since he will not wound the ephebus he longs for with his arrow.

Among the imitations of Anacreon—the "Anacreontea"—which are of later date, and in which mention is frequently made of the love of boys, may be specially noticed the little song in which the poet complains that a swallow by its early twittering has awakened him from his dreams of the beautiful Bathyllus. Another cleverly combines the matter of the love song with the manner of the song of war: "You sing of the deeds of the Thebans, of the war-shouts of the Phrygians, but I will tell of my conquests; it is neither horse, nor ship, nor foot soldier that hath destroyed me, but another new army launched from the eyes against me."

6. PINDAR

From Pindar, the greatest and most powerful of all Greek lyric poets, who lived from 522 to 442 B.C. we still possess, in addition to an imposing number of fragments, forty-five odes in nearly perfect condition—the songs of victory, which were composed for those who had won the crown in the great national games. The writer's piety made him recast in more respectful form some of the legends that had gathered irreverent accretions. Such a one was that which relates how Tantalus, having invited Zeus to dine, killed the All-Father's son, Pelops, and served him up as a meal as a test of the divine omniscience. But the gods saw through the horrible deception, put the pieces together again and restored the boy to life, and punished Tantalus severely. Such horrors are unendurable to the pious poet; according to his presentation of the legend Pelops has not fallen a victim to the shameful crime of his father, rather had his beauty so inflamed the heart of Poseidon, that he was carried off by him, as later Ganymede was seized by Zeus (*Olym.*, i, 37 ff.).

Pindar thought much the same as his contemporaries about friendship with the ephebi, and we owe to him what is unfortunately only a fragment of one of the most glorious poems ever written (frag. 123; see p. 431). The gods also rejoiced at his friendship for his favourite, Theoxenus. It was related that Pindar had prayed the gods to give him the most beautiful thing there was in the world; Theoxenus was the gift, and when, afterwards, the poet was present at a gymnastic contest in Argos he, during an attack of faintness, leaned on this boy's bosom and died in his arms.

Pindar's ashes were carried to Thebes, where, as Pausanias tells us (ix, 23, 2), they were buried in a tomb in the Hippodrome before the Proetidian gate.

7. THEOCRITUS

Of the thirty idylls preserved under the name of Theocritus, who lived about 310–245 B.C., no fewer than eight are exclusively devoted to the love of youths, and also in the others boys and love for them are frequently spoken of.

One, perhaps, the most beautiful of the poems of Theocritus about youths, inscribed *Τὰ παιδικά* (" the Favourites "), contains a conversation of the no longer youthful poet with his own heart. Certainly, his reason advised him to renounce all idea of love, but his heart teaches him that the battle with Eros is a useless enterprise. " For irresistible the life of the boy rushes in like the swift foot of the hind, and in the morning thou already seest him striving further after the fickle kiss of another love. Not lasting, however, was the most delightful enjoyment of youthful bloom. Yet thou consumest thy vigour in the torments of longing, and his charming picture is all that thy dream will paint for thee."

In another poem, which can hardly be Theocritus's own, we read the last complaints of an unhappy lover, who puts an end to his torments by suicide, and the revenge taken by the insulted Eros on the prudish boy who, while he is bathing in the gymnasium, is struck down by a falling marble statue of Eros.

A third poem, also inscribed παιδικά, is a complaint against the inconstancy of the loved one, an exhortation to remain faithful, and a reminder, while still in his tender youthful bloom, of the old age that threatens. He should therefore requite his love, so that their bond may be one day spoken of like the love of Achilles and Patroclus.

Tender and affectionate is a poem which gives expression to the joy of seeing the favourite again after three days of separation, and to the wish that their love may always be like that which flourished in Megara, where Diocles introduced the boys' kissing contest (p. 109), " about whose grave, so surely as spring cometh round, your children vie in a kissing-match, and whosoever presseth lip sweetliest upon lip, cometh away to's mother loaden with garlands." " How blessed are both in the joy of love! Their picture shines to us from ancient time—how he devotes his love to the boy!"

The charming poem entitled the " Harvest Festival", already called by old Heinsius the " queen " of the poems of Theocritus, is dedicated to the memory of a day joyfully spent on the island of Cos, and the poet relates how he wanders from the city into the country with two friends. On the way they meet a goatherd by name Lycidas, to whom the poet, after a brief conversation, proposes that he should rest and try his skill against him in a country singing-match. Lycidas gladly consents, and then sings a *propemptikon* (farewell song), in which he wishes his beloved Ageanax a happy journey over the sea :—

Ageanax late though he be for Mitylene bound
Heav'n bring him blest wi' the season's best to haven safe and sound;
And that day I'll make merry, and bind about my brow
The anise sweet or snowflake neat or rosebuds all a-row,
And there by the hearth I'll lay me down beside the cheerful cup,
And hot roast beans shall make my bite and elmy wine my sup;
And soft I'll lie, for elbow-high my bed strown thick and well
Shall be of crinkled parsley, mullet, and asphodel;
And so t'Ageanax I'll drink, drink wi' my dear in mind,
Drink wine and wine-cup at a draught and leave no lees behind.
My pipers shall be two shepherds, a man of Acharnæ he,
And he a man of Lycòpè; singer shall Tityrus be,
And sing beside me of Xénea and neatherd Daphnis' love.

After that Theocritus declares to his friend how much the song has pleased him, and answers with another, in which he contrasts his own happiness in love with the ill-luck of his friend Aratus, a famous physician and poet of Miletus, who had fallen in love with the beautiful but coy Philinus: "Yet you, winged host of the Loves, with cheeks red as peaches, now hit Philinus with curly hair, awake in him desire for my friend. After all, he is not so young now, already the girls chaff the fool—'Ay, ay, Philinus, you see your beauty is already gone!' So now take my heartfelt advice. Let the foolish boy run and let some other pretty ones, my dear friend Aratus, feel this deep sorrow."

To console his friend Aratus, whose art as a physician could not help him against the wounds inflicted on him by Eros, Theocritus wrote a longer epic poem, in which the passionate love of Heracles for Hylas, his rape by the nymphs of the spring, and the despair of the lonely hero are fully described. (Theocritus, 30, 23, 29, 12, 7, 13. Further paidophil passages in Theocritus are 15, 124; 20, 41; 6, 42; 3, 3: τὸ καλὸν πεφιλημένε—a form of address so sweet that (according to Gellius, ix, 9) it is impossible to translate it; 2, 77–80, 44, 150, 115; epigram 4.)

8. TRIFLES FROM OTHER LYRIC POETS

Praxilla, the amiable poetess of healthy merriment and sensual practical wisdom, had told in one of her poems of the rape of Chrysippus by Laïus, in another of the love of Apollo for Carnos (frags. 6 and 7).

According to Athenæus Stesichorus, "Who was to no small extent a sexualist," also wrote this kind of poem, which was already named in antiquity "a 'song about boys'". (Ath., xiii, 601*a*). But none of them is preserved.

Bacchylides (frag. 13) mentions among the works of peace the occupations of youths in the gymnasia, feasts, and the bursting forth of songs about boys.

"Skolia" was the name given to the drinking-songs, which were sung after the meal, when wine loosened men's tongues, chiefly by the guests in order, and composed *ex tempore*. Such an improvization runs as follows: "I would that I could become a lyre of ivory; then the boys would carry me to the Dionysian dance" (Skolion, 19).

The poetical remains of Bion of Smyrna, a younger contemporary of Theocritus, are trifling. From his poem on Lycidas I mention the lines: "I have sung of another than Lycidas, but my song then sounded like a lamentable stammer; I sang of the marvels of Eros and Lycidas, the beautiful and now my love-song would resound loftily and glorious."

In another poem (ix) he addresses Hesperus, the evening star: "Evening Star, which art the golden light of the lovely Child o' the Foam, dear Evening Star, which art the holy jewel of the blue blue night, even so much dimmer than the moon as brighter than any other star that shines, hail, gentle friend, and while I go a-serenading my shepherd love show me a light instead of the moon, for that she, being new but yesterday, is all too quickly set. I be no thief nor highwayman—'tis not for that I'm abroad to-night—but a lover; and lovers deserve all aid."

Lastly, the eighth poem is a list of famous

pairs of friends, praising those who found the happiness of mutual love, Theseus and Peirithous, Orestes and Pylades, Achilles and Patroclus.

III. *The Poems of the Anthology*

We have already so often had to quote by way of testimony passages from among the thousands of epigrams contained in the Codex Palatinus, that in this summary of homosexual literature only those supplementary ones need be given which furnish anything specially characteristic. Thus Antistius (Anth. Pal., xi, 40): " Cleodemus, Eumenes' boy, is still small, but tiny as he is, he dances nimbly with the boys. Look ! he has even girt on his hips the skin of a dappled fawn and a crown of ivy adorns his yellow hair. Make him big, O kindly Bacchus, so that thy little servant may soon lead holy dances of young men." The epigram of Lucilius (xi, 217) strikes us as almost modern : " To avoid suspicion, Apollophanes married and walked as a bridegroom through the middle of the market, saying : 'To-morrow at once I will have a child.' Then when to-morrow came he appeared carrying the suspicion instead of a child."

The twelfth book of the Palatine Anthology, which is quite exclusively devoted to the love of youths (258 epigrams of nearly 1,300 lines altogether) bears in the MS. the title " The boyish Muse of Straton ". Besides Straton, whose poems stand at the beginning and end of the collection, nineteen other poets are represented, amongst them good, indeed high-sounding names ; we have besides thirty-five epigrams without the name of the composer. The book may be called a hymn of Eros ; the same subject over and over again, but in as many forms and endless variations as nature itself.

1. STRATON OF SARDIS. (Anth. Pal., xii, 1, 2, 5, 244, 198, 201, 227, 180, 195)

This poet, who lived in the time of the emperor Hadrian, arranged a collection of epigrams on beautiful boys, and the twelfth book of the Anthology contains ninety-four poems under his name.

The collection does not begin with an invocation of the Muses, as the poems of antiquity usually do, but of Zeus, who in very ancient times had himself set the example to men by the carrying off of Ganymede and since then was regarded as the patron of the love of boys. The subject of which the poet intends to treat differs considerably from that which had hitherto been usual: "Look not in my pages for Priam by the altar, nor for the woes of Medea and Niobe, nor for Itys in his chamber and the nightingales amid the leaves; for earlier poets wrote of all these things in profusion. But look for sweet love mingled with the jolly Graces, and for Bacchus. No grave face suits them."

Straton's Muse also had to do with boys, but as there is no difference and no choice, he loves all who are beautiful. Nothing can resist this love, it is stronger than the poet, who no doubt would many times like to shake off the yoke, but time after time perceives that it is beyond him. If the boy is beautiful and above all his looks so charming that one can see that the Graces have stood by his cradle, then the poet cannot rejoice enough; certainly, the greater the beauty, the more speedy the complaint that it is only transitory and immediately disappears.

The great passion finds its expression also in poetry, and the twelfth book of the Anthology accordingly also contains a number of strongly erotic epigrams, many of them, indeed, highly obscene according to modern feeling.

2. MELEAGER. (Anth. Pal., xii, 86, 117, 47, 92, 132, 54, 122, 52 (cf. 53), 125, 137, 84, 164, 256, 154, 59, 106, 159, 110, 23, 101, 65, 133, 60, 127, 126)

Meleager of Gadara in Cœlo-Syria, of whose erotic poems to girls we have already spoken (p. 261), lived during his youth at Tyre. There he would have nothing to do with girls, and for that reason was the more susceptible to the beauty of boys, and although the number of those with love of whom he is consumed is very considerable it is a youth Myiscus whom he loves best, and whose name meets us most frequently in the epigrams.

Of the sixty poems of Meleager in the twelfth book of the Anthology, thirty-seven are addressed to boys whose names are given, and we find no fewer than eighteen to whom special poems are devoted; but in addition there are so many others mentioned, that one is astounded at the easy susceptibility of the poet, whether we conceive many of the poems to be exercises in poetry without any real background, or if we assume that the same boy perhaps appears several times, but under different names. In any case, Meleager is firmly convinced that preference is due to the love of boys, and he knows how to offer confirmation of his answer to the question by a new and unexpected argument: "It is Cypris, a woman, who casts at us the fire of passion for women, but Love himself rules over desire for males. Whither shall I incline, to the boy or to his mother? I tell you for sure that even Cypris herself will say 'The bold brat wins'."

When the marvel of Eros blazes up, then reason is done for and passion prevails. This is intelligible, for Eros has already played with the poet's soul in his tenderest age as with dice. But in everything it is the eyes of the poet, which eagerly drink in the beauty of boys so that Eros gains power over the soul, that are to blame.

Nothing is of avail any longer; the soul is captured and endeavours to escape, as a bird strives to flee from its cage. Eros himself has bound the wings of the soul, kindled a fire in it, and given the thirsty one nothing but hot tears to drink. All lamentation is in vain, as it has allowed Eros to grow up in its inmost parts.

But all that, thinks the poet, is quite natural, for the boy is so beautiful that even Aphrodite would prefer him to Eros as a son. He has obtained his beauty from the Graces themselves, who once met the boy and embraced him; this explains the charming grace of his youthful body, his sweet chatter, and the mute but yet eloquent language of his eyes. Longing for him takes the place of love, when he stays away afar, even when he has been obliged to set out on a journey by sea. Then the poet envies the ship, the waves, and the wind, which may enjoy the presence of the only loved one; and he would become a dolphin, that he might bear him on his back gently towards the longed-for destination.

(*a*) " Love brought to me under my mantle at night the sweet dream of a soft-laughing boy of eighteen, still wearing the chlamys; and I, pressing the tender flesh to my breast, culled empty hopes. Still does the desire of the memory heat me, and in my eyes still abideth sleep that caught for me in the chase that winged phantom. O soul, ill-starred in love, cease at last even in dreams to be warmed all in vain by beauty's images."

(*b*) " The South Wind, blowing fair for sailors, O ye who are sick for love, has carried off Andragathus, my soul's half. Thrice happy the ships, thrice fortunate the waves of the sea, and four times blessed the wind that bears the boy. Would I were a dolphin that, carried on my shoulders, he could cross the seas to look on Rhodes, the home of sweet lads."

It annoys the poet to be awakened prematurely from such dreams. The silly crowing of a cock, who puts an end to his life of dreams, sets him cursing the rude creature in a manner which because of its bathos has a comic effect.

On another occasion the poet has undertaken a sea-voyage. Already all the dangers of the sea are happily overcome, joyfully he leaves the rocking ship and sets foot on the mainland; then again Fate meets him in the form of a slender boy: new love—new life.

Another time he says: "Sweet it is to mingle the sweet honey of the bees with unmixed wine, but it is also sweet to be beautiful, if one desires boys. As Alexis loves the curly-headed Cleobulus such love is sweet, Cyprian honey-drink."

On Myiscus (little mouse)[1]: "Sweet is the boy, and even the name of Myiscus is sweet to me and full of charm. What excuse have I for not loving? For he is beautiful, by Cypris, entirely beautiful; and if he gives me pain, why it is the way of love to mix bitterness with honey"; and again, "One thing only appears to me beautiful, only one thing my eyes yearningly desire—to look upon Myiscus, for everything else I am blind."

It is especially the eyes of Myiscus, whose beauty the poet rapturously praises: (*a*) "Delicate children, so help me Love, doth Tyre nurture, but Myiscus is the sun that, when his light bursts forth, quenches the stars." (*b*) "My life's cable, Myiscus, is made fast to thee, in thee is all the breath that is left to my soul. For by thine eyes, dear boy, that speak even to the deaf, and by thy bright brow I swear it, if ever thou lookest at me with a clouded eye I see the winter, but if thy glance be blithe, the sweet spring bursts into bloom." (*c*) "It lightened sweet beauty: see how he flasheth flame from his eyes." (*d*) "Shining grace beams; like lightning thine eyes hurl sparks; has then Eros given thee lightning, O boy, as a weapon? Hail, Myiscus, thou

[1] Myiscus was also the name of one of the pages of Antiochus; see Polybius, v, 82, 13.

bringest to men the flames of love, beam thou on mortals, on me as an enchanting star."

Earlier, the poet has made himself merry over the fools who have easily fallen in love, yet Eros does not jest with him: "I am caught, I who once laughed often at the serenades of young men crossed in love. And at thy gate, Myiscus, love has fixed me, inscribing on me 'Spoils won from Chastity'."

Yet not only does Eros rejoice in his triumph, Myiscus himself also with glee congratulates himself, because he has succeeded in subjecting the stubborn one: "Myiscus, shooting me, whom the Loves could not wound, under the breast with his eyes, shouted out thus: 'It is I who have struck him down, the overbold, and see how I tread underfoot the arrogance of sceptered wisdom that sat on his brow?' But I, just gathering breath enough, said to him, 'Dear boy, why art thou astonished? Love brought down Zeus himself from Olympus.'" But he soon allows himself to be converted, and now, since he is sure of the love of his Myiscus, his happiness is only disturbed by the fear that Zeus may be able to carry off the boy from him.

Of the numerous poems which are devoted to other stars, a small selection may here be given: "When thirsty I kissed the tender-fleshed boy and said, when I was free of my parching thirst: 'Father Zeus, dost thou drink the nectareous kiss of Ganymede, and is this the wine he tenders to thy lips? For now that I have kissed Antiochus, fairest of our youths, I have drunk the sweet honey of the soul.'" "If I see Thero, I see everything, but if I see everything and no Thero, I again see nothing."

"I saw Alexis walking in the road at noontide, at the season when the summer was just being shorn of the tresses of her fruits; and double rays burnt me, the rays of love from the boy's eyes and others from the sun. The sun's night laid to rest again, but love's were kindled more in my dreams by the phantom of beauty. So night, who releases others from toil, brought pain to me, imaging in my soul a loveliness which is living fire."

" Pain has begun to touch my heart, for hot Love as he strayed, scratched it with the tip of his nails, and, smiling, said : ' Again, O unhappy lover, thou shalt have the sweet wound, burnt by biting honey.' Since when, seeing among the youths the fresh sapling Diophantus, I can neither fly nor abide."

3. ASCLEPIADES. (Anth. Pal., xii, 135, 162, 163)

Asclepiades of Samos was regarded as the teacher of Theocritus, by whom he was highly praised as a man and a poet. The epigrams handed down under his name are distinguished by graceful form and tender feeling ; eleven of them are preserved in the " boyish Muse " of the Anthology, of which the following is a specimen : " Wine is the proof of love. Nicagoras denied to us that he was in love, but those many toasts convicted him.

"Yes ! he shed tears and bent his head, and had a certain downcast look, and the wreath bound tight round his head kept not its place."

In another epigram the poet imagines how the little Love is introduced by his mother into the secrets of reading and writing. But the result of her efforts as a teacher are essentially different from what is expected ; instead of a text the docile pupil only reads over and over again the names of two beautiful boys, who are devoted to each other in hearty friendship—a tender glorification of boy-friendship, such as is also described in epigram 163 by the same author.

4. CALLIMACHUS. (Anth. Pal., xii, 102)

Callimachus of Cyrene in North Africa lived about 310–240 B.C. He is by far the most important epigrammatist of the Alexandrian period. After having studied in Athens together with the poet Aratus, already known to us, we find him in

Alexandria, first as a celebrated teacher and grammarian, and then at the luxurious court of Ptolemy Philadelphus as one of the most important collaborators in the business of the world-famed library with its many branches. His literary activity was mainly directed to the department of learning, but he was not disinclined to poetry. In the epigrams left by him, the erotic note is generally heard, and in the twelfth book of the Anthology, no fewer than twelve of them are preserved, which sing the praises of beautiful boys and are devoted to the mysteries of Eros. He knows how to vary the inexhaustible subject with a pleasantly surprising new point :—

" The huntsman on the hills, Epicydes, tracks every hare and the slot of every hind through the frost and snow. But if one say to him, 'Look, here is a beast lying wounded,' he will not take it. And even so is my love ; it is wont to pursue the fleeing game, but flies past what lies in its path.".

5. The Other Poets

Besides the great poets hitherto mentioned, in the twelfth book of the Anthology, twenty-four poets of the lower class are represented by epigrams on the love of boys.

From Dioscorides (second century B.C.) we have, among a number of other epigrams :—

" Zephyr, gentlest of the winds, bring back to me the lovely pilgrim Euphragoras, even as thou didst receive him, not extending his absence beyond a few month's space ; for to a lover's mind a short time is as a thousand years " (171).

Rhianus of Crete (flourished third century B.C.), a slave by birth, had originally been the inspector of a boys' wrestling school. His preference for youths is also to be recognized in his poetry : thus we know that he referred Apollo's service with King

Admetus to erotic reasons (cf. Callimachus, *Hymn*, ii, 49). Of the eleven epigrams preserved, six are upon boys, somewhat frivolous, but clever and full of grace. He was successful in the domain of philology, prepared worthy editions of the *Iliad* and *Odyssey* and became known as an epic poet, especially of the second Messenian war.

We have already quoted his poem on the " Labyrinth of Boys from which there is no escape ", but here is a further specimen : " Dexionicus, having caught a blackbird with lime under a green plane-tree, held it by the wings, and it, the holy bird, screamed complaining. But I, dear Love, and ye blooming Graces, would fain be even a thrush or a blackbird, so that in his hand I might pour forth my voice and sweet tears " (xii, 142).

An epigram of Alcæus of Messene (A. P., xii, 64) is tender and full of fine feeling : " Zeus, Lord of Pisa, crown under the steep hill of Cronus Peithenor, the second son of Cypris. And lord, I pray thee, beckon no eagle on high to seize him for thy cup-bearer in place of the fair Trojan boy. If ever I have brought thee a gift from the Muses that was dear to thee, grant that the godlike boy may be of one mind with me."

Alpheus of Mitylene (ibid., 18) makes a fresh point, when in the course of a six-line epigram he says : " Unhappy they whose life is loveless ; for without love it is not easy to do aught or to say aught. I, for example, am now all too slow, but were I to catch sight of Xenophilus I would fly swifter than lightning. Therefore I bid all men not to shun but to pursue sweet desire ; love is the whetstone of the soul."

Automedon (ibid., 34) strikes a humorously bantering note : " Yesterday I supped with the boys' trainer, Demetrius, the most blessed of all men. One lay on his lap, one stooped over his shoulder, one brought him the dishes, and another served him with drink—an admirable quartette. I said to him in fun, do you, my dear friend, train the boys at night too ?"

Evenus (Anth. Pal., xii, 172; cf. Catullus, 85), finds a new formula for the inimitable *Odi et amo* of Catullus: "If to hate is pain and to love is pain, of the two evils I choose the smart of kind pain."

Julius Leonidas (Anth. Pal., xii, 20) employs an idea of his own: "Zeus must be again rejoicing in the banquets of the Ethiopians, or, turned to gold, is stealing to Danaë's chamber; for it is a marvel that, seeing Periander, he did not carry off from earth the lovely youth; or is the god no longer a lover of boys?"

Lastly, we will select three of the thirty-five anonymous epigrams that are preserved in this twelfth book of the Anthology.

"Persistent love, thou ever whirlest at me no desire for woman, but the lightning of burning longing for my own sex. Now burnt by Damon, now looking on Ismenus, I ever suffer pain that will not be appeased. And not only on these have I looked, but, my eye, ever madly roving, is dragged into the nets of all alike" (ibid., 87).

Another time, longing leads the poet safely after a regular carousal: "I will go to serenade him, for I am, all of me, mighty drunk. 'Boy, take this wreath that my tears have bathed.' The way is long, but I shall not go in vain; it is the dead of night and dark, but for me Themison[1] is a great torch" (ibid., 116).

The author of the following is also unknown: "When Menecharmus, Anticles' son, won the boxing match, I crowned him with ten soft fillets, and thrice I kissed him, all dabbled with blood as he was, but the blood was sweeter to me than myrrh" (ibid., 123).

[1] Themison was also the name of the favourite of King Antiochus I. He came from Cyprus and was fond of dressing up as a young Heracles—naked with a lion's skin on his shoulders, armed with bow and arrows and a club. To him as such the people offered sacrifice (Pythermus in Ath., vii, 289 f.).

Having thus culled but a few of the flowers that bloom so profusely in the twelfth book of the Anthology, the "Musa puerilis" of Straton, we come now to the so-called "cinædic" poetry, whose most important representative, Sotades, has already been discussed (p. 266).

The earliest meaning of *cinædus* (κίναιδος) was "a lover of boys", with an obscene significance; then the name was given to the professional dancers of certain indecent ballets, as they are known to us from Plautus and Petronius and from the wall-paintings of the Villa Doria Pamphili in Rome, which were accompanied with very free, or even according to our ideas highly indecent songs. Only quite unimportant fragments of them have been preserved. The boxer Cleomachus of Magnesia had fallen in love with such a cinædus-actor and a girl kept by him and was thereby induced to take up similar dialogue character parts. (Cinædic Poetry: Plautus, *Mil. glor.*, 668 (iii, 1, 73); Petronius, 23; O. Jahn, *Wandgemälde des Columbariums in der Villa Pamphili* (Philol. Abhandl. der Münchener Akademie, viii, 254 ff.); for the story of Cleomachus see Strabo, xiv, 648*a*).

According to Athenæus (xv, 697*d*) "everyone sang a song glorifying the love of boys" by Seleucus (beginning of the second century B.C.) of which two verses are preserved: "I also love boys; this is more beautiful than languishing in the yoke of marriage; for in murderous battle your friend still stays as a protector at your side."

IV. *Prose*

It is superfluous to give a complete summary of the passages treating of pæderasty in Greek prose, since the Greek prose-writers have already been sufficiently discussed. Hence it will be enough to name some writings which were more especially occupied with the subject.

Under the name of Demosthenes a treatise called *Erotikos* has survived, which, obviously influenced by Plato's *Phædrus*, represents an enthusiastic eulogy in letter-form of a boy named Epicrates. However agreeable and worth reading this little work may be, it is, nevertheless, as philological criticism has shown, not the work of the great orator. The most important homosexual prose work in ancient Greek literature is, of course, the *Symposion* (' Banquet ') of Plato, written several years after the festive meal which the tragic writer Agathon had given to his friends Socrates, Phædrus, Pausanias, Eryximachus, and Aristophanes, on the occasion of his dramatic victory in 416 B.C. After the eatables had been removed and the drinking begins, on the proposal of Phædrus the importance and power of Eros is chosen as a subject of conversation. Thus this most beautiful writing of Plato, which is so rich in colouring and so stimulatingly illustrated and profoundly treated from so many different standpoints, assumes the form of a hymn of Eros unique in the literature of the world. By means of an ingeniously invented myth, Aristophanes defines love as the search of the one half of the once uniform original man (separated in two parts by the god) for its other part. The culminating point is the speech of Socrates, who defines love as the urge for immortality, which fructifies the body of women with the seed of children and the soul of boys and youths with wisdom and virtue. In the definition of Socrates, Eros attains the highest imaginable ideal : the sensual and spiritual melt in a wonderful harmony, from which with logical accuracy the demand results, that the really good teacher must also be a good pædophil (lover of boys), that is, that teacher and pupil must do their best by mutual love and common effort to reach the greatest perfection possible. No sooner has Socrates finished his speech, perhaps the most beautiful ever written in the Greek or any other language, than Alcibiades, coming slightly intoxicated from another banquet into the festive room, delivers the famous panegyric on Socrates, which overflows just as much with an enthusiasm glowing with passion for the beloved creature, as it lifts him up to the height of super-sensuous intellectuality and almost superhuman self-control.

By comparison with the *Symposion*, the Platonic dialogue *Alcibiades* seems colourless. It is connected with the love of Socrates for Alcibiades, the spoilt and idolized favourite of all, and develops the idea that a future counsellor of the people has first to decide with himself what is fitting and to their advantage.

The subject of the love of boys is also treated of in the *Phædrus* of Plato, named after the favourite of his youth. Under the towering plane-tree on the bank of the stream Ilissus, at midday, with the grasshoppers chirping around them, the dialogue takes place, which, gradually mounting higher and higher, leads at last to the Socratic definition of Eros, that pædophilia represents the demand for the originally beautiful and the world of ideas.

Whether the *Erastæ* ("The Lovers") is rightly attributed to Plato is not yet with certainty decided. It is named after the favourite one of two boys, with whom Socrates holds a conversation on the thesis that a smattering of various knowledge is by no means synonymous with true philosophical education.

A very favourite subject in philosophical literature is the examination of the question, whether the love of a man for a woman should always be preferred to the love of a man for a boy. Of the numerous passages devoted to this problem the treatise that has come down to us under Lucian's name, no doubt inaccurately, is to be mentioned in the first place—the *Erotes*: that is, the two kinds of love.

In a very charming framework the contest between two friends is brought forward, the Corinthian Charicles, who commends the love between a man and a woman, and the Athenian Callicratidas, who praises that between men and boys.

Lycinus, who acts as arbitrator, finally puts his judgment into the following words, which best characterize the Greek conception of love: " Marriage is for men a life-pressing necessity and a precious thing, if it is a happy one; but the love of boys, so far as it courts the sacred rights of affection, is in my opinion a result of practical wisdom. Therefore let marriage be for all, but let the love of boys remain alone the privilege of the wise, for a perfect virtue is absolutely unthinkable in women. But do not be angry, my dear Charicles, if the crown belongs to Athens, and not to Corinth."

That the *Erotes* enjoyed great popularity in antiquity, is clear from the fact that the little work found several imitators, the best known of whom is Achilles Tatius. In the concluding chapters of the second book of his romance the problem which is the foundation of the *Erotes* is treated of in the same manner in the form of two opposing speeches.

In the romance of Xenophon of Ephesus which contains the loves of Habrocomes and Antheia, there occurs a homosexual episode, in which Hippothoüs tells how, in his native place, Perinthus, he was passionately in love with a boy named Hyperanthus. But when the boy is bought by Aristomachus, a rich merchant of Byzantium, Hippothoüs follows him thither, kills Aristomachus, and flees with his favourite. Near Lesbos their ship is overtaken by a heavy storm, in which Hyperanthus is drowned, and there nothing remains for the utterly disconcerted Hippothoüs but to erect a beautiful memorial for his dead favourite, after which in despair he takes to a bandit's life.

The philosopher Maximus of Tyre, who lived in the time of the emperor Commodus (A.D. 180–92), has repeatedly examined the problem of the love of boys in his numerous writings. Thus we have from him διατριβαί, that is, discourses on the Eros of Socrates, a subject which the hermaphrodite Favorinus, the most learned and distinguished philosopher of the period of Hadrian, had already treated.

1. THE LOVE OF BOYS IN GREEK MYTHOLOGY

After all that up to this point has been said of Greek love of boys on the authority of written documents, the conjecture that it also played an important part in the mythology of the Hellenes is abundantly fulfilled. In fact, the entire body of legend concerning the gods and heroes of the Hellenes is so rich in motifs of pædophilia, that R. Beyer was able to write a monograph on the subject.[1] It would be a welcome task here to record these amours with boys of the Greek gods and heroes, since they in great part belong to the most beautiful flowers of Hellenic poetry, but considerations of space forbid any complete or connected presentation in this place of the pædophil myths of the Greeks, and we have moreover, in Beyer's valuable dissertation, a thoroughly sufficient, if not always complete, compilation of pædophil motifs in Greek mythology. We must therefore refer the reader to this work, and be content merely to mention here that as early as the times of antiquity more or less detailed catalogues of the beautiful boys of legend and their lovers were committed to writing. Traces of these lists have been preserved in several cases, as in Hyginus, Athenæus and others; but the fullest is that of the pious and learned Father of the Church, Clement of Alexandria,

[1] R. Beyer, *Fabulæ Græcæ quatenus quave ætate puerorum amore commutatæ sint* (Leipzig, 1910).

who has put together the following "Zeus loved Ganymede; Apollo Cinyras, Zacynthus, Hyacinthus, Phorbas, Hylas, Admetus, Cyparissus, Amyklas, Troilus, Branchus, Tymnius, Parus, Potuieus, and Orpheus; Dionysus loved Laonis, Ampelus, Hymenæus, Hermaphroditos, and Achilles; Asclepius loved Hippolytus; Hephæstus Peleus; Pan Daphnis; Hermes Perseus, Chryses, Therses, and Odryses; Heracles Abderus, Dryops, Iokastus, Philoktetes, Hylas, Polyphemus, Hæmon, Chonus, and Eurystheus."

From this list, which contains the names of but a few lovers among the gods, one gets a glimpse of the astonishing number of pædophil motifs in the mythology of Greece.

2. Joke and Jest, Based on Homosexuality

Hitherto we have treated the Greek love of boys from its serious side, but the well-known saying of Horace—that "nothing prevents one from telling the truth with a smile on one's lips", is true of the ephebophilia of the Greeks as well as of other forms of the phenomena of human life. There was also cause for many witticisms, a large number of which have been preserved. Since naturally it is not the spiritual content of love, but in a much higher degree its sensual impulse that is the target of jest and joke, I can here only reproduce a few of the sometimes very ingenious witticisms that have come down to us.

The word *cinædus* (kinaidos), already explained, gradually became the nickname for those half-men, who by their feminine behaviour and gestures, by painting the face and other tricks of the toilet, incurred general contempt. A satire in the Anthology (xi, 272) says of them: "They do not want to be men and yet were not born women; they are no men, since they allow themselves to be used as women; they are men to women, and women to men." The affected behaviour of such people is often ridiculed, as in Aristophanes: "I wish, O youth, to ask you who you are. Of what land, you weakling? What's your country, what means thy garb? Why all this confusion of fashions? What does the harp prattle to the saffron-coloured robe? What the lyre to the headdress? What mean the oil-flask and the girdle? How unsuitable! What connection then between a mirror and a sword? And you yourself, O youth, are you reared as a man? Why, where are the tokens of a man? Where is your cloak? Where are your boots? Or as a woman then? Where then are your breasts? What do you say? Why are you silent? Nay then, I'll judge of you from your song, since you are not willing to tell me yourself" (*Thesm.*, 134 ff.).

Menander describes the behaviour of a cinædus with a sly hint at Ctesippus, the son of Chabrias, of whom it was said that he had sold even the stones from his father's grave, to be able to enjoy his life of pleasure (frag. 363).

In Comedy such effeminate persons have women's names. Thus Aristophanes speaks of a female Sostratos, that is, instead of the masculine Sostratos he uses the feminine Sostrate, instead of Cleonymus, Cleonyme (*Clouds*, 678, 680). Cratinus ridicules "pleasure boys", calling them "little girlies"; or the feminine article was sometimes put before the masculine name (*CAF.*, I, 29).

A certain ready, if not always very seemly wit was, of course, required for the invention of actually new and appropriate nicknames, and from the abundant store we may first select the coarse word καταπύγων (from πύγη, bum), which is very common, and is known to every reader of Greek comedy; just as common is the still coarser abusive word εὐρύπρωκτος (broad-bummed).[1]

A nickname which needs no explanation στρόβιλος

[1] A grotesque exaggeration is λακκόπρωκτος, from λάκκος cistern.

(" pirouette ") occurs only once in Aristophanes,[1] while the name βάταλος is more frequent. The word is explained by a passage from Eupolis, in which it is used as synonymous with πρωκτός (" bum "). It also existed as a proper name, and Plutarch wrote of an effeminate flute-player " Batalos ", ridiculed by Aristophanes in a comedy. More harmless are παιδοπίπης (" ogler of boys ") and πυρροπίπης (" ogler of boys with golden curls "), also frequent in comedy.

A droll nickname for pædophils was ἀλφηστής, the first meaning of which is a kind of fish. The satirical transference of the name is thus explained by Athenæus (vii, 281): these fish, which are pale yellow in appearance, and in some places purple-coloured, " were always caught in pairs, one swimming behind the tail of the other." Since then one always follows the other, some old writers have transferred the name of these fishes to those who are immoderate and perverted in sensuality. The joke becomes still more effective from the fact that the word, in Homer and later writers, is of frequent occurrence, and is a distinguished epithet of men. In a clever but untranslatable epigram of Straton, in which terms from the theory of music are used in an obscene sense, the pædophil meaning of the word ἀλφηστής is also alluded to (Anth. Pal., xii, 187).

3. Trifles and Supplementary Remarks

Phanias of Eresus has told the following story: " In Heraclea, a city of lower Italy, a boy named Hipparinus, handsome to look at and of noble family, was loved by Antileon, who in spite of many efforts could not win his favour. In the gymnasia he was always by his side, saying again and again how much he loved him, and protesting

[1] *Peace*, 864, where the reference is to the "twirls and contortions" of the sons of Carcinus (three of whom were dancers). Στροβίλων is here used instead of παίδων.

that he would undergo any labour and do everything he ordered. The boy, for a joke, ordered him to bring the bell from a fortified place which was strongly guarded by Archelaus, tyrant of the Heracleotes, thinking that he would never be able to accomplish this task. But Antileon secretly entered the fort, ambushed and slew the keeper of the bell, and afterwards, when he had come to the boy—who kept his promise—they became very intimate, and henceforward loved each other greatly. It chanced, however, that the tyrant himself became enamoured of the lad and when he threatened violence Antileon, being angry, exhorted him not to imperil his life by refusing, since the tyrant had power to carry out his wishes and his threat; but he himself attacked and slew the tyrant when leaving his house, and having done this, he ran away and would have escaped had he not got mixed up with some herds of sheep and been captured. Wherefore, the city having been freed by the death of the tyrant, brazen statues were set up by the people of Heraclea to both Antileon and the boy, and a law was passed that in future no one should drive herds of sheep through the streets" (*FHG*, II, 298, 16).

Lastly, appreciating the beauty of boys, it is not to be wondered at that beautiful boys were also employed for paying tribute. As early as Homer, Agamemnon offers to present the insulted Achilles with some youths by way of expiation.

Further, we read in Herodotus (iii, 97) that the Æthiopians every other year were obliged to deliver to the King of the Persians, besides pure gold, 200 chests of ebony and twenty elephants' tusks, also five boys; every four years the Colchians sent 100 boys and 100 girls; and both these instances of tribute actually continued in the time of Herodotus.

These boys served the Persian nobles as pages, cupbearers, and favourites. That even a worse lot threatened such boys, is clear from another passage of Herodotus (iii, 48), in which he relates that

Periander, the well-known ruler of Corinth, had sent 300 boys from Kerkyra (Corfu), sons of the most distinguished men of the island, to the court of King Alyattes at Sardes, to be castrated and to perform the services customarily discharged by eunuchs. How the inhabitants of the island of Samos, on whom the duty of transporting them was imposed, saved the boys and in memory thereof instituted a feast which was still observed in the time of Herodotus, may be gathered from the historian himself. From a later passage, very interesting from the point of view of the history of civilization, it is clear that many persons made a profession of the castration of boys. Herodotus tells us (viii, 104 ff.): "Xerxes sent with these boys as a guard a certain Hermotimus, a native of Pedasa, who held the first place among the king's eunuchs. In the town of Pedasa, it is said that the following event happens: whenever all the neighbours living round are threatened by the approach of any serious disaster, the priestess of the temple of Athene grows a long beard. And this had already happened twice. Now Hermotimus was one of the inhabitants of Pedasa, to whom it befell to obtain the greatest vengeance that one can imagine upon a man by whom he had been wronged. Panionius, a citizen of Chios, who supported himself by most wicked acts, bought him when he had been captured by enemies and was put up for sale. For this Panionius, as often as he got possession of any beautiful boys, used to castrate them, take them to Sardes or Ephesus and sell them for a high price. For among the barbarians eunuchs are more valuable than those who are not castrated, and greater confidence is reposed in them in everything. When he had castrated many others, Panionius, who made his livelihood in this manner, then did the same to Hermotimus—to whom it did not come altogether as a misfortune, for he was sent to Sardes with other gifts for the king and in course of time of all the eunuchs of Xerxes he was held in the greatest honour." Under King Darius also eunuchs were given positions at the Persian court; Babylon and the rest of Asyria were obliged to send him as tribute besides 1,000 talents of silver also 500 castrated boys.

The town of Lebadea in Bœotia, unimportant in itself, was famous for the very old, highly sacred dream-oracle of Trophonius. Pausanias, who had himself questioned the oracle, tells us in detail (ix, 39, 7) the various preparatory steps, which, after the venerable ceremonial, were prescribed to one who desired information from the oracle. Among other things he was conducted to the stream Hercyna that flows through a valley, "where two boys from the town, about thirteen years of age, who are called "Hermæ", anoint him with oil and bathe and perform all kinds of services for him such as boys perform." The name is perhaps to be explained by the fact that Hermes was the patron god of boys and youths, for which reason no Greek gymnasium was without an altar and statue of the friendly god.[1]

A pretty epigram of Nicias in the Anthology of Planudes describes how boys crown the statue of Hermes in the gymnasium, "who stands there as the patron of the charming gymnasium, with evergreen, hyacinths, and violets."

From the last *Erotika* of Clearchus of Soli in Cyprus the following sentiment is preserved: "No flatterer can be a constant friend, for time detracts from the lie of him who pretends to friendship. But the true lover is a flatterer of love for the sake of the bloom of youth and beauty."

[1] According to Plutarch, *Numa*, 7, the boy who assisted the priest of Jupiter at the sacrifice was called Camillus, "as Hermes also as a helper was often called Kadmilos (Καδμῖλος) by the Greeks"; cf. Servius on Virgil, *Æn.*, xi, 543, and 558, and Scholiast on Apollonius Rhodius, i, 917. It is interesting to note that in the *Acts* (xiv, 12) after Paul had healed one who had been "a cripple from his mother's womb" at Lystra, the enthusiastic multitude regarded him as Hermes (Mercury) who had come down to earth.

CHAPTER VI

Perversions of Greek Sexual Life

How healthy the sexual life of the Greeks was is shown by the fact that those manifestations of sexual phenomena usually grouped together under the name of *Psycopathia Sexualis* played an extraordinarily small part in it. This assertion would not be just if homosexuality is reckoned as sexual psychopathy; but that this—at least for Greek homosexuality—is not allowable the previous chapter will have proved.

But there was no lack of the perverted forms of love in old Greece also, and their scientific representation may be justly demanded from the author of a sexual history; yet I may here be allowed to be brief, since well-known books by Rosenberg, Bloch, Vorberg, and others have already collected a quantity of material.

1. Mixoscopy[1]

Even as the name of this perversion is not ancient Greek, so the thing itself, which consists in stimulation and satisfaction by the secret observation of sexual acts, was so rare in Greece, that I can quote no passages in proof of it; whether any pictorial representation of a *voyeur* (those addicted to such practices) exists I am unable to say. When Candaules, as mentioned before, finds pleasure in showing his wife naked to his friend, we can only speak of mixoscopy in a wider sense, since it is not Gyges who desires to enjoy the sight, but the husband who tempts him to do so, whether it

[1] From *μῖξις* (sexual union) and *σκοπ-*, the stem from *σκέπτειν*, to look at.

be that he himself takes pleasure in expected sexual excitement of the spectator, or only wishes to satisfy his inordinate vanity in the possession of so beautiful a woman.

2. TRANSVESTITISMUS

For those who find sexual excitement or satisfaction in showing themselves in the dress of another sex, the term "Transvestites" has been invented. This perversion, which finally goes back to the embryonal-androgynous nature of every human being, was not foreign to the Greeks, although we hear comparatively little of it in our authorities. I have already frequently mentioned "transvestitic" usages in religious cult. At the festival Cotyttia in Athens, which was held in honour of Cotys or Cotytto, the goddess of sensuality, dance performances took place by men in women's clothes, in which the ceremonies, which certainly at first only referred symbolically to the sexual, gradually passed into orgies, so that, according to Synesius (*Calvitii Encomium*, 856) "one who participates in the orgies of Cotys was identical with a cinædus". Male sexual excitement seems to have been increased by wearing a wig in imitation of a woman's hair in addition to assuming feminine garb. The Italian festivals of Cotys, mentioned by Horace (*Epod.*, 17, 56) were specially infamous, but appear to have been only female orgies.

An epigram of Asclepiades (Anth. Pal., xii, 161) speaks of a beautiful girl named Dorcion (little fawn) who was fond of dressing up as a boy, and so "with the chlamys clearly revealing her naked thigh, to flash the fire of love from her eyes".

Ctesias related that Amarus, the governor of Babylon, was fond of appearing in a female dress and ornaments, and that, while he was so attired, 150 female singers and dancers enhanced the joys of the table (Athenæus, xii, 530).

3. EXHIBITIONISM

If by exhibitionism is understood the ostentatious uncovering of the sexual organs before persons of the same or a different sex, it is easy to understand that this perversion was very rare in ancient Greece. At that time there was often sufficient opportunity to see men completely naked; so that no one was conscious of sexual curiosity or of accompanying personal lustful feelings by partial uncovering. Contrary to the facts observed at the present day by physicians and jurists, in the older times of Greece it is female exhibitionism that is spoken of, if at all. The oldest example is Baubo, the wife of Dysaules at Eleusis, with whom Demeter and the little Iacchus took shelter when she was seeking her daughter Persephone who had been carried off by Hades. To cheer the sorrowing mother, Baubo strips herself, which drives Iacchus to such an outburst of delight, that Demeter also against her will is obliged to laugh.

The intentional uncoverings in the dance of the Cordax (see pp. 165 f.) are also not without an exhibitionistic character.

Diodorus (i, 85) says of the Egyptian women: If after the death of the sacred Apis-bull a new one is discovered, only women may look at him for forty days; but they do this "while lifting their clothes up and showing their private parts to the god".

Most of the images of Priapus and many of Hermaphrodites are intended to have a decidedly exhibitionistic effect (see p. 125).

All that we have mentioned would be only indirectly regarded as acts of exhibitionism by modern sexual science. The only passage known to me, where exhibitionism proper is spoken of, is in Theophrastus, where it is said in the character of the Immodest man (*Char.*, 11): "Such a shameless fellow, when he meets women, is fond of lifting up his *chiton*, and showing himself to them."

4. PYGMALIONISM

Pygmalion, the mythical King of Cyprus, was so delighted with the statue of the girl executed by him, that he fell in love with the ivory-work, and could not rest until Aphrodite, at his incessant entreaties, animated the statue, after which he begot Paphos with the young woman, from whom the well-known town in Cyprus was named. Hence the love of statues and other works of art was called " Pygmalionism " (see Ovid, *Metam.*, x, 243 ff.).

A case of Pygmalionism is given in detail in the *Erotes* of Lucian (xv ff.). A youth of excellent family who had fallen in love with the famous statue of Aphrodite in Cnidus by Praxiteles, spent whole days in the temple, and " was never tired of gazing without cessation at the divine images. Gently whispered sighs and passionate laments of stolen caresses with a struggle escaped his lips. As a token of his ever increasing passion every wall was filled with inscriptions of love, and on the bark of every tree he carved the words " Beautiful Aphrodite ". He adored Praxiteles as Zeus himself, and laid at the feet of the goddess as votive presents all that he possessed that was ornamental and valuable.

This was not the only time when a youth fell in love with the Cnidian Aphrodite. Philostratus (*Vita Ap.*, 276) relates that such a case was reported by Apollonius of Tyana, who caused the youth to visit him, and healed him of his passion. He told him that it did not befit men to love the gods and, by way of warning, reminded him of Ixion, who was undergoing severe punishment in the underworld because he had desired Hera. " Thus he succeeded in healing this madness, and the youth was allowed to go, after he had offered sacrifice to obtain the forgiveness of the goddess."

Ælian tells of a young and distinguished Athenian, " who fell madly in love with the statue of Agathe

Tyche that stood before the Prytaneum. He kissed and embraced it, then ran raving and half-crazy with desire to the councillors and begged them to sell him the statue for money. When his offer was refused, he adorned the statue with bands, garlands, and valuables, offered sacrifice and killed himself after unceasing lamentation" (*Var. hist.*, ix, 39).

According to Pliny (xxxvi, 22), Alcetas, a youth of Rhodes, fell in love with a naked statue of Eros by Praxiteles, at Parium on the Hellespont.

5. FLAGELLATION, SADISM, MASOCHISM

Flagellation is usually combined with religious motives, since a naïve or overheated state of mind believes that one performs a work that is especially well-pleasing to the gods if he voluntarily humiliates himself by flogging his body or even by partial self-mutilation. Thus are to be explained the floggings and castration already discussed, which formed part of different cults, such as the noisy orgiastic festivals of Cybele (see pp. 215 ff.). This self-emasculation has found its literary expression in numerous epigrams of the Palatine Anthology.

That such cruelties, however strange it may at first sound, finally have their reason in the desire for sexual excitement, has been proved by modern sexual science, whereby the connection between religion and sexuality finds a new and surprising confirmation. From this prime cause I also thought I could explain the well-known chastisement of Spartan boys at the altar of Artemis Orthia, to which the chastisements of the girls at the feast of Dionysus called Scieria at Alea in Arcadia form a counterpart, as also the already mentioned (p. 130) festival of the "unholy Aphrodite".

I have nowhere found sadistic or masochistic[1]

[1] Masochism is derived from the name of Leopold von Sacher-Masoch, who described the perversion, and added the termination -ism. Dunglison's *Medical Dictionary* (1893) gives the following definition: "Sexual perversion, in which a member of one sex takes delight in

scenes in ancient Greek literature. This is a fresh proof of the healthiness of Greek life again and again emphasized by the author who, however, would have little difficulty in quoting a few passages concerning them from Roman literature.

The story of Heracles and Omphale shows a masochistic character. The mighty hero becomes the slave of the Lydian queen Omphale, in whose service he so far humbles himself as to perform female tasks, while Omphale, clad in the lion's skin, looks on at him. Yet here we can hardly speak of masochism properly so called, since its special characteristic, the sensation of sexual pleasure felt by the sufferer, is nowhere emphasized in the story of Heracles and Omphale.

Also in the story of Demetrius of Phalerum, who bore on different parts of his body the evident scars of bites of the hetaira Lamia, not only is the express assurance that these bites had made Demetrius amorous wanting in Plutarch (*Demetr.*, 27), but it is in itself improbable.

6. Sodomy

Sodomy as, according to a completely false, but now naturalized definition, the intercourse with animals is named, is not seldom mentioned in Greek antiquity, but either only in fables and romances, or, as in the Sicilian herdsmen of Theocritus, as an occasional makeshift.

Of sodomitic stories I mention : Zeus approaches Leda as a swan, Persephone as a snake ; Pasiphaë falls in love with a bull and has intercourse with it, and the fruit of this passion was the Minotaur, " an ox that was half a man, a man that was half an ox," as Ovid calls him (*Ars am.*, ii, 24).

being dominated, even to the extent of violence or cruelty, by one of the other sex. Its opposite is Sadism (from the Comte de Sade), which is a form of sexual perversion specially marked by cruelty.—Translator's note.

7. NEKROPHILIA

In proof of the cruel malpractice of abusing corpses, I can only quote three passages from Grecian antiquity, one of which, by Dimœtes, who had connection with a drowned girl, has already been given (see p. 248). In the second passage it is a question not of Greeks, but of Egyptians. Herodotus relates (ii, 89) that an embalmer was informed against for having misused the dead body of a beautiful woman, who had been entrusted to him to embalm. After that it became the usual custom not to hand over the bodies of especially beautiful or distinguished women to the embalmers until three or four days had elapsed after death.

Lastly, the same Herodotus informs us that Periander, the well-known ruler of Corinth, committed an offence on the dead body of his wife Melissa after he had—perhaps accidentally—killed her (v, 92).

CHAPTER VII

Supplementary to the Sexual Life of the Greeks

1. The Sexual Organs and Kallipygy

From Meleager we have the epigram (Anth. Pal., v, 192): " If you see Callistion naked, you will say, here stands the double letter of the Syracusans upside down." [1]

Pastry was often made in phallic or ktenic form.

As already mentioned, men liked women to remove the hairs from their privy parts, which was done by pulling them out or singeing them off. The comic writer Plato spoke of " myrtle bunches pulled out by the hand " (*CAF.*, i, 648), and according to Aristophanes (*Lysistrata*, 827) women used a burning lamp, as, if the interpretation is correct, it is to be seen on a picture published by Moll ; hot ashes were also employed for the same purpose. Obvious depilation was the rule, for the strong growth of hair of southern women would otherwise prevent their private parts themselves from being seen, and in any case, many passages testify that it was but the smooth female bosom, not the bosom covered with hairs, that pleased the Greek man. Thus, Aristophanes in the *Lysistrata* (148 ff.) : " For if we women were to sit at home, painted, and approach them lightly clad in our vests of fine linen, having the hairs plucked off our bosoms, the men would become enamoured, and desire to lie with us ; and if we were not to come nigh them, but abstain, they would quickly make peace, I well know."

[1] According to the Scholiast, the double consonant *psi* (ψ) was invented by the Syracusan Epicharmus (Pliny, *Hist. Nat.*, vii, 56). If ψ be turned upside down, by a stretch of imagination it may represent the sexual organs ; hence Callistion would have been a hermaphrodite. It is less probable that two letters have to be changed, *K* into *Th* and *t* into *ch*, that is, Thallischion = " with large buttock muscles."

As a counterpart Aristophanes often describes scenes of female desire: "But if delightful Eros and the Cyprus-born Aphrodite breathe desire upon our bosoms and our breasts, and then create in the men a pleasing passion and voluptuousness, I think that we shall some time be called amongst the Greeks 'Lysimachæ'" (as having put an end to the war) (*Lysistrata*, 551 ff.).

Indirectly, since the play upon words is untranslateable, there are a number of lines in the *Thesmophoriazusæ* (esp. 246, 1119, 1185), in which the muscles of the buttocks are continually spoken of. In the *Lysistrata* (1148) the Laconian cries out in admiration: "Her buttocks are indescribably beautiful," and in the *Peace* (868) the servant says: "The girl has bathed, beautiful and smooth are her buttocks!" The coquettish movement of the same, with which according to a fragment of comedy women used to entice men, was called περιπρωκτιᾶν.

That this part of the body must also suffer when children had to be punished with a switch or a stick, is known from vase painting and a passage of Herondas (vii, 13); and there is a vase in the Museo Nazionale in Naples on which are painted two half-naked youths lying on a couch and turning their heads towards a woman who is pulling her clothes up to show her naked buttocks.

2. CASTRATION, CIRCUMCISION, INFIBULATION

Of the self-emasculation of the priests in the cult of the Syrian goddess Gallos, Lucian (*De Syr. dea*, 50) tells us: "On certain fixed days, the multitude assembles in the temple; many priestesses and the men consecrated to the gods whom I have mentioned, celebrate the mysteries, cut their arms and beat one another on the back. Many standing by accompany with the flute, many beat drums, others sing inspired verses and sacred songs. This takes place outside the temple, nor do any who perform these ceremonies enter the temple. In these days priestesses also are made; for when flutes have been played and the ceremonies performed, madness comes over many of them, and numbers of those, who came merely to look on, afterwards perpetrate such acts as I will relate. The youth, whose turn has come, having thrown off his garments with a loud shout leaps into the middle of the assembly and lifts up a sword—one of those which I imagine have for many years stood there for the purpose. Having grasped the sword he immediately castrates himself and runs through the city, bearing in his hands what he has cut off. From whatever house into which he throws it he receives a female dress and adornments." This is what took place at castrations. When the enthusiastic intoxication of self-emasculation was past, many oblations were offered by those castrated to the "great mother" such as cymbals and kettledrums, the knife with which the unholy deed was executed, and "the fair hair, which the youth before then threw back so proudly". Thus it is attested in an anonymous epigram in the Anthology (vi, 51), as well as in other authorities.

Although this orgiastic cult is of Asiatic origin, yet, like the kindred worship of Rhea Cybele, it early reached Greece, though in a milder form, so that self-emasculation can only have been very rare, if, indeed, it ever actually took place.

Self-emasculation could be carried out for other reasons, as has been described by Wieland—who certainly deviates from the ancient authorities—in his *Combabus* (Leipzig, 1824).

Lucian had had the following account given him of the priests of the "Syrian Goddess". When Stratonike, the wife of the Assyrian King, undertook a pilgrimage for building a temple, the king wished to assign his intimate friend Combabus to her as protector. In vain the young man, who owing to his youth was afraid of being alone for a long time with the beautiful woman, begged him to abandon the idea. All that he could obtain was an adjournment for seven days, and after these had expired he handed over to the king, in the presence of several witnesses, a small sealed box, with the request that he would keep it faithfully, since it contained the most valuable thing that he possessed. The king also seals the box and gives it to his treasurer to keep. Then they started on the journey and everything happened as Combabus had feared. Stratonike, who had so long been in want of the joys of marriage, fell in love with the handsome young man, but her advances are repulsed, and now the story of Potiphar or Phædra is repeated. The rejected woman in letters to the king falsely accuses her modest companion, or, what Lucian thinks more probable, the suspicion is suggested by others to the king, who orders Combabus to return and has him thrown into prison for seducing his wife. When the day of trial arrived, Combabus asks the king to open the box entrusted to him, since it contained the proof of his innocence. After the king had found the seal untampered with, he opens the box and finds therein the embalmed genitals of his unhappy friend. The king embraces him with many tears and distinguishes him with the highest honours. Later, a bronze statue of Combabus was shown in man's dress but of female figure. Hence it is said that the custom became naturalized, that many Galli emasculated themselves and ever after wore female dress and pursued female occupations (Lucian, *De Syr. dea*, 19 ff.).

Heracleides Ponticus in his book *On Enjoyment* had related that a certain Deinias, keeper of a perfumery, led a very dissipated life and had thereby wasted his property. When he had come to the end of his physical powers, he himself cut off the instruments of his lust, grieving that they could be of no further service to him (Ath., xii, 552).

As the *Odyssey* informs us, in ancient times there

lived "on the mainland" a king named Echetus (despot)[1] "the destroyer of all men". Tramps and beggars were threatened with being sent to Echetus "that he might cut off their nose and ears with merciless knife, tear out their private parts, and throw them raw to the dogs to eat" (*Od.*, xviii, 85).

Whether or not by Echetus[1] an historical person is meant, cannot be now decided. But it is certain that in ancient Greece castration was inflicted as a punishment. Thus Odysseus punishes the unfaithful goatherd Melanthius, cuts off his nose, ears, and hands, and gives his torn out genitals to the dogs to eat (*Od.*, xxii, 474).

If in the case of Melanthius we cannot speak of castration properly so called, but rather of cruel mutilation before being killed, there are, however, not a few examples of actual castration, that is of persons, especially boys, who it was intended should live on in that condition. Certainly it is nearly always a question of an Oriental, rarely of a Greek custom. Thus, according to Hellanicus (frag. 169, *FHG.*, I, 68), the Babylonians were the first to castrate boys, an atrocity introduced—according to Xenophon (*Cyrop.*, VII, v, 65)—into Persia by the elder Cyrus. According to a widespread notion the originator of the practice was a woman, no less a person than the Assyrian queen Semiramis (Amm. Marcell., XIV, vi, 17).

Eunuchs were also employed as temple servants at the sanctuaries of Cybele and Artemis in Sardes and Ephesus (Hdt., v, 102). By the threat of intending to castrate their boys, the Persians, before the naval battle off the island of Lade, endeavoured to bring the Ionians over to their side, and after their victory carried out their threat (Hdt., vi, 9 and 32).

Castration was also occasionally undertaken for

[1] The name means tyrant; and became proverbial, so that according to Eunapius 110 and Suïdas under Φῆστος the consul Festus in Asia was so named in the reign of the Emperor Valens.

lustful purposes; nothing of the kind is, indeed, known of the Greeks, but it is of the Medes who, according to Clearchus (Ath. xii, 514*d*), " castrated many of those who lived round about to excite lust ".

That sexual impulses—which, of course, are centralized in the brain and not in the sexual organs —were by no means extinguished by castration was well known to the Greeks, as is shown by an epigram of Straton (Anth. Pal. xii, 236) where a eunuch who kept a whole harem of boys is spoken of.

In Philostratus (*Vit. Ap.*, i, 33) we read: " Eunuchs also have feelings of love, and the yearning desire kindled in them through the eyes is by no means extinguished, but remains hot and ardent."

Castration was occasionally performed on women in order to make them barren. Certainly here also it is not a question of Greece proper. Thus Xanthus in his *Lydian History* informs us the " the Lydian King Adramyttes was the first who had women castrated, in order to use them instead of male eunuchs " (Ath., xii, 515*e*). The passage is not quite clear, but it may be conjectured that it is a matter of the removal of an ovary, whereby women may be rendered incapable of conceiving.

A note in Strabo (xvii, 284)—" that the Egyptians circumcise new-born children and take out the female part, as is also the practice of the Jews "— seems to have a different meaning; the reference here is evidently to a circumcision of the foreskin of the clitoris, a custom which still prevails among some Arabian, Coptic, Æthiopian, and Persian and Central African tribes. This circumcision was, perhaps, quite a reasonable proceeding in some cases, as " among African women the clitoris can be prominent and of importance as a cutaneous flap."

As the result of what has been stated we may

assert that castration was certainly not unknown to the Greeks, but that it was carried out by them only with extreme rarity. The fine feeling of the Hellenes strove against such barbarism, and they did not value, as was the case in the East, the effects of castration, which are thus described by Lucian: "But those wretched and unhappy creatures, that they may be longer boys, do not even remain men, a doubtful riddle of a double sex, who have neither preserved the nature in which they were born nor possess that into which they have changed; for them the flower of youth withers prematurely; they are reckoned at one and the same time among children and old men, without having passed the interval of manhood. So that cursed luxury, that teacher of everything that is bad, thinking out shameless pleasures one after another, plunges into that disgraceful disease that cannot be mentioned, in order that it may leave no kind of vice untried" (*Amor.*, 21).

Certainly we have a counterpart in Xenophon which expresses a very different opinion. In the *Cyropædeia* (VII, v., 60 ff.) Cyrus comes to the conclusion that there can be no more faithful or trustworthy friends than eunuchs. I need not go more closely into this highly interesting train of thought, as it would lead to a discussion not of Greek but of Oriental ideas.

Before carrying out the exercise of love, "infibulation" was very common in Greece. The prepuce, or foreskin, was drawn forward over the extremity of the penis and securely tied with a string or narrow band. This was intended to prevent the *glans* from being exposed to injury in the event of the prepuce slipping back during gymnastics or other active exercises.

If satyrs especially appear on vase-paintings "infibulated", this is generally intended as a joke, as a kind of "girdle of chastity", if it may be so expressed. Among the Romans, as is often mentioned, a stitching-needle (*fibula*) was drawn through the prepuce, in order to render copulation impossible, but I cannot remember to have read of this in any Greek author.

3. Aphrodisiacs

Many means of achieving erection and curing impotence were known in antiquity, and in classical authors the oldest passage is perhaps in Euripides, where Medea tells the old Ægeus, that she has medicaments that will enable even him to procreate (*Medea*, 718). The ancients had many nostrums for the promotion of frequent copulation, such as *satyrion* (probably a kind of orchis), or pounded pepper mixed with nettle-seed, or old wine to which triturated *pyrethron* (feverfew, or pellitory) had been added. These methods were pointed out by Ovid (*Ars*, ii, 415) as injurious to the organism; those he considers harmless are onions, wild cabbage (*brassica erica*), eggs, honey, and stone-pine apples.

All these as well as many other aphrodisiacs were also known to the Greeks. In the Greek papyri of charms numerous recipes having for their object a strengthening of the capacity for erection are preserved. Abundant material for such love-charms is also to be found in the great Louvre papyrus and *Anastasy* (Brit. Mus., Gk. pap., i, 90), both edited by Wessely.

It would serve no useful purpose to enumerate all the aphrodisiacs used by the Greeks or to discuss them more in detail, but we may offer a few samples.

Pyrethron by its name is to be recognized as a plant " that kindles the flame of love ". The onion is the most frequently named among Greek erotic stimulants, and, together with mussels, crabs, snails, and eggs, it is mentioned by the comic writer Alexis (*CAF*, II, 399) as specially effective. Diphilus says: " Bulbs (onions) are hard to digest, though nourishing and strengthening to the stomach;

they are cleansing but they weaken the eyesight, and they also stimulate sexual desire."

In an epigram of Lucian (46) a Cynic is spoken of, who refuses lupines and radishes, "since the virtuous man may not be a slave to his belly." But when acid snow-white onions are put on table, he eats them greedily. Wieland may be right in thinking that the sensuality of the Cynics is here ridiculed.

In 414 B.C. Aristophanes had put on the stage a comedy named *Amphiareus* in which it is described how a "highly pitiable old man" (δεισιδαίμονα ἐν τοῖς μάλιστα) with his young wife undertakes a pilgrimage to the oracle of Amphiaraus at Oropus on the borders of Bœotia and Attica, whose aid sick persons invoked, especially after fasting, abstinence from wine, and sacrifice, and how to these two in a dream the desired revelation was made. Thus also the old man in the comedy of Aristophanes has his longed-for youthful vigour restored. As to exactly how this happened, the scanty fragments afford no satisfactory explanation; but on piecing together certain disjointed portions we find that a dish of lentils, evidently considered stimulating, is put before the old man.[1]

If local massage also is mentioned in the comedy for the renewal of impotence, this was at all times a very favourite remedy which, although not always successful, is often mentioned by old authors.

The physician Theodorus Priscianus in the fourth century A.D. wrote a medical work which is still preserved, in which he had occasion to speak of the cure for masculine impotence. There (ii, 11) it is said: "Let the patient be surrounded by beautiful

[1] The comedy is not only a joke but, like all the comedies of Aristophanes, had a serious political background, for we may at least conjecture that it is fairly probable that by the old man who had become impotent the Athenian people is meant, who during seventeen long years of war, were considerably weakened, and to heal whom many more than suspicious means had been tried.

girls or boys; also give him books to read, which stimulate lust and in which love-stories are insinuatingly treated."

4. OBSCENE TERMS AND OBSCENITIES

The Greek language abounds in obscene terms and more or less ingenious obscenities and plays upon words, of which an imposing number has been collected by Moritz Schmidt in his large edition of Hesychius (v, 88). As is natural, they are mostly to be found in the remains of comedy, of which specimens have often been given, so that here I content myself with a few supplementary remarks.

In the *Knights* of Aristophanes (1384 ff.) occurs the following:

" *Sausage-Seller*: On these conditions then accept this folding-stool, And here's a stout youth to carry it for you. And, if anywhere you choose, make a folding stool of him.

" *Demos.*: Happy man! now am I reinstated in my former position.

" *Sausage-Seller*: You will say so, when I give you the thirty years' peace. Come hither, peace, quickly [*beautiful girl enters, representing Peace*]."

However, in Aristophanes and the old Comedy generally, αἰσχρολογιά, that is, the frank and unconcealed expression of indecencies is much more frequent than ὑπόνοια, the concealed obscenity and ambiguously wanton manner of expression, which is better adapted to the new comedy to which Aristotle has justly referred.

A characteristic example occurs in the love-romance of Achilles Tatius where part of the speech of the priest of Artemis (viii, 9) consists solely of obscenities conveyed by *doubles entendres*.

In an epigram of the Palatine Anthology addressed to a dancer, terms are employed belonging to musical technique, under which an obscene meaning is concealed (Anth. Pal., v, 99).

The custom, at all times and everywhere usual, of inscribing more or less obscene words, sentences, verses, and drawing pictures on the walls of public conveniences, may also be assumed with certainty as regards ancient Greece, although direct evidence on this point has naturally not come down to us. As Kalinka informs us, a non-obscene epigram has been found on the wall of a latrine at Ephesus.

5. Incest

The views of the Greeks on incest, like those of all naïve peoples, were less strict than those of the moderns, as their mythology shows, for Zeus, the father of gods and men, is the husband of his sister Hera. Nevertheless, incest was rejected by public opinion, although certainly nowhere and at no time in Greece do very severe penalties appear to have existed for it. From Isæus we learn that marriage between ascendants and descendants was forbidden, and in older times, as it appears, marriage between brothers and sisters was also interdicted; later, it was tolerated, if the spouses had different mothers. Apart from these restrictions, marriages between kinsfolk were not rare—indeed, even the marriage between brothers and sisters was not unheard of in noble conservative families until the fifth century, as we learn from the marriage of Cimon and Elpinike; indeed, the example of the Egyptians, among whom such marriages always existed, was imitated by the Greeks who lived in that country, with the proviso that the dowry should remain in the family. It is well known that King Ptolemy II (285–247 B.C.) after his marriage with his sister Arsinoë took the surname of Philadelphus. To keep the dowry in the family, it was also legally fixed that the hereditary daughter (ἐπίκληρος), that is, a girl to whom the property of her parents exclusively fell, was obliged to marry her next of kin who was still unmarried.

Naturally, here and there many instances of degeneration occurred. Thus an Athenian is reproached by Andocides (*De myst*., 124): "Thereupon he married the daughter of Ischomachus and after he had lived with her scarcely a year, he also took her mother, lived with the mother and daughter, and kept both in his house." Alcibiades is said to have acted even more madly, if we may believe what Lysias tells us, as already mentioned (p. 14).

In any case, public opinion disapproved of incest in general, as may be concluded from the numerous mythological stories in which it is represented as detestable. We need only recall the universally known and partly already discussed stories of Œdipus, who—certainly without suspecting it—married his mother Iokasta, or of Caunus, who loved his sister Byblis.

Motives of incest were not seldom brought upon the stage, as by Euripides in the *Æolus* (*TGF*., 365 ff.). The drama is not preserved but we know its object from the narrative of Sostratus. King Æolus had six daughters and six sons, the eldest of whom, Macareus, was in love with his sister Canace and forced her to yield to him. When the father heard of it, he sent the daughter a sword with which she killed herself. With the same sword Macareus also then took his life. When in the drama the line occurred, "For nothing is dishonourable or common, if only it pleases us," there was an instant uproar in the theatre, while the spectators were indignant at such a frivolous outrage, until they were calmed by Antisthenes, who altered the verse: "Dishonourable remains dishonourable, whether it pleases or not."

The *Æolus* is also frequently blamed by Aristophanes as indecent. In another passage he has associated the adjectives "objectionable" and "barbarian" with the noun incest; but he had found the motif already indicated in Homer, who makes the six sons of Æolus live with their six sisters in peaceful marriage.[1]

Lastly, it is worth mentioning that incest in a dream, even of the homosexual kind, was not by any means uncommon, at least if we may conclude from the detailed manner in which it is described and explained in the dream-books.

6. SCATOLOGY

The term scatology, usually employed in modern sexual science, comes from σκώρ (gen. σκατός), dirt, excrement. The unappetizing secretions of the human body, even the excrements themselves have an attraction for children and even for older people, who indeed all their life remain children, to a much greater degree than many imagine. The chief places where scatalogical wishes are made known and fulfilled, are the public conveniences, the walls of which are even to-day sometimes besmirched with coarse or erotic inscriptions and drawings. That it was the same in ancient Greece, is of itself intelligible, although we cannot of course prove it in detail. But the essential difference between the two periods is that scatology then found its open expression in literature and art, and not merely in furtive pornography as to-day. As may be easily understood, most instances of scatology occur in comic and satiric poetry, although serious passages concerning the process of secretion of the human products of matter are not wanting, e.g. the already mentioned instructions of the honest peasant-poet Hesiod on making water.

Similarly Herodotus informs us that among the

[1] Incest between father and daughter is occasionally found as a mythological motif, as in the story of Harpalyce, who is violated by her father and wreaks a terrible vengeance upon him (Parthenius, 13), or the horrible tale of Mycerinus and his daughter (Herodotus, ii, 131) : cf. also Lysias, *Alcibiades*, i, 41. Aristophanes (*Wasps*, 1178) mentions an unknown Cardopion, who lived in incest with his mother.

Persians it was forbidden to spit or make water in another person's presence (i, 133).

When little children wanted to make water, their mother or nurse said σεῖν, if they wanted to relieve themselves, they said βρῦν.

Making water is often spoken of in comedy. Thus in the *Clouds* of Aristophanes (373) the simple Strepsiades explains rain by the assumption that Zeus is making water through a sieve. In the *Lysistrata*, the leader of the chorus of old men complains of the women "who had wetted them with buckets, so that we have to wring our clothes, just as if we had bepissed ourselves" (402); and in the *Ecclesiazusæ* the citizen declares that he will now be on his guard against women, "that they may not bepiss him" (832). Boys making water are mentioned in the *Peace* (1266).

The chamber-pot is generally called ἀμίς in Greek. At licentious banquets it might happen that a guest cried out to the boy in waiting: "Bring the chamber-pot!" According to a passage in Eupolis (see *ante*, p. 12) this innovation was fathered upon Alcibiades, while Athenæus (xiii, 519*e*) ascribes it to the Sybarites.[1]

According to our ideas, we should hardly consider it possible that this vessel should be even mentioned by serious tragic writers. But Æschylus had already made Odysseus say: "Here is the knave who once threw a ridiculous missile at me, the stinking chamber-pot, and did not miss his mark; it hit my head and suffered shipwreck, split into fragments, smelling quite differently from vessels containing perfume" (frag. 180; *TGF.*, 59). We cannot decide whether this scene occurred in a tragedy, or, as Welcker conjectured, in a satiric drama. Athenæus,

[1] A still more tasteless instance is given in Petronius, 27, of the rich upstart Trimalchio. Two castrated boys stood by, one of whom had a silver chamber-pot (*matella*) in his hand. When Trimalchio snapped his fingers, he put the pot under him. After he had emptied his bladder, he called for water, washed his hands, and dried them on the hair of one of the beautiful boys.

who quotes the lines (i, 17*c*) blames Æschylus for making the Homeric heroes use the extravagancies of his time, but Sophocles in the *Assembling of the Achæans* (frag. 140; *TGF.*, 162), conjecturally a satiric drama, has also represented the scene and in similar words.

There were other names for the chamber-pot, such as οὐράνη, ἐνουρήθρα and οὐρητρίς; that for women had a boat-shaped form, hence called σκάφιον (Aristophanes, *Thesm.*, 633), which passed into Latin as *scaphium* (Juvenal, vi, 264; Martial, xi, 11). Of pictorial representations mention might be made of a vase in the Berlin Antiquarium, on which is seen a beautiful girl in a Doric chitōn, who, with bent head and the forefinger of her right hand outstretched, gives a signal to a youth in the form of Eros, who is hurrying up to her with a fairly large boat-shaped vessel; also, on a wall-painting in Pompeii we see the drunken Heracles with Silenus behind him pissing on his right leg. How dissipated, drunken satyrs use vessels originally intended for other purposes as a chamber-pot, is a fairly common subject of illustration in ancient Greek vase-paintings.

Now and again intemperance at banquets and drinking bouts led to the use of a spittoon, called σκᾱ́φη or λεβήτιον. In a fragment of the comedies of Aristophanes (49; *CAF.*, I, 404), a guest asks for a feather with which to tickle his throat, and a spittoon. On vase paintings, youths and men are frequently represented as vomiting.

Also excrements and their repulsiveness are often mentioned in comedy; the most usual Latin term is *cacare*, the Greek χέζειν or κακκᾶν, the latter being usual in children's language.

Not without spirit, and in the original having a very drastic effect through the tone-painting, is the description of the act of evacuation in the *Clouds* of Aristophanes (385 ff.). Socrates is telling Strepsiades that thunder is caused by the clashing together of clouds and endeavours to make it clear to him by the example of his body: "Were you ever, after being stuffed with broth at the Panathenæa, disturbed in your belly so that a tumult rumbled through it?" to which Strepsiades answers: "Yes, by Apollo! a little broth immediately plays the devil, and causes a grumbling and rumbling like thunder; at first gently—pappax, then—papapappax and when I relieve myself it thunders aloud—papapappax, just as the clouds do!"

The servant in the *Plutus* who has become well-to-do takes fresh garlic to clean himself every time after defecation (817).

The most grotesque scatological scene on the stage is perhaps that in the *Frogs* (479) in which the god Dionysus in his fear evacuates, and is wiped by Xanthias with a sponge.

Of pictorial representations I mention a Pompeian picture, thus described by Hellig: "In some rushes stands a hippopotamus staring up with wide-opened mouth at a naked dwarf who, standing on the edge of a boat and stretching forward his posteriors, evacuates down the animal's throat. At the same time he holds out his hands with satisfaction and looks round at the beast as if asking a question."

Almost more frequent than the secretion of the excrements, breaking wind, whether voluntary or accidental, becomes matter for jest and ridicule in grotesque poetry. The terms are ἡ πορδή for the noun, πέρδομαι for the verb, as well as βδόλος and βδέω.

There is a very amusing conversation, hardly translatable owing to the play on words, in the *Knights* of Aristophanes (639 ff.).

7. TRIVIALITIES AND SUPPLEMENTARY NOTES

In Greek literature we often meet with osphresiological passages, that is, passages in which sexual smells are spoken of (see *Lysistrata*, 686).

Philostratus writes to a boy, asking him to return

later the roses sent to him, which he had strewn over his bed, " since they then will have, not only the smell of roses, but also the fragrance of your body " (*Ep.* 18).

The inhabitants of Argyra in Achaia related that Selemnus was a beautiful youth, who was loved by the sea-nymph Argyra. It came to pass, however, that his bloom faded, whereupon the nymph deserted him and he died of love-sickness and was changed by Aphrodite into a brook with healing properties, so that any man or woman who bathed in it was for all time cured of the torments of love. Pausanias, who tells the story (vii, 23, 2, 3), adds: " If there is any truth in this great riches are less precious to mankind than the waters of the Selemnus."

According to Ælian (*Var. hist.*, xii, 63), Archedicus fell in love with an hetaira at Naucratis. " But she was very conceited and demanded a very large sum; when she had received the money, she only consented to his wishes for a short time and then would have nothing more to do with him. Thus the youth, who was not greatly blessed with earthly goods, could not secure the object of his wishes. But after he had dreamed one night that he held her in his arms, he was at once cured of his passion."

This story is also told by Plutarch (*Demetr.*, 27), who adds that the hetaira then demanded payment for the " night of love ", although it had been only a dream. The judge decided that the youth must bring the money in a vessel, but that the hetaira might only stretch out her hand for its shadow—a decision which Lamia, another member of the sisterhood, found most unjust, for while the dream had satisfied the youth, the vessel's shadow could afford no satisfaction to the hetaira.

On the couvade Diodorus Siculus (v, 14) says: " If a woman has borne a child in the island of Cyrnos (Corsica), no attention is paid to the woman in childbed. But the man lies down, as if he were ill and remains for a definite number of days in childbed." Apollonius, the writer of the *Argonautica*, confirms this (ii, 1011), and adds that the men lay in bed with their heads bound up, and that their food was cooked for them by the women in childbed and the childbed bath prepared for them.

Strabo (iii, 165) says the same of Celtic, Thracian and Scythian tribes, and then tells of a woman, who worked in the fields with men for a daily wage. Suddenly she suspected that she was pregnant, went a little aside, bore the child, and then returned to her work, so as not to lose her pay. When the owner of the field saw that the work fell hard on her, he sent her home with her pay, without knowing at first what the reason was. The woman then bathed the child in a brook hard by, made the absolutely necessary swaddling-clothes from just what she had, and carried the little thing home with them.

RETROSPECT

We have reached the end of our labours, in the course of which the author has tried to give a representation of Greek " morals " in the narrower sense of the word, and he hopes that he has at least in part fulfilled his task. In a work intended not only for the man of science, but also for the educated layman, material has been collected and worked, which can be afterwards checked, with the aid of the many references to authorities that are given throughout, by any person who knows something of the subject, and who will thus gain a deep insight into the morals of the ancient Greeks ; and for such a reader the conclusion would seem to be twofold. First, he learns that old Greek culture in all its divergences has its root and its prime cause in sexuality. Not only in the " life of love ", but also in religious aspects, in art and literature, in social as well as public life, in distractions and pleasures, in festivals and theatrical performances, in short, everywhere sexuality is the predominant component. Erotic is hence the key to the understanding of Greek culture generally, consequently the knowledge of Greek erotic is the indispensable assumption for a deeper knowledge of the life of ancient Greece. Hence the need and the object of the present work —to fill a no longer endurable gap in our knowledge of the Hellenic people.

But if erotic is the prime cause of old Greek culture and the centre of Hellenic life, with convincing force there logically results the further knowledge, that the attitude of the Greeks towards erotic as something that was a matter of course was naïve and natural, to an extent that seems to us to-day scarcely conceivable. As the word " sin " is foreign to the tongue of the Hellenes, so their " morality " was only concerned with what was unjust to others, with offences against the State, and with crime. To the Greek " morality " had no bearing on the problems of sexual life, except in so far as these reacted on immature boys or girls or when, in sexual matters, violence was employed. Otherwise, everyone among them had the right of disposal of his own body; what men who had passed the age of puberty did together, at that time troubled neither the judge nor public opinion: hence no one could take offence if sexual matters were spoken of with the greatest frankness and without any pretence of embarrassment.

The astonishingly perfect understanding of beauty possessed by the Greeks, of their Dionysiac joy in the glory of the human body, ennobled for them every act of sensuality, if only it was based upon true love, that is, on the yearning after beauty.

Hence, for them, pæderasty, instead of a vice was but another form of love which they regarded, not as the enemy of marriage, but as a necessary supplement to marriage recognized by the State; and it was publicly spoken of with just as much unconcern as it was brought into the sphere of their philosophical conversations by great intellects such as Socrates, Plato, and Aristotle. Because the fascinations of the sexual were not made still more alluring by being shrouded in a veil of mystery or branded as sinful and forbidden, and—further—because the almost unchecked sensuality of the Greeks was always dignified by the desire for beauty, their sexual life developed in overflowing force, but also in enviable healthiness. That this is so may be certainly adduced from the fact that sexual perversions, which play so lamentable a part in modern life, seldom occurred in ancient Greece, and that it is difficult to find even occasional traces of them in the classical writings.

We felt, while undertaking and discharging our task, that Greek morality must be known and understood by any who wished to form a right judgment upon the life and culture of the Hellenes; and that there must be added to this wish a serious will to transplant oneself into the spirit of the times of ancient Greece, rather than to make of the totally different views of modern men a standard by which to criticize the ethics of the Greeks. But anyone who is able to set himself free in the spirit from modern views, and to penetrate with unprejudiced mind into the thoughts of these ancient people, will comprehend the lofty ethics of the Hellenes, whose highest ideal expressed itself in *καλὸς κἀγαθός*, "the beautiful both in body and in soul."

GENERAL INDEX

General Index

General Index

General Index

General Index

General Index

General Index

INDEX OF AUTHORITIES AND QUOTED WORKS

INDEX OF AUTHORITIES

Index of Authorities

Index of Authorities